Leading Issues in Islamic Economics and Finance

Zubair Hasan

Leading Issues in Islamic Economics and Finance

Critical Evaluations

palgrave
macmillan

Zubair Hasan
International Centre for Education
in Islamic Finance
Kuala Lumpur, Malaysia

ISBN 978-981-15-6514-4 ISBN 978-981-15-6515-1 (eBook)
https://doi.org/10.1007/978-981-15-6515-1

This Palgrave Macmillan imprint is published by the registered company Springer Nature Singapore Pte Ltd.
The registered company address is: 152 Beach Road, #21-01/04 Gateway East, Singapore 189721, Singapore

In memory of my wife Raeesa

Preface

This work is not a 'book' in the usual sense of the term, i.e. a treatment of an academic subject in an integrated, cohesive manner; its chapters are not interlinked. Nevertheless, it is a book in an important and useful way. It adopts an inclusive approach, integrating Islamic positions with the mainstream where feasible. In addition, each chapter has some pedagogic features to facilitate understanding and absorption of the arguments without stressing the reader. These include an opening preview of each chapter and a clear statement of its learning objectives. The text is laced with attractive diagrams, well-structured tables, easy mathematical formulations, an explanatory glossary of important terms used, and searching end-of-chapter questions to enable readers evaluate if the learning outcomes have indeed been reasonably achieved. Hopefully, they will find this book far ahead of others on this feature alone.

The book deals with some leading issues in Islamic economics and finance that continue to remain in a fluid, non-consensual state in the profession. Regarding some issues, the differences are indeed sharp and consequential. Other issues are steeped in confusion or neglect. Contextually, this book does two things:

1. It examines each issue afresh in the light of updated literature, bringing data and documentation closer to the year 2019.
2. It keeps the feasibility aspect of its theoretical constructs in the forefront. For Islam it is a way of life, devoid of philosophical ivory tower thinking.

The book has 15 chapters—six on economic issues and six on financial matters. In between, Chapters 7 and 8 are a crossover insertion. The last chapter deals with an important accounting issue that has so far remained untouched in the literature on Islamic economics and finance.

The opening Chapter 1 examines the nature and significance of Islamic economics. It reviews the relevant literature on the subject, highlighting the deficiencies. It finds no fault with the mainstream definition based on the foundations discussed in the following chapter. It argues that mainstream economics, too, is not value-neutral and its framework allows the incorporation of all Islamic ethical norms of welfare including not only the mundane considerations of the present world, but also the concerns for the hereafter. The chapter presents a definition of economics centred on the Islamic notion of *falah*. It pinpoints its departures from the mainstream and shows that like the current mainstream discipline, Islamic economics also has positive and normative aspects. Principles of economics in each case are principles of economic policy. For that reason, both subjects have an art aspect as well. The chapter closes with a discussion on systemic differences between various economic orders.

However, to underline the efficacy of an integrative approach in the teaching of Islamic economics and finance, Chapter 2 of the book deals with three foundational concepts of mainstream economics—scarcity of resources, pursuit of self-interest, and maximization of economic results—to rehabilitate them for the Islamic discipline. The chapter argues that their age-long rejection by orthodoxy dominating the profession is not tenable. Islam indeed accommodates them all in essence as indispensable analytical tools albeit with modifications for conforming to Islamic norms.

Chapter 3 relates to development, the goal of unceasing economic activity over time and space, ever since Adam arrived on earth. The chapter has a historical perspective on the issues discussed. It draws its structure from some earlier writings of the author, including a concise book on the subject published in the year 2016; yet it wears an air of distinctive freshness. It focuses on poverty reduction, distributive justice, and sustainability as the primary goals and looks at questions of efficiency, motivation, and demographic aspects from an Islamic viewpoint. Further, it explores the role of the state in directing the economy towards achieving Islamic goals of development.

Environmental concerns are increasing across the globe but no one is willing to cut down on growth—least of all the developed countries—in order to keep the earth liveable in a highly competitive setting. We examine growth versus the environment as a distinct development issue in Chapter 4, from the Islamic perspective. The discussion includes the sources, types, and nature of pollution and the efficacy of various measures—market-oriented and interventionist—to control deterioration. The chapter emphasizes positive filters in the area of finance to bridge the gap between the mainstream and Islamic approaches. It brings in new versions of scarcity and efficiency commensurate with environmental concerns and points out the increasing devastation caused by wars across the globe that is emerging as a major and worrisome source of pollution.

Chapter 5 presents a comprehensive discussion on a central theme in Islamic economics—distributive justice. No topic in the subject has attracted so much attention as the distribution of wealth and income. The chapter is the longest in the book and the author had to resist the urge to divide it into two. The chapter presents a balanced integration of the mainstream and Islamic positions on the subject—theoretical and empirical. It examines the mainstream position with reference to the marginal productivity theory and welfare concepts the fiscal measures are supposed to strengthen. In contrast, it builds up the concept of distributive justice in Islam based on the all-pervading notion of *Amanah* or Trusteeship and shows how the Islamic attitude towards wealth and prosperity is conditioned by this foundational concept and how it moulds the various measures to work for distributional equity. The major focus is on factor relations built on sharing production gains between labour and capital. It ends with the role of the state in building bridges and trade-offs between conflicting objectives of development, especially growth employment and equity.

Consumption is considered as the beginning and end of all economic activity. Chapter 6 explains its micro foundations and macro modelling issues. The topic is important as it is closely related to both economic development and distributive justice, the fulfilment of the basic needs of the people in a country being an Islamic imperative. Transfer payments that Islam enforces tilt income distribution in favour of the poor, apparently reducing savings and investment, something that is detrimental to economic growth and development. The literature on Islamic economics was distinctly preoccupied with such debates and concerns during the decades before the turn of the century. The chapter streamlines this debate and allays such concerns. It incorporates several new developments recent research has added to the treatment of consumption.

Chapters 7 and 8 mark the transition from the economics section to the finance part of the book. Chapter 7 explains the role and consequences of deficit financing in developing economies in three forms: as a tool to mobilize real resources for planned development, use to bridging foreign exchange gap in balance of payments through external financing and seeking country bailout via borrowing from the international lender the IMF.

Chapter 8 explains how money evolved over time and space and its movement from a commodity to paper and eventually to just a promise to pay. In this evolutionary march, the crucial element was the general acceptability in society of anything as money; its linkage to something valuable or its legal backing ensured this acceptability, but its essential determinant was the stability in the value of money. The chapter discusses note issue methods and monetary standards, especially the advocacy for reinstalling the gold dinar in the Muslim world. It briefly discusses credit creation by commercial banks—its need and implications. It also discusses the rise of central banks to manage the volume of the base legal tender in an economy.

Chapter 9 builds upon the discussion in the preceding chapter and explores the nature and sources of *credit* money that conventional banks generate in modern economies. Loans create deposits and leverage gains lead to credit expansion beyond the limits of safety, thus exposing flourishing economies to devastating crises. The chapter discusses the role of the monetary policy the central banks enforce, with special reference to a dualistic system wherein Islamic and conventional banks operate in a competitive setting. Here, the chapter introduces a new credit control measure and demonstrates its effectiveness over other measures used for credit control. The discussion examines the claim that Islamic banks can face turmoil better than conventional banks, as the 2007–2010 experience shows.

Chapter 10 evaluates the details of the Basel Accords that set standards for banks to restrain them from taking imprudent risks and causing instability and turmoil across countries. The chapter argues that the Basel requirements are too elaborate and costly for Islamic banks to adopt at their present level of development. The distinctive character of Islamic finance in maintaining firm linkages with real economic assets, as well as the standards for safety internally developed, should suffice for their safe operation.

Chapter 11 looks at whether the issue of rapid convergence of the Islamic and mainstream banking systems is a boon or bane for the former. It argues that in the light of available evidence, this convergence is uni-directional; the Islamic system is being fast subsumed by the mainstream whirlpool. The Islamic banks have increasingly tended to become imitative of mainstream products, placing them in apparently Islamic wrappings. This puts the *Shari'ah* compliance of the products, indeed the very survival of the Islamic system, at risk. Such convergence must be resisted, or better reversed.

An important contention recently brought into sharp focus in several influential writings is that risk sharing is the *sole and inalienable* principle of Islamic banking, making it qualitatively different from the conventional and unsusceptible to crises. Chapter 12 refutes this claim using *Shari'ah* axioms. The emergence of risks in Islamic banking and the need to minimize them is not denied, but risk per se is neither productive nor a tradable commodity in Islam. The guiding principle of Islam is profit/loss sharing in participatory finance. Risk sharing is a consequence of such contracts, not their cause.

Chapter 13 demonstrates that the diminishing *musharakah* model commonly used in Islamic home financing violates Islamic requirements on two counts: first, the equal monthly instalments (EMIs) violate the ban on interest; these rather involve in the process the compounding of return on investment. Second, while instalment payments are pro rata with time, the ownership of the house passes to the buyer at a slower rate. The chapter presents a home financing model free of these blemishes. It is fully Shari'ah-compliant and cheaper for the buyer without being disadvantageous to the bank.

Chapter 14 deals with an issue that has eminently cropped up recently in the literature: the methodology of Islamic economics. The reasons for the subject currently being in a state of stagnation are attributed to failure at the methodological front. The chapter discusses the common usages of the term methodology and shows how ill-conceived interpretations of the term have led to confusion and controversy concerning the nature and significance of Islamic economics and led research into barren tracks. It finds the causes of slow progress of the subject resting elsewhere.

The last Chapter 15 is a contribution to the scanty literature on accounting in Islamic finance. It highlights the differences between accountants and economists, with reference to the definition and measurement of profit, a variable so vital to Islamic economics and finance. The chapter attempts to reduce the gap. It explains why the reconciliatory efforts have to originate from the economists rather than the accountants.

This book may well be the basis of introducing a one-semester course on Islamic economics and finance at the postgraduate level.

Finally, I must express my gratitude to Dr. Waleed Ahmad J. Addas, a senior official of the Islamic Development Bank, Jeddah, SA, who went through some chapters of the preliminary draft of the book and made valuable suggestions for improvement.

New Delhi, India Zubair Hasan

Contents

About the Author

Professor Dr. Zubair Hasan is an Indian economist. His teaching research and consultancy work spans over 58 years. During this period, he worked at the University of Delhi, Basra University of Iraq, International Islamic University of Malaysia, and INCEIF, the global university of Islamic finance, Kuala Lumpur. During this period, he won several academic awards; the main ones being the Islamic Development bank's coveted Prize in Islamic economics (2009) and the OIC Comsec Academic Award 2014.

During his long academic career, Prof. Hasan wrote over 125 working papers and articles in the area of Islamic economics and finance and published seven books listed below to promote the subject. His interest being mainly in student welfare, the books are mostly in a textbook mode. He has written *Microeconomics from Islamic Perspective* (2006), *Macroeconomics* (2009), *Fundamentals of Microeconomics* (2001), *Islamic Banking and Finance: An Integrative Approach* (2014), *Economics with*

Islamic Orientation (2015), *Theory of Profit with Islamic Directions* (2016), and *Islam and Economic Development* (2016).

In addition, Prof. Hasan has contributed chapters to about 20 edited works.

In June 2015, Hasan retired from INCEIF the institution awarding him their first professor emeritus title at that year's convocation. He continues his association with the institution in that capacity.

List of Figures

List of Tables

CHAPTER 1

The Nature and Significance of Islamic Economics: Integrative Approach

Preview

Disciplined knowledge is the result of human exploration of its sources. This exploration is invariably directed towards finding ways for making life comfortable and rewarding, including spiritual solace. It is an ongoing process, adding to our existing stock of knowledge. Over time, the tree of knowledge has spread into distinct branches of specialization because of the limitation of the individual mind to absorb the totality of knowledge expansion. The roots of the tree are the belief systems, reasons, and customs that have hardly changed over time and continue to serve the purpose of learning in various fields of human existence. Islamic economics is one of the latest graftings onto the knowledge tree. Being nascent, it has been mired in confusion and controversy. Today, much concern is voiced on the unsatisfactory state of the subject. The expression of concern is on the rise in the literature and needs attention. The cause for worry is the divergence in views on various aspects of Islamic economics—definition, nature, and scope. A cohesive and consensual thinking on the subject is yet to emerge. The present chapter examines these and related issues with a view to spelling out the nature and significance of Islamic economics.

During this exploration, we will show that Islamic economics—despite claims to the contrary—has similar structures, language forms, and issues for discussion as its mainstream counterpart because the basic mundane problems of human beings that both seek to address

Z. Hasan, *Leading Issues in Islamic Economics and Finance*,
https://doi.org/10.1007/978-981-15-6515-1_1

are essentially the same. The difference arises in the issues' identification and the methods of treating them. It would be helpful to see them both as supplementing each other with overlaps, rather than operating in conflict. An approach to the teaching of Islamic economics by integrating it with the mainstream would be of interest to learners and better enlighten them about facts around. An exclusivist all-or-nothing puritan approach to the subject would not be conducive to the general acceptability and growth of Islamic economics. A gradual step-by-step approach, based on filtering, adaptation, and absorption of the mainstream ideas, is required.

Learning Outcomes
The objective of this chapter is to enable readers understand, appreciate, and critically examine the scope, nature, and significance of Islamic economics vis-à-vis its mainstream counterpart. They are expected:

- To know why a subject must be defined and how Islamic economics differs from the mainstream version on the issue of definition.
- To have a fair idea of the evolution of Islamic economics as an academic discipline over time and space.
- To understand the concept of worldview, the difference between its mainstream and Islamic versions and the impact of these differences on the content and nature of mainstream and Islamic economic disciplines.
- To understand what we study in Islamic economics and in what way it is similar to, or different from, mainstream economics.
- What methodology of economics means, what role it plays in the development of the subject, and how it differs from the methods economists use to derive their theories and laws.
- What an economic system is and how the main elements of an Islamic system differ from those of its mainstream counterpart.

1.1 Introduction

One distinctive feature of Islam is its candid rejection of asceticism.[1] Islam exhorts mankind to enjoy all permissible things in life, albeit with moderation. To that end, God has stocked the Earth and Heavens with

[1] Yes and no, as it also rejects self-indulgence. Islam encourages moderation in pursuit of material goods and gains.

inexhaustible resources. He has made them submit to human beings' will and effort for their benefit. Thus, a sizeable part of Islamic jurisprudence, known as *fiqh al-muamalat*, deals with issues relating to the treatment of natural resources in the processes of production, consumption, and exchange. The distribution of income and wealth, questions of taxation, money matters, and financing are other matters of treatment and concern.

The evolution of the economic ideas enshrined in *fiqh al-muamalat* continued to grow as the Islamic renaissance movement gathered momentum during the struggle for freedom from colonial rule in Muslim lands. For the Islamic ideas provided a handy and non-provocative method to attack the Western ideologies of capitalism and socialism: these could be shown to be opposed to the Islamic ethos and exploitative of the masses. An important source of such preparatory writings was the Indian sub-continent.

The classical jurists discussed the *muamalat* in minute detail but were not always unanimous in their interpretations of the divine law. Interpretive differences were not a problem; they gave space and flexibility to the system while keeping its faith and ethical core undiluted. The term 'Islamic economics' seldom occurred to the classical scholars even as the evolution of the subject, in thought and methodology, shows a strong tendency of reverting to their writings.[2] This unceasing 'pull back' has indeed been a constant source of confusion and controversy as to the definition, nature, and scope of Islamic economics.[3]

The spread of works on economic ideas of Islam across countries began attracting much attention during the latter half of the twentieth century, when most of the Muslim nations had won their political

[2]A good account of their contribution is provided in occasional literature surveys, but a systematic historical analysis probably first appeared in a paper of Abdul Azim Islahi (2010). Nagaoka Shinsuke (2012) in his well-documented research provides a 'Critical Overview of the History of Islamic Economics.' The 'Current State of Knowledge and Development of the Discipline' is available in Khaled A. Hussein (2013).

[3]This apparently is common to the evolution and progress of various branches of knowledge. For instance, even mainstream economics has undergone and is undergoing this process since its acclaimed origin in Adam Smith's *Wealth of Nations* (1776). Even its name was not firmly fixed until the close of the nineteenth century. Alfred Marshall's *Principles* (1898) opens with the expression: 'Economics or political economy' that remains unchanged in the last (1924) edition of his *Principles*.

independence from colonial rule. This set the stage for the launching of Islamic economics in a formal way in the mid-seventies.[4]

The first International Conference on Islamic Economics held in Jeddah in 1976 endorsed a programme for erecting the infrastructure to launch the subject as a formal academic discipline. Three international Islamic universities were set up, one each at Islamabad, Kuala Lumpur, and Kampala; and new centres, institutions, and departments for teaching and research on the subject were added to existing universities. Two new academic journals were launched to publish, promote, and disseminate the literature on the subject worldwide. Islamic economics had formally arrived; the essential departing point from the mainstream discipline being its faith-based ethical foundations. The divergence derived its content and direction from the worldview underpinning each discipline.

This chapter is spread over eight sections including this Introduction. Section 1.2 discusses the Islamic worldview and identifies its points of departure from those that underpin mainstream economics. It shows how the worldview divergence impacts the nature and objectives of the two economic disciplines—Islamic and the mainstream. Section 1.3 surveys the literature on the definition of Islamic economics and presents a definition based on the mainstream fundamentals discussed in the following chapter. Section 1.4 elaborates on the character and scope of Islamic economics and in Sect. 1.5; we touch upon the methodology and methods of the subject. An economic discipline submits to, and articulates, the social organism in which it operates. Therefore, Sect. 1.6 outlines the main features of an Islamic economic system as compared to those of capitalism and socialism. Section 1.7 highlights some problems that presently confront Islamic economics. Finally, Sect. 1.8 discusses the challenges Islamic economics faces and provides a summary of how best to address them.

1.2 Worldview Differences

The notion of the worldview is Western in origin and contextual in nature. We cannot explain it without specifying whose worldview we are talking about, and at what point in time and to what end. The

[4]The term 'Islamic economics' was coined by Abu al-A'la Al-Mawdudi, whose students and followers worked to develop an ostensible Islamic social science. His influence on Arab Islamists began with the writings of Sayid Qutb, whose quasi-exegesis *Under the Qur'anic Shade* referred exclusively to Mawdudi's writings on economic matters (El-Gamal 2009).

term usually is taken to refer to an individual's perception of the world, although the role of external influences in shaping that perception is recognized.[5] However, for a social science like economics, we must see how a community looks at the purpose of life, especially the relationship with other human beings, with the Universe, and with the Creator of both. It is this collective social perception that distinguishes an economic discipline from others. Individuals may have their own variants but their overall behaviour would tend to conform to what has socially been settled.[6]

With the spread of education—including religious education—and changing social environs, individuals in a community tend to develop, rather unconsciously, a shared mental image of God's creation and its purpose, that is, of man's place and role in the universe and of their relationship with the social phenomena which they influence and which in turn influences them. Such a collective image constitutes the societal worldview. It is a compact structure from which various human activities generally follow.

Islam provides man with a worldview that is God ordained; it is shaped and conditioned by moral and ethical codes for individual and group conduct in various spheres of life, including economic, which the *Qur'an* and prophetic traditions prescribe. This code has interpretive flexibility, but cannot be altered or replaced by human will. In contrast, the West has developed what it calls a scientific worldview based on rationalism that is changeable by a social process of consent. Both these worldviews have distinct and largely divergent approaches to the material and spiritual aspects of human existence. Both create their own visions of truth and reality.

The Islamic worldview creates in believers a perception of their own significance in the divine scheme of creation.[7] The *Qur'an* tells us that *man*—a mix of earth[8] and the Divine (spirit)—is the best of all creations, even superior to angels. As man volunteered to work as God's vicegerent

[5] For an elaboration of this point, see Shari'ati (1982, pp. 22–25).

[6] Ibid., pp. 25–32. The author provides examples to clinch the point.

[7] Ibid., p. 18, n. 2. The author quotes the poet-philosopher Dr. Muhammad Iqbal's couplets in his explanation.

[8] 'It is He who created you from clay and then decreed a term and a specified time [known] to Him; then [still] you are in dispute (*Al-Ana'am*, verse 2). And when I have proportioned him and breathed into him of My [created] soul, then fall down to him in prostration' (*al-Hijr*, verse 29).

and co-worker on Earth, God handed over the planet with all its treasures to him in Trust. He provided human beings the *Shari'ah*, a code of conduct to run His trust. The code spells out man's rights and obligations in various spheres in managing this trust. However, the divine wisdom granted man freedom to follow or not to follow the instructions, but with the provision that he will be rewarded for submission to the rules and would be punished for their violation. In that sense, *Shari'ah* is a system of rewards and punishments for regulating man's conduct in running the trust[9] he undertook to manage (*Qur'an*, 2:38–39).

Thus, from its very inception, Islam is a religion that adores human life. It empowers one to enjoy all good things in this life and teaches one to do so in a way whereby the pleasures in the hereafter also remain open to him/her. Thus, the Islamic worldview inseparably links the life in this world (*al-dunya*) with life in the hereafter (*al-akhira*), the latter being of eternal significance. Everything in Islam is ultimately focused on the *al-akhira* aspect of human existence, without in any way implying the neglect of *al-dunya* within the prescribed norms. This stance centres around the Islamic concepts of *tawhid*, vicegerency, and *al-adl* (unity, trusteeship, and justice).

A worldview evolves and is locked in a reciprocal relationship with knowledge. The formation of the Islamic worldview itself attained maturity over the 23 years of revelation and its subsequent interpretative variants over the centuries. During this time, the process shaped, modified—and even changed at times—the content and direction of the expanding disciplines—science, jurisprudence, *tafsir* (interpretation), *kalam* (philosophy), literature, and history, economics entering the list only recently. However, the extent to which the modern expansion of knowledge was allowed to impact the Islamic worldview is difficult to say.[10] Nonetheless, there seems to be a sort of consensus about a hard core consisting of explicit non-controversial prescriptions that cannot be allowed dilution.

Thus, the main constituents of the hard core are explanations concerning the attributes of God, the nature of revelation, the purpose of

[9] 'Indeed, we offered the Trust to the heavens and the earth and the mountains, and they declined to bear it and feared it; but man [undertook to] bear it. Indeed, he was unjust and ignorant' (*Al-Ahzab*, verse 72).

[10] For instance, one finds that Al Attas is reluctant to admit modification or change compared to Shari'ati, who is more accommodative to fresh interpretations.

man's creation and his place in the universe, the faith imperatives, the notion of justice, and the meaning of reality and truth (*Qur'an*, 31:30). These elements and terms and the implications they unfold have a great bearing on the Islamic ideas concerning change, development, and progress.[11] They have been, and remain, open for interpretation and elaboration, lending flexibility to the Islamic worldview and its economic ramifications.

Other religions, too, project their own worldviews to guide their followers' conduct in this world in various spheres of life, including the economy, to achieve solace in the hereafter.[12] For instance, mainstream economics could not break free of its Christian moorings until the early decades of the twentieth century. The alienation process began with the Enlightenment Movement and completed the separation in 1929 when the Vienna Circle[13] published a position paper titled *The Scientific Worldview* (Redman 1991, p. 9).

What triggered this development was a new set of ideas within the rising entrepreneurial class with the significant political influence needed to remove the lingering feudal institutions and restrictive controls of the 300-year run of the mercantilist era. Ancient truths, such as the immorality of interest, the virtues of charity, and contentment with one's inherited station in life were considered barriers to progress and had to be abandoned. These ideas pushed social sciences, especially economics, closer to the thought processes and methods of natural sciences. Newton's science showed 'nature' as active and effective an agent as

[11] See Sadr (1983, pp. 7–9), Al-Atas (1995, p. 5), and Qutb (1978, p. 57).

[12] See for example Guide and Rist (1953, pp. 516–570) on the economic role and impact of Christianity through history. See also Redman (1991, p. 176, n. 11).

[13] The Vienna Circle was a group of philosophers who gathered around Moritz Schlick, after his coming to Vienna in 1922. They organized a philosophical association named Verein Ernst Mach (Ernst Mach Association). The group sought to re-conceptualize empiricism by means of their interpretation of the then recent advances in the physical and formal sciences. Their radically anti-metaphysical stance was supported by an empiricist criterion of meaning and a broadly logistic conception of mathematics. They denied that any principle or claim was synthetic a priori. Moreover, they sought to account for the presuppositions of scientific theories by regimenting such theories within a logical framework so that the important role played by conventions, either in the form of definitions or of other analytical framework principles, became evident (Stanford Encyclopedia of Philosophy, first published Wednesday, June 28, 2006; substantive revision Wednesday, February 17, 2016, https://plato.stanford.edu/entries/vienna-circle/).

the earlier Will of God: if the divine will had created the mechanism that worked harmoniously and automatically without human interference, then *laissez-faire* in economic activity was the highest wisdom. Natural law would best guide the economic system and the actions of people as well. However, it would be incorrect to attribute the origin of the change to the Vienna Circle. It was rather the crystallization of their position on the ideas that had been taking shape over the centuries. For instance, the emphasis on *naturalism* in Smith's *Wealth of Nations* or the later advocacy for *laissez-faire* in France. They forgot that the law of jungle—might is right—is the only natural *laissez-faire* law unsuitable for organizing and running human societies. This realization soon gave rise to constitutions and regulatory legal systems.

Adam Smith (1776) further darkened the clouds that Ibn Khaldun, a fifteenth-century Muslim scholar, had already cast on the mercantilist manipulations.[14] Smith, although a moral philosopher, articulated the pursuit of self-interest as the natural law for economic activity; he argued that the pursuit harmonized individual and social interests conducive to the overall progress and prosperity of mankind. He saw great *spontaneity* in the evolution of economic institutions such as accumulation of capital, division of labour, and the usage of money, combining in the production of wealth. The legitimacy of the *laissez-faire* system was derived from the natural order illustration of the solar system in Newton's mechanics. This was reinforced by the key ideas of Darwin focusing on natural selection based on individual mutations and differences leading by competition to the survival of the fittest. The impact of Darwinism led social scientists to the natural order from the biological end—the *competitive* evolution of species. Thus, naturalism rose to guide economics.

> Ideas illustrated from both ends—physics and biology—took the environment as given not to be manipulated or changed deliberately. The plea of maintaining the *status quo* suited those who had no grievance against the existing order; they saw benefit in its continuation. Interestingly, in economics a further but different influence from the natural sciences' side presumably came from Einstein's theory of relativity—what is true for an observer in one system may not be true for an observer in another system. The development of such terms as 'frames of reference', 'value systems' and 'points of view' illustrate such influence. (Hasan 1998)

[14]Ibn Khaldun (1967) is recognized as the founder of modern sociology but his contribution to economic thought is also well noted, see Jean David C. Boulakia (1971).

The three revolutions in natural sciences alluded to above induced major changes in social studies in thought, method, and direction, perhaps mostly in economics. Many saw in them a 'unity of method' applicable in equal measure to all the sciences—physical or social. Islam endorses this unity, but with a difference. The law for societal regulation is given by *Shari'ah*; it cannot be derived or based solely on observations of phenomena, natural or social. Such observations are encouraged to supplement *Shari'ah* norms and instructions as they too are in conformity with nature—the nature of humankind.

The difference in the unity of the scientific method and the natural law in the two worldviews—Islamic and secular—initiate major departures in Islamic economics from the mainstream discipline. The basic ones relate to the 'is or ought' controversy, reason-revelation relationship, doctrinal stance, and reality. These are briefly discussed as follows:

a. ***Is–ought controversy***: The secular worldview sought to expel all transcendental ideas from the purview of social sciences. Such ideas were attacked in economics on the plea that ethics and morality attempt to deduce illogically prescriptions from facts—an 'ought' from an 'is'. Economics as a science is concerned only with what is. What ought to be, it could admit only when supported by objective logic. This view of mainstream economics never lost significance once it occupied the centre stage.[15] The secular 'scientific worldview' thus thought of the universe as a self-acting machine following the natural laws, even when God was its original creator! This contention restricted man's vision to his existence in this world without any thought of the hereafter. It awakened the body and slumbered the soul, pushing life to chaos and anxiety.
   The so-called scientific worldview essentially projected rationalistic materialism, reflecting, and caring only for the mundane desires of humans. Thus, Alfred Marshall could talk of economics as catering only for 'the material requisites of well-being in the ordinary

[15] See, for instance, these two definitions: 'Science is science and ethics is ethics; it takes both to make a whole man; but only confusion, misunderstanding, and discord can come from not keeping them separate and distinct, from trying to impose the absolutes of ethics on the relatives of science' (Friedman 1953, p. 49).

'Morality, it could be argued, represents the way that people would like the world to work—whereas economics represents how it actually does work'.

business of life' (*Principles*, p. 1). In the absence of the hereafter and accountability to any superior being, man feels existence because he exists; he sees no difference in an act of suicide and a feat of sacrifice, as he faces no system of reward and punishment.

In Islam, the matter-spirit interlocks in human personality do not allow one to follow either asceticism or mammon worship. However, once the Enlightenment injected the scientific worldview into economics, the West separated ethics from it; capitalism never allowed them to rejoin. Secular economics overpowered human thought and action to the exclusion of ethical commitments; man could drop atom bombs on populous metropolises of Japan to hasten the end of an already ending war, just to test the new technology and view the unparalleled devastation with a triumphant smile and smug self-satisfaction.

Material progress unrestrained by ethics and morality has been indeed tremendous, but at an incalculable cost to humanity in terms of environmental damage and suffering. The fragmentation of the unitary religious worldview in the name of science has made the capital owners the dominant social class, perpetuating abject poverty and vulgar inequalities in the distribution of opportunities, freedom, and prosperity. To capital owners belongs power and wealth, and now even docile faith[16] One task of Islamic economics is to seek the restoration of the unity of its worldview that alien influences have dismembered and fractured in the Muslim mind. What is required is a closer look at the relationship between reason and revelation.

b. ***Reason–revelation relationship***: One may look at this relationship in two ways. First, reasoning operates as a tool of analysis *within* discussions on revelation. Second, reason confronts and questions revelation from *outside* the confines of religion. The first way of looking at the relationship is Islamic, the second secular. The meanings and arguments are not the same in the two cases.

Intellect, as defined above, is a faculty that goes beyond the realm of reason to provide principles for human guidance in worldly

[16]To be sure, Islam is one thing; what Muslims are doing is another. In this work, the focus is on Islam, not on the deeds of Muslims.

affairs. It makes comprehensible to humans the metaphysics of the visible and the invisible worlds and of their mutual linkage, thus enabling them to develop a holistic and integrated vision of life. Indeed, the intellectual foundations of the Islamic conception of God as enshrined in its scripture, the *Qur'an*. For, unlike secular rationalism, Islam does not see Nature as a material physical object merely meant for human exploitation and use; it accords it a further and deeper significance. The *Qur'an* upholds Nature[17]—the entire universe—as an open book that *intellect* alone, not rationality, can help read, understand, and interpret. Intellect makes one feel and grasp that Nature is bestowed with a cosmic purpose and relevance. It must be revered as it contains symbols bearing testimony to the existence of God and His supremacy over the universe. (On this, see Surah 55 Al-Rahman.)

Intellect invokes commitment to faith and ennobles ideas like creativity, beauty, love, altruism, empathy, and sacrifice. Intellect alone—not rationality—can appreciate why Ibrahim unhesitatingly plunged into the fire Nimrod lit; why Edward VIII abdicated the mighty British throne to marry the woman he loved; or why Nietzsche the great German philosopher sacrificed his life protecting a helpless, injured horse from the merciless beatings of its owner (Hasan 1998, p. 12). The *Qur'an* (30:39) declares: 'That which you give as interest to increase peoples' wealth, increases not with God but that which you give as charity seeking goodwill of God multiplies manifold'. Mainstream economic rationality cannot see how apparent loss here could be a gain in the hereafter. Intellect, however, can, as it would consider the non-pecuniary benefits like spiritual comfort and mental tranquillity. Indeed, intellect can create ideologies and systems, even revolutions, as history testifies. Intellect widens the span of knowledge and its sources. However, confusion in Islamic economics may arise, as it often

[17]These two verses in *Surah Fatir* sum up all possible branches of knowledge or that could ever be taught or learnt in any school, covering solids, liquids, plants, and animals, as well as the varieties of the human race: 'Do you not see that Allah sends down rain from the sky, and We produce thereby fruits of varying colors? And in the mountains are tracts, white and red of varying shades and [some] extremely black' (27). 'And among people and moving creatures and grazing livestock are various colors similarly. Only those fear Allah, from among His servants, who have knowledge'.

does, if the distinction between intellect and reason is missed in discussing the role of the latter in explaining the revelation.[18]

c. ***Doctrine versus reality***: Economic activity operates within some ideological framework; economics has an underlying doctrine that shapes institutions and prescribes goals, helps design policies, and gives content and direction to the ground reality. Thus, economies have an operable doctrine-reality circuitry. For example, in mainstream economic systems—capitalism or socialism—the doctrines resulted from the formalization of the observable ground realities. For instance, Adam Smith observed the accumulation of capital, technological breakthroughs, division of labour, and monetary institutions maturing in the country. In them, he could foresee the coming of the industrial revolution, characterizing Britain as the leading colonial power in the world at the time. His *Wealth of Nations* erected capitalism—its institutions and doctrine—from the ashes of the ground realities. Smith is rightly called the (capitalistic) triumphant system builder. Likewise, Karl Marx saw the dark side of capitalism: the exploitation and alienation of the working class, and the propensity of the system to spread mass income inequalities and abject poverty, deprivation, and denial. So he provided the initial design on which socialism was built. Over time, both capitalism and socialism assumed various shades and variations. The commonality between them is that in both cases the process went from reality to doctrine. What about Islam?

   The restraints of history apart, there was another challenge for Muslim economic thinkers. Here, one is confronted with a doctrine already in existence. The economic system must address the stated objectives (***maqasid-al-Shariah***). It must, for example, prioritize the fulfilment of basic needs, enforce the norms of justice, ensure fair play in business, tighten market regulations, and work for distributional equity. The process must move from doctrine to reality. The task is to make the existing realities reconcile with the doctrine; to get rid of the impurities that invaded it over time and continue to invade it even today. This is indeed an uphill task given the chaos and turmoil that plagues the Muslim world of today. Still,

[18] For a fuller discussion on the point, see Hasan (1998), the section on the reason-revelation relationship.

a beginning, however small, has to be made somewhere. It would be expedient to have a step-by-step approach to reach the destination over the course of time provided that the systems of governance in Muslim countries enable the minimum space required for such development.

With this background, we proceed with a discussion of some important topics on Islamic economics.

1.3 Definition of Islamic Economics

It is very difficult to define economics, more so in an Islamic framework, if it has to have and maintain linkage with ground realities. Economic activity is immersed in social dynamism. Thus, with multifarious types of social change, the scope of economics must keep on changing, or rather expanding, like the boundaries of a fast-growing metropolis. Still, for proper understanding of a subject, it becomes necessary to define it as precisely as possible.

A consensual definition of Islamic economics has not yet evolved even after more than six decades of its informal or formal existence (Iqbal and Muljawan 2007, p. 4). Social dynamism apart, several reasons have impeded progress in this matter.

First, the task of formalizing Islamic economics was initially taken up by religious scholars. They worked hard with devotion, earnestness, and humility. They successfully raised the edifice of Islamic economics, established and expanded educational institutions and developed teaching courses, published journals, and attracted professionals from the mainstream to enrich and give the subject a modern look and acceptability. Their contributions were great indeed.

New entrants into the discipline were sought and encouraged, although there was a discernible preference for those linked to the Islamic revivalist movements across countries in matters of recognition and reward. A school of thought of sorts had developed in Jeddah (Hasan 2005, pp. 12–13) having a common position on the approach, content, and thrust of Islamic economic ideas. With occasional departures, concepts like scarcity of resources, pursuit of self-interest, and maximizing behaviour on the part of economic agents, and what followed in their wake, was mostly thought external to Islamic economics. Nay, the denials were acclaimed to be the defining departures from the secular mainstream economics. This stance created much difficulty, confusion, controversy, and inconsistency in shaping the subject, especially its definition, nature, and scope.[19] There is no commonly agreed definition of Islamic economics; there is a profusion of them, characterized by ambiguity and confusion, if not absurdity.

The historical 'pull back' on the one hand and the resistance to it on the other has divided Islamic economists into two broad groupings: the regressive and the progressive. The regressive economists insist on a puritan *all-or-nothing* approach in developing Islamic economics. They reject mainstream economics lock, stock, and barrel. To them, it contains nothing worth Islamic approval.[20] To us, they are ivory tower thinkers and offer little that is operable in current times, even in Muslim countries. In contrast, there are those—the progressives—who argue that Islam never divided knowledge into Islamic and non-Islamic segments. Their approach takes the available stock of knowledge, advocates using Islamic filters to accept that which passes through, and reject what does not, even after modification in the light of *Shari'ah* norms. It is this sort of staggered 'step-by-step approach' that is gaining ground in the more recent writings on Islamic economics.

Then, there are writers who waver between these two more definitive group positions; not a few have preferred to revise their earlier postulates (see Khan 2013). There is increasing realization that mainstream economics contains much in terms of argument, analytical tools, and modes of presentation that can be adapted with advantage. The denial of resource scarcity, the condemnation of pursuing self-interest, and the

[19]The Islamic Development Bank (IDB) Prize Winner's Lecture by Dr. M. U. Chapra (1996) discusses the definition of Islamic Economics in pages 33–35. In his footnote 32, he has reproduced without comment the definitions of the subject in the writings of S. M. Hasanuz Zaman, M. A. Mannan, Khurshid Ahmad, M. N. Siddiqi, and M. Akram Khan, To Chapra himself, Islamic economics could be defined as 'that branch of knowledge which helps realize human well-being through an allocation and distribution of scarce resources that is in conformity with Islamic teachings without unduly curbing individual freedom or creating continued macroeconomic and ecological imbalances.' Necati Aydin (June, 2013) adds Hasan's definition of Islamic economics to Chapra's list and reviews them all in terms of what he calls a new paradigm in pp. 27–29.

[20]Of late, this group has become assertive and vocal, see articles in JKAU, *Islamic Economics*, vol. 26, no. 1, January 2013, 1 DOI: 10.4197 / Islec. 26-1.

rejection of maximizing behaviour have been common in Islamic economics. We shall discuss their efficacy in Chapter 2.

Despite the recent softening of attitudes on these basics of economics, many scholars continue to denounce any semblance of a proposal for defining Islamic economics that has the slightest affinity with the mainstream as touching the untouchable. This must be resisted. For it is hard to deny the 'want-scarcity' realism of human existence being a part of the Divine scheme. The definition we present below is doubtless in the post-Marshall-Robbins vein and yet its ramifications, we shall see, pull the two disciplines—Islamic and conventional economics—poles apart: One may presumably define the subject as follows:

> Islamic economics is a subject that studies human behavior in relation to multiplicity of human wants and scarcity of resources that have alternative uses, with a view to maximizing human *falah,* that is, best of well-being in the present world as also in the hereafter.

The incorporation of *falah* in the definition of Islamic economics is significant. The word is repeated twice in each call for prayers from the minarets five times a day. The word is the epitome of what Islam calls on mankind to observe, that is, to use material means to achieve peace in the hereafter. The notion is the essence of the request that most believers address to God after each prayer:

> Our Lord! Give unto us in this world that which is best and in the hereafter, that which is best, and save us from the torment of fire. (*Qur'an* [Al-Baqarah, 201])

In addition, the definition closes the gap between the mainstream and Islamic disciplines while keeping the two distinct because of their worldview differences. Several of the key mainstream concepts are in a process of revision for adaptation.

1.4 Nature and Scope

The nature of economics signifies the type of subject it is; appositive science or a normative science. This distinction between positive and normative has underlined the culture of mainstream economics since Lionel Robbins (1932), and has become the common property of textbook economics.[21] The scope of economics on the other hand, refers to its subject matter, that is, the areas of social concern it covers. The basic economic problems of people everywhere being alike, consumption, production, exchange, and distribution of goods and services (wealth) remain the basic concerns of economic studies (including Islamic) both at the micro and macro levels. Financing and public economics problems, including environmental issues, have of late shot into prominence. Scarcity of resources makes price theory pivotal to the discussion in all these areas. The main Islamic point of departure from mainstream economics is with reference to the concept of efficiency in various fields. Efficiency issues would indeed be a hard nut to crack in Islamic economics.

Scarcity of resources lends meaning to the notion of efficiency demanding extremism in the sense of maximizing gains. Such maximization per se is amoral: what is maximized and how are the deciding factors. For example, people may want to maximize the pleasure of God by doing virtuous deeds as the output from given inputs. We shall discuss the details in the next Chapter.

Following Adam Smith, mainstream economics was thought to be concerned with wealth alone, and the factors that promote its growth in a society, until the closing years of the twentieth century. However, ethical and moral considerations still had a perceptible influence on human conduct. The focus on wealth earned economics the title of a 'dismal science'. Marshall (1898) shifted the emphasis from wealth to the achieving of social well-being as the goal of economics; wealth becoming only a means to that end. Thus, economics became both a positive and a normative science with an artistic and *political* dimension added to it.

The position changed radically when in 1932 Lionel Robbins, a member of the Vienna Circle, projected a scarcity-based view of economics, making it neutral towards the ends. Positivism became its nature, empiricism its method. Consequently, its scope widened. Wherever scarcity raised a cost–benefit issue, there was seen an economic problem. Today, economic analysis is applied not only in the usual spheres of life but also

[21] 'In thinking about economic questions, we must distinguish questions of fact from questions of fairness ... Positive economics deals with questions such as: Why do doctors earn more than janitors? Does free trade raise or lower the wage of most Americans ... Normative Economics involves ethical precepts and norms of fairness; should poor people be required to work if they are to get government assistance?' (Samuelson and Nordau 2001, pp. 7–8).

in crime, education, marriage, health, law, politics, religion, social institutions, and war and peace studies. The expanding domain of economics in multiple social spheres is at times described as 'economic imperialism'. That description shows the nature and scope of modern economics. This may also be extended to Islamic economics with the *halal/haram* concepts as operative restrictions.

Islamic economics too, is a scientific body of knowledge, for it admits the use of reason and analogy to establish cause and effect relationships. The *Qur'an* shuns neither rationality nor positivism.[22] It is not averse to the use of metrics or empirical evidence. The scripture is replete with many positivist statements about natural phenomena and the real essence of human self and character. However, based as it is on religion, Islamic economics has of necessity a dominant normative aspect; it cannot move beyond its moral confines. Since Islam prescribes a way of living in this world, it avoids *idle theorizing*. Principles of Islamic economics are more the principles of economic policy. In sum, the subject holds both positive and normative content. Further, it also prescribes action programmes to achieve Islamic ends, as alluded to earlier.[23]

It is often contended as a point of distinction that mainstream economics is value-neutral while Islamic economics is value based. This is not true. For mainstream economics is not free of value judgments. Values are implicit in most of its assumptions, such as freedom of enterprise, private ownership of property, market arbitration, competition, non-intervention, and so on. All fall within this category. These assumptive values exist because of social approval and can also be changed or modified through social agreement. In Islamic economics, values are God-ordained; human beings can impart to them limited interpretive flexibility but they cannot abolish or replace them. Thus, both economic disciplines have values; the difference lies in their source.

[22] 'So have they not traveled through the earth and have hearts by which to reason and ears by which to hear? For indeed, it is not eyes that are blinded, but blinded are the hearts which are within the breasts' (*Al-Hajj*, verse 45–46).

[23] In a way, the positive/normative tangle had already been resolved for economics when J. N. Keynes (1890, pp. 34–35) observed: 'The problem whether political economy is to be regarded as a positive science, or as a normative science, or as an art, or as some combination of these, is to a certain extent a question merely of nomenclature and classification. It is, nevertheless, important to distinguish economic enquiries according as they belong to the three departments respectively; and it is also important to make clear their mutual relations'.

1.5 The Methods' Controversy

Economics studies human behaviour; thus, it cannot be as precise a study as of natural sciences like physics or chemistry. The latter subjects have the facility of designed experimentation in laboratories where the behaviour of relevant variables can be controlled to observe their mutual interactions. Social sciences, like economics, do not have such facility because they deal with living beings where stimuli can seldom be subjected to external control. Still, over a period of time, economic science has gained the maturity to develop its own *methods* that can be used for purposive analysis of economic phenomena. The role of these methods is to search for possible cause–effect relationships between the variables under consideration in order to generalize for explanatory purposes, as well as for making predictions with reasonable accuracy.

There are two broad methods used in economics for this purpose: deduction and induction. The positive-normative debate in economics has driven a wedge between the two; the 'battle of methods' was well known in the literature until it was realized that 'is and ought' can hardly exist without each other (Hands 2012).[24] It was argued, for example, that in the Pareto optimality postulate—making someone better off without making anyone else worse off—the fundamental postulate of modern welfare economics—the 'positive' incorporates a 'normative'. Norms of efficiency are purposeless without considerations of equity in the distribution of income and resources; the two must go together. These developments led to the conclusion that deduction and induction were both needed for scientific thought, as the right and left foot are both needed for walking.

In any case, one cannot imagine the existence of Islamic economics without a dominant normative content, thus raising concerns about increasing wealth concentration leading to mass deprivations, wage inadequacies, rent-seeking, land-related issues, suppressed or uncontrolled freedoms, environmental degradation, and so forth. The mainstream reconciliation on methods helps the cause of Islamic economics as well. Let us have a brief look at what these methods are and how they work.

[24] A related development has been the advent of the 'rational choice theory'.

1. ***Deduction***: In this method, certain hypotheses or postulates regarding human behaviour are taken to be true; for example, men are generally guided by self-interest. Then, logical reasoning establishes as to how they are likely to behave in a particular case. To illustrate: the pursuit of self-interest will tend to make consumers bid as low a price for a commodity as would be ***Deduction***: In this method, certain hypotheses or postulates regarding human behaviour are taken to be true; for example, men are generally guided by self-interest postulate. The important point is that in deduction we move from a general truth—real or assumed—to a conclusion. David Ricardo extensively used this method to establish many economic theories in the areas of distribution and foreign trade, theories that even to this day have explanatory and predictive values. Interestingly, Islamic economists could never explain the law of demand, neither by taking its existence as given nor by showing that it does not violate *Shari'ah* (Addas 2008). Mainstream economists took pains to put forth theories but could not justify a priori why the law of demand exists and behaves in the way it does.
2. ***Induction***: One need not deny the merits of the deductive method; it has proved useful in many cases and economizes on time and resources. However, it suffers from weaknesses. The main one is that the theories established via deduction often fail to keep pace with social dynamism over time and space. Ground realities increasingly tend to defy the assumptions underpinning deduction. Thus, the German historical school (and others) evolved induction or the empirical method, advocating its use in scientific inquiries. Induction involves deriving generalizations from the observation of commonalities in specific investigations concerning an economic phenomenon. Here we focus on facts to discover uniformities in relational behaviour to generate reasoning. For example, the output-cost data collected from the accounts of a large number of firms over time and space for short periods, defined by fixity of plant capacity, reveal similar U-shaped patterns of cost-output relationships and give rise to the law of variable proportions. Here is an attempt to arrive at a generalization from the known facts about ground realities. Note that here also social dynamism, variations in data elements, their definitions and recording within and between economic entities, choice of sample designs, and techniques of analysis can detract from the reliability of generalizations made. Empirical studies are increasingly found to be weak on the predictability front.

The preferred position on methods today is the use of what is known as the 'scientific approach', that advocates using deduction and induction at different stages within the same sphere of inquiry, if need be. Islam is supportive of this position; deduction and induction have both played their parts in the evolution of *fiqh al-muamalat*, especially in Moorish Spain.

1.6 Economic Systems

Islam prescribes, as said earlier, a way of living in this world in order to realize salvation in the hereafter. The divine law demands on ground demonstration in following the Path; idle theorizing has little value in *Shari'ah*. Thus, Islamic economics began with writings on the Islamic economic system.[25] In fact, the words 'economics', 'economic system', and 'economy' have been interchangeably used in the literature on the subject.

Economic activity operates in a broad organizational framework called the economic system. This framework consists of economic entities like households, business firms, public institutions, markets, and so on. Such entities consist of and are operated by a set of rules of conduct governed by the doctrine ingrained in the community's worldview. The main components of a system making it Islamic and different from the two others—capitalism and socialism—are as follows:

[25]The first systematic, comprehensive, and extensively documented treatise on the subject was *The Economic System of Islam (broad outlines)* in the Urdu language. Written by Sheikh Hif-zur-Rahman of Seohara, India, the then Secretary General of the Jamaat-e-Ulma-e-Hind, the book was published by Dar-ul-Mussanifeen, Urdu Bazar, Delhi-6 in 1936 and went into six *commercial* editions over a decade, the last appearing in 1946. Other writers, including Mawdudi, appeared on the scene much later.

Sheikh Rahman was doubtless *the* pioneer of Islamic economics in the Indian sub-continent. Regrettably, his *System* never won the recognition it deserved in the literature. This was because of a political divide: the Jamaat-e-Ulma-e-Hind of the Sheikh was with the Congress in the freedom movement and was against the partition of the country, while Islamic economics after the partition became the prime concern of the Jamaat-e-Islami (Pkistan Unit) controlling academic thought and agenda. Obviously, the *magnum opus* of Rahman—a truly encyclopedic effort—could not fall into the scheme of the Jamaat.

Original copies of the Sheikh's *System* with an introduction in English written by Zubair Hasan (2004), are available in the main libraries of the International Islamic University (IIUM) and INCEIF and the Global University of Islamic Finance, the two leading seats of Islamic instruction in Kuala Lumpur, Malaysia. Of late, an electronic edition of the book rendered by Prof. Ghaffari from Pakistan has also appeared on the internet. The book deserves translation into English at the earliest.

1. ***Axiomatic differences***: Axioms refer to what in a system is *believed* as self-evident truths; truths implicit in the worldview a society upholds. To illustrate, capitalism, in principle, believes in freedom of enterprise, public non-intervention in economic matters, market supremacy, and arbitration, with competition as a regulatory force for ensuring public good. In this setting, it sees no clash between individual and social interest in general. On the contrary, socialism, shorn of its shades and details, is opposed to freedom of enterprise which, it believes, must end up in a capital–labour clash resulting in the suppression and exploitation of workers. It believes in public ownership of productive resources and economic planning by central command and direction to ensure distributive justice resulting in social equality and eventual peace.

   Islam seeks to take the middle path between the two—capitalism, and socialism. It accommodates the axioms of capitalism, but in a reformed and socially conducive form as per *Shari'ah* norms and directions. In its thrust and focus, the system is, like socialism, pro-poor but without being anti-rich; it seeks to convert the mundane ambitions of people here into means for *falah* in the hereafter. Tolerance, patience, humanism, and justice are its guiding principles.
2. ***Property rights***: The Islamic system, like capitalism, allows the private ownership of property, but with an important departure. It enjoins property owners to hold it not only for self-benefit but also in trust to benefit others as well (*Qur'an*, 2:29). Unlike capitalism, Islam assigns rights to others in one's wealth, especially the poor and the deprived, that must be upheld and honoured. The scripture exhorts the believers to spend at least a prescribed minimum on social good.
3. ***Operational mechanism***: Allowing private ownership of property in Islam implies freedom of enterprise, pursuit of self-interest, and seeking of maximization of gains, of course, subject to *Shari'ah* constraints.[26] Islam approves competitive markets (for *halal* goods

[26]There has been much confusion and debate on the maximizing behaviour of economic agents in Islamic economics and the issue remains in a state of flux. Mohammad Akram Khan (2013, p. 42), commenting on the illogic of resistance to the proposition in his well-received publication *What is wrong with Islamic economics*, seems to have clinched the issue when he wrote, 'A respectable exception is Hasan (2005, 32) who argues that maximization behavior has to be seen in the context of "what" and "how" before a final verdict can be given'. We return to this issue, along with others, in the following Chapter 2 in detail.

only) and allows the price mechanism to operate *sans* interest, indeterminacy, and speculation that could mar the fair play of market forces. The system relies on regulation and control of markets.

4. ***Societal priorities***: Capitalism, as its name implies, works to promote and safeguard the interests of the owners of capital. In that, it gives more weight to individual liberty and freedom of action as compared to societal aspirations and well-being. Socialism seeks to reverse these priorities. Islam allows individuals *guided* liberty to develop and utilize one's full potential to benefit self and to help others. Philosophically, Islam sees the existence of individuals in society as waves in the ocean. Societal interest and well-being gains precedence over that of the individual in Islam should there be a clash between the two. Thus, scarce economic resources must be utilized to first produce those goods that meet the basic human needs of food, clothing, shelter, education, and health care (needs fulfilment).

1.7 Problems

Islamic economics is at present in a muddled state and lacks a clear direction. Part of the problem can be traced back to its originating in the writings of the clergy, who found themselves socially marginalized during the long spells of colonial rule over the Muslim lands. They did much laudable work that helped preserve the Islamic identity of the community and provided them with a living. Compared to their positive contributions to society, they also tended to keep the masses away from modern education to save them from absorbing the cultural values of the colonial masters. By the time foreign rule ended and independence dawned over the Muslim lands, mostly after the Second World War, the community had already been divided horizontally between those equipped with Western education and those remaining caught in religious orthodoxy without understanding its applications in modern times.

Independence transferred power to the minority with Western education, leaving the religious leadership far behind. The latter started Islamic movements across the Muslim world to capture political power. Islamic economics no longer remained a pious scholarly pursuit; it increasingly became part of the political arsenal of the relatively poor and those on the lower rungs of the intellectual ladder. However, Islamic movements could seldom gain political power, or retain it even where they could, because of Western machinations, including armed intervention to overthrow them.

Nevertheless, Islamic movements did succeed in extracting major concessions and massive financial support from the various state organs for Islamic economics and finance to emerge and attain quickly the status of an academic discipline, not only in Muslim lands but across non-Muslim countries as well.

This indeed was a great and laudable achievement of Islamic movement leaders across the world. However, on this road of progress, the discipline has also acquired some serious afflictions. With the passage of time and with wider recognition of the subject, the movements' dominance of Islamic economics and financial education slackened; they could not keep out, but rather had to welcome, non-movement professionals who entered and took over the discipline. This created some difficulties, as follows:

- The Islamic system having affinities with capitalism, the latter continued across Muslim countries. Consequently, the old guard sharpened its attacks on the situation, demonstrating the superiority of the Islamic order over capitalism. One need not go over their claim for it is flawed. One must ask: how valid is it to compare the *ideals* of an Islamic system with one operating *actual* economies? To us, it is an unfair chalk and cheese comparison, proving nothing and getting us nowhere.
- On the other hand, the new enthusiasts, the professionals educated in the West with their foreign degrees enjoying a premium in the emerging Muslim economies, have staked their claims on Islamic economics. Conditioned in the Western mode of thinking, they want Islamic economics, especially finance, to develop along the empirical route even as they are well aware that ethical norms and intentions limitations on quantification and the data they can, and do use, seldom have the needed Islamic content and essence.
- In between these, there has emerged a new group of so-called Islamic economists: the Muslims retiring from the international financial institutions such as the IMF and the World Bank. They do not always deserve the credit Islamic institutions add to them. Their appointment to international institutions is not essentially on

academic merit or through competition; it is principally political—governments of member countries appoint them as their representatives conforming to a quota system. They tend to make poor academics.

- The educational, cultural, and attitudinal differences among the academics working in higher learning institutions in the Muslim world are due to the fact that they come from heterogeneous backgrounds. They have limitations in developing a cohesive and directional body of literature in Islamic economics.

1.8 Challenges and the Future

Islamic economics faces some serious challenges for its survival as a distinct, respected academic discipline. Some of these are as follows:

- In the forward march of any educational system—Islamic or secular—the fear of change is the greatest stumbling block on the road to progress. The subject may remain rooted in the past but the past can never be the present or the future of a vibrant academic discipline. Conservatism is the millstone of Islamic economics, not contributing much in practical terms to the progress and prosperity of Muslims across the globe. There is no merit in finding fault with others unless one can show that what one preaches is superior on the ground. Demonstration wins conviction, not contentions.
- The rising overuse of econometric modelling in Islamic economics and finance is detracting from the cause of purposive research. It often lacks the needed theoretical basis and data compatibility with Islamic norms. The results are invariably confirmative akin to reinventing the wheel and, usually non-applicative. It seems a perilous imitation of the Western academic culture admiring Islamic economics and finance. It tends to kill creative thinking in young scholars and detracts attention from indigenous issues.
- A serious challenge Islamic economics and finance face is the lack of well-structured and graded course structures and the matching textbooks. Western course designs and textbooks in *social* sciences education do not always address the relevant issues nor provide cases and illustrations appropriate to Islamic disciplines. Students in Islamic institutions of higher learning should not be kept away from the learning of mainstream economics, as Islam does not shun

gaining that knowledge. However, it is advisable that writing textbooks on Islamic economics must be a priority and must adopt an integrative non-exclusivist approach.[27]

- Only a few of the journals brought out by Islamic educational institutions on research in Islamic economics and finance are refereed and well-recognized. Although the International Centre for Education in Islamic Finance (INCEIF) is acclaimed as the thought leader in Islamic finance, it surprisingly did not launch a journal to disseminate its acclaimed innovative thoughts and ground-breaking researches. However, its lesser-known sister organization, the International Shari'ah Research Academy for Islamic Finance (ISRA), regularly brings out a reputable bi-annual *Shari'ah*-oriented journal on Islamic finance. What is required is stricter scrutiny of articles for quality. There is uncalled for pressure on faculty and students to seek publication in Western journals for professional growth. New journals are mushrooming in the West to meet the rising demand; their publication has become a fast-expanding business. Many online 'journals charge hefty publication fees. Authors in developing countries, especially Muslims, tend to publish in such below par journals. They go in for group writing to share the publication charges' (Hasan 2018).
- The moral angle missing in mainstream economic theory and its alarming consequences[28] have increasingly been pushing economists to investigate the psychological aspects of human behaviour in the economic sphere (Hausman 2017)[29] The 'Nudge Theory' of the 2017 Nobel Laureate Richard Thaler has been hailed as a further vindication of the relevance of behavioural economics. Thus,

[27] On this, see Hasan (1998, 2005, 2015 prefaces). See also M. Akram Khan (2013, pp. 7–8).

[28] The global economy will confront serious challenges in the months and years ahead, and looming in the background is a mountain of debt that makes markets nervous—and that also increases the system's vulnerability to destabilizing shocks. Yet the baseline scenario seems to be one of continuity, with no obvious convulsions on the horizon.

[29] Ricardo Hausmann, former Chief Economist of the Inter-American Development Bank, Director of the Center for International Development at Harvard University, and a professor of economics at the Harvard Kennedy School.

here is an opportunity for Islamic economics to fill the gap, as it is a social science, not theology. However, to that end, Islamic economists must shun a retrogressive approach to the subject and promote interpretive flexibility to *Shari'ah*, while being assimilative of the changes that social dynamism initiates. This would enable the discipline to drop irrelevant economic content marring its future. Islamic finance may survive until there is demand for oil in the world, or other energy sources do not sufficiently replace it. Without the indicated changes, the future of Islamic economics looks bleak.

Box 1.1: Nature of Economics: Islamic vs. Mainstream

Islamic economics began as a challenge to and a fundamental critique of conventional economics, and the ambition of most Islamic economists of the first generation was the replacement of mainstream economics by a new paradigm based on, or at least consistent with, the comprehensive Islamic worldview. It is questionable whether this goal has been achieved. A growing volume of literature with an 'Islamic economics' label follows the same quantitative approach and differs from the mainstream only in so far as it deals with phenomena in Muslim countries, especially with aspects of *Shari'ah*-compliant banking and finance. Such studies of economic issues from an Islamic perspective are deeply rooted in conventional economics and lack the systemic or holistic dimension that is indispensable for the establishment of a new paradigm for the science of Islamic economics. Islamic economics as an autonomous discipline requires a systemic orientation, and it is conceptually inextricably linked with Islamic theology and law. However, the necessary intellectual interaction between economists and *Sharī'ah* scholars is deficient. While Islamic economists have come forward with models of a financial system based on participatory modes of finance and widespread risk sharing, many scholars of Islamic law have been more concerned with the replication of conventional instruments for risk-free, fixed-return transactions or with *Shari'ah*-compliant derivatives. Their efforts have moved Islamic finance closer to the conventional *status quo* and further away from an alternative system of financial intermediation. This does not contribute to the development of a new paradigm of Islamic economics, but this process is reversible (Nienhaus, V., 'Method and Substance of Islamic Economics: Moving Where?', *JKAU: Islamic Econ.*, vol. 26, no. 1, 2013 A.D./1434 A.H., pp. 175–208).

Test Questions

Q.1 Examine the nature of worldview and show how it affects theoretical structures and economic systems comparatively in the mainstream and Islamic disciplines.

Q.2 'The definition and scope of Islamic economics differs from the mainstream but the two have similarities as well'. Do you agree? Give reasons for your answer.

Q.3 'One common error in economics in both cases—Islamic and mainstream—is that the proponents of one compare their theoretical idealism with the operational blemishes of the other to claim superiority. This is akin to comparing apples with oranges'. Elaborate

Q.4 Methodology is a confused and controversial subject in economics. Do you agree? Argue your case.

Q.5 Write explanatory notes on:

a. Induction and deduction
b. Axiomatic differences
c. Property rights

What Next?

We have discussed the nature and significance of Islamic economics. The discussion has included mainstream positions resting on certain assumptions—scarcity of resources, pursuit of self-interest, and maximization of gains from economic activities. However, as these fundamentals are unacceptable to many writings on the subject, we examine them in some detail to assess their efficacy for use in Islamic economics in Chapter 2.

References

Addas, W. A. J. (2008). Methodology—Secular Versus Islamic. Kuala Lumpur: Research Management Centre, International Islamic University of Malaysia (IIUM).

Al-Atas, S. M. N. (1995). *Prolegomena to the Metaphysics of Islam: An Exposition of the Fundamental Elements of Islamic Worldview*. Kuala Lumpur: Malaysian International Institute of Islamic Thought and Civilization.

Aydin, N. (2013, June). Redefining Islamic Economics as a New Economic Paradigm. *Islamic Economic Studies, 21*(1), 1–34.

Boulakia, J. D. C. (1971). Ibn Khaldûn: A Fourteenth-Century Economist. *Journal of Political Economy, 79*(5), 1105–1118. https://doi.org/10.1086/259818.

Chapra, M. U. (1996). *What Is Islamic Economics*. Jeddah: IRTI.

El-Gamal, M. A. (2009). *Macro vs. Micro- Considerations in Islamic Financial Ijtihad*. Istanbul: Lecture IIFF.

Friedman, M. (1953). The Methodology of Positive Economics. In *Essays in Positive Economics* (pp. 3–43). Chicago: University of Chicago Press.

Guide, C., & Rist, C. (1953). *History of Economic Doctrines*. New Delhi: George Harper.

Hands, D. W. (2012). The Positive and Normative Dichotomy and Economics. *Handbook of Philosophy of Sciences, 3*, 219–239.

Hasan, Z. (1998). Islamization of Knowledge in Economics: Issues And Agenda. *IIUM Journal of Economics and Management, 6*(2), 1–40.

Hasan, Z. (2004). *The New World Order, Muslim Predicament, and the Way Out* (MPRA Paper 3009). University Library of Munich, Germany.

Hasan, Z. (2005). Islamic Banking at the Cross-Roads: Theory Versus Practice. In R. Wilson & M. Iqbal (Eds.), *Islamic Perspectives on Wealth Creation* (pp. 11–25). Edinburg, UK: Edinburg University Press.

Hasan, Z. (2015). *Economics with Islamic Orientation*. Kuala Lumpur, Malaysia: Oxford University Press.

Hasan, Z. (2018, June). Academic Sociology: The Alarming Rise in Predatory Publishing and Its Consequences for Islamic Economics and Finance. *ISRA Journal of Islamic Finance, 10*(1), 6–18.

Hausman Daniel, M. (Ed.). (2017). *The Philosophy of Economics; An Anthology*. UK: Cambridge University Press.

Hussein, K. A. (2013). *Islamic Economics: Current State of Knowledge and Development of the Ipline*. The Seventh International Conference on Islamic Economics, Jeddah.

Iqbal, S. A., & Muljawan, D. (Eds.). (2007). *Advances in Islamic Economics and Finance* (Vol. 1). Jeddah: IRTI/IDB.

Islahi, A. A. (2010). Four Generations of Islamic Economists. *Journal of King Abdulaziz University: Islamic Economics, 23*(1), 165–170.

Keynes, J. N. (1890). *Scope and Method of Political Economy*. Kitchener: Batoche Books.

Khaldun, I. (1967). *Muqaddimah: An Introduction to History* (F. Rozenthal, Trans., Bollingen Series XLIII, 1980 print, Vol. 2). Princeton University Press.

Khan, M. A. (2013). *What Is Wrong with Islamic Economics*. Northampton, MA: Edward Elgar.

Marshall, A. (1898/1949). *Principles of Economics*. New York: Macmillan.

Qutb, S. (1978). *Milestones*. Beirut: The Holy Qur'an Publishing House.

Redman, D. A. (1991). *Economics and Philosophy of Science*. Oxford: Oxford University Press.

Robbins, L. (1932). *Nature and Significance of Economic Science*. London, UK: Macmillan.

Sadr, M. Baqar-as. (1983). *Iqtisaaduna* (Our Economics) (Vol. 2, Part 1). Tehran: WOFIS.

Samuelson, P. A., & Nordau, W. D. (2001). *Economics* (17th ed.). New York: McGraw-Hill.

Shari'ati, A. (1982). *Man and Islam,* Lectures (G. M. Fayez, Trans.). Mashhad, Iran: University of Mushhad Press.

Shinsuke, N. (2012). Critical Overview of the History of Islamic Economics: Formation, Transformation, and New Horizons. *Asian and African Area Studies, 11*(2), 114–136.

CHAPTER 2

Scarcity Self-interest and Maximization: Efficacy for Islamic Economics

Preview
Modern economics is based on some fundamental assumptions believed to be realistic. These include: (i) that resources are scarce in relation to human wants; (ii) that people are normally spurred into action in pursuit of their own interest; and (iii) that they attempt to maximize the benefits of their efforts at minimum cost.

Islamic economics originated with men of religion, not as an academic discipline but as a socio-political element in their tools kit to educate and encourage Muslims in their struggle for freedom from their colonial rulers. Foreign plunder of their resources, devastation of local skills and crafts, and exploitation of farmers and workers were matters of common experience. Highlighting the economic sufferings of the masses was thought the best fuel to keep the freedom fire burning. It was relevant and expedient to demonstrate that exploitation causing the spread of poverty and aggravating income inequalities was inherent to the western economic systems. We shall argue as to how the Islamic system could get rid of these afflictions.

It was expected that after independence, objectivity and reason would guide the development of Islamic economics. Regrettably, this has not happened to the extent, and with the speed, that was expected. Orthodox rhetoric and unfounded apprehensions continue to cause a negative and rejectionist attitude towards many useful and logical mainstream ideas. The three fundamental concepts of economics mentioned above are still frowned upon, although some writers have of late relented on their use in Islamic economics for analytical purposes.

Z. Hasan, *Leading Issues in Islamic Economics and Finance*,
https://doi.org/10.1007/978-981-15-6515-1_2

This chapter argues that stocks of resources that God has created *are* inexhaustible. However, what is important is the availability of resources to mankind out of these provisions. Availability is a function of human knowledge about resources over time and space. In that sense, resources must be scarce in relation to the multiplicity of human wants in Islamic economics as well.

Self-interest must be distinguished from selfishness. This motive operates at both ends of human existence: the mundane and the spiritual. Its pursuit does not preclude altruism from human nature and living. In fact, counter-interests keep balance in society and promote civility. Islam recognizes this motive as valid.

Maximization relates to estimable *ex ante* variables. Although the uncertainty of future outcomes of human actions makes maximization a heuristic concept, it remains a useful analytical tool. The concept is value-neutral. What is maximized, how maximization is achieved and to what end, gives rise to moral issues. Modified in the light of *Shari'ah* norms the three concepts provide, as we have seen in Chapter 1, a firmer definition of Islamic economics, centred on the juristic notion of *falah*. We clarify the nature of these concepts in this chapter and provide a defence for their use in Islamic economics.

Learning Outcomes

A study of this chapter is expected to enable the reader to understand and explain the following:

- The implications of what gives rise to economic activities. That is, the multiplicity of human wants relative to the resources available to satisfy them against historical backdrop and population explosion.
- The true import of the concept of scarcity and its relevance for Islamic economics, in the sense of availability of resources as distinct from their providential provision.
- The impact of knowledge expansion and environmental concerns on the notion of scarcity.
- Self-interest, distinct from selfishness, as the dominant, natural, and legitimate motivational force in determining human conduct in human activities, mundane or spiritual.
- The nature of maximization a variable as a heuristic analytical tool useful for Islamic economics, co-extensive with altruism.

Scarcity of resources, pursuit of self-interest, and maximization of gains are the interrelated foundational concepts for erecting any economic system. For Islamic economics, they need modifications, not rejection.

2.1 Introduction

Islamic economics emerged as a formal academic discipline during the closing quarter of the preceding century. It has since moved forward rapidly even with conflicts in its content focus and presentation structure. While the juristic substance and ethical instructions of Islam have been the centre of attention, the writings on the subject—articles, books, or dissertations—have mostly picked up topics, terminology, and presentation styles of mainstream economics. Presumably, this was unavoidable for a variety of reasons. However, this could not soften the otherwise avoidable negativity towards some of the foundational concepts and methods of mainstream economics. It is however felt that the raising of the edifice of Islamic economics to newer heights could hardly ignore these fundamentals. The elaboration of this point is essential to reinforce the content of the preceding chapter and bolster the discussion of those that follow. These basics include scarcity of resources, pursuit of self-interest, and maximization of gains (Samuelson 1947).

The social order of Islam had been flourishing the world over for centuries before modern capitalism appeared on the scene with the dawn of the industrial revolution in England. However, it is seldom realized that the basic features of the capitalistic system had all along been evolving during the era away from the Red sea in Moorish Spain (Hasan 1992, p. 239). For instance the system allowed, as in Islam, the private ownership of property, granted freedom of enterprise, and approved a free play of market forces in the economy. Likewise, it also eulogized trade and held in high esteem business profits that Islam counted among the bounties of Allah (swt). But these features of the Islamic system became increasingly distorted as capitalism advanced on the secular path and eventually achieved *global* status.

Today, there has been a reversal of the historical sequence: Muslim scholars, oblivious to the past, emphasize the affinities of the Islamic system along these lines as borrowings from capitalism. Indeed, of late, they see and seek the fulfilment of their aspirations in reforming capitalism, not in erecting the Islamic order as an independent alternative.[1] Is it not then strange that Islamic economists are divided on admitting that resources for the satisfaction of wants are scarce, that human beings essentially seek to promote their own interests, and that they perforce want to maximize their gains? Their position on these issues and their ramifications, basic to economics, remain *inconclusive*, to put it mildly. We shall argue that these postulates have also to be the fulcrum of Islamic economics, for its own survival. What is required is a relook at the content and character of these postulates, not their rejection.

2.2 The Language of Economics

For a clear understanding of economic analysis, prior reference to a linguistic point may be helpful. Mainstream economics picks up its notions of consumption, production, firms, profit, demand, supply exchange, entrepreneurs, growth, and so forth mostly from the bin of common parlance. However, when economists construct the ideal or the abstract type out of these words of daily use to facilitate explanation or analysis, the meanings of these same words change, at times radically. Not many can always understand what economists may be talking about; they may mean something quite different from what the same word conveys to the man in the street. Even among economists, differences of opinion can, at times, be traced back to divergent meanings of the same term.

This happens because the terms tend to assume different meanings dependent on the goal of the model or the type of market structure one has in mind. For example, paper money is wealth for the one who sees it in the pockets of individuals. But the same money is not wealth for the community as a whole, for printing more notes cannot, by itself, remove poverty.

A brief explanation of the historical bearings of the concepts under review may help clear the confusion around them and enable us to

[1]For example, M. N. Siddiqi shifted from *the teaching of Islamic economics* to *teaching economics from the Islamic perspective* (Hasan 1998b). Professor Khurshid Ahmad pleaded in a recent lecture (2007) that Islamic reforms in the field of economics must be sought *within* the capitalistic framework. Also, the title of a recent book of Murat Cizaca is *Islamic Capitalism and Finance*. The process of one-sided convergence has been hastened more by the imitative expansion of Islamic finance.

see the issues in the right perspective. This we do in Sect. 2.3 below. Section 2.4 deals with 'population explosion and output expansion', a relationship contextual to distributive justice pertaining to the assumptions under discussion. In Sect. 2.5, we explain the meaning of scarcity, its social implications, and the Islamic position on it. Section 2.6 shows that pursuit of self-interest is ingrained in human nature and that Islam has no hesitation in recognizing this fact. Section 2.7 is devoted to explaining the maximizing behaviour of economic agents and its relevance in Islamic economics. Finally, Sect. 2.8 contains concluding observations on the linkage between the three basic economic notions and their collective efficacy in Islamic economics.

2.3 Pre-Islamic Context

Human beings have always desired and strived to improve their living conditions through increase in consumption. They instinctively desire more and more goods for use compared to what they command resources to produce. Thus, scarcity of resources in the face of unrestricted proliferation of human wants (including spiritual) gives rise to activities that we study in what has long been known as economics. However, a study of economics, as of any other subject, always relates to a *time span*—long or short—on its never-ending evolutionary path. It is vital to learn about the exact time when Islam joined the economics caravan in order to account for how it did or can contribute to the discipline.

It would perhaps be appropriate to start with the contribution of Greek thinkers to the history of economic thought, the leading lights among them being Hesiod, Democritus, Xenophon, and Aristotle. In their era (800–322 BC), the population of the world must have been tiny and scattered. Resources were plentiful at that time. There was no scarcity, nor was efficiency the focus of attention. Markets had arrived but played no role in the allocation of resources; that was regulated by tribal authorities, customs, or faith. As life was simple, there were few topics to discuss. And yet, the Greeks provided valuable insights into economic theory; their cohesive presentation of the *natural law* is notable. Greek contributions influenced not only Islamic thinking but left their mark far beyond on the path of knowledge expansion. For instance, their articulation of the *natural law* was revived centuries later in the French Physiocracy.

2.3.1 *The Greek Impact*

Two important themes emerged from the writings of the Greek thinkers. One related to the type of approach required for social inquiry. They believed that it was inappropriate to divide human activities into categories such as economic and non-economic for social inquiry and investigation. They held that social problems were interwoven, as shades in a painting, and could best be studied in relation to one another as parts of a whole. This view also found favour with early Islamic economists who insisted that Islam called for integrated studies of social phenomena in arriving at a correct understanding of the issues and in designing appropriate policy prescriptions. Such insistence was understandable at their time as populations were small and living simple.

Authentic records regarding world population are not available for the seventh century, the point when Islam arrived on the scene. Figure 2.1 shows that it was around 200 million at the dawn of Christianity, and grew to no more than 275 million by the year 1000. Thus, estimating the world population at 235 million, it may be inferred that the social environment of early Islamic scholars may not have been much different from that of the Greek writers and their immediate followers. Thus, they too could advocate for and indulge in an all-inclusive type of writing, taking a unitary view of social phenomena. However, the approach was by no means a faith compulsion. Subsequent population explosion and output expansion placed a question mark on these all-embracing types of studies.

Resources being abundant in relation to small populations, scarcity was not an issue for the Greeks. Thus, their next focus of attention was on the questions of fairness, justice, and equity. They examined exchange relations and prices essentially from an ethical prism. The dominance of moral sentiment could well be understood in economies where market activity yet remained inconsequential. Adam Smith spoke of 'moral sentiment' as a dominant social force even as late as 1758. Thus, the early Islamic scholars' focus on moral concerns could well be understood where market activity yet remained small and simple. Further, the early Islamic scholars also spoke more of social justice in the modern economic context of increasing complexities because the definitive core of the Islamic faith stays undiluted. In due course, population explosion and output expansion made such concerns more complicated, more urgent.

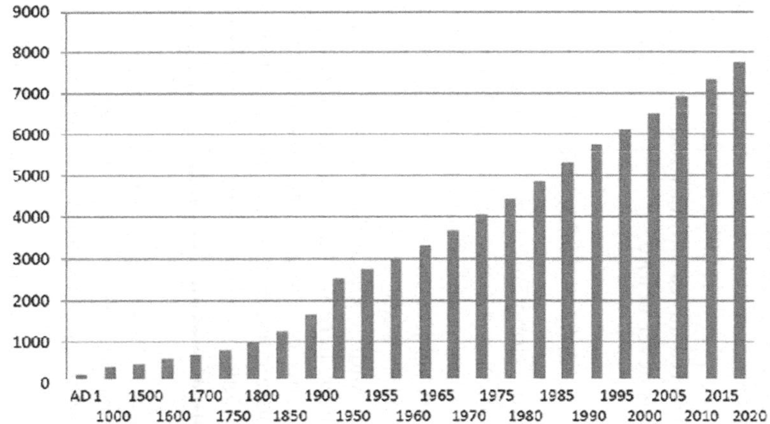

Y	P	Y	P
AD 1	200	1965	3,322
1000	400	1970	3,682
1500	458	1975	4,061
1600	580	1980	4,440
1700	682	1985	4,853
1750	791	1990	5,310
1800	1,000	1995	5,735
1850	1,262	2000	6,127
1900	1,650	2005	6,520
1950	2,525	2010	6,930
1955	2,758	2015	7,349
1960	3,018	2020	7,749

Fig. 2.1 World population growth over the centuries (*Source* Author's construction; Data from Wikipedia)

2.4 Population vs. Output

The world population grew at a significant pace after the industrial revolution. There was an explosion in numbers after the early decades of the preceding century (see Fig. 2.1). Today, world population is more than seven times what it was in 1750, that is, around 1500 years after the advent of Islam. The modern era has witnessed a vast expansion not only in numbers but in knowledge as well. These expansions have been accompanied by rapid developments in the means of transport and communication, making the world smaller in terms of time and distance. Consequently, humanity has produced more output since 1950 than it had during its entire existence prior to that year (AI 3 2006). Still, the world remains obsessed with the impending population explosion.

In addition, the prosperity the world has witnessed is not an unmixed blessing. The issues of war and violence, crime and corruption, tyranny and terror, poverty and plunder, affluence and bankruptcy, the rapacious exploitation of natural resources and environmental calamities now stare mankind in the face as never before.

2.4.1 *Holistic Studies*

Oblivious to these developments, many Islamic economists continue to insist that the subject must not restrict itself to the analysis of market forces alone. They assert that it must integrate the findings of other social sciences into its subject matter. Today, we do not have one physician to treat all human body parts—a whole array of specialists exists for different organs. And people welcome such specialization as it gives better results. However, here we have scholars insisting that Islamic economics must be holistic; covering every aspect of social existence—that is a million times more complicated an organism than the human body. Our brain *has* limitations. We have yet to come across such an integrative effort in the literature as is being demanded.

> Indeed, it was the very ability of man to make an abstract separation of human activities that represents the part of intellectual apparatus necessary for the 'birth' of economics and other social sciences. (Landreth and Colander, p. 25)

The fact that Islamic norms are not shaping realities in Muslim countries has led to many misplaced arguments between Islamic economists on the one hand and their mainstream critics on the other. Both sides have been oblivious to one principle of simple logic—that one must compare the ideals of one system with the ideals—*not realities*—of the other. Islamic economists invariably err in comparing the ideals of their system, based on what *ought to be*, with the '*what is*' of capitalism in operation.[2] Likewise, their opponents, largely from the West, attack Islamic ideals for erecting an economic system that has failed, citing conditions as they are in Muslim countries. Much of the criticism of Islamic economics coming from the West—for instance from Timur Kuran—falls in this category.[3] The critics fail to realize that the long colonial past of these countries, and its later continuation in different guises, seldom allowed their leaders the space to implement the Islamic agenda for social development, even when they desired to do so. Let us realize that Muslims may not always be doing what Islam requires and that what Muslims are doing may not always be Islamic.

Islamic economists can contribute to the effort by curbing the subjectivity colouring their thought process and by developing an objective understanding of mainstream economics in order to make more widely acceptable contributions to the discipline. Furthermore, emphasis is required on the substance rather than on the form of what Islam stands for. It is the understanding, not antagonism that will eventually win the day for Islamic economics.[4] Therefore, let us have a look at the foundation stones of mainstream economics from this angle.

[2] For example, suppose one had a magic wand that could be used for making competition perfect in all types of markets—the ideal of capitalism. Then, one could presumably venture the assertion that much of the divergence between the ideal Islamic economic structures and that of capitalism evaporates into thin air.

[3] Kuran (1989, p. 178) makes a rather eristic remark on my demonstration of how the profit-sharing ratio would be determined in Islamic finance under certain assumptions (Hasan 1985). He writes: 'Another author, using a mathematical model says that the shares are to be determined through the interaction of the supply and demand of contracts—as if, once again, an equilibrium allocation could never be lopsided.' Now, I have nowhere talked about the qualitative aspect of equilibrium, let alone held that the equilibrium ratio can, or will always, ensure a just division of profit between the parties. At the same time, is it not a fact that most of the theoretical constructs in mainstream economics rest on virtue-free equilibrium heuristics?

[4] It was in this context that I have long advocated a 'step-by-step' approach to Islamizing economics as opposed to the 'all-or-nothing' line implied in several major works on Islamic economics (Hasan 1988, 1998a, 2012). Haneef and Furqani (2004, p. 31) find me 'wrong' on the point. To them, the latter method never existed. I respect their opinion but I maintain my position that incidentally finds clarification and support in recent works. See, for example, M. Omar Farooq (2006, pp. 43–44).

2.5 Scarcity of Resources

The Greek writers did not care to give scarcity any precise meaning or explore its ramifications, as in their era population was small and resources plentiful. However, there were things during those times such as certain types of plants or rocks that they did not come across often; they were *rare*, i.e. very small in quantity. It was this experience of *rarity* that eventually led to the notion of *scarcity*. Senior (1790–1864) was presumably the first economist to lay stress on scarcity and regarded it as the basis of value. *Rarity* was not enough for a thing to assume value; it must also satisfy some human want. It must be rare in terms of utility. It was the same sense in which Walrus has used the term. 'scarcity' i.e. as a base of value. The term assumed new meaning when Lionel Robbins in his influential work, *An Essay on the Nature and Significance of Economic Science* (1932) projected the notion as the definitional base of economics.[5] He carried its relationship with human wants a step further. To him, resources, including time, could not be scarce unless they had alternative uses (pp. 13–14). This attribute of scarcity forces on human beings the compulsion of *choice-making* in the face of a multiplicity of wants: 'wherever there was a problem of choice, there was an economic problem'. Robbins thus saw scarcity as an aspect of human existence, widening the scope of economic science to cover a whole gamut of social problems, including even marriage, crime, corruption, and elections. There is room for the presumption that a remark in the *Essay* might have provoked Islamic economists to deny the existence of resource scarcity altogether. Robbins wrote[5]:

> The ends are various. The time and means for achieving these ends are limited and capable of alternative applications. At the same time, the ends have different importance. Here we are sentient creatures with a bundle of desires and aspirations with masses of instinctive tendencies all urging us different ways to action. But the time in which these tendencies can be expressed is limited. The external world does not offer full opportunities for their complete achievement. ***Life is short. Nature is niggardly***.... Human activity has not the independence of time or specific resources. There are only twenty-four hours in the day. We have to choose between different uses to which they may be put. (*Essay*, 1932, pp. 2–15, emphasis added)

[5]The second edition of the *Essay* was published in 1935. References given in this work are from a 1945 reprint of this version downloaded from the internet.

Presumably, the Islamic economists took Robbins' attributing niggardliness to nature as implying God, the Creator, and holding the entity responsible for scarcity of resources, as an affront to His benevolence. If this presumption is correct, their reaction was uncalled for. The statement could have been dismissed as a figure of speech.

It is difficult to identify Islamic economists who do or do not approve of the notion of scarcity as valid for their discipline. Many appear non-committal or take it for granted. Some appear to be on dubious ground. But there *are* those who still argue that resource scarcity is inadmissible from the Islamic perspective. Monzer Kahf (1992, p. 115) feels that the economic 'problem is not of scarcity; it is caused by human laziness and neglect'. The succinct work of Akram Khan (1994, pp. 44–45) provides a leading example of projecting a similar viewpoint. A reviewer of his book (Hasan 1996) found difficulty with the position Khan took on the scarcity of resources.[6] The point missing in the adversaries' argument is that the divine *provision* of stocks, however inexhaustible, is not a sufficient condition for the *availability* of resources to human beings in desired measure at any point in time or space.[7] Existence of resources is necessary but it is their availability to mankind from the store that lends content and meaning to the notion of scarcity as a basis of economics.

The availability of resources to human beings depends on the state of their knowledge; it expands as they strive to discover and have access to them and grows as they know more about their uses, location, methods of extraction, and cost-effectiveness through continued learning, research, and action. For example, see the role of humans' ingenuity and their relentless effort in harnessing a resource in just one area—energy. Note the sequence of developments under the pressure of scarcity from the point of commercial usage in each case: steam—1698; coal—1750; oil—1857; Hydroelectricity—1882; Nuclear energy—1960 Now, solar power has made its advent, India leading the pack. The great expansion in energy availability could not, of course, have been possible if Allah's mercy and provisions were not already in existence.

[6]The second edition of the *Essay* was published in 1935. References given in this work are from a 1945 reprint of this version downloaded from the internet.

[7]The *Qur'an* (12: 46–49) exemplifies the manifestation of scarcity in the sense of non-availability of needed resources. See the explanation of the king's dream that the Prophet Yusuf (peace be upon him) provided and the advice he gave to overcome the difficulty.

The holy *Qur'an* not only talks of Allah's bountiful resources; it also informs us that He alone is the source of knowledge. Divine wisdom releases that knowledge to those who seek; not all at once, but little by little, so that people are not carried away with pride and arrogance. Akram Khan's proposition (and he is not alone) that scarcity of resources is merely a man-made phenomenon resulting from the wasteful use and mal-distribution of resources, is not valid. The factors he mentions only aggravate scarcity; they do not cause it.[8] In fact, scarcity of resources in terms of their availability to mankind, as explained above, is conceivably a part of the divine scheme to spur human beings into creative action in making their living in the land of Allah, and at the same time to see how virtuously they do it.[9] Life, for that reason, is a trial in this world. The history of human civilization is the history of the march of human conquest of nature.[10] In essence, it is the history of pushing outward relentlessly the frontiers of scarcity through unceasing research, inventions, and innovations in science, technology, and social management.

2.5.1 *Knowledge vs. Scarcity*

Knowledge is the weapon that mankind uses in its quest for making resources available to it from the inexhaustible store of nature and the expansion of knowledge certainly knows no limits. The struggle of all peoples on Earth has indeed been between the growth of knowledge and resource availability for producing material requisites of well-being, in the face of the ever-increasing population. Malthus and Ricardo—the pessimists—were obsessed with the fear of an impending hell unless human

[8]The 'absence of scarcity' argument presupposes the availability to mankind of all resources needed, in appropriate quantities, and in ready-for-use form at each point in time and space. Once we give in to the naivety of this supposition, it is the wastage and mal-distribution of resources that could be claimed as the real economic problem, not their scarcity.

[9]Presumably, this was one reason why Allah stopped the falling of manna from the skies. Interestingly, Robbins sees the event as exemplifying the possibility of human beings remaining temporarily free of scarcity (*Essay*, p. 11).

[10]The ghost of scarcity that their logic unleashed continues to haunt humanity till today and has resulted over the centuries in chaotic top-heavy demographic structures that some nations are now trying to correct. Family planning cannot be a public policy in a Muslim country in view of the assuaging words of the *Qur'an*: 'Kill not thy children in the fear of want. We have provided for you. We shall provide for them too' (17:31; see also 11:7; 51:58).

beings adopted measures to keep their numbers in check.[11] In contrast, economists, like Seligman, saw in the birth of a child not only a mouth demanding food but also a pair of hands soon becoming capable of adding to output for survival. Such optimists were thus elated by the hope of a coming paradise. The elation came from the sight of the industrial revolution already flying high on the wings of scientific inventions and innovations—as the expansion of energy sources alluded to above illustrates.

In this non-stop race for knowledge vs. scarcity, the former has so far been winning, especially over the past 150 years. Efforts are being made to quantify knowledge and measure its rate of growth. League Table 2007 attempted to fix components of knowledge and explain how each could be measured. In this context, 23 variables were identified as determinants of knowledge. The measurement was the number of years each component took to double itself. It was found that various components had different time spans for doubling, but with the right inputs, investment knowledge doubled every five years. In this regard, there has been an explosive development in knowledge after the Second World War, more so in the field of science and technology.

The knowledge explosion has kept mankind ahead in the race against scarcity. The population of the world in 1999 was 2.7 times its size in 1950. During the same period, the real Gross Domestic Product (GDP) of the world measured in US dollars increased almost sevenfold, causing the per capita world income to improve to about three times. Within this broad spectrum, there have, of course, been vast differences over time and space. Muslim countries have been lagging far behind. They possess a major portion of global natural resources—both existing and potential—but contribute no more than 7–8% of world GDP. They are essentially sellers of resources, not their users. This correlates well with their meagre contribution to the stock of knowledge in the modern era.[12]

[11]There are roughly 1.6 billion Muslims in the world, but only two scientists from Muslim countries have won Nobel prizes in science (one for physics in 1979, the other for chemistry in 1999). Forty-six Muslim countries have combined contribute just 1% of the world's scientific literature; Spain and India each contribute more to the world's scientific literature than all these countries taken together.

[12]There are roughly 1.6 billion Muslims in the world, but only two scientists from Muslim countries have won Nobel Prizes in science (one for physics in 1979, the other for chemistry in 1999). Forty-Six Muslim countries combined contribute just 1 percent of the world's scientific literature; Spain and India each contribute more to the world's scientific literature than those countries taken together.

This reversal of ranks is rather lamentable for a community whose religion began with instructions to read.

Box 2.1: Scarcity vs. knowledge

Scarcity of knowledge is the mother of all scarcities that confront mankind on the planet Earth. The victory that mankind has so far achieved in the race against scarcity is not a cushion to sleep on. It is a race where temporal setbacks keep human beings constantly on track to stay triumphant. But worrisome is the fact that success has come at a cost that mankind may notice rather late in the day. The rapacious use of natural resources has resulted in almost irreversible environmental degradation.

'Sustainable Development from an Islamic Perspective: Meaning, Implications, and Policy Concerns', *JKAU: Islamic Economics*, vol. 19, no. 1, 2006, pp. 3–18.

2.5.2 Scarcity and the Environment

The holy *Qur'an* informs mankind that God has created things in measured proportions and that they are held together in a delicate balance. It warns mankind not to indulge in mischief lest the balance be disturbed.[13] But the warning goes unheeded. The environmentalists continue to express dismay over the decaying health of the planet. Diminishing biodiversity, shrinking supplies of fresh drinking water, the vanishing virgin forests, falling agricultural yields, and increasing frequency of natural calamities, all threaten to make human life miserable, if not extinct, with the passage of time.

In price formation, markets treat only those resources as scarce that have opportunity costs, and firms must pay for them. But there are also natural resources like fresh air and water.[14] These are used not only to produce goods and services but also for the disposing of the waste that the

[13] See, for example *Qur'an* 6:3; 30:41; 39:5; 54:49; 67:3–4.

[14] In the beginning when the population was small, the list of such free goods was long and included land, forest products, fruits, flowers, honey, grass, and water that were all freely available. The list shrank quickly with the growth of population and the resultant expansion of human wants and production.

production process emits. With the growth of population, there are hardly any environmental inputs available for production free of cost for either purpose. Environmental problems arise not from the use of resources the firms pay for producing valuable goods and services, but also from the release of wastes—poisonous liquids, gases, and solids—into the air, water, and soil. The disposal of waste imposes costs on people in various forms, such as enhanced medical bills for which no one compensates them. These social costs do not pass through the market (Silva et al. 2009); they are external to it. Arnold Coase's model (1960), based on creating property rights in environmental goods and allowing the polluters and sufferers to bargain in the market for compensation, looks neat in theory, but efforts to put it into operation in the United States and elsewhere have failed for a variety of reasons (Hasan 2015, pp. 327–331). Nations have repeatedly failed to agree on how to face the environmental challenges summed up in climate change: the recent pull out of the United States from the Paris Agreement illustrates the predicament. Anyway, an extension of the scarcity notion must cover environmental goods.

Finally, scarcity is the driver of life; a part of the divine scheme to make people work and test them in the running of affairs on Earth. In the absence of scarcity, what meaning would one put on patience, tolerance, and cooperation? Who would work for whom and why? Why would people not tend to hoard wealth or conversely, condemn the act? What would be the need for or the form of societal organization? Above all, would economics exist as a social science, and if yes, to what end? In fact, it is the scarcity of resources that gave meaning and significance to the debate on the efficacy of the pursuit of self-interest as the driving force of economic activities in the world.

2.6 Pursuit of Self-interest

People seek to enhance their lives through increased want satisfaction. Wants being unlimited, the scarcity of resources forces people to keep self-interest in the forefront. But this priority does not imply a denial of the existence of other motives, including altruism, as affecting human conduct,[15] nor does it demand the renunciation of such ends.

[15] For instance, Adam Smith wrote: 'How selfish soever man may be supposed, there are evidently some principles in his nature, which interest him in the fortune of others, and render their happiness necessary to him, though he derives nothing from it, except the pleasure of seeing it' (quoted in Coase 1984, p. 546).

Economics, as a science dealing with social behaviour, studies human activities *en mass*—of society as a whole, not of individuals. Mainstream economists hold that of the various motives which actuate human conduct, the pursuit of self-interest tends to override others. It is relatively more universal and stable. Thus, the pursuit of self-interest spurred by scarcity emerged as the focal point in economic modelling and analysis.

2.6.1 Containment, not Rejection

Islamic economists made a mistake in accepting the bifurcation of human motives into self-interest and altruism—a division that originated from the West. In the Islamic faith, man is bipolar in creation: a combination of the dust and Divine. He has traits both noble and ignoble residing and conflicting within his self. Islam recognizes this fact. Thus, *Shari'ah* encourages people to acquire and enjoy all good things in life in gratitude to divine benevolence. However, mankind is instructed to observe moderation in consumption and avoid waste and hoarding.[16] If people are greedy and exceed the limits, the pursuit of self-interest requires containment, not rejection. After all, why should the believers meet their religious obligations—praying, living the way God wants them to, fasting, going for the pilgrimage, and performing good deeds, if not in self-interest: that is, seeking from the grace of their Creator escape from the punishment of fire after death. Indeed, the *Qur'an* instructs them to work towards that end *in self-interest*.[17]

The pursuit of self-interest demands that one should be conscious of the interests of others and avoid hurting those interests. This requirement invokes mutual respect and calls for cooperation—not conflict—in promoting the interests of each other. On this, the following quote from Adam Smith's *Wealth of Nations* (1776) is indeed illuminating:

> It is not from the benevolence of the butcher, the brewer, or the baker that we expect our dinner, but from their regard to their own interest. We address ourselves not to their humanity but to their self-love, and never talk to them of our necessities but of their advantage.

[16] Khan and Mirakhor (1992, p. 4) regard the pursuit of self-interest both as an obligation and a right of an individual, flowing from the Islamic concept of justice.

[17] 'But seek with the (wealth) which Allah has bestowed on thee the home of the Hereafter, and forget not thy portion of lawful enjoyment in the present world' (*Qu'ran*, 28:77).

We are immersed in a social milieu of opposing (self-)interests that can stay in harmony only by being based on reciprocal accommodation. There seems to be some sort of affinity in the depths of our selves between self-interest and moral conduct. Ironically, the best Islamic defence against self-interest is self-interest itself; 'Cause no injury, receive no injury' is a well-known Islamic maxim. Thus seen, the pursuit of self-interest ushers in morality; it promotes civility and consideration for others. Enlightened self-interest is the root of altruism.

2.6.2 *Self-interest Is Not Selfishness*

Most Islamic economists naively treat self-interest identical to selfishness even as a demarcation does separate the two. Self-interest can be pursued within the ambit of morality, but selfishness would always violate this ambit. In a race, every participant attempts to surge ahead using his own strategy and power; he is promoting self-interest. However, if he puts his hand on the shoulder of a rival who is pulling ahead and holds him back to win the race, he is selfish. For defying the rules of the game. Zola Budd—the South African/British runner—was temporarily suspended on a suspicion of tripping the one ahead of her during the 3000-metre race in the 1984 Olympics at Los Angles.[18] The demarcation line between self-interest and selfishness may at times be very fine; for intention could be the pen that draws it.

Pursuit of self-interest is both moral and legal. Self-interest and selfishness are not identical in principle but in practical affairs of the world, the demarcation may blur beyond recognition. However, it is not for this reason that the pursuit of self-interest came into disrepute, even in mainstream economics.[19] There were other difficulties as well.

2.6.3 *The Harmony of Interests Fallacy*

Society being a collection of individuals, there has been a strong presumption in economics that whatever promotes individual interest would *automatically* promote that of the society. Adam Smith not only brought

[18] See the BBC Report dated 11 August 1984 on their news website for the full story.

[19] Interestingly, the psychologists especially rose up in arms against the behavioural mentality scarcity they say this creates (Ahmad and Pandey 2010).

self-interest to the fore in economics, he was also the author of the 'harmony of interests' thesis. He wrote in his *Wealth of Nations*:

> An individual generally neither intends to promote the public interest, nor knows how much he is promoting it, he intends only his own gain, and he is in this, as in many other cases, led by an *invisible hand* to promote an end which was no part of his intention. ... *By pursuing his own interest, he frequently promotes that of the society more* (Emphasis added).

Empirics prove that the harmony of interest thesis is questionable because the pursuit of self-interest could cross limits. For, visionless self-interest becomes the snake eating its own tail. To illustrate, take the case of the much talked about 'win-win situations' these days.

Such a situation need not automatically be just and conducive to social well-being unless the division of gains can be shown as equitable. The spectre of poverty and overwhelming inequalities in income distributions within and across nations provide ample evidence falsifying the proposition, despite growth being a win-win situation for all, this much Table 2.1 candidly demonstrates. Despite GDP growth being twice as fast in developing economies their per capita income with the developed ones has been on the rise (See row A).

Table 2.1 Per capita income in current US Dollars for selected years for country groups

Type of countries	*Year*						
	1990	*1995*	*2000*	*2005*	*2010*	*2015*	*2015/1990*
Developed countries (a)	19,590	24,930	27,510	34,962	38,360	40,617	2.07
Developing countries (b)	840	1090	1230	2363	2781	3372	4.0
A. Income gap (a)–(b)	18,750	23,840	26,280	32,599	35,579	37,246	2.0
B. Income ration (a)/(b)	23.32	22.87	22.37	14.80	13.79	12.0	

Source World Development Reports and world indicators. High income countries have been treated as developed ones; all others are grouped as developing countries

2.6.4 Rationality Exaggerated

The fallacy concerning self-interest leads to exaggerating rationality in economic decision-making. One is supposed to be rational if he works to promote *only* his own interest. This view has long been dubbed in economic discourse as egoistic rationality. Its criticism—scathing at times—is well known and much documented in the mainstream literature; we need not reproduce it here. In Islamic economics, this proposition led to the coinage of a few reactionary terms; some sought to replace the invisible hand of God for the invisible hand of self-interest in Adam Smith. Others attempted to paint the picture of an 'Islamic man' to pale the mainstream 'economic man' into insignificance. Such efforts were presumably amateurish, if not absurd. However, the evaluation of the proposition by Syed Omar Agil (1992) has been somewhat balanced. But it was Professor A. K. Sen (1977) who in his *Rational Fools* drove the last nail into the coffin of the rationality propositions. One cannot but enjoy the sarcasm the very title of his essay carries.[20] That it has been reproduced in many different places is a measure of its vitality.

With the emergence of free markets as the driving force of the fast-paced Western economies, rationalism took little time to replace faith in choice-making and ethical concerns perforce took a back seat. However, it is interesting that the significance of ethical conduct in business is now resurfacing in mainstream literature on corporate governance after the worldwide devastations the financial crisis of 2007–2009 brought in its train, unveiling the moral bankruptcy of big business.

Furthermore, not only does the pursuit of self-interest contain the notion of rationality, there is also insistence that conduct is rational only when the system single-mindedly works for maximization of that interest; businesses must maximize profits and consumers must maximize utility.

This maximizing behaviour has attracted much criticism, even in mainstream economics, while its Islamic counterpart just rejects the principle out of hand. We examine the debate in the following section, taking profit maximization as an illustrative case.

[20]The figure of the young, handsome Sen as I first saw him on 8 September 1965, chairing a selection committee meeting, rises to my mind's eye even today as that interview brought me to the once-famous Delhi College of the University of Delhi. The institution is currently named the Zakir Husain Delhi College and is housed in a new building on Nehru Marg, New Delhi.

2.7 Maximizing Behaviour

Maximizing behaviour may relate to an economic magnitude such as utility or profit; it may also relate to a non-economic magnitude like goodwill of neighbours or the pleasure of God. To denounce the conduct in the first case and appreciate and promote it in the second must make the Islamic stance on the issue internally inconsistent. This point has not received due attention in Islamic economics.[21]

The pursuit of profit maximization is apparently avaricious and seems to conflict with moral conduct. For this reason, the maximization notion has received much criticism in mainstream literature itself. Still, it survives, and for two reasons. First, price formation under varying market conditions is difficult to explain without a maximization hypothesis, both on the side of demand and supply in the market. Second, the critics of the assumption have not so far been able to produce an alternative rule of behaviour having the same explanatory or predictive value that maximization carries.

However, most Islamic economists denounce maximizing behaviour on the part of economic entities. A typical condemnation comes from Professor M. N. Siddiqi (1996). Among the basic points of departure of Islamic economics from the mainstream, he accords first place to the rejection of any maximizing effort of producers or consumers. He writes:

> The maximization hypothesis is not very helpful in understanding the economy, any economy. But it is entirely unacceptable as an aid to the understanding of an Islamic economy, any Islamic economy. Even some understanding of Islam and some compliance with its teachings is sufficient to create a society which defies the maximization hypothesis. Something else is needed. (p. xiii, see also, pp. 17 and 28)

This is rhetoric; the author provides little reasoning or documentation for his opinion and says not a word on what the 'something else' that he mentions could possibly be.[22] We find that scarcity of resources perforce

[21]There are Islamic economists who approve, albeit grudgingly, the act of profit maximization, but join the consensual condemnation of utility maximization. The confusion is further exacerbated when there are yet others who change their position without notice.

[22]Siddiqi (1996) approves of the use of conventional analysis of a firm's equilibrium via the marginal cost and marginal revenue curves, based on the maximization of profit assumption. However, he believes that the assumption can be relaxed to incorporate objectives relating to the good of society. How, he does not show.

makes maximization a behavioural norm for human beings in most spheres of socio-economic activity. To illustrate, let us consider the following line of argument.

Should a farmer not choose a crop to grow on his piece of land that he expects to bring him more income than others? Or, having made that choice, should the farmer not attempt to raise the maximum output from his piece of land? In the same way, should not a carpenter who is to supply certain pieces of furniture—tables, chairs, beds, or cupboards—attempt to minimize the use of wood and other inputs to fill the order? To maximize output with given inputs or to produce a given output with minimum input expense are the sides of the same coin of rational conduct that only the naïve would oppose. But such obvious cases have escaped the attention of Islamic economists, presumably because they were obsessed with the desire of finding fault in the capitalistic economic system in order to claim superiority for the Islamic. This led them to focus only on condemning the profit maximization hypothesis in mainstream economics. Let us examine the maximizing behaviour in this narrower context.

2.7.1 *Profit Maximization*

Islamic economists plead for some reasonable or fair profit as a *Shari'ah* norm for business firms, not maximum profit. One comes across diagrams showing how fair profit can replace the maximization norm. We have demonstrated the un-tenability of such diagrams earlier (Hasan 2012, p. 116, n. 20). Here we shall argue why the fair profit norm cannot be used for the price determining process in free market operations that Islam upholds. Under perfect competition, price is determined by the forces of aggregate demand and aggregate supply. Individual firms have no pricing power; they are just price takers. In the long run, firms are able to make only normal profit, that is, just equal to implicit opportunity costs of the factors their owners supply to the firm. Probably no Islamic economist will dispute that normal profit is fair profit. In the short run, firms can earn more than normal profit but it is soon competed away.

The long run position is no different even when competition is not perfect and firms enjoy some pricing power; profit is again normal and therefore fair (Hasan 1992). In the short run, the price that would give fair profit is difficult to determine (see Fig. 2.2). Here, the profit of the

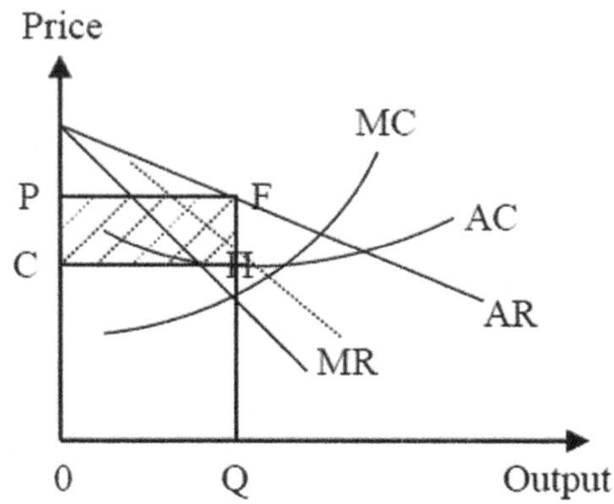

Fig. 2.2 Short-run equilibrium of the firm under imperfect competition

firm—the shaded area PCHF—is the maximum under given market conditions. Now the firm, following the advice of Islamic economists, wants to have only fair profit, not the maximum the figure shows. Its difficulty is that in the absence of an externally available benchmark, it does not know by how much it should shrink the rectangle PCHF to make profit look fair. It is willing to reduce the price but does not know what price cut would make profit acceptable as fair. Again, reaction of customers, as well as of the rivals, to a price reduction is difficult to gauge.

Islamic economists plead for some reasonable or fair profit as a *Shari'ah* norm for business firms, not maximum profit. One comes across diagrams showing how fair profit can replace the maximization norm. We have demonstrated the un-tenability of such diagrams earlier (Hasan 2012, p. 116, n. 20). Here we shall argue why the fair profit norm cannot be used for the price determining process in free market operations that Islam approves. Under perfect competition, price is determined by the forces of aggregate demand and aggregate supply. Individual firms have no pricing power; they are just price takers. In the long run, firms are able to make only normal profit, that is, just equal to implicit opportunity costs of the factors their owners supply to the firm. Probably no Islamic economist will dispute that normal profit is fair profit. In the short run, firms can earn more than normal profit but it may be competed away.

The long-run position is no different even when the competition is not perfect and firms enjoy some pricing power; profit is again normal and, therefore, fair (Hasan 1992). In the short run, the price that would give fair profit is difficult to determine Here, the profit of a firm—the shaded area PCHF in Fig. 2.2—is the maximum under given market conditions. Now the firm, following the advice of Islamic economists, wants to have only fair profit, not the maximum the figure shows. Its difficulty is that in the absence of an externally available benchmark, it does not know by how much it should shrink the rectangle PCHF to make profit look fair. It is willing to reduce the price but does not know what price cut would make profit acceptable as fair? Again, the reaction of the customers as well as of the rivals, to price reduction is difficult to gauge Sadiq (1996) tried to demonstrate how profit could be made fair. In his diagram he shifted the marginal revenue curve MR to the right, as the dotted line in Fig. 2.2, cutting AC in H. But he did not shift AR. This is erroneous, as MR must bisect the horizontal line from C to AR in equal parts.

The moral code of sellers going for a fair profit, however defined, could be beneficial in a small-time social scenario (refer to Sect. 2.3 above) when production was mostly to fill standing orders while adding a margin to the procurement cost of inputs—this was a common trade practice. It was also easy then to have an idea of fairness in transactions. Today, we are in an era of mass production for the markets. The number and variety of goods has increased tremendously. Producers or sellers are subject to market discipline (or indiscipline). They have limited control over the determination of the prices for their goods. Also, let us ask if the Islamic banks of today can use mark-ups yielding only fair profits? The fact is that the concept of a fair price or profit is largely external to modern business. The required information is rarely available, let alone accessible. Purchasers' associations, NGOs, and ultimately public authorities work as watchdogs for consumers on issues such as fair trade practices, quality, price, or profit. The matter falls within the domain of state policy. Thus, the limitations of a fair profit notion in theory and in practice take us back to the maximization of profit issue.

2.7.2 *The Defence: Two Aspects*

Profit maximization has two broad aspects: motivational and operational. The key questions are: do firms want to maximize their profits, and if yes, can they achieve this goal? Much controversy has centred on these issues in the mainstream literature.[23]

[23]For a literature review and fuller discussion of these points, see Hasan (1975), Chapter IV, 'Profit maximization as a business objective', pp. 59–82.

On the question of motivation, it is agreed that in the case of small owner-operated firms, profit maximization has always been the guiding star of the decision-making process over time and space. However, with the rise of modern corporations to dominance, this objective has long since paled into insignificance. Managers are well-compensated professionals. The common shareholders are a scattered lot. They are not interested in knowing, nor have the means of knowing, if the profits of their company are indeed being maximized. They are happy with dividends so long as they find them satisfactory. Managers are more interested in their reputation, peace of mind, leisure, and unsuspecting rivals. Corporations, after crossing a profit threshold, become more interested in growth of variables such as size, sales, and share of the market. However, careful observation and analysis of internal happenings in corporations will convince us that the clouds of alternative goals shine only in the light of the good old moon of profit behind them. In any case, other motives that are claimed to have replaced profit maximization in large corporations are mostly situational; they lack global character and stability.

We probably face greater difficulties on the feasibility side of the divide. Profit maximization lies in the future; it is an *ex ante* concept. The future consequences of most decisions are uncertain. It is thus argued that even if firms desire maximum profits, they do not have the means of knowing which of the alternative courses of action—often overlapping—would ensure achievement of the goal. Realized profit may fall short of the expected (maximum); it could even be negative. Uncertainty must be taken as a fact of life, like sunshine or rain. It can make most rational decisions look idiotic if expectations fail. But that does not deter people from trying to peep into the future. All planning in human life would be non-existent if we were so possessed with the possibility of failing expectations due to uncertainty. Profit maximization under uncertainty can only be a directional concept. It only states that due to scarcity of resources, firms should not miss taking a chance if there is a legitimate opportunity to enhance profits. Maximization spurs efficiency.

2.7.3 The Final Word

Maximization per se is value-neutral; what is maximized, how to do it and to what end, are questions that can have ethical labels assigned to them—good or bad. In addition, it is a mathematical concept inapplicable to variables that cannot be measured and divided infinitesimally.

Within those criteria, profit maximization is a heuristic notion. Roads carry goods far and near to facilitate growth, but on their own add nothing to them. Likewise, maximization has no content, yet it is a powerful tool for economic analysis: it moves markets to equilibrium. It can be used with legal provisions to safeguard against potentially undesirable consequences. *Shari'ah* provides ample protection to both consumers and the hired factors of production against profit/rent-seeking. Islamic economics need not throw away the baby with the bathwater.

2.8 Concluding Remarks

This preliminary discussion has attempted to correct some misconceptions in Islamic economics concerning a few foundational terms—scarcity of resources, pursuit of self-interest, and maximization of gains. These concepts are interrelated as the foregoing discussion must have amply demonstrated. They constitute a minimal, but essential, toolkit needed to explain and investigate economic phenomena from the conventional or Islamic perspective, and help to formulate theories with the predictive value required to guide economic policy to fruition.

The misconceptions probably cropped up for two reasons. First, the earlier Islamic scholars were jurists who mostly had little knowledge about mainstream economic theory and policy. Second, the desire of believers to demonstrate, after the independence of Muslim lands from foreign rule, that Islamic economic thinking was independent of, and superior to, the Western position. Both reasons hindered the growth of the discipline.

The situation has significantly changed with the passage of time. Islamic economics has grown out of its nascent confines, especially in finance. The subject has assumed the stature and status of an academic discipline. Colleges, universities, and institutes promoting instruction and research in Islamic economics have cropped up all over the globe, including countries in Europe and America. The publication of journals, articles, and books is on the rise. This development, however, lacks balance, variety, and coverage. While Islamic finance is in the ascendency, Islamic economics seems to be losing ground. The main reason is that the subject grossly lacks theoretical cohesion and operational appeal. It is a rudderless, unstable, ship.

To impart stability and direction, the resistance to using the concepts foundational to the subject must be eliminated. Scarcity of resources, pursuit of self-interest, and maximization estimation is inevitable in order to raise the structure of economics—secular or Islamic. What is required is the spelling out of their *Shari'ah* specifications and confines, not rejection. In this chapter, we have endeavoured to exemplify how an attempt in that direction is possible.

Islam is different and distinct from other religions in several important ways. This eternal message of Allah was not meant for any specific time, place, or people. It was addressed to humanity at large, and for that reason it was final and its Prophet, the last in the chain. The development of Islamic economics must be cosmopolitan in outlook and universal in appeal. The essential economic problems of mankind are the same, independent of time and space, and in the effort to solve them, scarcity of resources, as we have explained, is a perpetual hurdle, and makes the pursuit of self-interest and maximization imperatives of human conduct. They can be modified as per Islamic norms. Currently, Islamic economics is based upon negative-screening methodology; relying upon averting conventional concepts considered contrary to Islamic law, rather than their positive adaptation, with possible modifications of what is foundational for both disciplines. Unless the professionals imbibe this stark truth, Islamic economics cannot halt its plunge into oblivion.

Box 2.2: Scarcity, self-interest, and maximization implicit in *zakah* disbursement?

The aid that comes from payable *zakah* is meant for those who do not have enough means to maintain themselves or their businesses—those who suffer from shortage (scarcity) of resources.

It is recommended to prioritize penurious relatives over others in extending *zakah* aid to needy neighbours. People of knowledge (*Ahlul-'Ilm*) and the virtuous are to be preferred over others if needy. Even sons and daughters can be the beneficiaries under some special circumstances. A Persian proverb declares that: '*awwal khuesh baadho derwaish*' ('first self, later one who asks for'). This suggests links with self-interest.

Finally, this all contributes to maximize earning the pleasure of Allah (swt) in order to gain a place in Paradise.

Test Questions

Q.1 Account for the contribution of the Greek writers to the evolution of the concept of scarcity. Does the concept of scarcity violate the dictum that Allah (swt) has stocked the earth and heavens with his inexhaustible resources for all times to come? Argue your case.

Q.2 'Pursuit of self-interest is not un-Islamic; rather, it promotes civility'. Do you agree? Give reasons for your answer.

Q.3 The maximization of profit hypothesis is extrinsic to Islam. The concept should be banished from Islamic economics, argues M. N. Siddiqi. Comment.

Q.4 Write critical notes on the following:
a. Scarcity and environment
b. Self-interest and welfare

Q.5 Scarcity of resources, pursuit of self-interest, and maximization of economic results are foundations of mainstream economics. Can Islamic economics discard them? Give reasons for your answer.

What Next?

The primary object of economic activities is to enhance the living comforts of people. These efforts crystallize in what is called economic development. In Chapter 3, we shall examine the various issues in this area within the Islamic framework we visualize in light of the discussions in the preceding chapters.

References

Agil, S. O. S. (1992). Rationality and Altruism in Islam. In S. L. Tahir (Ed.), *Microeconomics*. Malaysia.

Ahmad, K. (2007). *Capitalism. Socialism and Welfare State*. IRTI Jeddah Power Point Slides.

Ahmad, M. M., & Pandey, D. (2010). *Are Islamic Banks Better Immunized Than Conventional Banks in the Current Financial Crisis*. 10th Global Conference on Business and Economics, Rome, Italy.

Al 3. (2006). *The Biggest Disruption in History: Massively Accelerated Growth Since the Industrial Revolution.* http://www.nikbergman.com/250/the-biggest-disruption-in-history-masively-ccelerated-growth-since-the-industrial-revolution/.

Coase, R. H (1960). The problem of social cost. *Journal of Law and Economics, 3*, 1–44.

Coase, R. W. (1984). Adam Smith's View of Man. In J. C. Wood (Ed.), *Adam Smith: Critical Assessments.* London: Croom Helm.

Farooq, M. O. (2006). *Islamic L aw and the Use and Misuse of Hathith.* New Horizon.

Haneef, M. A., & Furqani, M. (2004). Contemporary Islamic Economics and Missing Directions of Genuine Islamization. *Journal of Thoughts on Economics, 19*(4), 28–48.

Hasan, Z. (1975). *Theory of Profit.* New Delhi: Vikas Publishing House Pvt. Ltd.

Hasan, Z. (1985). Determination of Profit and Loss Sharing Ratios in Interest-Free Business Finance. *Journal of Research in Islamic Economics, 3*(1), 13–27.

Hasan, Z. (1988). Distributional Equity in Islam. In M. Iqbal (Ed.), *Distributive Justice and Need Fulfillment in an Islamic Economy* (Chapter 1, pp. 35–62). Leicester, UK: Islamic Foundation.

Hasan, Z. (1992). Profit Maximization: Secular Versus Islamic. In S. Tahir, A. Ghazali, & S. O. S. Agil (Eds.), *Readings in Microeconomics: An Islamic Perspective* (Chapter 20, pp. 239–255). Petaling Jaya, Malaysia: Longman.

Hasan, Z. (1996). Book Review of Akram Khan's *An Introduction to Islamic Economics. American Journal of Islamic Social Sciences, 13*(4), 580–585.

Hasan, Z. (1998a). Islamization of Knowledge in Economics: Issues And Agenda. *IIUM Journal of Economics and Management, 6*(2), 1–40.

Hasan, Z. (1998b). Book Review of M. N/ Siddiqi's *Teaching Economics in Islamic Perspective. Islamic Economic Studies, 6*(1), 111–132.

Hasan, Z. (2012). Money Creation and Control from Islamic Perspective. *Journal of Islamic Banking & Finance, Karachi, 29*(1), 70–85.

Hasan, Z. (2015). *Economics with Islamic Orientation.* Kuala Lumpur, Malaysia: Oxford University Press.

Kahf, M. (1992). The Theory of Consumption. In Tahir et al. (Eds.), *Readings in Microeconomics in Islamic Perspective* (pp. 61–68; 90–105). Petaling Jaya, Malaysia: Longman.

Khan, M. A. (1994). *An Introduction to Islamic Economics.* Islamabad, Pakistan: International Institute of Islamic Thought and Institute of Policy Studies.

Khan, M., & Mirakhor, A. (1992). The Financial System and Monetary Policy in an Islamic Economy, 1989. In *Principles of Islamic Financing: A Survey.* Jeddah: IRTI.

Kuran, T. (1989). On the Notion of Economic Justice in Contemporary Islamic Thought. *International Journal of Middle East Studies, 21*(2), 171–191.

Robbins, L. (1932). *Nature and Significance of Economic Science*. London, UK: Macmillan.

Sadiq, M. (Ed.). (1996). *Economic Development and Islam*. Malaysia: IIUM Press.

Samuelson, P. A. (1947). *Foundations of Economic Analysis*. Harvard University Press.

Sen, A. K. (1977). Rational Fools: A Critique of the Behavioral Foundations of Economic Theory. *Philosophy and Public Affairs, 6*(4), 317–344.

Siddiqi, M. N. (1996). *Teaching Economics in Islamic Perspective*. Jeddah: Scientific Publishing Centre, King Abdulaziz University.

Silva, S. S. da, Reis, R. P., & Ferreira, P. A. (2009). Concepts of Nature Value: Are the Particular Characteristics of Nature Goods Being Considered? *VII International PENSA Conference*. Sao Paulo, Brazil.

CHAPTER 3

Islam and Economic Development: Mundane Effort for Spiritual Solace

Preview

> *Our Lord; Give unto us in this world that which is the best and in the hereafter, that which is the best … (Al Baqarah, 201)*

We have argued in the preceding chapter that the ultimate goal of economic activity across the world has been to enrich human life by increasing the availability of resources in the face of ever-increasing wants and utilize them to maximize benefit in terms of production and its distribution among the masses. During the long spells of foreign occupation of the now-developing countries, the rulers exported these resources home to boost domestic production and sold the surplus in their colonies' markets for self-enrichment.

However, since the end of the colonial era around the middle of the preceding century, there has been a notable economic resurgence and expansion in emerging countries, though progress in the Muslim world has been slower and uneven. A contributory reason has probably been that the initial development model was conceived by the jurists leading the pre-independence revivalist movements in various countries. No cohesive thought and design could emerge. Instead, the colonial hangover clouded fresh thinking on the subject, pulling the Islamic perspective in different directions. Compulsions of orthodoxy are now fast yielding to modern designs and technological breakthroughs, especially in the mid-east and South East Asia.

Z. Hasan, *Leading Issues in Islamic Economics and Finance*,
https://doi.org/10.1007/978-981-15-6515-1_3

The present chapter projects an integrative approach to development issues from an Islamic perspective. The discussion is within a comparative setting for dealing with the concept, objectives, and priorities of development. In addition, several contextual matters such as the issue of motivation, the role of the state, and the population problem are addressed. The discussion keeps the puritan flavour of the earlier writers on the subject.

3.1 Introduction

The human struggle for survival in the world began as soon as Adam set his foot on the Planet Earth. Food, clothing, and shelter were the immediate needs calling for action but wants multiplied fast with population growth and fired up aspirations. Resource availability being the roadblock, fight against scarcity dominated the history of human struggle for survival on Earth. This struggle is unending. Through advances in knowledge effort and exploration mankind presently seems running ahead of scarcity in a perpetual race albeit many doubt it. In any case, that struggle remains the essence of human development, economic and non-economic. There are billions even today waiting for satisfaction of their initial requirements of food, clothing, and shelter though not because of availability but due to distributional fault lines.

Economic development is part of a complex, rather perplexing social dynamism which in itself is difficult to comprehend. It becomes more complicated a matter when an attempt is made to add an Islamic dimension to it. Yet, we venture to define that:

> Economic development is a societal process that seeks a continual and sustainable uplift in the economic variables – output, investment, savings, employment and financing with a view to generate social prosperity through wealth creation and its distribution on an inclusive and equitable basis without harming environment with long-run stability. From Islamic viewpoint the process must observe its prescribed moral and ethical prescriptions.

The history of human civilization, of its rise and fall, of its achievements and deprivations, of the making and unmaking of its grand institutions—social, political, and economic—has essentially been the history of man's conquest of nature, making wealth acquisition the *sine qua non* of economic development.

The emphasis on development was considered all the more relevant after the Second World War for reconstruction and to bring up countries newly becoming independent from the colonial rule. Indeed, the endeavour was successful; during the three quarters of the preceding century ending 1975, the GDP of developing countries grew at an annual rate that was higher than for developed countries (Todaro 1986). However, the fruits of this growth were not evenly distributed. Let us elaborate on this problem.

3.1.1 Growth Versus Welfare

It was soon realized that wealth was not an end in itself; it had to promote human welfare evenly. The size of the GDP packet was important, but more important was what it contained—more of guns or butter; more of clothing or cosmetics; more of dwellings or racecourses; more of medicines or wine; more of textbooks or comics; and so on. Moreover the social cost of producing the packet was important; how fair was the treatment of labour? Was the allocation and use of resources efficient? Was the sharing of the pie equitable across the board? Was the system stable, running smoothly without obstacles? Questions of this sort have not been satisfactorily answered over decades of impressive growth.

The failure on several fronts has indeed been agonizing. The widening distributional disparities within and among nations have been worrisome, with the rich becoming richer, and the poor, poorer. The fact that the focus of development on growth alone was inadequate was voiced out as early as 1971 when Professor Mehboob-ul Haque in a UN Seminar observed:

> We were taught to take care of our GDP so that we may take care of our poverty. Let us reverse it; let us take care of our poverty such that we may take care of our GDP.

The alarm that he raised has only intensified with the passage of time. Piketty (2014) has shown that the rising of profit rates on capital ahead of GDP growth has accentuated the problem of poverty and income inequalities in *developed* economies. He warned that the malady might soon afflict the developing economies as well. And unfortunately, it has already happened. The problem is so real and alarming that various world organizations have become obsessed with designing remedial measures to mitigate poverty and the riotous inequalities. Various indices are in circulation; most in vogue being the cut off poverty lines expressed per day per head incomes measured in current US dollars. These lines are periodically revised to adjust for changes in dollar value.

Efforts at reducing poverty and income inequalities across and within countries have gathered momentum and this change in policy has begun bearing fruits. 1.75 billion people were reported to be living in poverty worldwide in 1990. According to the latest World Bank estimates, this figure has decreased to 702.1 million for the year 2015, meaning a 60% fall, averaging 2.4% a year over the past 25 years.

The rapacious use of natural resources has led to numerous environmental problems, globally, regionally, and locally. Species extinction, ozone erosion, depletion of non-renewable recourses, global warming, rising sea levels, spread of new diseases, and food chain disturbances epitomize the alarming climate changes. This has eventually forced mankind to think about the environment, take steps to arrest the deterioration, and attempt to roll back the process as much as possible. Environmental consciousness has added a new adjective to development—'sustainable' Most writings on the subject now talk of *sustainable* development. Unfortunately, they seldom care to explain what sustainability in this context precisely means. Islamic economists are no exception; more on this in the following section.

3.1.2 The Un View of Development

The attempt to define development has run into difficulties even in mainstream economics; it is easier to say what development is not than to state what it precisely is. However, the concept no longer remains as lopsided as it used to be when it centred on *growth*. Even as there is still insistence to keep the definition distinct from the overall comprehensive development of society, its interrelationships with other aspects of improvement—social, cultural, legal, political, and ethical—are now being emphasized. The concept of sustainable human development is gaining ground. In this regard, it is indeed interesting to quote an explanation from the United Nations Development Programme (UNDP) Report, 1994:

> Sustainable human development is development that not only generates economic growth but also distributes its benefits equitably; that regenerates the environment rather than destroying it; that empowers people rather than marginalizing them. It is development that gives priority to the poor, enlarging their choices and opportunities and providing for their participation in decisions that affect their lives. It is development that is pro-people, pro-nature, pro-jobs and pro-women.

The focal points in this view of development are the same i.e. poverty, unemployment, inequalities, and the environment as in our definition above and constitute the problems that afflict most the masses in developing economies. The solution envisaged is to enable grass-root participation in the decision-making that affects peoples' lives. Implementation of such development programmes as is for example now underway in India requires political will and action that is pro-poor and can convince the rich at the national and international levels that it is in their own interests to provide succour to the underprivileged voluntarily. For history teaches us that people do not always starve in silence.

Development programmes must promote work effort, protect freedom of individuals and dignity of democratic institutions; they ensure a compensating relationship between nature and production. Islamic culture and civility already have the main ingredients of the recipe; lacking is the will to act. Nevertheless, the *Islamic* view of development remains different from that of the UNDP The main difficulty with any mainstream concept of economic development is that it remains firmly anchored in the mundane aspect of human existence to the neglect of the spiritual.

3.2 More on Islam and Development

The Islamic view of development centres on two broad aspects of its belief system: the Divine and the human, with a mutual relationship. It sees life and death as parts of its unitary view of creation. It does not consider the mundane and spiritual/moral aspects of human existence in separation, not even conceptually, or for analytical convenience. Asceticism is suffering and stagnation; amoral materialism is exploitative and anarchic. Both are unacceptable to Islam. The Islamic position is that man was created to operate as the trust-keeper and the co-worker of Allah (swt) on Earth (*Qu'ran*, 2:29; 6:165; 8:27–28). To that end, he was made the best of all creations from a combination of dust and the Divine (*Qu'ran*, 30:6).

The earthly pole of the two-dimensional man is symbolic of expressing his mundane aspirations, his lower passions—the Devil within that binds him to the state of his *being*. In contrast, his upper or spiritual pole radiates his self-awareness, will power, and creativeness—attributes Allah (swt) breathed a little into his being. These qualities are the essence of man, the freeing force in him. This force urges him to soar into the skies towards its Fountainhead. Man perceives himself as moving from a state of being (*bashar*) into a state of becoming (*insan*). Human evolution from the state of being to the state of becoming has no limits (Shari'ati 1982, pp. 62–75). Thus, Islam envisages man as broadly having two types of wants or urges: the mundane and the spiritual. His mundane desires urge man towards the acquisition, consumption, and enjoyment of material facilities, as well as towards seeking to produce them in abundance. Regarding spirituality, he seeks an environment that will permit full and free expression to humanistic urges to choose ideals—moral, ethical, economic, and social—and facilitate his achieving them. This will enable him to create not only what nature does not provide, but also beauty in the widest sense of the term, and to cultivate love, expressed in his willingness to sacrifice of the highest order.

These two types of urges—the mundane and the spiritual—seem conflicting but are in fact interrelated and interact within the unity of human existence. Real progress means their harmonious, supportive balance, and progressive satisfaction—*the growth of human personality*. The Islamic system aims at providing this sort of growth—it is the essence of development in Islam.

Thus, material progress is an inalienable ingredient of the Islamic scheme of living (*Qur'an*, 62:10). It is, indeed, internal to the divine design of creation (Qutb 1948, p. 197). It is also true that the material needs of mankind are on the rise; especially because of the increasing demand for variety. However, most individual wants have a limit. The human stomach cannot take in food unabated. Nor does one require thousands of dresses, hundreds of rooms, and so on. 'Going beyond reasonable limits in want satisfaction no longer remains consumption but something opposite—consumerism, consumer gluttony—that leads to degeneration and impoverishment of the individual instead of his real development' (Ursul 1983, p. 108). Notice that what is being denounced today as consumerism, the *Qur'an* had damned centuries ago when it declared:

> And those who do *kufr* (mischief) avail of material things and eat as do the animals; their abode is Hell. (*Qur'an*, 47:12)

Excessive attention to materialistic desires breeds egotism, causing more frustration and futility, and not fulfilment. Man tends to recede into asceticism and passive reflection. Even in our history, a similar type of materialistic era (as in the West today) gave rise to an ascetic phenomenon—Sufism. It is indeed a tribute to the timeless horizon of Islamic philosophy that ideas like 'quality of life', 'self-esteem', and 'freedom of choice' are now making inroads into the mainstream development literature to loosen the strangulating hold of the Gross National Product (GNP) syndrome and escape the dead end of the materialistic path (see, for example, Todaro 1986, p. 524).

However, increase in consumption (and production) proves counterproductive only when it becomes an end in itself instead of remaining a means to promote the satisfaction of human needs in the sense of transforming man from his *being* to his *becoming* an *insan*. Such needs would ever remain unlimited. There are, for example, no limits to human understanding or creativity—material or spiritual. 'There is none either for corresponding social needs be that of individuals or of society as a whole' (Ursul 1983, p. 109). There being an inverse correlation between the two types of needs—the mundane and the spiritual—the idea of placing limits on growth becomes defeatist, inhuman, and un-Islamic, provided the rules of the game are observed. Through visualizing a positive relationship between the two, Islam intends to help men rise to never-ending heights in personality development.

Islam's attitude towards numerous matters concerning development—consumption, resource allocation, production structures, technology, investment patterns, market exchange, finance, and distribution- is geared to this end. Decisions on these and related matters cannot be the same as for other economic systems.

Time and space constraints do not allow us to discuss how various systems differ in issues that have remained obscure in the current literature on the subject. Of significance here are the following:

1. The role of consumption in development;
2. Work effort and output levels;
3. Productivity and distributive shares.

3.2.1 Consumption and Development

Islam's concern for the poor and the weak remains the main appeal of the social order it envisages implementing (Levy 1957, pp. 54–55). Islam insists on the provision of the means of subsistence to all—Muslims and non-Muslims—living in an Islamic state. Some Muslim countries have a constitutional provision making it an eventual state obligation to meet the basic needs of their citizens and their record on this score, overall, has been better than others (Hasan 1997).[1] Indeed, Islam invokes a share for the poor in the wealth of the rich, which they are obliged to use for helping the needy.[2] Hence, much of the current income in Muslim countries would, some fear, be spent on consumption, reducing savings to invest for future growth and prosperity. Thus, many do not consider expedient even the mitigation of distributional inequalities, at least in the initial stages of development. They argue that with low per capita incomes, any attempt at equalization would only lead to a redistribution of poverty.

Although mainstream literature questions this hypothesis, Islamic economists have seldom examined its validity. Rather, the contention that consumption under Islamic dispensation could reduce investable funds and retard growth finds support. Let us investigate if the proposition is indeed valid. We shall argue that there could be a case where an increase in consumption could possibly lead to an increase in production.

Many support the contention, based on empirical evidence, that in poor countries, improved standards of living are a precondition for higher labour input and efficiency. They argue as for example, Hasan (1994):

> Where the level of living is as low as in a LDC (less developed country), the distinction between consumption and investment becomes overdrawn in so far as private consumption may well have a positive marginal productivity. The reason is not that consumption will augment resources but that a rise in consumption may improve labour quality and efficiency and hence allow better use to be made of the existing labor resources.

[1] These needs include food, clothing, shelter, education, and health care. The concept is flexible; the content and quality of the package depend son the level of income and prosperity a country may have reached.

[2] The *Holy Qur'an* unequivocally grants such rights in the wealth of the rich to others, especially the needy and the deprived (7:24–25; 16:141; 17:26; 30:38; and 51:19) and insists that these rights must be honoured.

Given the desired motivation and cooperating factors, a selective increase in consumption can become an instrument for development. Some of the components of consumption that can improve labour quality are, for example, calories per head, investment in education and training, health care, and social security programmes. The resultant increase in labour productivity may more than compensate for the output loss due to a relative fall in investment. Indeed, the same principle of circular and cumulative causation that is shown to accentuate poverty on the demand side of the market may begin operating in the reverse direction.

An even more consequential relationship was envisaged between consumption and production. It initially began with an understanding that producers would produce 'to order', i.e. what the consumers would demand—consumer being the king, so to say. The instructional flow would be from the consumer to the market. But consumers' sovereignty soon evaporated into thin air with the industrial revolution spreading across the world. Advertising emerged on the scene to tame the customers. Today, we are not sure if we buy what we *want* to or what the demand managers make us buy. There is now a well-established revised 'sequence' of instruction: from the market to the consumer (Galbraith 1969). It is thus being questioned if the current consumption-production axis is indeed sustainable.[3]

3.2.2 Work Effort

Development models pay much attention to achieving efficiency in the allocation of resources to various uses. Such efficiency need not per se produce optimal results. The human performance also matters.

[3]Sustainable consumption and production (SCP) is an overarching objective of, and an essential requirement for, sustainable development, as recognized in the Johannesburg Plan of Implementation (JPOI) of the 2002 World Summit on Sustainable Development. The summit called on all stakeholders to 'encourage and promote the development of a 10-year framework of programmes (10YFP) in support of regional and national initiatives to accelerate the shift towards sustainable consumption and production to promote social and economic development within the carrying capacity of ecosystems by addressing and, where appropriate, delinking economic growth and environmental degradation through improving efficiency and sustainability in the use of resources and production processes; and reducing resource degradation; pollution and waste'(10-Year Framework of Programmes on Sustainable Consumption and Production).

Performance on the job is a function of the work effort workers put into the process of production. The neglect of this factor in planning development has resulted in performance shortfalls being experienced in many developing countries. It is significant that work effort has become an integral element in discussions on efficiency since Leibenstein (1978).

Briefly, the issue is posited like this. A firm would like its employees to work as hard as feasible, while the employees would prefer to take it easy on the job. The difficulty from the firm's perspective is that it may not be able to observe at all times how hard the employees are actually working. In contrast, in a simple textbook presumptive model, this gives rise to a moral hazard problem—the level of work effort of the operator remains an unknown quantity. The issue as shown above presumes immorality operating at both ends of the employment equation. Islamic economics does not begin with such an assumption. Islam assumes that people are basically honest, hard-working, and sincere with their employers. The employer on his part is supposed to be caring and generous in treating his workers—the relationship between the two is one of mutual trust, kindness, and accommodation.

Mainstream economics also has several market responses for dealing with this moral hazard. For example, employers may use performance-based compensation packages. However, no method can make a legal contract to ensure the desired solution; only moral conditioning of the individual can deliver. For decisions influencing performance depend on something internal to their makers, whether they operate on their own or as members of an organizational unit, e.g. a firm. Attitudes, motives, and morals of the individuals shape the results; hence the Islamic emphasis on the development of human personality to achieve *falah*.

Case Study 3.1

Unemployment in India has been on the rise since 2009 despite growth pacing over the years. The impact is more on urban centres and female suffering is almost double. Differences on a religious basis are notable. Table presents some facts in percentages drawn from the Periodic Labour Force Survey (PLFS) 2017–2018.

Religion	*Rural %*	*Urban %*	*Female %**
Hinduism	5.7	6.9	10.0
Islam	6.7	7.5	14.5
Christianity	6.9	8.9	15.6
Sikhism	6.4	6.4	16.9

Figures are for urban unemployment only
Source of data The Indian Express August 2, 2019, p. 13 ◄

Ethical doctrine in Islam is intimately connected with law. *Fiqh* makes no distinction between rules concerning conduct and those that other systems consider as pertaining to civil and criminal law. Innumerable illustrations are available on this point. A government warning erected near some cotton fields outside Cairo in 1942 read: 'Beware of wetting cotton (before weighing) for it is fraud of which the consequence is loss for this world and punishment in the next' (Levy 1957, n. 197; see also pp. 204, 255–256). We can likewise publicize the Islamic obligations of giving (*infaq)*, of condemning temptation to greed or parsimony, and of observing honesty in contracts of all types, including those involving work effort, exploitation-free labour relations, prohibition of interest and speculation, opposition to hoarding and amassing of wealth. This would be a much better utilization of the modern means of mass communication to create social awareness of commercial ills.

3.2.3 Productivity and Distribution

Combinational or total factor productivity—output per composite unit of factors employed—is commonly used as a measure of growth. However, microeconomic theory continues to harp upon the productivities of *individual* factors as determinants of their distributive share in production. This concept, and its use as a just measure of factor contributions to production, is arbitrary and unjust. Furthermore, the theory emphasizes individualism, weakening social cohesion, and cooperation. Thus viewed, the concept of combinational productivity—participation in the productive effort as well as participation in sharing the fruits—is commensurate with the Islamic norm of fair play (Hasan 1975). It is combinational productivity that is the source of a firm's output and factor shares ought to be decided in accordance with the preagreed rules of the game (Fora reiteration of the concept, see Hasan [2016, pp. 152–155]).

3.3 Growth Versus Welfare

Broad identification of policy objectives for development is rarely a problem. Growth, employment, distributive justice, stability, self-reliance, and of late, environmental care and poverty eradication, complete the list.[4]

In this regard, Meier (1985, p. 6) makes an interesting observation that any statement of policy objectives is a definitional of development. These objectives could differ over time and space, defying unanimity on what development means. For that reason, the Islamic concept of development may be different from others, although some parallels cannot be ruled out.

However, perplexing difficulties are encountered when an attempt is made to spell out the precise meaning, range, and rankings of the objectives. This task is complicated, as most of the developing countries, impressed by the records of developed nations, often tend to base their decisions on Western prescriptions that are not always in harmony with the local needs or conditions.

The centrepiece of Western economic development prescriptions has been the acceleration of the GNP per head growth in real terms. Other policy goals are subjected to this imperative (*Human Development Report 1994*, p. 15). Emphasis on growth may suit the developed economies as they are reasonably sure of the input supplies and markets for their products and the lucrative returns on investments. Thus, in principle, the 'Made in India' programme of the Modi government.

[4]Contextually, Meier (1985, p. 6) makes an interesting observation. He says that any statement of policy objectives implies a prior fixation of the definition of development—the stated objectives condition, thus defying unanimity on what development is. We think he has a point here. For that reason, the Islamic concept of development is different from others, although some parallels cannot be denied.

As stated earlier, growth-centric policies did succeed in developing countries. However, the experiment failed on many other fronts such as poverty alleviation, reduction in income disparities and unemployment, and economic and socio-political stability. In fact, these problems poverty, deprivations, job deficiencies, and inequalities are required to remedy the situation before it is indeed too late.

The literature on economic development no longer places growth at the top of the hierarchy of development goals. To be meaningful, these goals must perforce follow the Islamic approach to development that focuses on basic needs fulfilment as a developmental priority. The programme aims at minimizing poverty along with growth. But to that end, it may turn out to be quite a radical proposition, demanding a drastic reshuffling of socio-economic priorities in resource allocation—its implementation presupposes iron resolve and determination for its successful implementation.

The relationship between growth and equity is one of the most talked-about issues in development. Yet it remains the least explored in the literature, more so in Islamic economics. Here, it is sufficient to state that the Islamic system would opt for a relatively slower rate of GNP growth should that bode better for distributive justice, compared to a system where faster growth could only be ensured at the cost of aggravating the existing inequalities.[5]

3.3.1 Employment Provision [B]

Another question closely related to growth is that of employment. Social security networks like *infaq, zakah*, and *awqaf* are at times thought to make people shun work and live on charity. This idea is unfounded, as it faces resistance from the need for self-esteem characteristic of humans. In addition, the *Qur'an* exhorts people to work for a living (31:34; 71:20). Of the many traditions on the point, one declares that 'striving for permissible living is the greatest human obligation next only to the worshiping of Allah' (quoted by Rahman 1936, p. 62).

The Islamic preference for engaging in trade signifies the relative importance of self-employment. The rising proportion of youth in developing economies' populations has forced public authorities to

[5] See Hasan (1988, p. 59). It is interesting to note that less than 150 years ago, J. S. Mill expressed a similar preference (see Osar and Blanchfeild 1975, p. 159).

expand opportunities for self-employment. The establishment of ministries for entrepreneurial development, on-the-job-skill-improvement programmes, aid to 'start-ups', liberal financial assistance to SMEs, and no-limit working hours for proprietary businesses in India are in line with the far-sighted Islamic view of being 'your own masters.' The financing of such programmes via *grameen* (rural) banks in Bangladesh has changed the face of the village economy in that country.

Islam sees the employment issue in the wider context of human resource development. Indeed, Islam was the first social order that made learning for knowledge compulsory for all its followers—men and women—whatever the hardships. The learning of the humanities, abstract sciences, and arts of various types, as conditioned by the *Shari'ah*, is a *fard kafaya*, i.e. sufficiency obligation in Islam. The implication is that Muslims must have among themselves knowledgeable people in all fields, to meet the *umatic* (communal) requirements. So long as deficiencies in any area of expertise remain, the entire community stays sinful (Qutb 1948, p. 203). An Islamic development programme must aim at providing adequate facilities for education, training, and research.

A human resource development programme, its vocational training component in particular, must partly depend on trade-offs the economy envisages between employment and output and the linkages it seeks between the choice of technologies and the basic needs-fulfilment requirement. Intuitively, the requirement may force the initiation of projects where people actually reside, rather than at far-off sites, keeping workers and families together. Migrant workers create many problems—economic, social, and political—in overcrowded industrial centres.

What is essential is a non-discriminatory social order for the fuller development of human capabilities for societal well-being. Social equality is fundamental to Islam. History tells us that the non-partisan attitude of the state enables the community to harness talent from far and near, from the high-born and the low-born, and from all races, to bring unparalleled expansion, glory, and prosperity to Muslims; and that the reversal to discriminatory ways led to decay and disintegration.

Central to social equality in Islam is its notion of distributive justice. *Shari'ah* insists on a wider percolation of wealth 'in order that it may not make a circuit merely among the rich of you' (*Qu'ran*, 59:7). However, people being prone to avarice, the concentration of wealth may be in fewer hands. *Shari'ah* thus makes it obligatory for the state authorities to take corrective action.

Box 3.1: Labor reforms in Saudi Arabia: End of discriminatory treatment

Rapid reforms discarding orthodoxy on the socio-economic front in favour of modernity has recently been trending in the Kingdom of Saudi Arabia. The latest in the series is allowing women to travel at home and abroad without a male escort. As an extension of the provision, it is also declared that work is the right of a citizen and employers could not discriminate against employees on the basis of sex, age or handicaps.

(*Source* The Indian Express, August 3, 2019, p. 16)

3.3.2 Systemic Stability

Social phenomena are dynamic and susceptible to tumultuous changes. Not all variables change at the same time, in the same direction, or proportionately. Dynamic changes alter relative price structures, resulting in unexpected income fluctuations. System instability retards societal progress. Containing such fluctuations—that are increasing in frequency and intensity—is a major problem confronting modern economies. Maintaining economic stability is perhaps the most ticklish of issues in modern economies. We are not aware of any counter-cyclic policies specific to Islam. The system must share the usual mainstream monetary and fiscal policies, with the necessary modifications to meet *Shari'ah* requirements.

Most countries—both developed and developing—that experienced fast growth in recent decades were particularly stable; many of the slowest were not (Meier 1985, p. 501). It is well known that after the Great Depression of the 1930s, the world economy never witnessed such a long period of stability—both political and economic—as from 1950 to 2000. Consequently, the world output also never expanded as fast—it tripled during this period. In contrast, the global instability unleashed by the 2007 US sub-prime debacle has not yet allowed a stable global recovery.

Finally, *Shari'ah* is a code of conduct that emphasizes creating harmony between human behaviour and nature. Man is allowed to partake of nature with joy as long as he is 'a benefactor, not a corruptor a cultivator not a destroyer' (Caliph Ali b. Talib, as quoted in Liewellyn 1984,

p. 6).[6] Islam insists on maintaining a balance of the biosphere; ecological care is its integral element. History showers praise on Muslim contributions to the beautification of the environment through landscaping, the raising of orchards, water management, and air circulation in the vastness of their architectural designs. Crop patterns, land usage, animal rearing, etc. were all geared towards ecological conservancy (However, Islam and the environment is a separate topic for discussion that we cannot take up here).

3.4 More Issues

The policy objectives discussed above are interwoven into the socio-economic developmental fabric of Islam; the system must push forward on all fronts simultaneously. Basic needs fulfilment, full employment, and human resource development with the focus on character building must promote one another in a cycle. Together they make a direct and cumulative assault on poverty and social inequalities; for the deprived, the unemployed, and the illiterate are mostly the poor. Equality and equity fortify the process of development as minds are freed from the tyranny of a discriminatory class and caste culture. People must become imbued with a sense of confidence in their own abilities and self-esteem so as to reignite in them that elation and pride which has ever been the hallmark of the believers. This type of Islamic development programme would stimulate people to grow while maintaining the balance between their mundane and spiritual urges.

3.4.1 The Question of Motivation

People are guided to action by a multiplicity of motives. However, an economic system usually identifies a basic one that urges its adherents to initiate action for improvement. Capitalism and socialism share the pursuit of self-interest with Islam as a motivational force, but with a difference. This difference arises from the divergence of their systemic constituents, as we examined in Chapter 1. We noted that Islam does not approve of most of the socialist goals or methods to achieve them. However, it accepts some

[6] It is agreed that the ultimate purpose of the *Shari'ah* is '...the universal good, the welfare of the entire creation ... This means that all the measurable effects of an action both immediate and ultimate on all beings must be weighed ...to maximize benefit and minimize harm to the totality of the creation' (Liewellyn 1984, p. 28).

features of capitalism in a unique relationship between affinity and divergence. Self-interest serving as a motivational force is one of them, but its place and its implications in the two systems are not the same.

The foundation bricks of the social values of capitalism were baked in the rationality-fuelled secular oven, Adam Smith installing self-interest as the system's motivational engine. Lux thought Smith invented economics and killed morality. This assertion may seem harsh as Smith had much ethical substance in his postulates; he candidly condemned avarice and the exploitation of the weak.[7] Still, there is no denying the fact that *he* made self-interest the guiding star of the free enterprise system.

For Smith, the pursuit of self-interest not only promoted individuals' well-being but also that of society. In his earlier work—*The Theory of Moral Sentiment* (1758)—Smith thought that sympathy and benevolence could overcome avarice and selfishness in humans; people wish to see their faces shining in the social looking glass. Why he dropped these ideas some twenty years later is not known. One is therefore inclined to agree with Lux that it was the beginning of an attack on the moral and ethical values of religion.[8]

One may not agree with the critics of Adam Smith in charging him with the creation of an 'economic man', but the impact of his views on motivations in mainstream economics, giving them a self-interest orientation, is undeniable. A popular textbook, for example, observes as follows.

> Capitalism presumes self-interest as the fundamental *modus operandi* for the various economic units as they express their choices. The motive of self-interest gives direction and consistency to what might otherwise be an extremely chaotic economy. (McConnell and Brue 1990, p. 41)

[7] Although Hutchinson (1978, p. 31) makes the following observation in another context, it serves the present purpose well. He writes: '[It was] natural that the church should have opposed the adoption of business customs that were not only contrary to Christian teachings but tainted with Judaism'. More damning is the charge that oppression was the objective of the expanding colonialism of the Christian West.

[8] Interestingly, after Lux, the 2009 work of Thaler and Sunstein, that won them the 2017 Nobel Prize in economics, seeks to create a bridge between the two subjects. It signifies the role of psychological analysis in individual decision-making. It is the recognition that 'economic agents are human and economic models have to incorporate that'. Maintaining freedom of choice, society must guide economic agents in the right direction, they argue. This reduces the distance between the Islamic and mainstream disciplines. Islam seeks to set that direction.

The difficulty is that the pursuit of self-interest tends to annihilate the competition, the force that seeks to discipline it (Hasan 1992, pp. 241–242). Monopsonic market structures have become an integral part of capitalist economies. The case for pursuing self-interest as a behavioural norm must rest, therefore, on the social efficacy of such structures, not on the virtues of a non-existent type of competition.

Lux traces the failures of societies based on self-interest from the misery of Charles Dickens's England through the Great Depression in the United States to the latter's culture of selfishness in recent years. He fully acknowledges the glorious achievements of modern capitalism in the field of scientific exploration, technological breakthroughs, and the advancement of material prosperity, but also shows that the unconstrained pursuit of self-interest has led to unprecedented social strife, ecological damage, and abuse of power. Pursuing self-interest may lead to'traits such as lack of self-control and fear of losing what you already have prompt decisions that may not have the best outcome in the longer term' (Thaler and Sunstein 2009).

Islam sees the behaviour of the bipolar man of its perception (as explained earlier) as determined by an array of motives that may broadly be thought of as a continuum of hate, selfishness, self-interest, and benevolence, with love at the pinnacle in ascending order. The conflict of interests in the world is, in fact, the conflict between the lower- and upper-end motives of human personality—between good and bad; between virtue and vice (Lux 1979, pp. 91–92). Adam Smith dealt only with the middle range of this sequence—selfishness, self-interest, and benevolence. Even here, he reversed the order: he held self-interest supreme and slighted benevolence.

Contrary to Smith, the regulatory force of the system in Islam is the believers' passion to follow the divine path. This path epitomizes the behavioural norms that *Shari'ah* prescribes for them in various walks of life. These norms are not averse to the pursuit of self-interest for worldly gains, but they have a rider that the means for acquiring riches must remain honest and *halal* and, more importantly, that the *amanah* view of wealth is never neglected or violated. *Amanah* seeks to convert the material ambitions of people into the means of attaining spiritual heights—their ultimate goal in life (*Qur'an*, 28:77). The instrument of conversion is not Smith's competition but benevolence, that finds expression in the grand Islamic principle of *infaq* i.e. spending on the prescribed, the needy, and the poor, for the pleasure of Allah (2:263; 3:86).

Human development is an increasing function of *infaq* and must motivate the believers to work more—not less as some perceive—to increase earnings, both for maintaining their own lives and for spending more on less fortunate members of society. This is to serve the cause of Allah, avoiding waste and extravagance on the way (6:142; 7:27). This approach could not only be promotive of growth by expanding markets, but could also encourage the evolution of honest production-exchange relations that have been so rare in recent times. *Infaq* as a behavioural norm must rest, therefore, on the social efficacy of such structures, not on the virtues of a non-existent type of competition.

Thus, in Islam, *amanah* adds a social dimension to the urge for personal gain. It seeks to harmonize individual and social interests. For without their adequate synchronization, the potentialities of freedom of enterprise ingrained in the Islamic religion can rarely become an instrument of mass amelioration.

3.4.2 The Role of the State

In an Islamic economy, as in others, major development problems include a discussion on the relative roles of the state and the market-led private sector in achieving the given goals. The division between the spheres and responsibilities of the two sectors is neither intuitively obvious nor objectively fixed. It is case-specific. In principle, the division in an Islamic state has to be commensurate with *Shari'ah* norms, as well as flexible, and must be decided through a consultative process among the mature, knowledgeable members of the community at various levels. Islam being a system based on voluntary dynamism, the role of grass-roots participation in social decision-making cannot be ignored.

Western society has been divided on the role of the state in the economic sphere since the mercantilist era; liberalism being its overtone following Adam Smith (1776). This has occasionally been disrupted by circumstantial compulsions, especially after the onset of the economic turmoil that devastated the globe beginning in 2017. Some Muslim economists have dragged the debate into discussions on Islamic finance. What is required is thinking out of the box. Developing economies may do well to stay clear of these controversies and think indigenously. However, a few remarks may not be out of place.

To begin with, one has to remember that in practice the market system does not always work efficiently. This reminder is needed in view of the present race towards privatization in the developing economies. Privatization is an integral part of globalization of economic freedom, but it is a dress that does not fit all sizes.

Also, the current wave of privatization need not always be a catalogue of virtues. The shrinking of the state's entrepreneurial activities must tend to enhance its supervisory role. It is worth noting that the size of the public sector as measured by the proportion of the federal (central) government's total revenue to GDP remains much higher in the advanced economies as compared to the developing ones, over time and space. Between 1992 and 2015, public revenue as GDP share has in general increased in advanced economies, implying a decline in privatization, while the reverse has been the position in developing economies—ironically, because of Western political manipulations.[9]

Asset distribution in contemporary Muslim countries being what it is, the participation of the state in economic activities to improve the situation has to be substantial. Market regulation must be tightened in the initial stages. Islamic values are also to be protected from alien policy norms coming in the garb of promoting global culture.[10] For example, public enterprise may gradually be converted to public regulation and intervention may decline with the passage of time.

The areas, forms, and extent of state intervention in Muslim countries must respond to the broad priorities of development in order to realize the objectives of *Shari'ah*. These include, for instance, provision for meeting the minimum basic needs, demanding production of sufficient wage goods, especially food. This would mean giving priority to rural development where conditions permit. Detailed schemes for land reclamation, cropping patterns, landscaping and usage, irrigation, improved seeds, and farm machinery, together with tiller-friendly land tenure systems, have to be introduced. Input/output prices must be kept in a reasonable relationship, using meaningful subsidies and support incentives where necessary. Adequate infrastructural services, including institutional financing facilities, have to be arranged. For example, cooperatives suit the Islamic temperament and are cost-saving in rural development. Finally, agriculture must be integrated with manufacturing; the two cannot be seen as competitors.

[9] Consider, for example, controversial discussions in the works of Robert Higgs (2012), who describes a pervasive lack of confidence among investors in their ability to foresee the extent to which future government interventionist policies will adversely alter their private property rights. In contrast, Robert Piketty (2014) argues that state intervention is needed to keep the economy on the stable trajectory of development.

[10] Table 3.1 provides the evidence. Notice that during the period from 1992–2015, public revenue as GDP share has in general increased, implying a decline in privatization, while the reverse has been the position in the developing economies because of Western pressure (source: World Bank Reports). See also Case study 3.1.

Table 3.1 Comparative percentages of federal revenues to GDP as privatization measure

Countries	*1992%*	*2015%*	*Countries*	*1992%*	*2015%*
Australia	27.6	25.8	India	24.4	17.7
France	40.9	47.8	Indonesia	19.7	12.0
Germany	30.3	40.6	Malaysia	30.1	15.5
Italy	40.7	43.5	Pakistan	16.7	12.4
Norway	47.8	43.8	Philippines	17.4	14.4
USA	37.5	28.9	Turkey	22.9	32.5
Simple mean	37.5	38.4		22.1	14.1

Case Study 3.2

Internationalization, privatization and liberalization have been the pillars of modern capitalism now sweeping across the world. Developing economies are finding the dress fitting all sizes. Of the three privatization is easier to measure. A rough and ready measure is the ratio of Tax revenue to the GDP of the country. Higher this ratio is the lower tends to be the degree of privatization in an economy and vice versa. The following three sets of countries testify the efficacy the efficacy of the measure.

Developed countries	%	Developing countries	%	Muslim countries	%
Germany	44.5	Argentina	37.2	Turkey	24.8
Italy	43.5	Brazil	34.4	Pakistan	16.8
France	41.9	Australia	34.3	Egypt	15.8
UK	34.4	China	20.1	Malaysia	15.4
USA	26.2	India	17.7	Indonesia	12.1

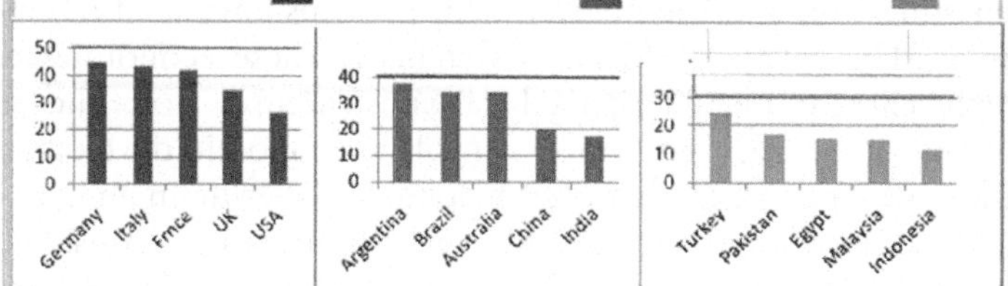

Source: Construction id based on data in World Bank publications

Source of Data: Revnue statistics 2019
https://www.oecd.org/tax/tax-policy/revenue-statistics-highlights-brochure.pdf

To improve coordination, the industrial development programme can accord importance to the production of goods of mass consumption, curbing resource-absorbing luxuries. Production of common use goods employs relatively more labour and helps relieve unemployment pressures. The application of more, if appropriate, technology is encouraged in populous Muslim countries. Local skills may also be put to good use.

Housing is another important component of basic human needs. Provision of dwellings in the countryside may lessen slum expansion in urban centres. This issue can be addressed by public sector initiatives in specific areas and in partnership with the private sector. Group housing cooperatives can also alleviate the problem. Priority should be given to low-cost, simple, but comfortable dwellings. Having high-rise fancy structures, as is the fashion today, is not the answer to the housing issues in many Muslim countries, where availability of land is not a problem for reasonable horizontal expansion. Such expansion cuts costs, and may be unsafe during natural calamities or wars. A revolving National Housing Development Fund may be established to help finance these projects.

To the list may be added a minimal provision for health care. Modern state-of-the-art medical facilities are of course needed, but cannot be the only goal of a popular mass health care programme in most developing economies. Medical personnel in mobile dispensaries with basic knowledge of common ailments may make regular visits to rural clusters and suburban neighbourhoods. In addition, there is a strong case to revive and encourage the traditional medicine systems. A corps of footloose doctors as in China may be raised to fan out to the interior. Cities may also have street corner clinics, as recently introduced in the Union Territory of Delhi.

A well-grounded education policy must be a core element in any Islamic development programme. There is an intimate relationship between education and the development patterns envisaged in emerging economies. The existing education systems in these economies tend to perpetuate elite non-egalitarian education structures from the colonial era. Suitable reforms in education can place economic development on the right course in an Islamic order, helping in ushering in an overall ethical social and economic change. Muslim countries may consider introducing the following in their educational systems to strengthen them from within:

a. A moral orientation to basic and general education;
b. Family improvement education;
c. Community improvement education; and
d. Occupational instruction and training.

Such diversified education will help develop a well-balanced societal structure.

Adequate resources must be allocated to promote education on a priority basis. The introduction of scholarship schemes and subsidies, merit recognition, and transparent staff promotion processes are also important. Entry quotas for weaker and underprivileged, but potentially good students, must be arranged. Strengthening of infrastructure is needed. Over-emphasis on specialization absorbs more resources relative to benefits; it also attracts less intelligent students to higher education, raising the overall cost–benefit ratios. Reforms from outside the system may include the following:

- Adjusting the emerging markets imbalances, indicators and incentives.
- Modification of job rationing by educational certification, if needed; and
- Curbs on brain drain by making educational qualifications less stringent than global requirements and arresting the exodus by other means.

The use of local languages for instruction can also help. Arabic can easily replace foreign languages as a medium of instruction in many non-Arab Organization of Islamic Cooperation (OIC) countries. Selective exceptions can meet special requirements.

Finally, Muslim countries must forge closer social, economic, and cultural ties with each other, especially to jointly face the global machinations being engineered against Islam and Muslims by vested interests. Cooperation alone can bail them out of their current predicament.

3.4.3 Demographic Issues

Today, the adherents of Islam constitute the second-largest religious group in the world, second only to Christianity. Significantly, Muslim populations are growing the fastest compared to the adherents of other

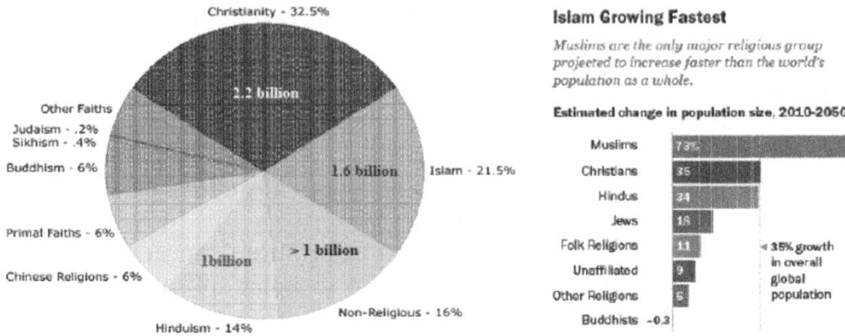

Fig. 3.1 World religious adherence in 2012 (*Source* The future of world religious population growth projections 2010–2050)

faiths, especially due to conversions. Figure 3.1 highlights the latest available position. It is rather surprising that in the writings on Islamic development, the population issue is considered too sensitive for debate. However, the issue need not invoke anxiety, especially discussions on birth control. The matter is vital to provide for the basic needs of people—an Islamic imperative. Demographic insights are crucial as the base for planning. In many developing countries, efforts are being made to monitor family sizes. Even developed economies prefer to keep families small. This is a vast and complicated topic but a few observations may not be out of place.

Mainstream economists seldom refrain from raising the alarm on the population issue. Across nations, this issue has helped mill-owners blame the poor for their low wages and the deprivations they suffered. The uncritical acceptance of this argument placed the developing economies unceasingly on the defensive and made population control a worldwide movement. Islamic economists sought refuge in silence.

Fortunately, the opinion that has long been gaining ground in developing countries is that 'scarcity verses population' is not so much a question of numbers as of distribution (Todaro 1986). The average per head income of the global village (as some fondly prefer to call the world) was over US$10,000 in 2015, estimated from World Development Report 2017 data. Why must there then be so much misery and destitution in the vast majority of its lanes? What would have been the result if the colossal amount of resources spent on armaments, on the engineering of conflicts to sell arms, and on exploring space had been otherwise used? The lot of the global poor could have been significantly improved even if a fraction of this wasteful expenditure was diverted to welfare schemes for the deprived.

The density of population in the Muslim world is estimated at around 30,000 per square kilometre[11] This is much lower than most of the densely populated developed economies. More land resources can possibly be a contributory factor to the economic development of the Muslim world vis-à-vis other developing countries. The density is especially thin in the Middle East, North Africa, and the Muslim countries of Central Asia. Many of these are rich in resources but short of labour supply. On the other hand, countries like Bangladesh, Indonesia, and Egypt are labour surplus areas deficient in resources. A coordinated development effort can benefit both categories of countries and some progress in that direction is already visible. Cheaper labour supply can lend products a competitive edge in the world markets. Regrettably, the preference for high-rise construction is leaving less for investing in high-end-value manufacturing. A change in priorities may promise faster and more beneficial development, especially to the extent it helps cut imports of goods for daily use.

3.4.4 Population Management

Coordinated efforts can help kick-start development in the Muslim world. Eventually, however, each country would like to grow according to its own needs and compulsions. Thus, the problem of population numbers would confront individual countries differently. For instance, countries like Bangladesh, Egypt, and Indonesia must face the numbers issue. Should these countries resort to modern ways of population

[11]The estimation is based on the population densities of the following countries: Bahrain, 1235; Maldives, 309; Lebanon, 4224; Cameroon, 676; Pakistan, 193,870; Kuwait, 3566; Nigeria, 154,729; Uganda, 32,710; Malawi, 15,263; Qatar, 1409; Indonesia, 237,596; Albania, 1195; Azerbaijan, 9165; Turkey, 77,804; Malaysia, 28,307; Egypt, 88,057; Ethiopia, 79,221; Brunei, 400; Tunisia, 10,327; Uzbekistan, 27,488; B. Faso, 15,757; Tajikistan, 6952; Tanzania, 43,739; Afghanistan, 29,863; Iran, 74,194; Yemen 23,558; Guinea Bissau, 1611; Djibouti, 864; Kyrgyzstan, 5482; Algeria, 34,895; Somalia, 9133; Niger, 15,290; Saudi Arabia, 8260; Mali, 14,517; Turkmenistan, 5110; Oman, 2845; Chad, 11,274; Kazakhstan, 17,010; Gabon, 1475; Libya, 762; Mauritania, 3291; Surinam, 520 (source: World Bank Statistics).

management? We are not quite sure if Islamic religion and sociology would permit family planning of the modern type. However, the issue can be examined from the viewpoint of an individual or as a matter of public policy. Presumably, family planning as a state programme would not be permissible, for the *Qur'an* unequivocally declares:

The *Qur'an* on population.

> No creature is there crawling on the earth but its provision rests on Allah (*Qur'an*11:7) and slay not your children for fear of poverty. We will provide for you and them (*Qur'an* 17:31). Satan threatens you with poverty and bids you to indecency. Allah promises you forgiveness and bounty. (*Qur'an* 2:268)

Population control may have some serious consequences. It is the richer and educated sections of the community that tend to be more receptive to the idea although they require it the least. In contrast, the poor, who need it most, shun it. These tendencies are likely to reduce the *quality* of population in the long run. There is a shift in numbers towards the older age groups; population pyramids tend to become wider at the top with the passage of time, as is now the case with many developed countries. The shift tends to tilt the output-mix in favour of the older generations. Overall, labour productivity may decline. Unemployment and frustration among the youth may cause social problems, even political turmoil.

At the individual level, modern population control could perhaps be permissible, but the methods in vogue may not all be granted unreservedly. It may be noted, for example, that the condom is not just a contraceptive; the popularization of its use is likely to promote a culture of unfaithfulness and permissiveness that Islam abhors. Likewise, the use of abortion as a family control measure is clearly unacceptable. What seem allowable are measures before conception, but rarely anything thereafter.[12] Finally, the population issue is inseparable from the overall concern for development. Reduction in fertility comes about from investment in education and health care measures for women. On a philosophical plane, population control as a policy seems to conflict with the concept of human freedom and dignity.

[12] Life is a principle of growth that needs nourishment, respiration, and expansion. However, it also faces the possibility of extinction. The availability of life support to avoid extinction is required by a child from day one of conception. Thus seen, abortion at any stage equals termination of life.

3.5 Concluding Remarks

The fact is that the concept of development—and its objectives and priorities—in mainstream economics and Islam are divergent, although similar. This chapter has presented an integrated view of the subject with a focus on Islamic departures from the mainstream.

On the ground, most developing countries have attempted to imitate development designs and strategies of the Western countries, albeit with modifications. This has tended to make their economies, at times, serve alien interests rather than their own. Developing countries have become markets for the products of the leading developed counties, as well as suppliers of materials and workers for their factories and profitable investment avenues for their surplus funds.

Muslim countries, in general, were steeped in poverty when Allah opened the doors of wealth and prosperity to many of them in the form of petroleum—black liquid gold. Western countries, having the technology to explore and extract oil for commercial use, soon dominated the oil-rich tracts of the Muslim world. Easy wealth made the owners lethargic. The money obtained was either left in foreign banks or spent on conspicuous consumption. Armament sales being the most lucrative of all trades, Western machinations soon succeeded in dividing Muslims within and between countries. Since the Second World War, Muslims have probably killed more Muslims than have the non-Muslims. They emerged as the top buyers of Western weaponry as well as of operators and trainers (Liewellyn 1984, Table 3). This in-fighting led to the *Arab spring* in most of the Middle East at the turn of the century. After the first wave of elation subsided, the West discovered to its dismay that it was not spring but in fact autumn that was unleashed from the mosques of countries antagonistic to their interests. The process was reversed. Another round

Of mutual bloodshed ensued until submissive governments were restored.

The *Qur'an* had told the believers that Allah divided them into clans and tribes so that they could recognize each other and warned that unless they remained united, they would lose honour and dignity in the world. Over time, Muslims reversed what the *Qur'an* had stated: clans, tribes, and lineages meant for recognition became divisive forces pitting one against the other. The community (*ummah*) lost its respect and glory.

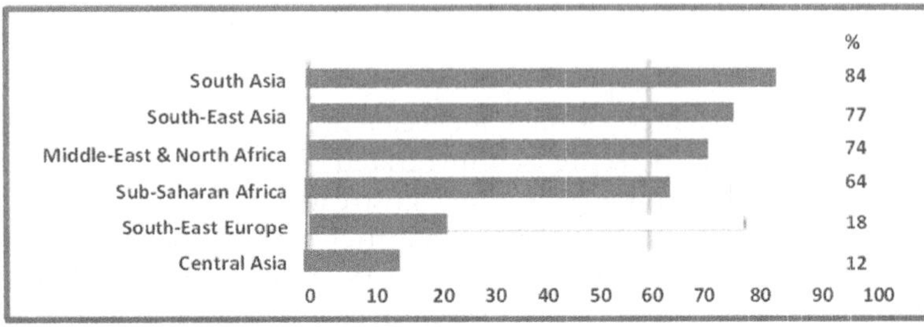

Fig. 3.2 Many hold Shari'ah as equivalent to Islamic law albeit they differ (*Source of data for construction* Pew research center 2015)

Nowadays, new sources of energy are being found, petroleum prices are falling, and oil extraction approaching limits: where do we go from here? Interestingly, the Muslim masses wish to go back to their religious culture and ethos, if the survey in Fig. 3.2 is to be relied upon.

Is it not surprising that despite a vast majority of Muslims opting for the implementation of *Shari'ah* norms in public administration, authorities continue dragging their feet on the issue?

Historically, over time and space, a multiplicity of mundane wants kept outstripping resource availability and acquiring wealth became the *sine qua non* of economic development, more relevantly to countries that became independent of colonial rule after the Second World War. Indeed, between 1950 and 1975, the GDP of the developing countries grew at a faster annual rate (5.5%) than of the developed countries (4.6%) (Todaro 1986). But it soon became clear that the escalating growth rates concealed many faults and failures of development planning, and poverty and inequalities worsened.

Test Questions

Q.1 Explain the concept of economic development in Islam. Is this concept entirely different from the mainstream concept of development? Give reasons for your answer.

Q.2 Examine the concept of sustainability contextual to economic development. Is sustainable development an operable concept in your opinion? Justify your answer.

Q.3 'Goals of development are always not mutually compatible.' Explain. How would you reconcile growth with distributional equity and full employment?

Q.4 'Best economic results are obtained when the state does not intervene in the market.'. Critically evaluate this claim. What role does Islam assign to the government in an economy?

Q.5 Write explanatory notes on the following within an Islamic perspective:

a. Efficiency in resource allocation
b. Cost of production
c. Basic needs fulfilment
d. Nudge theory

What Next?

We have referred to environmental issues in the discussion above. These issues are fast becoming graver and stand at the centre of development. Chapter 4 examines environmental concerns, the nature of the problems that confront the world, and the remedies proposed to arrest the deterioration of the situation.

References

Galbraith, J. K. (1969). *The New Industrial State*. USA: Princeton University Press.

Hasan, Z. (1975). *Theory of Profit*. New Delhi: Vikas Publishing House Pvt. Ltd.

Hasan, Z. (1988). Distributional Equity in Islam. In M. Iqbal (Ed.), *Distributive Justice and Need Fulfillment in an Islamic Economy* (Chapter 1, pp. 35–62). Leicester, UK: Islamic Foundation.

Hasan, Z. (1992). Profit Maximization: Secular Versus Islamic. In S. Tahir, A. Ghazali, & S. O. S. Agil (Eds.), *Readings in Microeconomics: An Islamic Perspective* (Chapter 20, pp. 239–255). Petaling Jaya, Malaysia: Longman.

Hasan, Z. (1994). Economic Development in Islamic Perspective: Concept, Objectives and Some Issues. *IIUM, Journal of Islamic Economics, 1*(1), 80–111.

Hasan, Z. (1997). Fulfillment of Basic Needs: Concept, Measurement and Muslim Countries' Performance. *IIUM Journal of Economic and Management, 5*(2), 1–38.

Hasan, Z. (2016). Risk-Sharing: The Sole Basis of Islamic Finance? Time for a Serious Rethink. *Journal of King Abdulaziz University: Islamic Economics, 29*(2), 23–36.

Higgs, R. (2012). *Delusions of Power: New Explorations of the State, War, and Economy*. Oakland, California: The Independent Institute.
Hutchinson, M. G. (1978). *Economics Thought In Spain, 1177–1740*. London: George Allen & Unwin.
Leibenstein, H. (1978). *General X-Efficiency Theory and Economic Development*. New York: Oxford.
Levy, R. (1957). *The Social Structure of Islam*. London: Cambridge University Press.
Liewellyn, O. A. (1984). Islamic Jurisprudence and Environmental Planning. *Journal of Research in Islamic Economics, 1*(2), 25–49.
Lux, K. (1979). *Adam Smith's Mistake*. US: Shambhala (1990).
Meier, G. M. (Ed.). (1985). *Leading Issues in Economic Development* (4th ed.). Delhi: Oxford University Press.
McConnell, C., & Brue, S. (1990). *Economics, Principles Problems and Polices* (11th ed.). New York: Mcgrew Hill.
Osar, J., & Blanchfeild, W. C. (1975). *The Evolution of Economics Thought* (3rd ed.). New York: Haarcourt Brace JovanVish Inc.
Piketty, T. R. (2014). *Capital in the Twenty First Century*. Spiegel.
Qutb, S. (1948). *Milestones*. Beirut: The Quran House.
Rahman, M. H. (1936). *Islam ka Iqtisadi Nizam ek ajmali khaka (Urdu)—The Economic System of Islam (An outline)*. Dar-ul-Mussan-e-feen, Urdu Bazar, Jama Masjid, Delhi.
Shari'ati, A. (1982). *Man and Islam*, Lectures (G. M. Fayez, Trans.). Mashhad, Iran: University of Mushhad Press.
Smith, A. (1776). *An Inquiry Into the Nature and Causes of Wealth of Nations*. University of Glasgow Press.
Thaler, R. H., & Sunstein, C. R. (2009). *Nudge: Improving Decisions About Health, Wealth and Happiness*. New Haven & London: Yale University Press.
Todaro, M. P. (1986). *Economic Development in the Third World*. Longman, UK.
Ursul, A. D. (1983). *Philosophy and The Ecological Problems of Civilization* (2nd ed.). Moscow: Progress.

CHAPTER 4

Growth Versus Environment: Pollution and Its Mitigation

Preview
The notion of sustainability emerged in development economics literature in the wake of the environmental devastation rapid growth has inflicted on human beings and other life forms across the planet Earth. However, the roots of the notion can be traced back to various faiths, especially Islam. Several Islamic economists have studied the debate on the meaning of sustainable development and related environmental issues the world now faces. This chapter examines several interpretations of sustainability and attempts to put forth a concrete, Islamic definition for sustainable development. It argues that any definition of sustainable development ultimately ends with environmental concerns. On this and other issues discussed the Chapter has a strictly *theoretical* orientation.

The linkage assumes importance as sustainable development, however defined, is related to finance. Product fund-bounding is increasingly being used to serve environmental ends. Islamic finance has so far been based essentially upon negative screening. The focus has been more on averting the investments and actions contrary to Islamic law, rather than think positively about investing in socially responsible and compliant concerns. While organizations such as the Islamic Development Bank do engage in such projects, positivism, and particularly the safeguards required to protect the environment, have been inadequate in most of the criteria of Islamic financial institutions.

Z. Hasan, *Leading Issues in Islamic Economics and Finance*,
https://doi.org/10.1007/978-981-15-6515-1_4

The formulation of a definition of Islamic sustainable development this chapter presents implies an opportunity for convergence between Islamic and other ethical investments. With the growing emphasis on socially responsible investment in the financial world, an Islamic alternative would provide an opportunity for collaboration, particularly in view of ample liquidity available in the Gulf region. The effort may help evolve a systemic framework for some sort of positive screening. Finally, the chapter looks at the type of theoretical problems contextual to the environment and the solutions for resolving them, especially the viability of the Coase theorem.

Learning Outcomes
The study of this Chapter is expected to make the reader aware of:

- The theoretical issues relating to sustainability vis-a-vis the environment.
- To evaluate the market and non-market solutions to environmental problems.
- To understand the nature of environmental concerns expressed in Islamic sources of knowledge.
- To appreciate the positive role of finance relative to environment.

4.1 Introduction

Economic development and the factors that promote it have been the prime concern of economics from its very inception. Essentially, development acquired the status of a formal discipline after the Second World War for a variety of reasons.[1] But the innate human urge to produce increasing volumes of goods and services to meet the demand of expanding population to maintain and raise the living standards already attained worldwide, forces a conflict between material prosperity on the one hand, and environmental sustainability on the other. The conflict has resulted in intensifying the debate on how the benefits of growth

[1] The reasons included the colossal reconstruction requirements of the war-devastated economies, and the poverty eradication demands of the people in many countries that had won their political freedom from colonial rule after the war. Thus, the talk of planning for economic development became the order of the day, especially after 1945. Regrettably, wars have since become more frequent and destructive, demanding colossal rebuilds.

in output, and its negative impact on environment, should be reconciled. The difficulty is that neither the population increase nor the urge to improve living standards can be halted, let alone reversed, to remain commensurate with maintaining the balance in the provisions Allah created for supporting life on the planet. Eventually, growth of output became the top priority for countries, especially Islamic, for reducing poverty and distributional inequalities. Thus, the patterns and processes of production were sought to be *modified* to resolve these problems and related issues.

The modification was the attachment of an attribute to the development: countries must work for *sustainable* development. However, this only added more ambiguity to an already murky notion. If growth could not be frozen, one could legitimately ask: what is it then that we need to *sustain* in the development process to neutralize the adverse consequences of growth?

4.1.1 Versions of Sustainability

There seems to be no agreed definition of sustainability contextual to economic development, for this is a recent concept attempting to assimilate the dynamism of change, but that cannot ignore local concerns, needs, and interests. The question in essence here is: what is it that we want to sustain? We can identify three broad answers in the literature. Sustainability implies:

a. Maintaining the long-run rate of economic growth;
b. Achieving intergenerational equity in the use of natural resources;
c. Restricting, as far as possible, the increase in pollution to sustain the present quality of the environment i.e. do not harm or deteriorate it.

The three versions of sustainable development listed above are interlinked. For example, a sustainable rate of growth implies that the pace of development should be slower than its present rate. Moderation would help conserve resources, lower pollution, and improve distribution. Emphasis on temporal equity would demand a more even spread of resources, prosperity, and environmental damage over time. The notion implies putting the brakes on consumerism and expanding credit card culture i.e. borrowing from the future to spend in the present. Again, the focus on environmental sustenance would eventually help in conservation of resources and may also improve the intergenerational distribution of incomes. In summary, whichever of the above forms one conceived of sustainability, one would end up with environmental concerns.

Having discussed the versions of sustainability as stated in the literature, Sect. 4.2 of this chapter takes a brief look at the growth-equity conflict and its ramifications for sustainable development. In Sect. 4.3, we deal with the environmental problems that modern warfare unleashes. Section 4.4 describes the Islamic position on the environmental issue. Section 4.5 explains how the instrument of finance—conventional and Islamic—can converge to make a positive contribution to environmental improvement. Section 4.6 lists the types of environmental problems the world now faces and various policy prescriptions are put forth to resolve them, especially the Coase theorem. Section 4.7 contains several final observations. We conclude that the Islamic approach is notably agreeable to environmental protection and that issues surrounding sustainable development have moral, ethical, social, and political complexities that economics alone cannot resolve.

Passion for growth is rarely abated. Indeed, the total output of the world during the latter half of the twentieth century far exceeded that which humanity could produce during the entire span of its existence before the Second World War. The plates on the global dining table had multiplied 2.75 times during the period (Fig. 2.1) yet on an average they were better filled. However, the expected trickle-down did not take place: the gulf between the rich and the poor widened both within and among, nations. Likewise, the centres of growth did not radiate prosperity everywhere: they became whirlpools of affluence, sucking in men and material from all around.

4.2 Growth vs. Welfare [a]

The focus on growth derives its inspiration from the classical, steady-state, long-run development model. The model depicts the pessimism unleashed by Malthus and Ricardo, who visualized scarcity of resources as slowing growth under a faster expansion of population until output expansion would no longer be possible—growth having reached a stationary state. Figure 4.1 outlines the operation process of the model

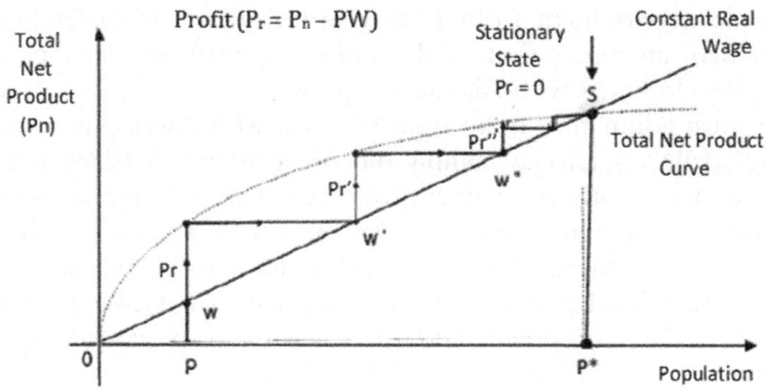

Fig. 4.1 Classical model of stationary state

and the consequences of the classical approach. History belied their fears, leaving far-flung areas in deep deprivation.

In addition, rapid development brought in frightful degradation of the environment, including ozone depletion, the melting of ice caps, global warming, rising sea levels, deforestation, and species extinction. In sum, fast growth was characterized by aggravated poverty and inequalities, together with immense environmental deterioration. A review of the concept of development was required. Growth, of course, could not be ignored, but it did lose its pride of place among the objectives of development. Ideas like the quality of life, the upward movement of the entire social order, eradication of poverty, mitigation of inequalities, reduction of regional imbalances, and above all, environmental concerns, all invaded the notion of development. The result was the addition of the word *sustainable* to development, even as the maladies of the notion increased.

4.2.1 *Sustainable Growth*

What is development with 'sustainable growth' and what are the policy implications of such a concept? Substantive writings dealing with the subject from that angle are hard to find. Whatever little is available discusses the allusions that scripture and the prophetic traditions about environmental care contain. To claim that one can deduce the concept of sustainable development from Islamic jurisprudence is far-fetched.[2] We attempt here an integration of the various mainstream versions of sustainable development with Islamic positions.

One must admit that Islam does not deal with development issues as they are spelled out today, simply did not exist when Islam arrived on the scene. To do otherwise may involve the risk of being apologetic or irresolute in argument. However, *Shari'ah* contains many unmistakable, albeit generic, warnings that the world is likely to be overwhelmed by development-related problems of the sort it is now facing if people do not resist selfishness, greed, and the rapacious exploitation of natural resources.

Repetto (1986) defined sustainable development as one that aims at managing all-natural, human, and financial resources of a country to sustain its wealth and welfare over the long run. Following a similar line, Pearce et al. (1990) saw development as a vector—a list of elements—that society sought to maximize. In Islamic dispensation, the fulfilment of basic needs of all nationals is a social imperative. The vector will doubtless include growth factors such as improvement in food and nutrition, accommodation facilities, medical care, educational attainment, and an increase in basic freedoms. Thus seen, sustainable development is a situation where the specified vector elements must increase over time, without limits. In this formulation, GNP growth remains at the forefront as other elements of the vector essentially depend on this variable. This approach has several difficulties; the 1992 World Bank Report does not mince words when it says:

> Sustainable management of the environment and natural resources is vital for economic growth and human well-being. When managed well, renewable natural resources, watersheds, productive landscapes and seascapes can provide the foundation for sustained inclusive growth, food security and poverty reduction. Natural resources provide livelihoods for hundreds of millions of people and generate sizeable tax revenue. The world's ecosystems regulate the air, water and soil on which we all depend, form a unique and cost-effective buffer against extreme weather events and climate change.

[2] For such claims, see, for example, Llewellyn (1984), Akhtar (1996), and Khalid (2002). All three are valuable contributions to Islamic economics on the environment, although their coverage and thrust is very different from the present exercise.

This view of development implies an infinite time horizon. However, decision-making operates within specified time scales. Planning for achieving pre-fixed targets may thus be difficult. In a dynamic socio-economic scenario over the long run, the elements of the development vector may undergo sharp changes in content, range, and quality, destroying intertemporal comparability. Again, the concept is silent on the direction of change in the vector; the rate of change is assumed to remain positive for each time segment, and that may not be valid. Only the overall trend may be conceived as remaining positive. Most writers prefer to work with this, rather weak, view of sustainability.

Case Study 4.1: Land Beneath the Silicon Valley Sinking

Climate change is the mother of all environmental problems the world faces today. The earth is heating up, with average temperatures rising year after year; wind belts are sliding and with that local climatic norms in terms of heat and rainfall levels changing, affecting diverse life forms, life forms impacting human life. Here is a simple illustration:

'The San Francisco Bay area's Silicon Valley is home to a plethora of wealthy tech companies, but the sinking land beneath risks leading to far worse floods in the years to come,' researchers said.

This sinking, or subsidence, doubles the territory in Silicon Valley at risk of flooding by 2100, said the report in the journal Science Advances.

Most of the San Francisco bay shoreline is sinking by less than two millimetres a year, but 'in several areas we discovered subsidence rates of half an inch a year and more', said the study. Source *Times of India*, Friday, 9 March 2018.

4.2.2 Intergenerational Equity

The World Commission on Environment and Development (the 'Commission') presented the definition of sustainable development in 1987, focusing on the concept of inter-generational equity. It believed that such development is one that meets the needs of the present population without compromising the satisfying of our material needs. It must

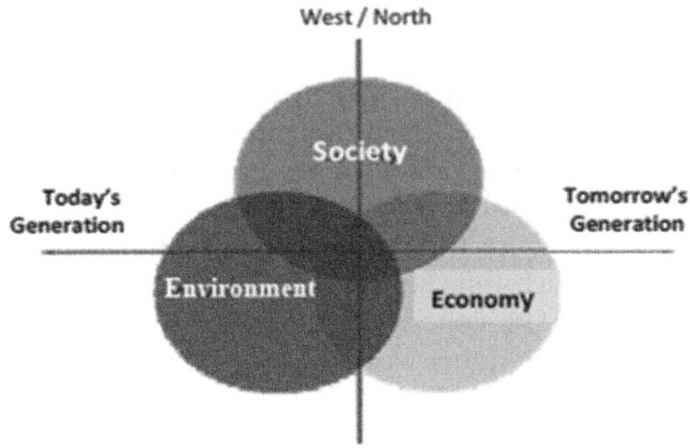

Fig. 4.2 Economy, society and environment interaction (*Source* Report of World Commission on Environment and Development 1987)

aim at preserving the natural foundations of life and calls for sustainable development in three domains: the economy, the environment, and society, in equal measure. This is depicted in Fig. 4.2 (reproduced with some modifications from the Commission Report). This rendition of sustainable development echoes the Islamic position on the issue.

This depiction puts the spiritual or non-material needs of people on the same footing as their material needs when measuring economic performance. Islam also puts such needs on the same footing as the material needs of people when measuring economic performance. We shall have occasion to present in some detail the Islamic stance relative to the environment in Sect. 4.4. This depiction puts the spiritual or non-material needs of people on the same footing as their material needs when measuring economic performance. Islam also puts such needs on the same footing as the material needs of people when measuring economic performance. We shall have occasion to present in sòme detail the Islamic stance relative to the environment in Sect. 4.4.

We shall see that the Islamic ingredients of sustainability are more potent than what the Commission bargained for in its report. Its deliberations did not go far enough and were not free of weaknesses. In the first place, there is little agreement on the objective criteria to test if development is indeed progressing at a sustainable pace, let alone for knowing the needs of future generations on a comparable basis. The time dimension of the concept remains unspecified. It is more rhetoric than offering a workable plan of action.

4.2.3 *Curbing Pollution*

Finally, there is the perception that sustainable development is an effort to forge a compromise between demands for economic growth and environmental protection. True, this approach is narrower, but it is more realistic than those discussed earlier. In fact, it provides the foundation for all the shades of environmentalism that have been so vocalized in recent years. The credit for its formulation goes back to the Earth Summit at Rio de Janeiro in 1992, especially to its Agenda 21, a programme of action for sustainable development worldwide. This agenda still inspires the thought process on environmental issues. The definition of sustainable development it projects seeks to limit the rate of growth to a level that would allow it to continue without aggravating the resource position. It focuses on recycling of resources, their renewal where possible, and their conservation if non-renewable. However, this view, too, has difficulties similar to those we noted related to the other two versions of sustainable development.

4.3 War and the Environment

There have been many and varied causes of environmental degradation, but writings on the subject, textbooks especially, seldom include wars (including civilian unrest like that in Syria, Iraq, Libya, or Kashmir) among its leading causes. The impact of modern warfare, including scorched-earth methods, has indeed been devastating to landscapes, ecosystems, and people. The progression in weaponry from chemical to nuclear has increasingly put stress on the environment. The literature is full of the environmental damage inflicted by recent wars such as those in Vietnam, Korea, Rwanda, the Balkans, the Gulf, and Afghanistan.[3]

Wars in various parts of the world, especially in the Gulf region, reveal that the ecological consequences of conflicts often remain written upon

[3]Widespread concern about the environmental effects of warfare began with the American attack on Vietnam; the US military sprayed 79 million litres of herbicides and defoliants over about one-seventh of the land area of southern Vietnam. A variety of chemicals, including the infamous Agent Orange, were aimed at destroying the country's inland hardwood forests and the mangroves that fringed the Mekong Delta, so as to deprive communist Viet Cong guerrillas of the cover that enabled them to move freely and launch ambushes against American forces. US actions in Vietnam gave rise to the concept of 'ecocide'—the deliberate destruction of the environment as a military strategy. It was disastrous for these tropical forests.

the landscape for decades. Efforts at regeneration or development do apparently scrape the landscape clean, concealing the scarring effects of war; yet if one looks carefully and in the right places, one can read the post-war history in the landscape. Problems often tend to be swept under the carpet but one may need only to scratch the surface to find the remains of the continuing environmental damage. For example, even decades after the American-led invasion of Kuwait, the Persian Gulf oil spill of 1991 is regarded as one of the worst-ever cases of sea pollution. Moreover, the oil has been found percolating through the porous soil and is threatening the country's meagre freshwater resources.

Of course, wars alone are not the events that leave their footprints on the ecosystem. Natural calamities—floods, hurricanes, earthquakes, volcanic eruptions, and tsunamis—are no less devastating. Thus, it is argued that armed conflicts fall into the same category as these natural disasters.

Yet, warfare is not the same as other disturbances that buffet natural ecosystems, and there are reasons to be concerned about the long-term ecological effects of war, particularly of the modern variety. For one thing, there is the sheer firepower of current weapons technology, especially its shock-and-awe deployment by modern superpowers:

> 'Our capacity to destroy now is so much greater than it's ever been before,' notes World Conservation Union chief scientist Jeffrey McNeely. 'The involvement of guerrilla groups in many recent wars draws that firepower toward the natural ecosystems—often already circumscribed and endangered ones—where those groups take cover. And the targeting of civilians can touch off mass migrations of refugees, which on an overcrowded planet can have a devastating environmental effect.'

4.4 The Islamic Position

Islamic economists often claim that centuries ago, the Holy Scripture had already voiced these concerns. This seems a bit far-fetched. Environmental issues, as we see them today, confronted mankind centuries later than the advent of Islam. However, it is notable that the scripture did contain candid prohibitions of acts relevant to the environmental issues of today. Islam is a universal religion imbued with rationality. Thus people, irrespective of their faith, may unconsciously think, at times, along Islamic lines. One finds, for instance, the approach of the Commission (above) largely in consonance with the objectives (*maqasid*) of the *Shari'ah*.

The main objective Islam seeks to achieve is the well-being of mankind, and it urges the protection of their faith, self-respect, intellect, progeny, and wealth. Such protection needs wisdom, mercy, and justice. Muslims, as others, must be strong enough both materially and morally to achieve these goals. Rapid economic growth with a priority on the fulfilment of basic needs and avoidance of wasteful expenditure is imperative to help move in that direction. Safeguarding of intellect implies that the community can resist polluting cultural influences from alien sources and must hold on to what remains relevant in their heritage. It has to pay special attention to educational attainments, research, and critical valuations. The insistence of *Shari'ah* on the preservation of the progeny is intended to ensure intergenerational equity in the distribution of wealth and prosperity, conservation of resources, and sustenance of the environment, all links of one chain.

The moderation and balance in worldly pursuits that the verses of the *Qur'an* repeatedly emphasize are intended to support this basic Islamic concept of sustainable development. We shall have occasion to present such verses later on in this discussion. The achievement of the *maqasid* calls for dynamic interaction between socio-economic processes and environmental priorities. If Muslim countries could produce even a replica of such interaction and its benefits, they could possibly send a positive message to humanity that such a framework is imperative to produce an equitable economy, a better society, and a world that is worth living in, for present and future generations. The Islamic ingredients of sustainability are more telling than the Commission Report contains.

4.4.1 Policy Concerns

Our discussion of some of the variants of sustainability shows that the concept of development seems to have thrown up more haze than light. Development by nature is a value-loaded term and implies the achievement of stated economic and social objectives at a perceived pace. Sustainability, on the other hand, refers to the ability of development to continue indefinitely. Thus seen, sustainable development is a constrained process of dynamic change for social betterment. The common element underpinning the indicated approaches to such development is the conservation of resources and maintenance, if not reduction, of pollution levels.

The debate on sustainable development thus centres on concerns about the deteriorating environmental quality; deterioration that continues unabated in the Muslim world as well, even as Islam preaches moderation in consumption, exhorts us to avoid wasteful use of natural resources, reminds people of the delicate balance of forces in the universe, and instructs them to maintain that balance. The following verses of the *Qur'an* bear ample testimony towards working for sustainable development, as discussed earlier.[4]

> *6:3—It is He Who created the heavens and the earth in true (proportions).*
> *30:41—Mischief has appeared on land and sea because of (the need) that hands of men have earned.*
> *39:5—He created the heaven and the earth in true (proportions).*
> *54:49—Verily, all things have We created in proportion and measure.*
> *67:3—He Who created the seven heavens one above another; No want of proportion will thou see in the Creation of Allah Most Gracious. So turn thy vision again. Seest thou any flaw?*
> *67:4—Again turn thy vision a second time (thy) vision will come back to thee dull and is comfited, in state worn out.*

Here, a clarification may not be out of place. It is sometimes argued that the Islamic concern for the environment follows automatically from its leading maxim: 'Receive no injury, inflict no injury'. Some support the contention that there are hundreds of verses in the *Qur'an* instructing us to avoid injury to environmental resources (Hassan and Cajee 2002). This seems implausible, if not irrelevant. The maxim was presumably intended more to regulate relations between men, rather than between them and the environment.[5]

The environmentalists continue to express dismay about the decadent health of the planet. Among other concerns mentioned earlier, they lament the diminishing biodiversity. It is estimated that there are as many as 30 million distinct species of living organisms in the world, constituting a vast source of genetic information that could be useful for the development of medicines, natural pesticides, and resistant varieties of plants and animals. Human activities have taken a heavy toll on

[4]The translation of the verses given here in support of the stated Islamic position is reproduced from *The Holy Qur'an Text, Translation and Commentary* by Abdullah Yusuf Ali (New Revised Edition, 1409 A.H./1989 A.C.), Amana Corp., USA.

[5]It must however, be emphasized that the *Qur'anic* instructions are not confined to Muslims alone; they are addressed to the whole of humanity.

biodiversity, increasing the rate of species extinction. For example, estuarine water pollution reduces fish regeneration. The conservation of habitats and species preservation poses another resource problem. Examples can be multiplied ad infinitum.

The issue of property rights in environmental goods remains unsettled even on the theoretical plane: do individuals have, or should they have, these rights, or should the societal entity? If the two have to share these rights, when shall they do so, and how? Again, in many cases, it is not possible to pinpoint the sources of the pollution affecting air, water, or land. Even if the sources were satisfactorily identified, the contribution of each source to total pollution is difficult to determine. Furthermore, there are the problems of estimating the cost of the damage caused, identifying the victims, and ascertaining the damage each has suffered for granting compensation. And the criteria or the form the compensation should take is a question that has yet to be answered. Decisions on issues of this sort usually involve a measure of arbitrariness and thus tend to raise grave concerns about justice.

Added to these problems are the difficulties of putting policies into operation. Here, adequacy of laws and efficiency in executing them are the issues. Islamic economists sometimes raise what they consider a more fundamental issue, i.e. why is the world characterized by glaring inequalities in the distribution of wealth and incomes within and among nations, that are the prime sources of increasing pollution. Today, in 2016, the projected GDP of the 'global man' is over US$10,000 per annum, double what it was in 2000. Is it not good enough for a comfortable living for people on this globe if the distribution were more equitable?[6] But the story has been very different: widening income and opportunity disparities have put immense pressure on world resources, giving rise to wars, armed conflicts, corruption, and mounting environmental degradation.[7]

[6]The per capita GDP projection for the year 2016 is based on the data reported in the World Development Reports—World GDP: US$75.21 trillion and population: 7.4 billion. Interestingly, the global economy as of date is 1.58 times greater in Purchasing Power Parity (PPP) terms. The PPP version of income shows the poor-rich gap being notably small.

[7]Strictly speaking, environmental economics is distinguished from ecology on two grounds. First, ecology is systemic; it focuses on preserving natural capital that cannot in any way be substituted by man-made resources. Second, and it follows from the first, sustainability is puritan or strong as opposed to diluted or weak.

4.4.2 *Finance and the Environment*

Using financial incentives and restrictions to address environmental problems is a recent phenomenon. Environmental or green finance, its common name, is fast emerging both as an academic discipline and policy tool. It may be defined as being concerned with supporting investment in ecological systems and environmental preservation. It is being used to induce business activities to arrest damage and falls within the domain of corporate social responsibility.

Environmental finance involves funding conservation initiatives to mitigate the impact of businesses on the environment without sacrificing profitability. It is leading the shift from isolated environmental regulations to their internationalization in market-driven economies. It envisages corporate strategies that financial service providers, as well as their clients, must understand in order to improve their environmental performance. New markets are being created to help companies manage environmental risks, including weather derivatives, catastrophe bonds, and emissions trading permits.

London is emerging as the global centre of green finance. The government has established a task force to oversee the implementation of climate-related finance recommendations. A set of green standards is being developed to provide clarity to financial institutions for certification of green financial products. Lenders are receiving support for developing low-risk green mortgage products. Financial allocations are being made for new investments to support clean technologies. Due to these measures, London tops the global index of green financial centres.[8] Further, the Australian carbon market has been lauded for 'full compliance' among the largest carbon emitters, and the company Climatic Energy seeks to use green bonds to retrofit buildings in California.[9]

[8]A *financial centre* is a location that is home to a cluster of significant financial service providers such as banks,investment managers, or stock markets. Such a centre can be of domestic, regional, or global importance. AGlobal Financial Centers Index (GFCI) ranks them based on assessments of competitiveness from an online questionnaire, together with over 100 indices from organizations such as the World Bank and the Organisation for Economic Co-operation and Development (OECD). The index covers 29,000 financial centres from across the world and was first issued in 2007.

[9]Sovereign issuers gave a major boost to the green bond market in February 2018 with inaugural issues from Belgium (€4.5 billion) and Indonesia (US$1.25 billion) and a repeat issue from Poland (€1.0 billion) (Environmental Finance, Green bond round-up, 14 March 2018. https://www.environmental-finance.com, accessed 15 March 2018).

In evaluating the projects, effort is first made to avoid adverse environmental impacts. If satisfactory results cannot be obtained, alternatives are examined. Even then, if avoidance is not possible, ways to minimize the damage are considered. An example is the shortening of the distance between western and southern Europe for fast and smooth movement of men and materials by the opening of a rail tunnel through the Swiss Alps. This will certainly help energy conservation. Tunnelling is indeed becoming popular to serve that end. Other ways include reducing inventory and capitalizing on just-in-time delivery, and reducing emissions in product fabrication processes. The US$46 billion China-Pakistan Economic Corridor (CPEC), once operational, will also cut energy consumption in a big way.

Public sector agencies across countries have environmental funding centres. The Environmental Protection Agency (EPA) in the US, and similar institutions in Indonesia, Mongolia, India, and in many European countries, promote environmental finance. Many colleges and universities in the developed world have a designated environmental finance centre. Some colleges and universities offer environmental finance degrees that focus on economic and policy analysis, financial analytics, science and technology, and markets and regulation. However, developing nations, especially Muslim countries, lag far behind in environmental teaching and research. Environmental economics and environmental finance are sister disciplines, although with different shades; they supplement each other. We discuss in the following section some theoretical bases and policy prescriptions relevant to both.

4.5 The Sources of the Problems

The natural resources that Allah (swt) has provided on/in planet Earth include all sorts of minerals, animals, vegetation, and liquids for humans to utilize to create things for their comfort and enjoyment. Some of these resources, like vegetation, fish, and animals, are renewable and can be maintained at the existing level of availability if the rates of their renewal and consumption remain the same. But most of these resources, especially forest cover, are being used up faster than they can be replaced. They are on the verge of extinction. Even more serious a problem confronts mankind in the swift depletion of non-renewable mineral resources such as iron ore, tin, coal, oil, and natural gas. The situation calls for a well-conceived conservation policy, which falls within the ambit of environmental policy.

Case Study 4.2: Commercial Vehicles Over 20 Years Old to Be Deregistered from 2020

India has decided to cap the life of commercial vehicles to 20 years. This means commercial vehicles such as taxis,trucks, and buses that were registered before 2000 cannot run on Indian roads from 2020 onward, putting at least 700,000 commercial vehicles off the roads on that date. Since this will be a regulatory mechanism, the government will give some tax relief to those who scrap their old vehicles and buy a new one as a replacement. Seven million electric vehicles are planned to be on Indian roads by the same date. The greening programme will involve huge financial commitments, both for the public and private sectors of the economy (*Times of India*, 2019).

However, the core environmental issues arise in the case of resources that are not priced in the market, such as air and water; these are used for free in the production processes. But this use is unique. It does not form part of the output to deplete its volume. Instead, human beings use them as receptacles of their personal discharges and wastes, flowing out of their consumption and production activities. Examples are domestic garbage, hospital waste, construction dust, and emissions from automobiles, power plants, chemical factories, and nuclear plants. They all find their way into the air and/or water—running or still, on the surface or underground. Allah gave these receptacles great absorption and self-cleansing power for what we throw into them. However, we were naïve in believing that this power of the natural agents was unlimited. We learnt rather late that we could use them as waste receptacles only at the cost of reducing their availability for the healthy living of all life forms on planet Earth. What reduces this availability is summed up in one word—pollution. To maintain a balance between the two—health and pollution—is the core issue of environmental economics.

Pollution alters the characteristics of natural agents so as to inflict or threaten damage to the health, safety, and welfare of all life forms or property. This harm can assume various forms and temporal distances. An important question contextual to pollution is: who has property rights in natural agents—the common people or public authorities? The

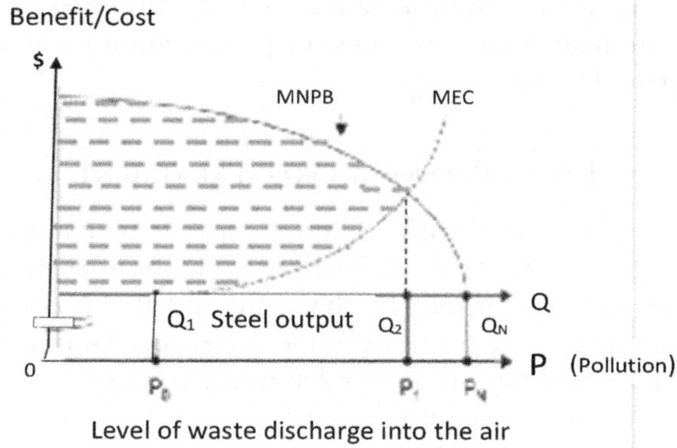

Fig. 4.3 Property rights in fresh air

answer affects the rights to pollute. If one takes the position that air and water are free gifts of nature, governmental action can be taken against the polluters only after the absorption capacity of, say, air has been exhausted. Figure 4.3 illustrates the case of a steel producer. Here, as output increases along the Q-axis, so does pollution. The curve MNPB measures the marginal net private benefit in the figure.

4.5.1 *Pollution and Property Rights*

The term 'pollution' refers to the contamination of air, water, or soil caused by the discharge of substances harmful to living beings and their possessions. Such substances may consist of particles of gases, liquids, or solids. Energy—heat, noise, or radiation—could also be a source form of business profits as output increases. MEC, in contrast, measures the marginal external cost the corresponding pollution imposes on the people around. Assume that society has property rights in the fresh air; a right that the government must protect by penalizing the polluter, here the steel factory. A property right question is: should the entire equilibrium output Q_2 be penalized? Arguably, production up to Q_1 output is within the pollution absorption capacity of air; the red curve turns up from that point. Thus, Q_1 is part of output and should carry no penalty. Only Q_1Q_2 as part of output must bear penalty, if any. However, the argument, although valid, poses insurmountable difficulties in application.

Hence, the rule of the thumb is that as public authorities have property rights in the fresh air, businesses must be penalized on the entire Q_2 output, to mitigate the pollution.

4.6 Proposals for Treatment

The choice of ways to deal with pollution depends on its type and intensity, technologies available, costs involved, and the societal response to programs authorities sponsor. To these are added the commitments a country makes or askance from over time and space. Thus, it is a multidimensional choice with serious imponderables involved.

4.6.1 Pollution Types

Pollution problems are classified as local, regional, and international. Domestic waste disposal, noise control, and waterways maintenance are examples of local problems. Regional typically involve cross-border pollution. Local bush fires, volcanic eruptions, floods, tornadoes, tsunamis, and toxic leakages often cause serious cross-border environmental problems, at times needing dispute resolution requiring international arbitration and cooperative settlements. The river water-sharing treaty between India and Pakistan brokered by the World Bank in the 1960s is one leading example.

International environmental issues affect the whole globe and are equally worrisome for different countries. These include ozone depletion, global warming, rising sea levels, and vanishing forest cover. These problems usually feed upon each other. They are the roots of most environmental problems the world faces today. The United Nations and its various agencies have remained constantly anxious about the degrading health of the environment. Not much has emerged from periodic world deliberations until recently because a just distribution of responsibilities and cost sharing has been obstructed by the gross inequality in economic and political power sitting around the negotiation table. The more powerful parties did not have the same perception of costs and benefits involved as the weaker parties.

Over the past fifty years or so, it has been a story of vague national commitments and non-performance. Many sensible reports have only gathered dust after gaining momentary applause. Eventually, the world reached the point of 'now or never'. Then, the 2015 United Nations

Climate Change Conference was held in Paris and attracted the largest number of countries ever; past attitudinal obstinacies gave way to rationality, rigidities to relaxation. They negotiated the Paris Agreement, which contains realistic evaluations, pragmatic policy content, and a collective resolve to act. It was hoped this would stand the test of time, until Donald Trump, the new US President, announced that the United States would cease participation in the Agreement. However, other countries have continued launching 'save the environment' programmes unperturbed. For example, special plans are in the pipeline to tackle pollution in major Indian cities, especially through developing non-conventional and sustainable clean energy sources as a national commitment, not a compulsion. China is making concerted efforts to control pollution—a US$2.6 billion plan has been announced to fight pollution in Beijing alone (*Hindustan Times*, 16 January 2017, pp. 7, 14).[10]

4.6.2 Remedial Plans

Conflicts between private gain and public interest in free market economies have made the remedial measures contextual to environment regrettably a doctrinal concern. There is a preference, if not insistence, that the measures to arrest the damage to the environment must be market-driven; public authorities should not impose them from outside the system, as has generally been the case. Professor Coase presented a market-based solution suggesting the creation of private property rights in environmental goods and encouraging their trading in the open market. We explain and illustrate his theory below and show its limitations. We also support the current governmental action and global cooperation to resolve the situation.[11]

[10]A recent article in the influential international journal *The Lancet* reports that the rising pollution-related deaths touched 2.5 million in 2015, air and water pollution being the main culprits. The article also says that such mortalities cost the world US$4.6 trillion in the reference year. India and China alone accounted for about 44% of pollution-caused deaths.

[11]India is implementing a well-conceived, graded plan to arrest the spread of pollution (see *Times of India*, 17 January 2017, p. 2).

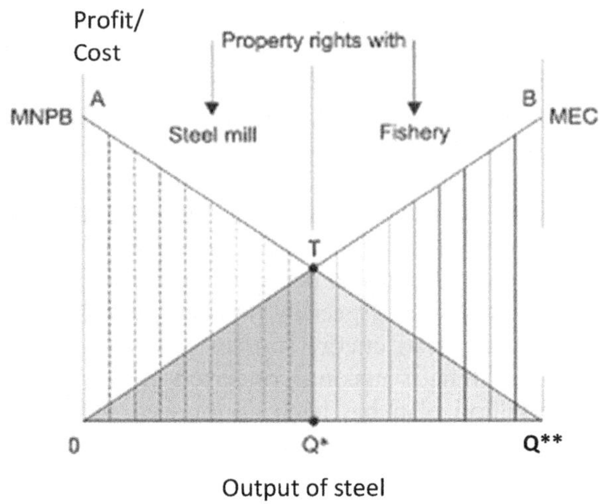

Fig. 4.4 Property rights in fresh air bargain between the steel mill and the fishery

4.6.2.1 The Coase Theorem Explained

We will take the case of a steel mill operating close to a fishery. The gas emissions from the mill cause acid rain to fall on the fishery's waters, reducing the fishery's output and profits. Coase suggests the government may grant property rights in fresh air to either the mill or the fishery (or even to third party). Evidently, no one can store fresh air or reduce its availability to others. Suppose the property rights in fresh air are granted to the steel mill. The fishery must compensate the mill for the loss of profit it would suffer in curtailing output to reduce pollution. The amount of money the two will settle on in the negotiation will be determined at such levels

money to the mill of steel output where the loss of revenue to the mill will equal the money the fishery offers to the mill. Interestingly, the outcome of this bargain will be the same even if property rights were granted to the fishery. Figure 4.4 explains the operation: property rights in fresh air are with the steel mill, and the fishery must make an offer to curtail output.

Prior to negotiations, the mill was producing Q** of steel with AOQ** profit. The fishery was losing TQ*Q** of profit because of the pollution the mill generated. The fishery would gain so long as it pays the mill to reduce its output to less than or equal to what it gains in terms of increased profit. On the other hand, the mill will accept from the fishery any amount, so long as it is more than or at least equal to the shrinkage in its profit from output reduction. The settlement would be at point T, where the marginal gain of the mill would equal the marginal payment of the fishery. The equilibrium output would be Q*. Pollution would be reduced proportionately. The net profit of the mill plus the compensation received from the fishery would be AOQ*T and the fishery's profit minus compensation paid would be Q*TBQ**. We can easily reverse the argument if the property rights in the fresh air are with the fishery to arrive at the same result. For more details, see Hasan (2015).

The Coase theorem widens the concept of the resources that firms use in production, including those that they use, for example, air and water, as receptors of waste. Firms do not pay for these, but they impose various types of costs on society. Thus, the theorem widens the concept of scarcity and extends the meaning of efficiency. The passing of resources not paid for through the market internalizes the harmful externalities. It raises the cost of production for individual firms, which they attempt to pass on to the consumers by charging higher prices. The changes in concepts mentioned are incorporated into the fundamental theorem of welfare economics derived from the Pareto optimality conditions, i.e. MRTYX = MRSXY.[12]

Figure 4.5 depicts these implications in operation. To keep matters simple, we assume that the marginal external cost (MEC) the firm imposes on society remains unchanged for all levels of output. Before internalization of the externalities, the firm produces Q_0 output, selling it at a price of P_0, given by the intersection of the demand and supply curves at point T_0. When we add MEC to the private cost curve S_P, we get the marginal social cost curve S_B. The equilibrium point shifts to T_S, price rises to P_S and output contracts to Q_S. The shaded area shows the efficiency gain, enhancing social welfare.

The Weaknesses of the Coase Theorem

The main points of criticism are as follows:

- *Narrow outlook*: One serious pollution problem which the Coase theorem fails to take note of is global dimming—the increasing

[12]For more details, see Hasan (2015, Chapter 12, pp. 318–321).

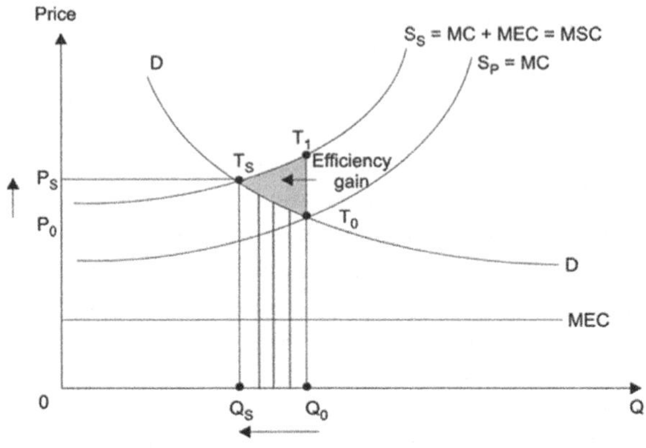

Fig. 4.5 The impact of internalizing externalities

day-by-day reduction in the volume of sunshine reaching the crest of the earth. This phenomenon is caused by clouds absorbing the chemical droplets and gas particles hanging in the air due to fuel-burning in airplanes, as well as the devastating carpet-bombing places like Afghanistan, Syria, Iraq, and Yemen have witnessed in recent years. To illustrate, the pollution coming from industrially advanced Europe and America smog-blankets the Indian Ocean south of Africa, causing the rising dimming effect and not allowing enough cloud formation over North Sahara, leading to crop failures, famines, and diseases. The desert is on the march, impoverishing people even in places rich with unexplored natural resources. The Coase theorem is powerless to deal with such grave issues.

- *Non-availability of information*: Even at the domestic level, one seldom comes across examples of successful bargains in environmental goods, except in a few cases of nuclear power stations indulging in negotiations with people in their neighbourhoods. Pollution-mitigating market solutions are severely handicapped by the non-availability of the needed information and the moral hazards of the parties involved. In our mill-fishery illustration above, the fishery would rarely know the reduction in the mill's profit the curtailing of steel output would cause, nor could it be sure of the value of the damage acid rain, and rain alone might be inflicting on the fishery. The negotiation takes place in an information vacuum.

- *Transaction costs*: Pollution is pervasive. We would require numerous negotiations all the time. In case the polluters are not willing to bargain or the bargains break down for any reason, legal action may have to be taken, involving more costs in terms of time and money. Court cases may be slow, identification of polluters may be difficult, and the estimation of the damage caused for compensation may not be easy. For example, in our illustration, the mill alone may not be the cause of the pollution harming the fishery. Moving automobiles could also be the culprits, partially at least, but they could easily evade the negotiations between the steel mill and the fishery. Costs involved in handling such situations may keep people away from bargaining.
- *Free riding*: Victims suffering the effects of pollution, even after seeing it publicised in the media, may not automatically file a public interest litigation suit; they usually wait for someone else to spend the money and time and then reap the benefits automatically free of cost, if their side wins. In business as in politics, free riding may bring in enormous gains.
- *Identification problems*: Even when transaction costs are not prohibitive and negotiations promise net gain to the parties, a bargain may not take place for two reasons. First, many pollutants hang in the air for a long time and the damage they cause is only unveiled after decades, even centuries. Toxic chemicals, radioactive waste, global dimming, and greenhouse gases fall, for example, within this category. Victims may even have died before they could have known the cause, let alone think of taking action. Second, the victims may not know which pollutant has affected them and what or how much damage it has caused. Regulatory authorities may fail to identify all the polluters or fail to estimate the monetary value of the injuries they inflict.
- *Market imperfections*: Finally, the Coase theorem rests on the assumption of perfect competition in both the product and factor markets. Under perfect competition, we have $MNPB = P - MC$ in conventional economics. However, in the environmental context, we find $P = MC + MEC$ where MEC is, as we know, the marginal external cost. Thus, $MC + MEC$ constitutes social cost (SC). This puts $MNPB = P - SC$ in a state of equilibrium. It is this formulation of MNPB that constitutes profit for the mill in our illustration. But recall that for a firm operating under perfect competition $MR - MC$

gives the marginal profit curve. The equation MNPB = P − MC is valid under perfect competition only because AR equals MR. The condition does not hold under imperfect competition: MR = MC is less than AR. Here, P − AC is the measure of per unit profit, not P − MC. This detracts much from the basis of the Coase theorem. Theoretically, the bargain is feasible under imperfect competition (Pearce et al. 1990), but would be very complicated, beset with many imponderables. Its practical utility is very restricted.

Pollution Taxes

Pollution charges are imposed per unit of output. The charge is usually equal to the estimated social cost. The producer attempts to shift the tax to the buyer by adding it to the price. The point here is that the tax imposed per unit of output equals the cost pollution is estimated to impose on society. Normally, taxes reduce equilibrium output, curtailing pollution, and raising the price of the commodity. Figure 4.6 illustrates the mechanism. Social cost is assumed constant to keep matters simple. The pre-tax equilibrium of demand and supply based on private cost only is at point P0 for the P0Q0 combination. The imposition of per unit tax T_1P_0 equal to SC internalizes externalities. The equilibrium price remains unchanged, the demand being perfectly elastic; the entire tax is paid by the seller. Tax sharing between the buyer and the seller would depend on the relative elasticity of demand and supply.

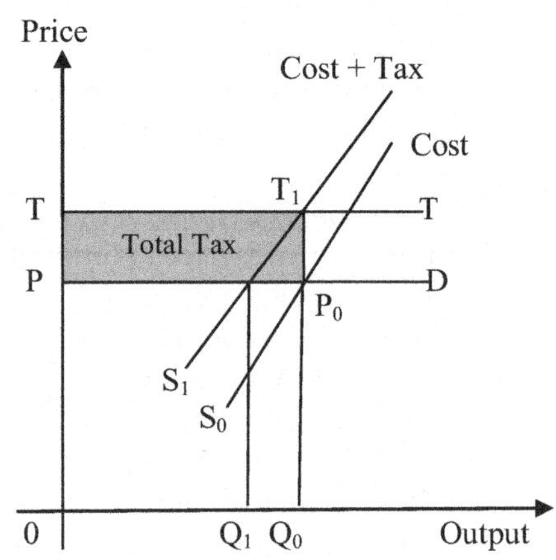

Fig. 4.6 Taxing polluters to cover damage cost keeps price unchanged, and reduces output

There are two limiting cases here. If the demand is perfectly elastic as in Fig. 4.6, the seller will have to bear the entire tax. In contrast, if the supply is perfectly inelastic, the seller will be able to shift the entire tax to the buyer.

Taxes may be applied indirectly as well, e.g. on consumer goods that can damage the environment, such as excise taxes on gasoline or cigarettes. Environment-related provisions can be inserted in other taxes also. There are, however, a few problems with taxation.

First, the charges do not exempt the pollution absorbed by the natural agent—air or water. To reiterate, this issue stands resolved arbitrarily assuming that public authorities have property rights in the environmental goods. A more serious difficulty is that once a firm under the threat of taxation has already curtailed the output to optimal pollution level, why should such output be subjected to tax? The firm would be burdened with two types of losses. It loses profit on the output voluntarily foregone but even so, the product must carry the tax. Finally, it is difficult to estimate the damage and its monetary value.

Of late, several innovative ideas have caught the attention of authorities. One gaining ground is the prescription of subsidy grants to encourage the polluters to use more efficient technologies for damage control. The use of scrubbers or filters in coal-burning mills or the technique of passing smoke through water before it is released into the atmosphere are some examples attracting subsidies to meet full or partial cost of equipment.[13]

Figure 4.7 illustrates how subsidies work. Here, the vertical axis measures both the marginal abatement cost (MAC) and the marginal external or social cost (MEC). Likewise, both pollution and output are measured on the horizontal axis. The initial equilibrium is at T_1, the firm incurring some cost to control pollution. The regulators feel that emissions must meet the standard at point T_0. They offer the firm a subsidy sufficient to meet that end without reduction in output Q_1.

[13]A global example in this context is of carbon credits. The Kyoto Protocol commits certain developed countries to reduce their emissions of GHGs (greenhouse gases), including carbon dioxide, through an industrial entity switching over, for example, to renewable sources of energy or by using energy-efficient technology. The reduction entitles the entity to credit in the form of a Certified Emission Reduction (CER) certificate. The CERs are saleable in the market.

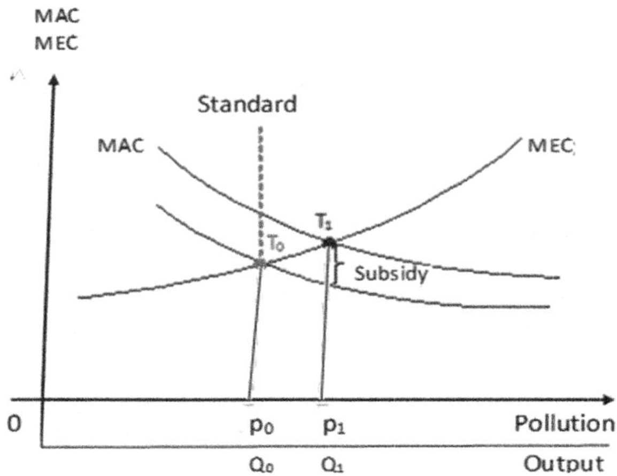

Fig. 4.7 How subsidies work as pollution abates

Emissions Trading

Emissions trading is a market-based approach for curbing pollution that operates via tradable pollution permits. The scheme combines the profit motive with incentives for environmental care. Developed between 1970 and 1980, emissions trading was applied in the US in 1990 to combat acid rain. More recently, it has assumed significance in fighting greenhouse gas effects linked to climate change. In this measure, a cap on emissions is set and permits are created to cover the cap. The companies or other entities included in the scheme need to hold one permit for every specified unit of pollution, e.g. to emit a certain number of tons of CO_2. The price placed on a permit multiplied by the number of permits purchased is the cost the buyer has to bear. Each firm is free to buy permits for as much pollution as meets its production needs. The market for permits thus imparts flexibility to the distribution of permissions among firms and over space. There are two main considerations that influence decisions of business firms in the matter.

These are (i) the criterion public authorities adopt to ensure an efficient distribution of emission rights between firms and (ii) how this criterion is put into operation. Figure 4.8 helps us fix and explain the criterion for an efficient distribution of rights between two hypothetical

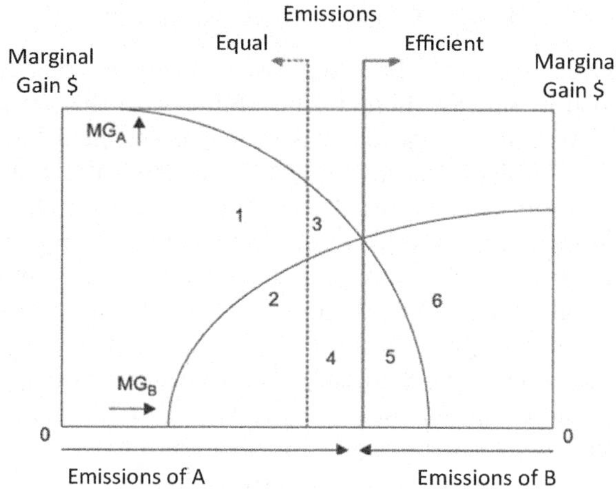

Fig. 4.8 Efficiency in emissions trading

firms—A and B. The firms are in an efficient permit distribution state regarding their rights, depending on the value each puts on them. Emissions of firm A increase from left to right and of firm B from right to left. Likewise, the curves MG_A and MG_B provide the marginal value A and B, respectively, place on emissions. The lower segment of MG_B (i.e. before crossing MG_A) indicates that B places a smaller profit value on emissions than A. After the intersection point, the position is reversed. If the dotted perpendicular line shows an equal distribution of rights between A and B, then with reference to that line the total gain for firm A would be 1 + 2 and for B, the area 4 + 5 + 6. An efficient allocation of rights takes place when the marginal gains of the two firms equalize at the point of the curves intersection. Now, firm A gains 1 + 2+3 + 4 and firm B 5 + 6. It is easy to see that total gain is maximized under an efficient distribution regimen. Emissions trading was a central element of the Kyoto Protocol in the form of the Clean Development Mechanism (CDM) and has been the cornerstone policy of the European Union, who's Emissions Trading System (ETS) is the largest in the world. However, its progress has slowed down in the United States due to inter-state differences on implementation.

4.7 Concluding Remarks

In the foregoing pages, we have discussed the nature of environmental problems and how serious these are becoming with the passage of time. The measures that are, or can be, taken to handle them have also been discussed. The problems centre on climate change, the result of global warming. The world has eventually become concerned about this. The 2016 Paris Agreement was a big deal. The world saw the United States, the biggest polluter, sign such an agreement for the first time. However, the country pulled out even before the ink dried on its signature. President Trump thought 'the idea of climate change was of "Chinese creation"'. However, it is gratifying that resistance from the countries with the two largest populations in the world—China and India—has ceased and that the other signatories stay committed.

Finally, we have shown that modern warfare is a major contributor to international pollution. As per estimates recently released by the Council on Foreign Relations (CFR), in 2016 alone, the US administration rained at least 26,171 bombs on seven different countries, averaging three

per hour, every day, every month, over the entire year. The figures, says the report, are relatively conservative, meaning the number of bombs dropped in 2016 could have been much higher.[14] The report concludes that there was no legal validity for this action save through stretching the interpretation of an old authorization for the use of military force. Further, Trump admits that costly wars are responsible for the current economic troubles of the United States, not the trade with Beijing (Fig. 4.9).[15]

[14]Following the charge, at the recently held G20 finance ministers' conference in Germany, the United States refused to sign the Paris commitment, in addition to the anti-protection clause (*Times of India*, 19 March 2017, p. 14).

[15]Former French prime minister Dominique de Villepin, speaking at the Global Leadership Forum organised by Sri Sri Ravi Shankar's Art of Living Foundation, said, 'Military intervention is stupid, war on terrorism is stupid. The global leadership has been wrong in responding to Afghanistan, Iraq, Libya and Mali.' He said that the world needs new weapons of peace and not weapons of war (*Times of India*, 13 March 2016).

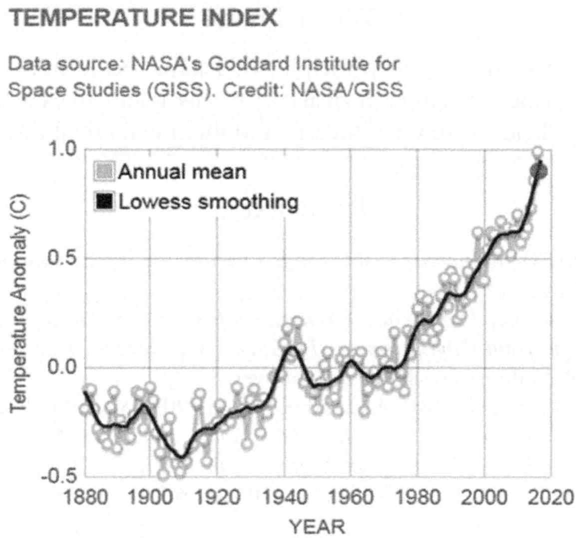

Fig. 4.9 Global warming over the years (*Source* Google maps)

Test Questions

Q.1 Why is there is a clash between growth and distributive justice? Explain. How can the issue be resolved?

Q.2 It is claimed that Islam provides solutions to various environmental problems the world faces today. Do you agree? Argue your case.

Q.3 Explain the Coase argument for market solutions of environmental issues. Do you agree with him? Elaborate on the weaknesses of the theory.

Q.4 How can finance be linked to help resolve environmental issues? Evaluate the current performance of financial institutions in this direction.

Q.5 Which one do you prefer—standard fixing or taxation to curb pollution? Explain. How far can subsidies help in the matter?

Q.6 Write critical notes on the following:

a. Pollution and property rights
b. Tradable pollution permits
c. War and pollution

What Next?

One of the most important principles of Islamic economics is to ensure distributive justice. Chapter 5 deals with this issue. It examines Islamic norms and policies to reduce poverty and income inequalities.

References

Hasan, Z. (2015). *Economics with Islamic Orientation*. Kuala Lumpur, Malaysia: Oxford University Press.

Hassan, A., & Cajee, Z. A. (2002). *Islam, Muslims, and Sustainable Development: The Message from Johannesburg, IMASE*. www.webstar.co.uk/~imase/Old/index.php?fcontent=article9&content=yes.

Pearce, D., Barbier, E., & Markandya, A. (1990). *Sustainable Development: Economics and Environment in the Third World*. Aldershot: Edward Edgar.

Repetto, R. (1986). *Skimming the Water: Rent Seeking and the Performance of Public Irrigation Systems*. Washington, DC: World Resources Institute.

CHAPTER 5

Distributive Justice: Foundation and Measures

Preview

The gap between the rich and the poor is on the rise within and across countries. This is an alarming situation. How to stem the rot is the question. Indeed, this has been *the* question at all times but the problem now seems getting out of hand. The present chapter attempts to address the income distribution issue—a vast and important terrain—from the Islamic perspective. It highlights that the Islamic system seeks ensuring distributional equity through reliance on two sets of controls. First, there is a set of ethical and regulatory measures that would prevent the emergence of undesirable inequalities. Essentially, these *preventive* measures are obligatory and voluntary expenditures from their income by the affluent Muslims to ameliorate the lot of the poor. The second is a set of *corrective* measures that the Islamic state would activate if unwelcome inequalities do in fact arise.

These corrective measures are quite varied and include most of the familiar monetary, fiscal, legal, and administrative tools of modern economic policy, subject to Islamic constraints. The foundation of Islam's scheme of treating distributional issues is its all-pervading philosophical notion of *amanah* that seeks to convert the material ambitions of man into the means for attaining spiritual heights. It invokes altruism. Studies now show that acts of generosity confer health benefits like lower blood pressure and improved longevity. In the light of the argument developed, the chapter evaluates the mainstream approach to the problem, discusses factor relations, and presents a macroeconomic model for

Z. Hasan, *Leading Issues in Islamic Economics and Finance*,
https://doi.org/10.1007/978-981-15-6515-1_5

attaining equity in the functional distribution of income. In the concluding section, we deal briefly with the trade-off between various goals of economic policy contextual to distribution.

Learning Outcomes
Students are expected to learn and explain the following:

- Distribution of income and wealth in a society has always been the most controversial area as sharing among stakeholders invokes conflict of interests.
- Islam supports an income floor but the position on income ceilings is unclear.
- In Islam, policies to ensure distributive justice include growth designed to address the fulfilment of peoples' basic needs, lifting people out of poverty, reducing inequities of incomes via *infaq*, moderation in consumption, and avoiding frivolous expenditure.
- Islam does not trust free markets to ensure distributive justice; it finds the marginal productivity theory vague, circular in reasoning, and inoperable.
- State intervention in economic activity is essential at both ends—production and distribution—in meeting the social goals of economic activities.

5.1 Introduction

No area in economics has perhaps been more complex and challenging than the distribution of income and wealth within and among nations, ever since David Ricardo's *On the Principles of Political Economy and Taxation* (1817) opened the subject for formal discussion.[1] Adam Smith's *Wealth of Nations* (1776) was mostly concerned with production, an area where one could talk of capital accumulation, technological improvements, division of labour, and money cooperating in harmonious

[1] Earlier economists were mainly occupied with concerns about production. In contrast, Ricardo thought that production offered few challenges. Factors had to cooperate; the main problem of political economy was to determine the laws that regulated the distribution of wealth in a society. Thus, he opened an entirely new vista for economic inquiry but landed himself in fierce controversy.

productive combinations under market discipline. However, his book though discussed factor rewards; distribution was not his primary area of concern or contribution. Staying in the realm of production was one of the main factors that made Smith the great master that he was.

Ricardo chanced to read Smith's influential work about 23 years after its publication. He thought that it was not production, but issues relating to output distribution among the cooperating factors that are more complex, controversial, and closer to social interest. In fact, it was the debate on distribution that had played the key role in dividing the world into different economic systems, mainly capitalism and socialism.

Adam Smith, the builder of capitalism, and Karl Marx, the socialist, both agreed on some core ideas; they differed on the method of production of goods and services essentially because it determined the patterns of the value product distribution among the participating factors. Marx went as far as suggesting revolution by the proletariat against the *bourgeoisie* for an equitable distribution. Adam Smith preferred societal stability to chaotic upheavals. He believed in peace which in his view competitive free markets could ensure. We have shown in Chapter 1 that Islam prefers following the middle course; it modifies capitalist institutions to achieve socialistic ends. We shall see that the Islamic scheme of income and wealth distribution differs from that of capitalism and socialism both in thrust and content.

5.1.1 Policy Goals

One basic question concerning distributive justice is what ought to be the policy goal: equal division of unequal incomes, division according to contribution, or division based on needs.[2] As people are not alike either in need or efficiency, equal distribution of incomes in society would evidently be as unjust as are the current distributive inequalities. It would be a valid question to ask how much inequality would then be allowable. Can we set a floor for, and put a ceiling on, incomes, as is sometimes suggested, to make differences look reasonable? Let us examine the Islamic position on the issue.

The *Qur'an* reminds us time and again that people may *differ* from each other as to the *quantum* of *rizq*, i.e. sustenance granted to them

[2] For an illuminating discussion on the three alternative approaches, see Boulding (1963, Chapter 4).

but all creatures of the Almighty have an *equal right* to sustenance from His inexhaustible treasures of Earth (and the Heavens). The obvious inference is that one prime consideration governing money income distribution in Islam is the fulfilment of the minimum needs of all members of the community. These needs may include, according to Ibn Hazm (and he is not alone in this opinion), legitimate food requirements, clothing for summer and winter, and reasonable accommodation. It may be added that any concept of minimum needs has to be flexible. Their coverage and standards in a particular society would have to be spelled out from time to time in accordance with the level of economic development reached.

Thus, in Islam the fulfilment of the basic needs' imperative makes the approval of an income floor very clear. However, the position regarding income ceilings is not so explicit. One can perhaps build up a case on some presumptive sort of argument. A distinction between 'restriction' and 'intervention' as corrective measures might be enlightening. Intervention seeks to alter or modify the consequences if necessary after the event has taken place. Restriction, on the other hand, does not allow the event to happen. It impinges upon the individuals' freedom, so dear in Islam, even in matters of religion (*Qur'an*, 2:256, 10:99, etc.). A ceiling on incomes is not only restrictive of human freedom but also attempts to block the operation of the verse: '... Allah does provide whom He wills without measure' (24:38). Thus, putting ceilings on incomes appears repugnant to Islam unless one can conclusively show it to be otherwise. Floors improve income distribution. Ceilings are prone to encourage black markets and corruption.

We have ruled out perfect equality of incomes and income ceilings; can we have distribution according to needs as a policy goal? There can be special circumstances for using this norm, but under normal circumstances, the rule would perpetuate injustice. For once the basic needs of all have been provided for, wants of people would be indeterminate. Furthermore, the criterion would reward efficiency and inefficiency or activity, and lethargy at equal rates. Overall, payment according to contribution is seen as a just norm. Islam also approves it. The *Qur'an* (45:22) declares: 'Allah created the heavens and the Earth for just ends and in order that each soul may find the recompense of what it has earned'. Also, it instructs to give 'to each his due' (2:279. 11:85, 28:183, 45:22), that is, as per contribution to output.

We shall see that the Islamic approach to distributional equity is qualitatively different from the customary mainstream approach of making income distributions less skewed and more flat-topped. Islam aims at preventing the emergence of the malady rather than treating it after it appears. The elements of its grand scheme flow from its all-pervading concept of *amanah*. We shall explain this foundational concept soon; for now, let us briefly examine the current state of inequalities in income distribution across countries, including Muslim nations.

This we do in Sect. 5.2. In Sect. 5.3, we evaluate how mainstream economic theory deals with the distribution issue, especially with regard to the return to capital. Section 5.4 explains the Islamic concept of *amanah* and its ramifications for income distribution. In Sect. 5.5, we lay bare the Islamic structure to implement its distributive programme in an economy. In Sect. 5.6, we deal with some redistributive measures of Islam and in Sect. 5.7 we examine the role of the state with reference to distributive issues. Finally, Sect. 5.8 contains a few concluding remarks.

5.2 Extent and Nature of Inequities

It was stated in the World Development Report 2016 that over the past 25 years ending 2015 per capita incomes unceasingly rose in both developed and developing countries, making a noticeable impact on poverty across the world. The number of people living in extreme deprivation was slashed from nearly 40% of humanity to fewer than 10%, an unprecedented feat indeed. However, the just-published World Inequality Report (2018) regrettably paints a dismal picture of income distribution across countries.

The ground realities mock the egalitarian claims of Islamic theory on distributive justice. Figure 5.1 is revealing on the point. Note that in the Islamic Middle East income inequalities are the highest, while in secular Europe, the lowest.

Section B of the figure testifies that it is not merely a point of time position but also a long-run trend (1990–2016), although with a difference.[3] Overall, inequalities show a rising trend across the globe, being the sharpest in India and slowest in Sub-Saharan Africa. Deliberating on

[3]The figures are from the recently published World Inequality Report 2018. They have been edited and juxtaposed here to facilitate comparisons.

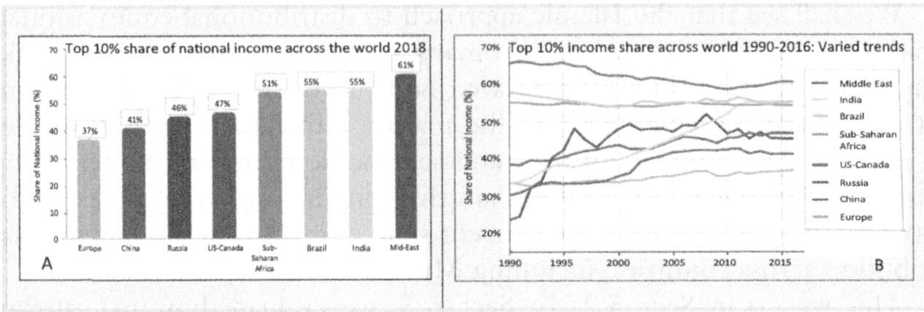

Fig. 5.1 Current state of income inequalities over space and time across the globe

such issues is urgent than hair-splitting debates on philosophical issues of methodology as some insist. On that, let us rest with the saying that 'anything goes ... let a thousand flowers bloom'. On this more in Chapter 13.

Historical Context
People were long aware of poverty and distributional inequities as characteristics of market economies, but by the close of the nineteenth century, the position turned worrisome and invited scathing attacks on moral and ethical grounds, especially from men of letters. The exploitation of the workers on the one hand, and of the consumers on the other, had become rampant. In addition to the Marxian attack on the system, Henry George in the United States was clamouring for nationalization of land because the landlords, he thought, reaped where they never sowed.

Capitalism needed a defence. That defence came from J. B. Clark, an American economist (1847–1938). He identified—as in Islam—contribution to output as the criteria for just factor payments.

5.3 Marginal Productivity and Distribution

J. B. Clark argues in his *The Distribution of Wealth* that payment to a factor according to its ***marginal productivity*** would be a just compensation for its contribution to output. We will explain and evaluate this theory to assess its worth.

The marginal productivity theory of distribution assumes the existence of perfect competition in both product and factor markets, wherein

Table 5.1 Physical and revenue product of labour with fixed land (amount in US$)

Units of labour employed per week L	*Price of wheat per tonne ($)* P	*Physical product of labour (Q)*			*Revenue product of labour MPR_L per unit of MP_L*		
		Total product (tonnes of wheat) TP_L *(TQ)*	*Average product* AP_L *TQ/L*	*Marginal product* MP_L ΔTQ	*Total revenue product* TRP_L P × *TQ*	*Average revenue product* APR_L P *(TQ/L)*	*Marginal revenue product* MRP_L P (MP_L)
0	240	0	0	0	0	0	0
1	240	10	10	10	2400	2400	2400
2	240	22	11	12	5280	2640	2880
3	240	39	13	17	9360	3120	4080
4	240	64	16	25	15,360	3840	6000
5	240	100	20	36	24,000	4800	8640
6	240	120	20	20	28,800	4800	4800
7	240	133	19	13	31,920	4560	3120
8	240	144	18	11	34,560	4320	2640
9	240	144	16	0	34,560	3840	0
10	240	140	14	−4	−960	3360	−35,520

a firm can readily adjust to changes in demand or supply conditions. An implication of the assumption is that constant returns to scale operate in both the markets. The firm is a price taker in either case: it can sell as much or as little of its product as it may choose without affecting the price of the commodity. Likewise, it can hire any amount of a factor service at the going price, for example, as much of labour hours as it may want at the current wage rate.

To keep matters simple, we assume that there are only two factors—labour and land—that the firms employ for producing wheat in the agricultural sector of an economy. A firm will hire labour until the dollar value of its marginal revenue product equals the current wage rate *W* a week. Its marginal revenue product MRP_L would equal the price of wheat per tonne in the market times the tonnes of wheat (*Q*) its marginal unit produces. Assuming that the farmland area the firm hires remains fixed, the law of diminishing returns must apply to labour's contribution to the wheat output *Q* that the firm produces.

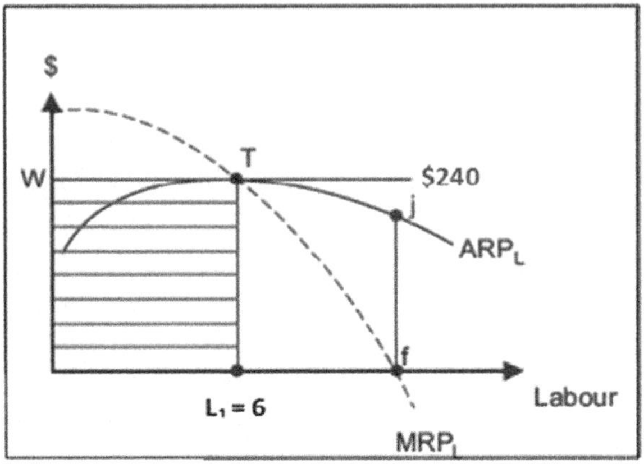

Fig. 5.2 Labour market equilibrium of firm

Given the data commensurate with the stated conditions in Table 5.1, we see that the average and marginal revenue values for labour vary with units employed. These values are then used to draw the curves shown in Fig. 5.2.

Here, we find that with wage level WW_1 per week, the firm would employ L_1 units of labour to maximize its profit. If the firm employs more labour than L_1 units at the going wage rate WW_1, the ARP_L would fall, reducing the profit of the firm. On the other hand, if it employs less than L_1 labour units, it would lose the opportunity to earn more. The lined rectangle shows the total wage bill at $WT \times TL_1$.[4] Check the relevant values from the table.

We can construct, in the same way, the revenue product curves for any of the factor combinations. Figure 5.3 puts the cases of labour and land side by side. In panel A, the curve MRP_L is the marginal revenue product of labour obtained as the multiplication of its physical product MP_L and the dollar price of wheat at US$12 a tonne in the market. The price will be constant for the firm as competition in the wheat market is by assumption perfect. In panel A of the figure, MRP_L is the marginal revenue product curve of labour and W is the wage rate prevailing in the labour market. The firm will continue hiring workers until W equals

[4]Expenditure on labour is a cost element. Its reduction increases profit and vice versa, other things remaining the same.

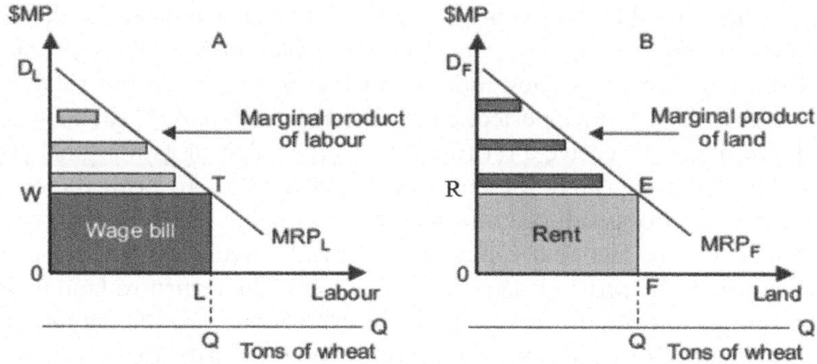

Fig. 5.3 Marginal productivity theory is circular in reasoning

MRP_L at point *T*. Thus, it would employ *L* units of labour to produce *Q* tonnes of wheat at the minimum labour cost per tonne. The total wage bill ($W \times L = \$1440$) is shown by the lined rectangle OWTL. The remaining portion of total dollar product, i.e. the area of the triangle D_LWT, is rent for the farmland, the fixed factor.

We employ the same procedure in panel B as in A to determine the payment of rent. MRP_F is the marginal revenue product of the farmland, now the number of labour units employed remaining constant. Here, the white rectangle OREF gives the total amount of rent paid to landowners. The remaining area under the curve MRP_F, i.e. D_FRE, represents wages. Thus, it follows that in terms of the marginal productivity theory; wages can be depicted as rent and rent as wages. *The theory suffers from circular reasoning.*

Even so, the theory is considered elegant in showing that the sum of factor rewards equals the total revenue product of the firm. In Fig. 5.3, the sum of marginal revenue product of labour multiplied by its units employed (*L*) plus the marginal revenue product of land multiplied by its units (*F*) used in production, equals the dollar value of its total output *Q*. In physical terms, we have:

$$Q = \frac{dQ}{dL} + \frac{dQ}{dF} \tag{5.1}$$

This means that given the market price (*P*) of the product, we get:

$$PQ = P.\,MP_L\,L + P.\,MP_F\,.F$$

$$TR = MRPL\,.L + MRP_F F \tag{5.2}$$

Note that in the long-run equilibrium, PQ also represents the total production cost to the firm, including normal profit. The sum of the shaded areas showing wages and rent in Fig. 5.3 exhausts the total revenue product PQ. Under perfect competition in the market, each factor of production would receive a return equal to the value of its marginal product. The return measures the contribution of a factor to both the output of the commodity produced and to society (why?). The return to capital is justified by the fact that capital too, is productive. Competitive profits being normal, the return is fair and just as well. The return to land is, similarly, not an unearned income, but a return for the productivity of land. The same applies to the return to labour. Thus, the marginal productivity theory demonstrates, it is claimed, that capitalism is a just economic system. Theories of exploitation and unearned income are erroneous; they fail to understand the working of freely competitive markets. We must have a look at the logical and ethical aspects of these claims.

5.3.1 Evaluation of the Theory

Marginal productivity theory has attracted a lot of criticism from its very inception, and much of this criticism remains valid. The earlier critics were unsure whether the theory applied to labour, capital, or land because of the circular nature of its reasoning indicated above. Special problems arose when attempts were made to determine profits and interest in terms of marginal productivity. We shall discuss these problems later on in the chapter. For now, we will examine the difficulties in its *generic* application. The main points raised are as follows:

1. The final output of a firm, industry, or economy is the result of a combinative effort of land, labour, capital, and enterprise; it is impossible to separate their individual contributions to the aggregate. In the simple process of driving nails into wooden panels in the furniture industry, how can one separate the productivity of labour from the productivity of capital, the hammer? Again, if one hammer alone were added to the stock, what shall be its marginal productivity until a worker is also added to use it? When a farmer and his worker sow and reap a field of tomatoes, how do we determine the quantity each has grown? Or how would one determine the marginal productivity of a teacher in a university department?
2. The demonstration that under perfect competition, a factor is paid equal to the value of its contribution to output does not by itself

prove that marginal product *determines* that payment, because it is not the contribution of a factor to output, but its scarcity relative to other factors that determines both its marginal product and return.

3. Even if we concede for a moment that perfect markets equate payment to contribution, we cannot draw an ethical conclusion from an ethically neutral analysis. For what a person *actually* earns need not be equal to what he *should* earn. His actual earning may, for example, equal his contribution to output, but it may not equal the minimum he should receive to meet his minimal needs. Also, even when there are visible differences in the productivity of workers, they are paid the same amount at each time point of the pay scale.
4. We cannot derive long-run conclusions from a short-run analysis, if the conditions imposed do not remain intact over time. The argument based on Eqs. 5.1 and 5.2 above assumes the division of factors into fixed and variable, a short-run imperative. The distinction would not hold good in the long run. What can be shown as valid in one case may not be valid for another. This removes the very base of the marginal productivity theory.

5.3.2 *Interest, Profit, and Marginal Productivity*

The weaknesses noted above of marginal productivity theory apart, cannot explain either the attribution of interest or of profit to capital providers alone. Islamic economists need not deny that capital—real or nominal—can be productive in a factor combination to deserve a return. A more fundamental question is whether interest payments match their productivity? It is well known that the level of interest rates in modern economies is determined by the policy decisions of the central bank of a country and placements on the bonds market. What has the productivity of capital to do with either? Also, how can one measure the productivity of a purely financial transaction departing continually from real sector economic activities (Hasan 2015, p. 304).

Profit is by definition a residual that can also be negative. It will be hard to justify its accrual to a factor of production with reference to its productivity. Furthermore, *ex post* profits are history. There is no conclusive empirical evidence of their equitable linkage to the functional productivity of the receivers. It is *ex ante* profits that are the guiding stars for future action. But to link expected profits to productivity of capital investment is all the more difficult, if not impossible.

5.3.3 *Profit, Islam, and Equity*

The claim of mainstream economics of achieving distributive justice via the marginal productivity theory subsists, as explained, on the assumptions of perfect competition and constant returns to scale. The claim also disregards the existence of uncertainty contextual to the outcome of human activity. These assumptions face many difficulties. Perfect competition tends to hang itself by a noose of its own making (Hasan 1992). Certainty in the economic sphere cannot survive while uncertainty infests other walks of life. Most of the merits claimed for free market economies flow from this heuristic construct. Presumably, it was because of this that Galbraith declared recently that most economic theories are falsehoods.

We have indicated that Islam approves freedom of enterprise. It puts no ceiling on incomes, including profits, and is not averse to competitive market arbitration. If so, how can Islam achieve what market capitalism cannot? We need not seek far for the answer. Islam regulates human conduct in all spheres of life through a well laid out, coordinated, code of conduct. Islam's is not a theoretical construct. It remained in bold operation for centuries after its advent, reaching its zenith during the thirteenth century, bringing peace and prosperity to vast tracts of the globe it influenced. In contrast, the perfect competition model and its perceived merits have never been demonstrated. Indeed, they could not be, for uncertainty being a part of the divine scheme for shaping human destiny could never be made external to human destiny. So on the criteria of applicability, the Islamic model of human conduct has a much better record than the model of perfect competition. Let us now explain how the Islamic moral code, *if put into operation* once again, could promote equity that the perfect competition model, inherently inoperable, can never.

5.4 Amanah (Trusteeship)—The Bedrock of Equity

The concept of *amanah* or trusteeship makes the Islamic approach to the issue of equity in distribution qualitatively different from that in mainstream economics. It lends an edge to the preventive prescriptions of Islam, rather than treating the malady after its emergence. Let us explain the notion briefly.

Amanah is fundamental to Islam, although other religions also subscribe to the notion. In Islam, it seeks to convert the mundane *ends* of man into the *means* for attaining spiritual heights—his eventual goal. The *Qur'an* instructs believers:

> But seek with the wealth which Allah has bestowed on thee the home of the hereafter and forget not thy portion of this world. (*Qur'an*, 20:77)

The notion of *amanah* inspires the entire socio-economic programme of Islam and encompasses human activities of individuals and the community in their relationship with Allah and His creation. The last part of the verse above clarifies that Islam is not a religion of renunciation; it exhorts believers to enjoy all good things in life. Commonly, *amanah* refers to something tangible that a person entrusts to another in good faith for safekeeping, to be returned to the giver when requested. The keeper can also be allowed to use the item(s) subject to the obligations the trust imposes.

According to the Islamic faith, all things in heaven and earth belong to Allah (*Qur'an*, 31:26, 42:2). He handed over the earth with all its treasures to man, and gave him the intellect and the ability to understand, subdue, tame, and harness resources of nature for his use. He made His bounties flow to him in vast measure (*Qur'an*, 31:20). For man alone agreed to run affairs on the planet as His trust-keeper (*Qur'an*, 33:72). The concept implies that the Creator of the trust expects man—the trustee—to manage it according to a prescribed code, spelling out obligations in return for rights to benefit from the treasures of the trust.

The most important part of the code consists of one's obligations towards fellow human beings (indeed the whole of creation). Obligations of one person become the rights of others. Islamic *Shari'ah* (law) is essentially an aggregation of these rights and obligations; it is a code of conduct prescribed for man by the Almighty for running the show according to His Will. Islam is nothing but total submission to this Will. But human beings were granted the discretion to either meet their obligations or ignore them; if they meet them, they will be rewarded, but if they do not, they will be punished by the same code. *Shari'ah* spells out a system of such rewards and punishments.

According to the Divine proclamation: 'He is Who created for you all that is in the Earth' (2:29). Things in the universe are the common property of Adam's progeny; there is no reason given in the origin of resources as to why anything must belong to a particular person or a group. Even the wealth produced is deemed, in light of the above verse, as accruing in the first instance to the entire human society. It is to avoid disputes and motivate individuals to produce for a better living that the acquisition of resources through permitted means is allowed and recognized. As long as one is in legal and safe possession of something, no one else can deprive the owner of its rightful use and enjoyment (*Qur'an*,

4:29). If property still remains a cause of dispute among people, it is not because the right to own property is in principle disputed, but because people have different perceptions about the *actual* and the *ideal* distribution of property and the gap between the two.

Since wealth in origin is common to all, it must not remain concentrated in a few hands (*Qur'an*, 59:7). The possessor himself should not hold what he perceives as being in excess of his legitimate requirements. He must voluntarily surrender the surplus in favour of the less fortunate members of the community, for to that extent, their rights are clearly invoked in his wealth. The surplus belongs to them; he holds it as their trustee. This is why he is not permitted to indulge in frivolous expenditure or idly hoard wealth. The *Shari'ah* confronts the holder with a serious trial (*Qur'an*, 26:151, 70:18, 64:15). The *Qur'an* reminds people time and again of those powerful men who, blinded by their riches, defied the divine instructions only to meet their total destruction.

The view of property rights in a pure *amanah* model is much different from their notion in capitalism. Islam grants explicit *rights* to the weak and the deprived in the wealth of the rich. *Shari'ah* insists that one must honour these rights; the excess wealth owned by a person beyond his own requirements belongs to others. What the 'legitimate' needs of a person are and how much excess wealth he has are matters for his own moral perceptions; their external determination is difficult.

Amanah is an attitude of mind, a sort of self-discipline. It promotes in man the feeling that he is at the centre of an oceanic circle that consists of a family, a neighbourhood, a group, a community, a nation and humanity at large. We cannot be self-contained as we are not pure individualists. We are bound together in a social web; we cannot be completely independent of, or non-accountable to, one another (*Qur'an*, 4:37–38). *Amanah* is not an isolated idea. It is the soul of religion. Without this base, many Islamic principles would not fit into a pattern as neatly as they do, without conflict or contradiction. On this foundation is raised the superstructure of Islamic economics.

5.5 The Structure for Distributive Justice

The extent of departure of *actual* income distribution in a society from its view of the *ideal,* however defined, would broadly depend on the place of wealth in its value system, factor return norms in production, and the redistributive institutions it has in place. Let us briefly examine the Islamic position on each of the three.

5.5.1 *Attitude Towards Wealth*

The notion of *amanah* tends to bring about harmony between individual interests and societal concerns in the pursuit of wealth because without this, the freedom of enterprise that Islam encourages can rarely work as an instrument for improving the lot of the masses. *Amanah* refines one's attitude towards material pursuits. Islam advises that one should be moderate in one's pursuit of wealth, that the means to acquire it must be honest, and that if there is a conflict between wealth and virtue, one ought to be content with what can rightfully be obtained, even if it was little (*Qur'an*, 5:103).

In contrast, pure rationalistic concepts are atomic; they are based on a split view of human personality, pitching the individual against society. Islam projects a different vision of man. It focuses on his self-developmental qualities wherein his social, economic, political, and spiritual activities are all fused for achieving a balance between his inward ambitions and external obligations. The pursuit of self-interest does not operate as the sole driving force of human conduct. Amassing wealth no longer remains the primary objective of life. The temptation to become rich through deceit, corruption, or exploitation is dampened.

The notion of *amanah* leads to the Islamic norm of *al-adl* or justice and fair play. It has wide implications for dividing the fruits of their combined effort among the factors of production. We have already noted that Islam regards as just the payment made to each factor according to its contribution to total output (*Qur'an*, 2:279, 11:85, 28:183, and 45: 22). We shall discuss in the following section how Islam addresses the issue through profit-sharing schemes.

5.5.2 *Redistributive Measures*

Because surplus wealth with the rich is viewed as held in *amanah* for others, Islam introduces into the picture a number of redistributive measures. The main ones are: spending in the way of Allah (*infaq* and *sadaqaat*)' *zakah*, being the obligatory floor meant for spending on specified objects. In addition, *awqaf* or public trusts are welfare institutions the members of the community are encouraged to establish. In *awqaf* there is voluntary transfer of wealth from private ownership to social custody to promote community welfare. *Awqaf* provided inns, wells, and rest houses along the highways. The schools, colleges, hospitals, mosques, burial grounds, and even production units Awqaf established have dotted Muslim lands during the era of Islamic glory until the fourteenth century, and beyond. The revival of *awqaf* is of late on the rise in Muslim communities. This voluntary sector is expanding, in addition to the public and private sectors, in the Muslim world.

5.5.3 Factor Relations

Amanah may impact the relations of factors in production, including the sharing of the fruits of their combinational productivity, thus improving distributive justice. The Islamic norm for factor reward is: 'To each his due' (*Qur'an*, 2:279, 11:85, 28:183, 45:22) as per contribution to output. Relations among production factors must minimize the chance of rewards being vitiated by indeterminacy (*gharar*), speculation, or interest.[5]

The outcome of modern businesses is characterized by uncertainty, meaning unmeasurable risks in transactions. Also, the market forces are not well equipped to dispense justice in apportioning output value among the contributing factors. Even if the market could somehow bring factor prices in reasonable relationship with their marginal revenue product, such prices, as we have seen, may not be just on contribution criteria. To reiterate, the marginal revenue product of a factor is a function not of what it contributes to output, but of its scarcity relative to other factors.

Under these circumstances, predetermined factor prices must, in principle, be distasteful to Islam. However, they have a customary sanction that faith may honour. But custom does not compel society to accept the consequences of such prices as non-adjustable if distributive justice so demands. This presumption finds support, for example, in the fact that Islam explicitly prohibits, nay condemns, the giving and taking of interest in any form. One of the reasons is that the outcome of the productive effort being uncertain, a predetermined payment could involve *gharar*. In the case of rent for agricultural land too, the dominant view seems to be that Islam would *prefer* sharecropping, i.e. giving to the landowner a negotiated proportion of the yield or its cash equivalent.

Thus, capital owners can participate in the production process only for profit. However, one has yet to come across a convincing reason in Islamic economics for excluding the workers from sharing the positive consequences of modern business operations.

[5]Islam aims at designing all exchange relations on the principle of mutual benefit, cooperation, and fair play (*Qur'an*, 4:29–30). Thus, as a general rule, it does not permit transactions wherein avoidable chance could cause any of the parties a loss to benefit the other. This, in essence, is the celebrated concept of *gharar*.

5.5.4 *Wages and Islam*

It is true that Islam allows the employment of workers on a fixed piece or time wage rate independent of business results. But to insist that the fixity of the rate is the essence of the Islamic position would be misleading. Interestingly, such insistence would put wages and interest at par. The simultaneous permission for one and the condemnation of the other would be hard to defend.[6] However, such a defence is not required. For what Islam really requires is to give labour a just wage for its contribution.[7] Customarily, fixed wages could reasonably conform to a fair play norm in days when production was carried out on a small scale to fill standing orders. However, in modern mass production, the payment of the market-determined wage in the final settlement of workers' compensation, before the result of the productive work is known, can rarely be shown to meet the ends of justice.

It may sometimes be argued in defence of pre-fixed wages that the workers, as human beings, have in any case to be sustained. But this compulsion can be overcome by ensuring workers payment sufficient to maintain them over the span of a production cycle. The notion of such minimum payment (wages) can be deduced from the Islamic insistence noted earlier that the basic needs of all nationals—working or out of work—have to be met. Minimum wages have to be an essential component of production cost, like depreciation allowance for maintaining capital assets intact.

Subject to a minimum wage constraint, Islam requires labour participation in profits of a firm. For then alone can one hope that the earnings from work have a reasonable chance of being just and *gharar*-free. The presumption is further strengthened by the Islamic principle of ***mudharabah*** or participatory finance, so commonly used in early Muslim societies (Rodinson 1974, p. 51) and that is currently being revived in Islamic finance. In fact, ***mudharabah*** is not only a form of business organization, it is a principle of deeper and wider import (see Qutb, n.d., Chapter 4).

[6] The question of such similarity between the two was raised by Dr. W. A. Kabuli and has been referred to in Zarqa. He provides reasons why Islam allows fixed wages to workers, but not fixed returns to capital as interest. Interestingly, a similar difficulty with interest is raised vis-à-vis fixed cash rent for land.

[7] According to a prophetic tradition, of the three persons who are certain to attract the wrath of Allah on the Day of Judgement, one would be who takes full measure of work from the workman but does not pay him his due wages (Bukhari, Volume 3, p. 112).

Thus, we have to treat the entire value product resulting from the *combinational productivity* of participating factors—labour and capital—minus the minimum wage bill, as profit to be shared by them. The workers may receive the market wage rate during the production period, but their post-production earnings must be adjusted in the light of the final business results.

5.5.5 *The Distribution Model*

The macro-level model of income distribution that emerges from the above discussion can be neatly fixed and explained using a few simple notations. Let $\mathring{Y}$ be the net value added in a yearly production cycle, P be the profit, $\hat{W}$ the minimum wage, and W the market wage. Thus, we have:

$$\mathring{Y} = P + \hat{W} \tag{5.3}$$

Suppose P is shared between capital, including land, and labour in k and $(1 - k)$ ratios, respectively. The above equation would become:

$$\mathring{Y} = kP + (1 - k)\,P + \hat{W} \tag{5.4}$$

However, the market wage W that the workers would have already received must be more than the minimum $\hat{W}$. The excess payment must be deducted from their profit share $(1 - k)$ P. With this adjustment, Eq. 5.4 becomes:

$$\mathring{Y} = kP + [(1 - k)\,P + (W - \hat{W})] + W \tag{5.5}$$

Let us suppose $[(1 - k)$ $P + (W - \hat{W})] = B$, which we may term as bonus payable to workers. We then obtain:

$$\mathring{Y} = kP + B + W \tag{5.6}$$

where kP accrues to the capitalists, and $(B + W)$ to workers, B being the bonus payable to them.

Here, $\hat{W}$ and k are policy variables and can be a matter for either juridical determination, or a committee may be constituted (with stakeholders' representation on it) for periodic review of k. Industry-wide differences in k may be created. Alternatively, a domain may be specified for it, leaving the parties free to negotiate on its specific value. Differences in k values may be used to make resource allocation match social priorities. $\hat{W}$, too, may differ for various worker groupings, as is the current practice. Workers can share B volume among themselves accordingly via their unions. Anyway, such specifics are matters for internal settlement in an organization. *Sharing of profit is a matter of principle, not of details.* The following quotation from Jan Pen (1971, p. 17) places the significance of our adjustment to wages in sharp focus:

> The high incomes of top executives can in fact be understood only if we bear in mind that they are in position in which they can fix their own remuneration. Supply and demand do not take us far here, nor does the concept of productive 'contribution'... Here 'power' is a more enlightening term than the force of the market. And perhaps something of the same kind applies to wages fixed by collective bargaining.

The adjustment seeks to neutralize the consequences of this 'power' but rather erases the temptation to take advantages of 'position' It intends to bring the ultimate earnings of the top executives into some reasonable relation with those lower down the scale, thus reducing vertical income inequalities. Above all, it establishes the necessary equation between remuneration and the paying capacity of industry.

The model contained in the above equations is equity oriented. It is based on Islamic rationality, and can be put into operation. It attempts to mitigate *gharar* and minimizes the chance of exploitation of one factor at the expense of others. Thus, it must help *ceteris paribus* in reducing the emergence of sharp inequalities in the distribution of incomes.

Those inclined to support the case of profit sharing by labour as a system fear that wages-plus-profit would raise the remuneration of new entrants to the labour market. Thus, profit sharing may not improve the distribution of incomes. In capital-short and labour-surplus Muslim countries, sharing could lead to unemployment.

Such apprehension stems from the static theoretical construct wherein the marginal physical product can be shown to be reflected in the wage rate under some heroic assumption. In real-world situations, there is no single unequivocal price system in which the various contributions and corresponding rewards would match, and marginal revenue product could unambiguously determine either the contribution or the reward of the participating factors. Also, distributive justice must not be compromised for increasing employment. For as a logical extension of that argument, one could presumably ask: why then are wages not allowed to fall, or rather, be pushed below even the marginal value product of labour in the capital-scarce and labour-abundant Muslim countries to raise employment?

About three decades back, the industrial scene in most of the developing economies—Muslim and non-Muslim—was characterized with disquieting labour unrest: both trade unions and industrialists becoming increasingly wary and distrustful of each other. The centre of dispute was mainly the industrial wage structure. It has been calculated, for example, that in the overpopulated and capital-short Indian economy, disputes on this count have accounted for the highest percentage of man-days lost. The perception gained currency that if capital employed labour, the reverse was no less true: labour too, employed capital, for machines would stand idle if workers did not cooperate. The underlying spirit of the Islamic model pictured above is to help build bridges of goodwill and mutual trust on a shared basis.

Even mainstream economics is now favourably inclined towards the idea and profit-sharing schemes are becoming increasingly pervasive in various forms in most capitalistic economies. These schemes now form an important part of an attempt to build responsibility and participation, and therefore loyalty, into the workers' relationship with the firm. A recent study finds that profit sharing and wage levels have an effort-augmenting effect and, therefore, increase productivity (Kosekla and König 2010, Abstract).

Critics have also argued that profits are primarily returns for risk-taking and labour is not involved in that act. As such, workers cannot be rightful claimants for a share in profits. However, factors are paid for because they are productive. Risk-taking is barren, by itself, incapable of producing even a blade of grass. More importantly, risk invariably includes an immeasurable component called 'uncertainty' (Knight 1921). The two are inseparable. Thus, in its *totality*, risk can never be measured and profit cannot be shown in a one-on-one relationship with risk-taking (Hasan 2016).

The fact is that both capital and labour become productive only when combined to work in a firm. The combination is exposed to risk and uncertainly as a composite unit; in case of failure being total, if financiers lose their capital, the workers lose their jobs. Who would suffer more depends on their relative circumstances and contractual position. Even in a going concern, the workers face the risk of exploitation because of their restricted staying power and mobility. They are vulnerable to retrenchment, being exposed to health hazards, becoming unemployed, and so on. The risks borne by the two factors—capital and labour—may be different in nature and magnitude but neither is completely independent.

Box 5.1: Measuring income inequalities

There are several techniques for measuring income inequalities but most are based on the Lorenz curve. It is a graph wherein cumulative income proportions are plotted upward against the corresponding cumulative population proportions on the horizontal axis as in Fig. 5.4. If the income proportion and its corresponding population were identical, all incomes would be the same, as the line of equal distribution in the figure shows. The departure of the actual distribution curve from the equality line measures the prevailing inequality. Thus, in our illustration, incomes are more unevenly distributed in country B than in country A. A numerical measure of inequalities, the Gini coefficient, is mathematically derived from the Lorenz curve (see Hasan, Z., and Laher, H. 2009. *Macroeconomics*. Kuala Lumpur: Oxford University Press).

Fig. 5.4 Lorenz curve measures the inequalities in income distributions

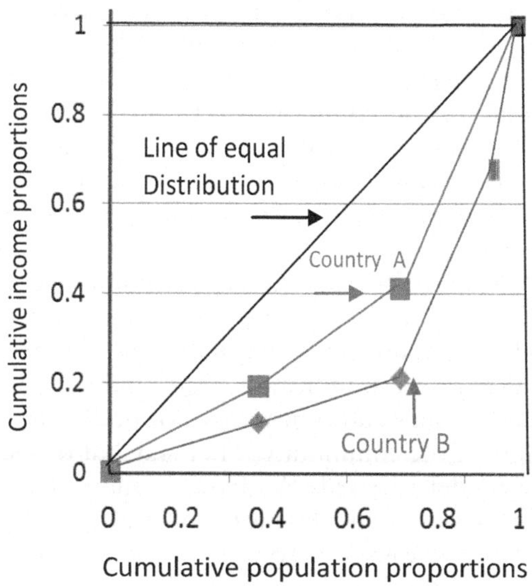

5.6 Some Redistributive Measures

The sharing model we have presented above is based on *functional* distribution of incomes. This must be distinguished from *personal* income distribution. In the latter type of distribution, the focus of attention is on an individual; we are interested in knowing how much a person earns from various sources. A teacher receives a salary from a university, but he may be earning profit from investments, receiving royalties from his publishers, and may also be drawing some money from consultancy. His receipts from these varied sources would constitute his personal income. Equitable wealth distribution can go a long way in narrowing down personal distribution inequalities. Personal income statistics are generated from income tax records or through special-purpose surveys to determine the living conditions of particular groups of people, say, industrial workers, fishermen, shop assistants, and so forth. Data on personal incomes is vital for studying the extent and nature of poverty in a country. Also, the structure of income distribution is a guide to public policy. Functional income distribution, on the other hand, is classification of personal data according to specific sources, e.g. wages, rent, interest, profits, etc. To illustrate, the salary in the above example will form part of the national wage bill, profit will be counted in return on capital, and any unspent amount will be added to national savings. Thus, personal incomes are broken down to give national macroeconomic aggregates like investment, wages, savings tax revenue, etc., for use in planning various national policies.

However, the functional distribution scheme of Islam as outlined in our model does not cover some important sections of the population—children, housewives, the infirm and the disabled, the unemployed, and victims of social upheavals, wars, and natural calamities so frequent now. These groups and others may not be able to contribute to the productive effort of the community. They stay out of the market processes on which the model is based. We have to support these non-contributing members because they belong to us. A carpenter does not deny his feet shoes because he earns his living by working with his hands. The marginal productivity theory is disarmed. These non-contributing members have to be provided for as a matter of survival and are linked to national output in some manner in all communities.

5.6.1 *Infaq, Sadaqah, and Zakah*

Under such circumstances, and because we have accepted contribution as the basis of reward, the income-levelling effect of the model is not likely to go far enough to meet the ends of social justice. Even through honest means, many acquire great riches, while many others remain needy and poor. But since the surplus with the former is viewed as *amanah*, Islam introduces into the picture its grand principle of *infaq*. God promises his *fadl* or bounties (*Qur'an*, 2:268) to people but warns that in no case will man attain righteousness unless he spends freely from his wealth in the way of Allah for the needy and the poor (3:86). *Fadl* and *infaq* are inseparable in a pure Islamic model. Broadly, *infaq* begins from one's own self at the centre of the circle and spreads out in a ripple effect to cover the family, the group, and the community, until it reaches humanity at large at the circumference (4:37–38).

For spending in the way of Allah, the *Qur'an* uses the words *infaq*, *sadaqah*, and *zakah* as synonyms. Its unceasing mention of them is not a mere exhortation for the pious act of generosity. Rather, their observance is a form of worship that ranks only third among the five fundamentals of Islam. So great is the significance of *infaq* in the Islamic system that *Qur'anic* wisdom could not leave it entirely to individuals' discretion. Allah instructed His messenger (saws) that he must extract *one sadaqah* from peoples' material possessions (*Qu'ran*, 9:13). The minimum exemption limit as well as the rates applicable in case of various assets were left to be decided by the Prophet (saw). As such, he laid down the system and his decisions on both counts continue to be sacred and unalterable. This obligatory part of the payment has since become known as *zakah* and is kept distinct from *infaq and sadaqah*, which constitute a voluntary category. It is not relevant for our purpose to elaborate on the details of the system as they are already well known. However, a few observations may not be out of place:

a. First, the coverage of *zakah* is wide. It covers cash in hand, in the bank, or on loan; gold, silver, or ornaments made of them; all property (save residential houses), even if under dispute or on auction or mortgaged; insurance and provident funds; agricultural produce; animal husbandry; goods for trade; the output of manufacturing units; minerals, including crude; buried treasures as and when found; goods on hire; and so on. Even this incomplete list is quite formidable. Thus, despite many exceptions and low rates, the amount collected would be fairly sizeable for the purposes it is meant for.

b. Second, *zakah* is a pure transfer operation that siphons off from the rich part of their wealth and current incomes and gives it to the poor and the needy. There is no material return whatsoever to the payee, either directly or indirectly. *Zakah* funds can only be used for explicitly specified purposes (*Qur'an*, 9:60, and elsewhere). They have a social security dimension.

5.7 The State and Income Distribution

Islam's is not a *laissez-faire* system leaving economic affairs entirely to private decisions. It is well aware of humans' love of material gains (*Qur'an*, 100:8), of their avarice and miserliness (41:128, 7:100). Despite warnings, people are tempted to acquire riches through oblique means, neglecting their *trusteeship* duties and obligations. The provisions discussed above that are built into the system may fail, as currently, to keep them on the right path. Thus, Islam makes it obligatory on the part of the state authority to intervene in the economic deliberations of the nation and keep the economy on the right track. Individual freedoms are not a sacred cow in Islam if wider social interests are threatened. An honest and efficient government, as Islam envisages, can do miraculous work in several areas. We discuss below several matters related to reduction in poverty and income inequalities.

Islam sanctifies the role of markets as they have long been hailed as valuable societal institutions. Mainstream economics holds market arbitration supreme in matters of production and the distribution of its fruits, for, it sees no clash between individual and social interests. Islam sanctifies the role of markets as they have long been hailed as valuable societal institutions. Mainstream economics holds market arbitration supreme in matters of production and the distribution of its fruits, for, it sees no clash between individual and social interests. However, this clash does arise frequently, free markets producing and distributing.

Interestingly, a recent empirical work (Piketty 2014) establishes that when the rate of return on capital runs higher than the rate of economic growth over the long run, there is a rise in the concentration of wealth in fewer hands. He sees in this proclivity the cause of social strife and economic instability in the developed world and advocates public regulation of economic activity, with measures including steeper progression in taxation. He warns that developing economies may soon fall victim to this malaise.

Implicit in Piketty are two points relevant to the present discussion. First, how hard should the developing economies push for growth with reference to poverty alleviation and inequality reduction? A trade-off has to be struck. We feel that if the choice is between distributive justice and pace of growth, a slower growth with better distribution would probably be preferable to faster growth with increased inequalities, from an Islamic viewpoint (Hasan 1988, p. 59). This may also allow the use of relatively labour-intensive local technologies and expand employment in densely populated Muslim countries.

It is not that distributional and other market failures are not recognized in mainstream economics. Economists do at times produce analyses of such failures and suggest possible methods of correction. They plead for public action to initiate taxes, subsidies, takeovers, bailouts, wages, and price controls. But others oppose intervention and regulations on the plea that the measures may lead to inefficiencies in the allocation of resources or in distribution of income. Thus, the choice often falls between imperfect market outcomes and imperfect results of government intervention. Islamic economists can use mainstream analyses on market failures and suggested remedial action with advantage on a selective basis.

Human resource development must be at the top of any Islamic developmental agenda. There are many aspects to the issue, but here we briefly discuss one component that is most emphasized and is fairly determinate—the fulfilment of the basic needs of people alluded to earlier.

5.7.1 Basic Needs Fulfilment

It is not that distributional and other market failures are not recognized in mainstream economics. Economists do at times produce analyses of such failures, and suggest possible methods of correction. They plead for public action to initiate taxes, subsidies, takeovers, bailouts, wages, and price controls. But others oppose intervention and regulations on the plea that the measures may lead to inefficiencies in the allocation of resources or in distribution of income. Thus, the choice often falls between imperfect market outcomes and imperfect results of government intervention. Islamic economists can use mainstream analyses on market failures and suggested remedial action with advantage on a selective basis.

Human resource development must be at the top of any Islamic developmental agenda. There are many aspects to the issue, but here we briefly discuss one component that is most emphasized and is fairly determinate—the fulfilment of the basic needs of people alluded to earlier.

The fulfilment of basic needs is the most important of the ingredients in human resource development, closely related to mitigating poverty and distributive inequalities in emerging economies. The United Nations Development Programme (UNDP) has published a Human Development Index (HDI) since 1989. The index is a composite criterion consisting of three indicators of human development, to measure its level for individual countries and to rank them. These indicators are:

1. Expectancy Life;
2. Education;
3. Standard of living.

The first two elements in the index take care of food, health care, and education, but leave out clothing and shelter of the minimal Islamic list. Presumably, the same are taken as covered in the third, the standard of living as measured by income. But the income level also affects the first two. Thus, the definition of the index has elements of a circuitous dependency. It does not focus on basic needs per se.

The basic needs package cannot be the same in content and quality for all countries and for different levels of economic development. Nor can dollar 1 or dollar 2 per capita income be realistic poverty lines for all economies. For Muslim countries, an objective demarcation line seems to be the *zakah nisab*. Rightful *zakah* claimants may be treated as the poor (P) in an economy. Average expenditure in the country on the identified basic needs (E_B) may constitute the poverty line. The average resource gap (G) for poverty eradication at any point of time would be $[E_B - Y_P]$, where Y_P is the average income of the poor (P). The total resource requirement for poverty eradication can be found by multiplying G by P. This may help to plan a phased programme to eradicate poverty.

The most complex issue concerning basic needs is of their standardization. In matters of food, for example, the calorie requirement of various professional groups—children, women, intellectuals, blue-collar workers, and sportspersons—is not the same. The requirements of individuals in the same group may differ. Even the UN Food and Agriculture Organization has put forth different views in various reports over the years. Shelter is no less difficult to define for the fulfilment of basic needs. How many rooms and of what size should a dwelling have? What materials and of what quality should be used? What facilities should each unit have, for example in matters of running water, lighting, and sewerage?

Medical care is very personal to the average person. Education at all levels has varying facilities needing improvement. In some countries, even primary schooling is not available to a large proportion of the population. In India, with its second-largest population in the world, over 30 million children do not go to school. Basic needs are hard to define and provide for, yet we cannot shun them. They have to be addressed and are being addressed.[8]

5.8 Concluding Observations

The two world wars during the first half of the preceding century, hardly 20 years apart, had geared the economies of most Western countries towards the invention and production of lethal arms, including atomic and chemical weapon arsenals. The industry proved lucrative. The United States emerged as the largest beneficiary from this expanding industry. However, the end of hostilities confronted this industry—presumably the most lucrative in the world—with prospects of decline. So, the cold war between capitalism and communism was begun, and arms production was boosted by the division of developing countries between the rivals. Meanwhile, among the emerging economies, petroleum brought unprecedented wealth to the Muslim countries; mountains of petro-dollars piled up.

The Muslim world is in the grip of a resource drain. To illustrate, in 2015 alone, Muslim countries purchased arms worth about US$10

[8]For a detailed discussion on basic needs measurement and poverty line specification with illustrations, see Hasan (1997).

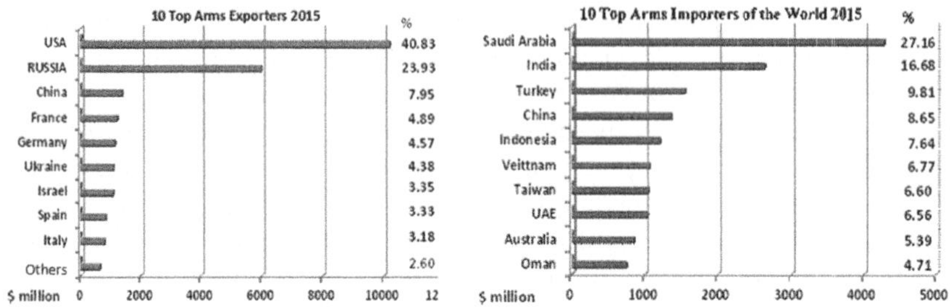

Fig. 5.5 Muslim countries dominate arms purchases, having almost 57% as imports

billion, which is 36% of total arms sales and 56% of total global purchases. The information in Fig. 5.5 is revealing.

Evidently, the petro-dollars the developed countries paid to Muslims by one hand have been taken back in a large measure by the other for supplying arms. And against whom are these arms being used, if not against the non-Muslim opponents.

The need of the hour is to forge the *umatic* unity that Islam so vehemently emphasizes, to stop this unproductive drain on resources, and also for poverty alleviation and inequalities reduction in the Muslim world. This calls for political will and sagacity to put welfare-related economic decisions into operation.

Test Questions

Q.1 'The concept of distributive justice implies that the current state of income distribution within and across nations is not satisfactory'. Elaborate on this statement, supporting it with facts and figures.

Q.2 'Free markets have failed to distribute incomes equitably'. Do you agree? Give reasons for your answer.

Q.3 Explain the marginal productivity theory of income distribution. Examine its efficacy as a defence of free markets.

Q.4 Explain the profit-sharing model in this chapter. Would you support it? Argue your case.

Q.5 'The Islamic scheme for ensuring distributive justice rests on the notion of *amanah*'. Discuss the redistributive measures favouring the poor that follow from this notion.

What Next?

There is an old saying that consumption is the beginning and end of all economic activity. After all, for whom does the bell toll? The next chapter deals with this interesting topic and also brings several production-related issues into the picture.

References

Boulding, K. E. (1963). *Principles of Economic Policy*. London: Staples Press.

Hasan, Z. (1988). Distributional Equity in Islam. In M. Iqbal (Ed.), *Distributive Justice and Need Fulfillment in an Islamic Economy* (Chapter 1, pp. 35–62). Leicester, UK: Islamic Foundation.

Hasan, Z. (1992). Profit Maximization: Secular Versus Islamic. In S. Tahir, A. Ghazali, & S. O. S. Agil (Eds.), *Readings in Microeconomics: An Islamic Perspective* (Chapter 20, pp. 239–255). Petaling Jaya, Malaysia: Longman.

Hasan, Z. (1997). Fulfillment of Basic Needs: Concept, Measurement and Muslim Countries' Performance. *IIUM Journal of Economic and Management, 5*(2), 1–38.

Hasan, Z. (2015). *Economics with Islamic Orientation*. Kuala Lumpur, Malaysia: Oxford University Press.

Hasan, Z. (2016). *Theory of Profit with Islamic Directions*. UK: Paragon.

Knight, F. H. (1921). *Risk, Uncertainty and Profit*. USA: Mifflin.

Kosekla, E., & König, J. (2010). *Can Profit Sharing Lower Flexible Outsourcing?* (HECER Discussion paper No. 310).

Pen. J. (1971). *Income Distribution: Facts, Theories, and Policies*. New York: Praeger.

Piketty, T. R. (2014). *Capital in the Twenty First Century*. Cambridge, MA: Belknap Press.

Qutb, S. (n.d.). *Islam, the Misunderstood Religion*. Beirut: Quran House.

Rodinson, M. (1974). *Islam and Capitalism*. London: Allen Lande.

World Inequality Report. (2018). Harvard University Press.

CHAPTER 6

Consumption: Micro Foundations and Macro Modelling

Preview
This chapter deals with the treatment of consumption in Islamic economics. However, consumption presupposes the existence of a system of producing goods and services that people need to consume to satisfy their wants. Thus, it opens with a brief look at how consumption and production are interrelated, before passing on to an examination of the issues specific to the former field.

Next, the chapter examines the microelements of consumption theory to clear several cobwebs concerning the nature of human needs, the conceptual efficacy of the utility analysis, and its maximization for consumer equilibrium. The treatment seeks to narrow the conceptual gaps on the subject between the mainstream and Islamic economic disciplines.

The chapter then reviews some selected macromodels resting on a division of income, based on *nisab*, between the upper (rich) and the lower (poor) classes of society to analyse the impact of Islamic institutions on economic growth via the saving-investment mechanism. It is demonstrated that, contrary to the claims based on the models surveyed, a helpful impact of the Islamic scheme on economic growth and distribution is uncertain, to put it mildly.

Finally, attention is drawn to some recent developments in the treatment of consumption in economics, and also to the interest in the subject currently shown by other social sciences. This interdisciplinary

Z. Hasan, *Leading Issues in Islamic Economics and Finance*,
https://doi.org/10.1007/978-981-15-6515-1_6

approach seeks to detach consumption from income and link it to wealth. This new linkage also draws attention to some environmental and ethical concerns.

Learning Outcomes
A study of this chapter is expected to help students learn and appreciate the following:

- The circular relationship between consumption and production, and its significance.
- The basic issues in the area of consumption from an Islamic perspective. These, for example, include the nature of human wants—necessities, comforts, and luxuries—from the viewpoint of faith *vis-a-vis* their mainstream conceptualization.
- The fact that demand determines and shapes supply is no less valid than the popular perception that supply creates its own demand—there is a two-way interaction between the variables.
- How the gap between the micro and macro treatment of consumption can be narrowed down to make the two mutually compatible.
- How an interdisciplinary approach improves the understanding of consumption-related issues in an Islamic setting.
- How human longing for variety in consumption has made people surrender their sovereignty to market arbitration and the consequences of this surrender.
- How an interdisciplinary approach improves the understanding of consumption-related issues in an Islamic setting.

6.1 Introduction

For a country, production is what it produces. Consumption is what its people consume. The ultimate goal of economic action is to have production meet consumption requirements so that the population remains well off. If production falls short of the goal, a nation has to import what it needs to carry on. This happened to the Soviet Union when the communist regime could not feed its people despite having Ukraine (then part of the Soviet Union) as the 'breadbasket of Europe'. The Soviets had to import grain from the United States, Canada, and Argentina. This was one factor that led to the collapse of the Soviet Union and showed the world the failure of socialism. India had a similar experience during the 1960s when the United States refused to sell wheat to the country for want of foreign exchange to pay. The Russians came to her rescue, supplying two million tonnes of grain as a loan, to tide over the situation. This is not to deny the fact that most countries do not meet their production goals for domestic consumption and rely on importing what they need, usually facing imbalance in their external balances.

For example, presently both India and the United States have chronic trade deficits with the rest of the world. Both import many more goods from other countries than they export, the deficit running into worth billions of dollars a year. Persistently large deficits are not good, as domestic money flows out to other countries leading to adverse consequences: local currency weakens and employment slackens. However, favourable trade balances may also not often be welcome. The country piles up foreign IOUs in exchange for *real* commodities. There is an upward pressure on the local currency, eating into its competitiveness in foreign markets. Japan has long suffered from this malady and China seems to be moving in a similar direction.

Sticky imbalances are, however, the consequence of the modern transformation in the production–consumption relationship its historical evolution had obscured. The obscuring has found manifestation in the dominant expansion in the *variety* of consumption goods compared to growth in their *availability*. This development has weakened the positive impact of consumption on human resource development. This has been revealed in a variance analysis of the connection between scale of individual consumption and labour productivity in European countries, the United States, and Japan. Beyond such considerations, production is more a matter concerning technology and sociology than economics—mainstream or Islamic. We shall revert to this point later.

One interesting aspect of the consumption–production relationship is the habit in mainstream economics to look at it as if the supply side of the market is the arbiter in economic matters. Say's law of markets states that supply creates its own demand; this may have substance. However, it is equally true that demand creates its own supply—necessity is the mother of invention. For Islamic economics, it would be a constructive and conducive way to start from this perception. It is in harmony with its view of development.

However, change seems to be the undercurrent. Most of the writings on consumption in Islamic economics have shown interest in investigating the determinants of consumer behaviour from the demand side of price formation in microeconomic settings. However, some macro formulations have also attempted to explain the processes of incomes' determination and their distribution in the same vein as microanalyses of consumption provide the necessary foundation for dealing with the phenomenon at the macro level. There is, therefore, advantage, or rather propriety, in reviewing both types of discussion together.

Economics, as currently taught in Muslim institutions of higher learning across countries, is mostly anchored in the mainstream tradition in terms of curricula frames, course structures, reading materials, and the researches initiated. This tradition is likely to continue far into the future for a variety of reasons. Indeed, there is now realization that greater attention must be paid to the 'teaching of economics from the Islamic perspective' than to the 'teaching of Islamic economics'.[1] The available Islamic analyses, therefore, hardly move out of the orthodox mainstream groove in approach, method, or textbook content. But not a few writings in the area, including on consumption, take a rather puritan approach, assuming that an Islamic socio-economic order is already in place. They derive their inspiration from the past and often lose sight of the great and irreversible changes that have been taking place in Muslim countries over the centuries. This is not to deny the validity or value of heterodox writings in Islamic economics, including those on consumption. The concern is that such writings often overlook the critics who raise the point that their views do not, or cannot, reconcile with the temporal requirements of the community.

The chapter is spread over five sections including the Introduction. Section 6.2 evaluates the treatment of consumption in the literature at the micro level. This includes a look at what is usually presented in the literature under the title 'Theory of consumption', or as a preface to the macromodels they present. Here, the key issues discussed are the distinction between wants and needs, utility as a guide to consumer behaviour, and the impact of the variety syndrome on the production–consumption linkage. Section 6.3 looks at modifications of the consumption concept for income determination at the macro level. An attempt is made to show the impact of the abolition of interest, introduction of *zakah*, and avoidance of *israf*, i.e. excessive consumption on savings and investment, in an Islamic economy. Section 6.4 deals with the relationship between

[1]For explanations of the compulsions leading to this situation, see Hasan (2002, pp. 97–98).

consumption and social welfare as desired by Islamic ethics—an emerging topic that has scantly been touched upon by Muslim economists. Section 6.5 provides a summary of the review, and contains a few concluding remarks. The chapter deals with the literature produced in the English language on a selective basis; it focuses on the issues, rather than on the author-wise contribution.

6.2 Microeconomic Foundations

What Islamic economics deals with under the 'theory of consumption' is largely the hierarchical setting of human wants, and what regulates consumer behaviour in the process of their satisfaction, given a resource constraint. Islamic departures from the mainstream positions in consumer theory are broadly set up regarding these two matters. The law of demand remains untouched.

There is a natural feeling of some non-fulfilment that constitutes what is called a 'human want' in mainstream economics. Wants being psychic, are unlimited. Individually, many of them are satiable but are, at the same time, recurring. These characteristics of wants put pressure on a person to seek their satisfaction, and have in that aspect been the primary wellspring of human toil and progress. These facts are well recognized in the religious writings. Writings on Islamic economics also include these discussions on needs and wants—their definition, characteristics, and nature. What is usually highlighted in the literature is their classification and relationship with income in macro-level modelling.

6.2.1 Wants, Needs, and Scarcity

The relationship between unlimited wants and scarcity of available resources that gives rise to the issues of choice-making in human life is the foundation of economics. This relationship gives the subject its nature and content under the secular dispensation. Islamic economists, in general, endorse this type of scarcity underpinning the discussions, but there are scholars who candidly denounce any relevance of the notion of scarcity to Islamic economics. We have already shown in Chapter 2 that the reasons they advance for this denunciation are not valid.

To reiterate, we need goods and services to satisfy our wants. However, Islamic scholars tend to confuse needs with wants. More intense wants could probably be called needs; otherwise, forcing a distinction between them is confusing and uncalled for. The two terms can be used interchangeably. Islamic economists classify needs into three categories, providing linkages between them.[2]

To begin with, there are the *daruriyat* or necessities of life, like food, clothing, shelter, education, health care, and so on. Their satisfaction is basic to human life. However, there are things that, if available, take life beyond just survival. The urge for them to improve the quality of living gives rise to*hajiyat*, i.e. complementary needs. Lastly, we have *tahsiniyat* or the needs whose satisfaction accords us social status and recognition. The latter categories are conceived of as a sort of expansion of the necessities of life. The three are thus interlinked and their satisfaction pictures a graded improvement in the quality of life. The focus of attention is on goods that satisfy needs falling in each category.[3]The needs remain the same, but the consumers' satisfaction improves as we move from *daruriyat* to higher up the scale.

In mainstream economics, the corresponding terms are necessities, comforts, and luxuries. To replace these more familiar words with Arabic terms is futile and confusing. However, missing in their Arabic narration is an objective criterion for distinguishing between the categories of needs to facilitate analysis. The mainstream classification of wants—necessities, comforts, and luxuries—rests on an objective and measurable criterion. Necessities are wants whose non-satisfaction would result in a reduction of a person's work efficiency, while the addition of comforts is likely to improve it. Satisfaction from luxuries may have negligible impact on efficiency, but may improve creativity, unless their consumption is injurious to health. Here, the categories need not have a linkage or layering, as is mentioned in the literature on Islamic economics.

Furthermore, the same commodity may fall within any of the categories, depending on the nature of the want it satisfies for an individual. The point is, in mainstream economics, there is an external criterion for classifying wants and measuring the impact of their satisfaction on work efficiency. It is difficult to see how this approach is opposed to Islamic norms. Adaptation would help avoid many pitfalls in constructing a

[2]Jurists usually discuss this classification. See Khan for an interpretation (1995, Chapter 2).

[3]See the chart and discussion in Khan (1995, pp. 39–40), also Siddiqi (1992, p. 21), and Chapra (2000, p. 307).

microtheory of consumption and erecting macromodels for Islamic economics. It would eliminate the conceptual wedge one finds between the micro- and macro-level treatment of the consumption variable.[4]

Now, the question is: what shapes the behaviour of a consumer for attaining equilibrium in mainstream economics, and how do Islamic economists react to the process? Put briefly, the consumer is assumed to be a rational being in the sense that he seeks to maximize his satisfaction from a given income. Several approaches—utility calculus, indifference curve technique, and revealed preference theorem—have been used to explain the process of achieving this objective. These approaches do have weaknesses,[5] but they have served well the purpose of erecting the law of demand for mainstream economics. The law states that normally, there is an inverse relationship between the price and quantity demanded of a commodity, under the assumption that certain things—the income of the consumer and his tastes, the prices of related goods, the number of consumers in the group, and the market conditions of competition—remain unchanged.

Islamic economists raise several objections to the above formulation of mainstream consumption theory. To begin with, they are mostly averse to a maximizing behaviour on the part of any economic agent, let alone the consumer. Others find it just alien to Islamic norms.[6]

A blanket rejection seems untenable. We have shown in Chapter 2 that maximization per se is value-neutral. What is maximized, how, and to what effect, are the questions to be answered before passing judgement in a particular case. Scarcity forces maximization on economic agents for an efficient use of resources and lends meaning to the

[4]Most of the elementary economics textbooks in India and elsewhere contained this classification and its basis during the middle of the twentieth century. One finds a cursory mention of necessities, comforts, and luxuries in Siddiqi (1992, p. 56) as well as in Chapra (2000, p. 307)

[5]Interestingly, Islamic economists conveniently ignore the microeconomic positions they so laboriously erect when they cross over to the macro side of the fence. There, they tend to grab on to the same concepts of growth, consumption, savings, and investment as we have them in mainstream economics, except that interest is eliminated from, and *zakah* introduced into, the models.

[6]Microeconomics textbooks usually discuss these approaches and their weaknesses. Nevertheless, one may find their critical evaluation also in Hasan (2002, pp. 109–111).

avoidance of their overuse or wasteful use, in consumption as well.[7]Islamic economists often cite the following verses from the *Qur'an*, arguing that a believer is not to be a miser or extravagant in spending his wealth, he is to follow the middle path:

> And let not your hand be tied (like a miser) to your neck, nor be stretched forth to its utmost reach (like a spendthrift), so that you may become blameworthy, and in severe poverty. (17:29)
>
> 'And those who when spending, are neither extravagant nor niggardly but hold a medium (way) between those (extremes)' are the true believers. (25:67)

Explaining the second of these verses, Monzer Kahf observes that extravagance as a limit becomes non-applicable when one is 'spending for charity, for the improvement of the community, and for the propagation of the message of Islam' (1992, p. 65). The interpretation seems a bit debatable if the two verses were taken together. In normal circumstances, expenditure, even under the abovementioned heads, should not leave one in destitution.[8] Siddiqi too, regards minimum consumption essential (1992, p. 54). In any case, these verses, and others quoted on the point in the literature, refer to the apportioning of one's wealth between spending on one's own needs and in the way of Allah. They do not refer perhaps to how one must spend on permissible goods the amount one eventually decides to spend on self.[9] The latter has rarely been discussed in Islamic economics. Another dubious notion that has permeated Islamic theory is that the basket of goods in the case of a Muslim consumer would be smaller than that of a non-Muslim, as the former will keep away from the consumption of non-permissible (*haram*) goods. Clearly, it is the money value of the basket, not the sort of things it contains that determines the size of expenditure on it. A believer can spend

[7]See Siddiqi (1996, pp. xiii, 17, and 56) for his total rejection of the proposition in any economics.

[8]The author has argued in defence of the mainstream maximization hypothesis for Islamic economics. See Hasan (2002, pp. 95, 101, and 112). MonzerKahf also strikes a positive stance (1992, p. 65).

[9]Khan (1995, pp. 47–48) has the same position as Kahf on this point. However, the conclusion does not follow from the verses cited. Verses 2:15 and 2:19 also refute this position.

much more on permitted goods alone than a non-Muslim would on a basket containing non-permissible goods as well.[10]

Finally, there are some misgivings about the role that utility plays in the mainstream analysis of consumer behaviour. Part of the difficulty arises because of the already-stated confusion between wants and needs, and the insistence on the hierarchy of needs. It is seldom realized that the hierarchy was a matter of temporal thought and expression, not a belief imperative. One can reasonably demand evidence for the hierarchy being eternal for Islamic dispensation. Neither human wants, nor goods that satisfy them, can be ordered as suggested by anyone for individual consumers. Of course, public policy can rank societal needs and review the ranking periodically to address the *maqasid*.[11] Characteristic of the position Islamic economists take on utility analysis of consumer behaviour are the following observations of Siddiqi (1992, p. 21):

> The assumption that the consumer maximizes utility or satisfaction implies that all goods and services have a common *denominator* called utility or satisfaction, which can be measured or at least compared with one another. This idea is not acceptable in view of the hierarchy of human needs and the fact that the same commodity may serve a number of needs. This makes a generalized analysis of consumer's equilibrium impossible.[12] (emphasis added)[13]

[10] See Hasan (1985, p. 79; 1990, Section 1) for comments on Iqbal, who is in agreement with Khan on the point.

[11] Take, for example, the case of keeping wealth secure. The individual may spend on doors, grills, locks, etc., depending on the costs he deems fit to incur for the purpose. The state would provide police protection and a system of dispensing justice; it will maintain a defence force to ward off external aggression, within budgetary constraints set by the community. Would one regard the individual's need as a *Shari'ah* imperative, and if so, of which category?

[12] It is argued that the concept of utility involves value judgement, regards desires as the best criterion for the formation of preferences, and does not distinguish them from needs. In Islamic economics, *maslahah* is a more objective concept for analysing the behaviour of economic agents than utility (Khan 1995, pp. 31 and 35). However, he does not establish his claim. Rather, he negates it in the next breath by admitting that *maslahah* is as subjective as utility in the sense that the individual consumer himself is the best judge of whether a particular good/service is *maslahah* for him (p. 35). This is a *faux pas* par excellence.

[13] It is one unit of money spent on each commodity that is the common denominator, not utility, in the determination of consumer equilibrium. See Box 6.1.

Box 6.1: The equilibrium condition for the consumer

Utility is the satisfaction one *expects* to derive to have one more unit (marginal) of some commodity, starting from zero. The measure of utility is indirect; it is the price one willingly pays for it. In comparing marginal utilities of different commodities, the familiar formula for consumer equilibrium is:

$$\frac{\text{Marginal Utility of A}}{\text{Price of A}} = \frac{\text{Marginal Utility of B}}{\text{Price of B}} \text{ and so on}$$

Thus, the equilibrium condition is that the marginal utility per unit of money spent on each commodity must be the common denominator.

What a consumer pays for an item is the difference between the price he actually pays for it and the price he would be willing to pay rather than do without it. Alfred Marshall called this consumer surplus. It is a useful concept to compare location advantages. For example, a given income would yield more consumer surplus in a big town than it would in a small, far-off village.

If money can be a common denominator for measuring the exchange value of goods and services as expressed in their prices, why utility cannot be used for measuring their value in use is not clear. One reason possibly is that utility is seen as ingrained as intrinsic to commodities and is not distinguished from satisfaction. The fact is that the locus of utility is the human mind; it does not reside *within* commodities. Thus, a glass of water may have no utility to one who is not thirsty. Also, the utility of identical successive units of a commodity for a consumer would not diminish as he has more of them. Again, utility is the satisfaction one *expects* from consuming a commodity; it is an *ex ante* concept. Expectations guide the consumer in allocating income to various uses, including savings. Satisfaction, on the other hand, is an *ex post* notion; how one feels after consuming a thing. Utility—expected satisfaction—need not equal realized satisfaction. Thus, we experience at times a pleasant surprise or disappointment after spending money on a commodity. The source of both may often be incomplete information in an uncertain world.

6.3 Macroeconomic Modelling

In this section, we shall mainly deal with three publications. First is the work of Khan (1984) followed by some searching comments on it by Tag-el-Din, Seif-el-Din (1985). His study later appeared unchanged as Chapter 3 of a book in 1995. Second, is the work of Iqbal (1985). followed by a comprehensive review by Hasan (1990). These works have much in common. They essentially attempt to modify the elementary Keynesian structure to construct an Islamic departure. Here we shall examine briefly the gist of the controversy these writings raise. Third is a recent work (Gassan 2016) that reviews the literature, places the need–want issue in a fresh light, and presents an Islamic consumption model incorporating new ideas.

Figure 6.1 provides the starting point. Here, C is the initial consumption function, with A_0 the minimum consumption-income requirement in the economy, its slope being the overall marginal propensity to consume. People save TT_0 out of a given income $\ddot{Y}$.

When income E_2 is transferred via *zakah* to the poor, i.e. the lower income classes, it may have one of the two consequences. As no saving is assumed out of E_2 transference in the literature under reference, C* must rise parallel to C, as A_0 remains unchanged. Now, the income transfers from the rich to the poor may give rise to one of the following two possibilities.

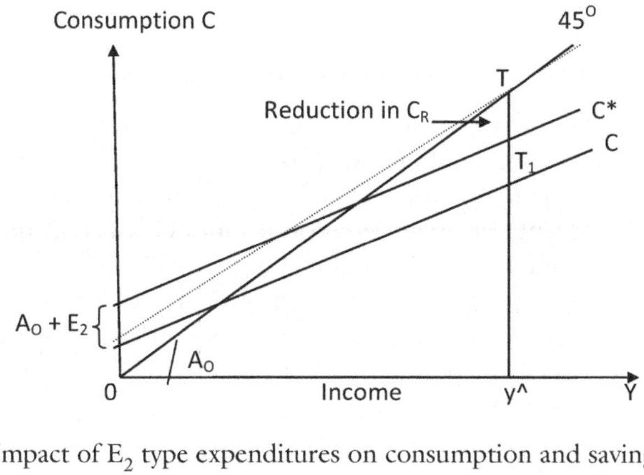

Fig. 6.1 Impact of E_2 type expenditures on consumption and savings

First, it is claimed that consumption in the economy could remain the same as before, the savings of the rich falling appropriately by T_1T_0. The propensity to consume would remain unchanged. Lower savings would slow down growth. Islamic economists refute this claim. They maintain that the propensity to consume would decline, such that the savings would remain intact, and may even increase. This rests on two assumptions: (i) the fear of Allah is expected to curtail wasteful expenditure on frivolous wants, and (ii) moderation would curb ostentatious lifestyles. Thus, the transfer of income from the rich to the poor would be at the cost TT_1 of consumption of the rich, not their savings.

The overall average propensity to consume would re-adjust appropriately, growth remaining unaffected. The consumption curve C would rotate upward at its lower end, passing through the point T, as shown by the dotted light line with a slope greater than that of C. Thus, maintaining savings equivalent to the reduction in consumption of the rich by $C_r = TT_1$.

The above argument is in line with mainstream consumption models having a short-run perspective to fit into their stabilization policy framework. They assume constant propensity to consume as at A_0.

In contrast, the second conjuncture is that the rich, having become accustomed to particular consumption levels, are more likely to maintain them; they would rather reduce savings to meet that end. C* would rise to pass through reducing savings, not consumption. However, there is no conclusive evidence to show which of these two possibilities is closer to ground reality in Muslim countries.

6.3.1 Consumption and Income Layers[14]

Interestingly, the reconciliation between the conventional and Islamic want classifications we made in Sect. 6.2.1 above is revived in a recent well-researched article Professor Gassan published in September 2016. The author presents a macroeconomic model of consumer behaviour and social welfare based on the writings of Shibani, a seventh- or eighth-century Islamic jurist from Iraq. In raising the microeconomic façade for his exercise, Gassan goes over afresh the entire literature on consumption, the salient points of which we have already covered above.

[14]This section draws on the work of Gassan (2016) wherein the translation of the Arabic text from Shibani (1997) is his rendition.

His value added is the coverage of relevant elements from the mainstream discipline since the early writings on the subject.

Gassan sees Shibani as one of the pioneers in the analysis of economic issues from the Islamic viewpoint. Shibani explored, in particular, topics related to earnings, savings, and spending in a macro frame. He regarded savings as fundamental to capital accumulation and to increasing wealth through 'permissible abstinence'.[15] He developed the notion of income being distributed among individuals in layers corresponding to different types of consumer needs: (a) necessities; (b) comforts; and (c) luxuries. Thus, some earn enough just to meet (a), others to meet both (a) and (b), while there are some others who can meet all three, and more. It is akin to income layering in the World Development Reports.

Gassan (2016) presents a macroeconomic model based on Shibani's income layers. All the writers he mentions in his paper (p. 244) use such sort of aggregate income divisions. But their division is only between two groups—payers of *zakah* and its recipients. However, Gassan (p. 249) uses three groups for constructing his model.[16] First, are the poorest who receive *zakah* from the second, a middle-income group, and the third, the richest. Gassan does not make use of *nisab* as the demarcation line between the payers and the recipients of *zakah*. The omission makes his second and third income groups analytically indeterminate.

6.4 Consumption and Social Welfare

The income distribution models in Islamic economics usually incorporate consumption by proxy, that is, as income minus savings. Islamic economists have shown almost complete ignorance of some far-reaching developments

[15]The term is useful for it separates savings from the abhorred miserliness. One wonders if this term, which is attributed to Shibani, could be taken as the precursor of Senior's *abstinence* theory of interest in mainstream economics.

[16]The macro consumption function in the long run can be formulated as follows:

$$\begin{aligned} Ct = {} & cste + \beta 1\,[(1 - \mu 2 - \mu 3)\,Yt + z1\mu 2Yt + z1\mu 3Yt] \\ & + \beta 2\,(1 - z1)\mu 2Yt + \beta 3\,(1 - z1)\,\mu 3Yt + \varepsilon t \end{aligned} \tag{6.1}$$

where the coefficients β, 1, 2, and 3 are the MPCs of the three income groups in that order. The model ignores the savings and assets of the wealthiest third group, why and with what implications must have been explained.

that have been taking place over the past decades in mainstream economics in general, and in the treatment of consumption, in particular. It is, of course, well recognized in the literature that to the extent Islamic transfer payments—*zakah* and *infaq*—increase labour productivity and enlarge the size of the market, the rise in consumption they cause is a sort of *real* investment and contributes to making up for the possible shortfall in savings. But the type of changes we are talking about is different.

There is an ever-increasing interface between economics and other social sciences—sociology, political science, psychology, and, of late, ethics. Their mutual understandings, areas of common concern, and shared research interests are on the rise. Mainstream economics seems moving closer to the Islamic insistence on the interdisciplinary approach to the seeking of knowledge, use of ethical filters, and giving a human face to economic relations between sectors, groups, and economies.[17] Working within and across disciplines, social scientists have begun to seek consensus on the dimensions of well-being and its appropriate measurements. These developments can have a profound impact on findings regarding relative well-being across groups, and trends therein. The choices can affect conclusions about the consequences of social and economic policies (Beverly 2002, p. 1).

Notice the effect of these developments on the issue of consumption. Slesnick (2001) produces empirical evidence from the US economy to challenge some of the normally accepted facts in the area. His estimates, based on family income data, show that living standards in the United States have made little improvement over the decades,[18] inequalities have increased, and poverty remains high. He argues that consumption

[17] It is time that Islamic economists shed their misconceptions that mainstream economics is value free, has no altruistic elements in its applications, and is seized with the money-making 'economic man' alone. This is not to say that all is now well with mainstream economics. Its own proponents are its most informed and vocal critics. The point is that things are changing in some ways, even if slowly, in a welcome direction from an Islamic viewpoint.

[18] Aspiration gaps, which consumerism creates, are eating into the vitals of American life. In middle-class families, parents experience an almost threatening pressure to keep up, both for themselves and their children. 85% of the population cannot earn the six-digit figure income necessary to support the upper middle-class lifestyles. Inability to save much is a constant source of stress and worry. Somewhere between a quarter and a half of all households lives hand to mouth. Bankruptcy rates continue to set new records, rising from 200,000 a year in 1980 to 1.4 million in 1998 (Schor 2003, p. 6).

compared to income is a better measure of economic well-being. It can be spread more evenly over time; people can, and do, save when income exceeds consumption requirements and can liquidate savings or run debts if income falls below consumption needs. Income elasticity of consumption is in general, less than unity. Also, national income figures, because of product-mix differences over time and among nations, are not so much reflective of welfare as are the data on consumption. On this count too, there seems to be a close relationship between consumption levels and social welfare. This presumption lends meaning and content to the Islamic emphasis on the fulfilment of basic needs, restraint on consumption, and achievement of distributive justice.

For an objective analysis of the consumption–welfare nexus, the two concepts have to be measurable. Slesnick (2001) includes in consumption, out-of-pocket expenditures of consumers plus market rental equivalents of owner-occupied houses, and durables. To measure intertemporal changes in welfare, he rejects the consumer price index in favour of a social cost of living index.[19] When the standard of living is based on consumption rather than on income, one finds the elderly having an edge over the young in terms of economic well-being. This finding is relevant to recent debates among sociologists on economic hardships across the course of life.

6.4.1 The Craze for Variety

People could not relish for long manna that fell free from the skies, however delicious it was, and asked for variety; Allah told them through Prophet Musa, peace be upon him to search for variety in His land. Thus, desire for variety is part of human nature. As perfect competition did not permit businesses more than the normal profit, they found human longing for variety handy in eliminating competition for larger and more stable earnings. Today, each firm attempts to convince buyers that what it sells is better in some important way than what its competitors are selling. Brand names, trademarks, and packaging make its product look different from others. A loyal and expanding clientele is then built around the brand name through what has now come to be known

[19]The social cost of living index is the ratio of the minimum expenditure needed to attain a given level of welfare at one set of prices, to the minimum expenditure needed to attain the same level of welfare at a different set of prices. For technical details, see Nagar and Das (1997, Section 12.5, pp. 301–305).

as the *management of demand*.[20] This involves expenditure on advertising, dealership models, salesmanship, and other supporting services. Indeed, TV advertisements have become serious health hazard via noise pollution.

Product differentiation essentially has a psychic appeal: it preys on the judgement of the customers. Everyone knows what soap is and what it does. Yet there are significant buyers' preferences for Maharani, Sandalwood, Hamam, Lux, and other brand names in South Asian markets. Product differentiation has clearly subdivided the soap market, where each firm has the discretion to vary the price of its product, within limits. A monopoly shelter for its profits has emerged.

In contemporary American culture, consumption has become as authentic an indicator of social status as the level it attains. Advertisements, bargain hunting, garage sales, and credit cards[21] have become well-entrenched pillars of the American way of life. This shopping mania brings considerable unease; there is a growing preoccupation with and anxiety towards, 'getting and spending'. There is a realization of losing touch with more worthwhile values and ways of living. Unfortunately, these feelings of discomfort have not intensified enough to cohere into an effective weapon against the proliferating consumerism.

This culture is catching up fast in emerging economies. There too, the emphasis is turning quickly from availability to variety, as alluded to earlier. The massive and expanding marketing machinations have unleashed self-cancelling competitive advertising costs onto the hapless consumer. Consumer sovereignty is an illusion. Sales management has reversed the direction of instructions. It used to be from the consumer to the market; it is now from the market to the consumer. Advertising has perverted consumers' choices. Frequently, we are not sure if we have bought what we actually wanted, or if the acumen of the seller has made us buy something else.

[20] 'The control or management of demand is, in fact, a vast and rapidly growing industry in itself. It embraces a huge network of communications, a growing array of merchandising and selling organizations, nearly the entire advertising industry, numerous ancillary research, training and other related services and much more' (Galbraith 1969, p. 200 and *passim*).

[21] In the United States, distribution of income and wealth has shifted decisively in the direction of the top 20% since the 1970s. Their income share rose from 41.4% in 1979 to 46.8% in 1996. Likewise, the share of wealth they controlled went up from 81.3% in 1983 to 84.3% in 1996.

The resurgence of interest in the theory and evolving patterns of consumption at the macro level possibly draws inspiration from the much-debated lifecycle theorem in the literature and the criticism of income hypothesis on which it rests.[22] However, two of its dimensions—environmental and ethical—are certainly of recent vintage.

The popular discourse on sustainable development is not clear on what it is that has to be sustained: long-run economic growth, intergenerational equity in distribution of incomes and wealth, or the quality of the environment. A closer look at the first two items would reveal that their requirements make them converge on the third, sustainability of the environment. The greatest source of environmental degradation can be traced to the grossly uneven consumption levels within and across nations. About 15% of the population of the world living in developed countries enjoys no less than 77% of the global output. Now, even if the rich could remain content with their current consumption levels, global production of goods and services must increase to ameliorate living conditions and reduces poverty in the world's population. Output expansion cannot be slowed. These facts pose some serious challenges for mankind.

As availability of resources invariably lags behind demand for them, and the bulk of them are located in developing countries, the interests of the rich and the poor of the world conflict. The increasing wars, clashes, and violence witnessed around the world today are but manifestations of this conflict. The underlying factors are essentially economic. Again, as production must increase, pollution volume cannot be reduced, although its generation could be slowed down. If the cake and the poison are both to grow, how the rich and the poor would share each must be a bone of contention.[23] The rich and powerful want most of the cake but little of the poison. This reminds us of the universal and eternal nature of the *Qur'anic* injunctions. The Scripture expresses abhorrence for what we now call consumerism in these words:

[22] Consumer credit is fast becoming the most lucrative business for the commercial banks in the West. The Islamic banking system too, wants to follow suit, without caring to identify the welfare implications of the credit card culture—the impact of borrowing from the future to spend now. There is a lot of transformation without much discretion.

[23] Caliph Ali b. Talib, explaining the *Shari'ah* requirement of maintaining harmony in the nature–man relationship observed: 'Partake of it (nature) with joy as long as you are a benefactor not a corruptor, a cultivator not a destroyer'.

And those who do *kufr* (mischief) avail of material things and eat as do the animals; their abode is Hell. (Qur'an, 47:12)

Consumerism—excessive attention to materialistic desires—breeds egotism that ultimately brings in more of frustration and futility than the bliss of fulfilment.

Interestingly, the need for ethical and moral controls on the behaviour of economic agents is of late being recognized in mainstream research.[24] In the area of consumption, a variety of issues are often defined as ethical concerns, including environmental care, health and safety risks, fair trade, labour conditions, animal welfare, and human rights. Informed research into motivations for ethical consumption is relatively scarce, in Islamic economics as well. We can proceed here by raising two questions: first, how do academics, policymakers, and organizations understand ethical decision-making? Second, what types of ethical conduct would Islamic norms encourage in the area of consumption?

Some types of ethical values, determined by the cultural patterns of people, are already implicit in their routine consumption behaviour in all societies. Examples are priority for the fulfilment of basic needs, equitable distribution of consumption among family members, spending on religious and social ceremonies, saving for a rainy day, altruistic expenditure, and so forth. Researchers in mainstream economics seek to collect and examine data on how such values tend to become the object of explicit policies and campaigns for their own reinforcement, and how far such reinforcement improves the attitudes of people to continue manifesting these values in their daily lives.[25] (Such research, albeit useful and revealing, is of a matter-of-fact sort, dealing mostly with static circular relationships; it has little reformative content.)

Scholars in other social disciplines—sociology, anthropology, cultural studies, and human geography—have moved a step further. They demonstrate that consumption is one area where autonomous action to discipline the market is required, as the market allocates resources and distributes commodities in accordance with the purchasing power of people, not their needs. Individuals require reflective monitoring of their own conduct: they must indulge in fashioning relationships between

[24] For a brief presentation of this criticism, see for example, Hasan (1990, pp. 98–99).

[25] The economic value of ethical conduct for corporate strategy in purchasing, retailing, and policymaking is well established and is likely to grow. See, for example, Bernett and Clock (2003, p. 14).

themselves and others. This is the message of Islamic economics as well, but with a difference. The choice of behavioural norms, or their modification, is much less flexible in Islamic economics, compared to secular dispensations. It has to observe the confines of *Shari'ah*, and is regulated by its foundational all-pervading notion of ***amanah***. These norms have been extensively discussed in writings on Islamic economics. The main ones relevant to the present discussion we have already mentioned in Sect. 6.2 and need not be repeated here.

Although conceptualization has not always been logical, one does come across some worthwhile discussions on basic Islamic notions like needs, moderation, the impact of pursuing Islamic norms on propensity to consume, savings, and investment, and the like, as the chapter addresses. Scholars are now also inclined to shed their aversion to using utility tools. This need not support the acceptance of the ideas in mainstream economics. They can be, and are, being successfully modified to meet Islamic norms and requirements. Their retention will reduce, if not entirely eliminate, the conceptual divergences in the meaning of the same terms while passing from the micro to the macro part of economic analysis, from the Islamic perspective.

There have also been laudable efforts to examine basic macroeconomic models in the Keynesian tradition and incorporate into them some key Islamic variables as well as the consequences of disaggregating consumption and income, using *nisab* as the dividing line. However, some of the conclusions are probably ambiguous and do not stand the test of logic. For example, the argument that there is a *trade-off* between the pleasures of this world and the gains in the hereafter is not convincing. It is also purely presumptive to insist that moderation would more than make up for the fall in savings due to the transfer of income from the rich to the poor through the *zakah* mechanism.

The major difficulty is not with the knowledge of the norms; it is with their ***measurable*** conceptualization. Frivolous expenditure (*israf*), moderation, legitimate requirements, basic needs fulfilment and so on, all need quantification. It is a difficult task, but by no means impossible. Many of the value-loaded concepts—normal profit, minimum wages, productivity, efficiency, quality of life, and the like—have been provided in measurable forms in mainstream economics. Islamic economists too, have quantified in money terms some of the concepts such as *nisab*, or the fulfilment of basic needs. Let us take up this task in a more earnest way, if not individually, then by forming research teams.

6.5 Concluding Remarks

The foregoing appraisal of the treatment of consumption in Islamic economics over the past 25 years or so has been rewarding in several ways. The scholars have rightly followed an evolutionary approach in preference to puritan formulations. They have based their work on mainstream concepts, modifying them to meet Islamic requirements. There is much confusion concerning the impact of these transfers on the propensity to consume. The clarification of this point provided in this regard is perhaps one of its main contributions. It also demonstrates in this context that for the economy as a whole, the *difference* between the two marginal propensities to consume (MPCs), i.e. before and after the introduction of the *zakah*-moderation mechanism into the picture, is independent of the division of income between the rich and the poor.

The chapter also draws attention to certain developments in mainstream economics and other social sciences that are welcome from an Islamic viewpoint. Of special interest is the integration of environmental and ethical issues into the discussion on consumption. We think that Islamic scholars will do well to keep track of these welcome events.

Case Study 6.1: US curbs on consumption

The US plan to impose about $60 billion worth of annual tariffs on imports from China constitutes the strongest ever trade action against any country. What the United States is doing is purportedly in retaliation to Chinese 'economic aggression' robbing the United States of technology, jobs, and incomes.

The 1300 items from China targeted for tariffs include everything from shoes and clothing to electronics. Exclusively targeting daily use items in the list can be interpreted as an effort to curb rising consumerism among Americans that the low prices of imported goods promote all the more. For that reason, the story may not end with China. Imports from Asian countries such as India, South Korea, Vietnam, and Taiwan may receive similar treatment. Is the history of the colonial era repeating itself?

Source: *Times of India*, Friday, 23 March 2018, p. 24.

Finally, we have not included a chapter on production in this book for two reasons. First, consumption is the beginning and also the end of economic activity. In Islamic economics, demand for goods and services determines or must determine the character and content of production. Beyond that, it is largely a matter of science and technology, guided by Islamic ethical norms. Second, the essentials of labour-related issues we have already discussed in the preceding chapter.

Test Questions

Q.1 'Consumption is the beginning and end of all economic activity'. Do you agree? Argue your case, providing supportive examples.

Q.2 Examine critically the relationship claimed between the level of consumption and the lifecycle income theory.

Q.3 Survey the major developments in the consumption theory in Islamic economic literature.

Q.4 Critically evaluate Shibani's income layers consumption relationship theory. Do you think it is a useful contribution to the literature? Justify your position.

Q.5 Explain and illustrate using an appropriate diagram how income transfer from the rich to the poor would affect savings and growth if the rich maintain their 'before transfer' consumption level.

Q.6 Write critical notes on the following:
(a) Consumer sovereignty
(b) Demonstration effect
(c) Consumerism
(d) Management of demand

What Next?

The bridge to cross over from economics to finance is the institution of money. Modern exchange economies operate with money as a go-between in real transactions. Thus, the next chapter deals with the evolution of money, and its forms, expansion, and significance in economies, within and across countries.

References

Bernett, C., & Clock, P. (2003). *Governing the Subjects and Spaces of Ethical Consumption*. Internet, Research Projects, Oxford University.

Beverly, S. G. (2002). Consumption and Social Welfare; Living Standards and Their Distribution in the United States (Book Review). *Journal of Sociology and Social Welfare, 29*(4), 172–174.

Chapra, M. U. (2000). *The Future of Economics: An Islamic Perspective* (pp. 305–308). UK: The Islamic Foundation.

Galbraith. (1969). *The New Industrial State*. USA: Princeton University Press.

Gassan, H. B. (2016). A Consumer and Social Welfare Model Based on the Writings of Shibani (750–805 AD, 131–189 AH). *PSL Quarterly Review, 69*(2), 235–266.

Hasan, Z. (1985). Determination of Profit and Loss Sharing Ratios in Interest-Free Business Finance. *Journal of Research in Islamic Economics, 3*(1), 13–27.

Hasan, Z. (1990). Munawar Iqbal; Zakah, Moderation, and Aggregate Consumption in an Islamic Economy-Comments. *KAU Islamic Economics, 2*(2), 91–100.

Hasan, Z. (2002). Maximization Postulates and Their Efficacy for Islamic Economics. *American Journal of Islamic Social Sciences, 19*(1), 95–118.

Iqbal, M. (1985). Zakah, Moderation, and Aggregate Consumption in an Islamic Economy. *Journal of Research in Islamic Economics, 3*(1), 45–60.

Kahf, M. (1992). The Theory of Consumption. In Tahir et al. (Eds.), *Readings in Microeconomics in Islamic Perspective* (pp. 61–68; 90–105). Petaling Jaya, Malaysia: Longman.

Khan F. M. (1984). Macro Consumption Function in an Islamic Framework. *Journal of Research in Islamic Economics, 1*(2), 3–25.

Khan, M. (1995). *Essays in Islamic Economics*. UK: Islamic Foundation.

Nagar, & Das. (1997). *Basic Statistics*. India: Oxford University Press.

Schor, J. (2003). *The New Politics of Consumption: Life Cycle Thinking as a Solution*. Research Projects, Oxford University.

Shibani, M. I. A.-H. (1997). *Book of Earning* (1st ed.). Explained by Mohammed Sarkhasi, verified by Abdul Fattah Abu Ghuda. Beirut: Dar Albachaer Alislamia, and Aleppo: Office of the Islamic Publications.

Siddiqi, M. N. (1992). Islamic Consumer Behavior. In Tahir, et al. (Eds.), *Readings in Microeconomics in Islamic Perspective* (pp. 49–60). Malaysia: Longman.

Siddiqi, M. N. (1996). *Teaching Economics in Islamic Perspective*. Jeddah: Scientific Publishing Centre, King Abdulaziz University.

Slesnick, D. T. (2001). *Consumption and Social Welfare: Living Standards and their Distribution in the United States*. UK: Oxford.

CHAPTER 7

Deficit Financing in Developing Countries: Applications and Consequences

Preview

Budgetary deficits and adverse external payments have emerged as major public policy issues recently in developing economies. The purpose of this chapter is to discuss briefly the various aspects and forms of deficit financing to examine their range and consequences as fiscal tools. Thus, deficit finance processes raise some serious policy concerns because of their potential to inflict harm on the economy at the domestic and external levels. An examination of these concerns is among the focal points of this chapter.

History bears evidence that controlled deficit finance could be a useful tool to mobilize physical resources for economic development. Borrowings from the IMF are available to meet revenue deficits during a financial turmoil. Chronic balance of payments deficits may raise debt burden of a country requiring an international bailout.

This chapter underscores the potential dangers of reckless indulgence in deficits for any reason—internal or external—and indicates precautions to avoid the pitfalls. It puts, presumably for the first time, deficit finance for various purposes—(i) resource mobilization, (ii) crisis management, and (iii) insolvency cover—in a single framework in Islamic economics.

Z. Hasan, *Leading Issues in Islamic Economics and Finance*,
https://doi.org/10.1007/978-981-15-6515-1_7

Learning Outcomes
The contents of this chapter are expected to help the reader understand:

- The various forms of deficit financing and their implications contextual to specific situations.
- How deficit financing has been used and can be used to mobilize physical resources for economic development but with caution.
- In case of capital flight from the country during a crisis, one way is to borrow from external sources, usually the IMF. However, the measure is not an unmixed blessing.
- At times, the balances of payment deficits accumulate to unmanageable national debt making a country virtually bankrupt. The deficit problem is much bigger than in the above cases. The situation is perilous. The economy must be bailed out. The source of relief is again the IMF But conditions imposed are stringent for ensuring the eventual return of the loan granted.

7.1 Introduction

The term 'deficit financing' has wide applications even extending to TV shows. In economics, it connotes the amount by which a resource falls short of a given target; indicating most often a difference between cash inflows and outflows or the shortfall by which expenses or costs exceed income or revenues. In the context of developing countries, the term refers to government budgetary deficits. To define:

> Deficit financing is a practice in which a government spends more money than it receives as revenue the difference being made up by borrowing or minting new funds. (Britannica.com)

Having a balanced budget—equating revenues and expenditures of a government—seems an ideal fiscal policy. However, even as socio-economic dynamism may not usually allow a perfect synchronization of the two variables, there are occasions when circumstances may force governments to run into a deficit. There are others when they may find it expedient to run a deficit. This has been true with reference to both developmental effort and crisis management. The concept of deficit is not as simple as it looks. Various indicators of deficit in the budget may be noted, as delineated by Jose (2016):

- Budget deficit = total expenditure – total receipts
- Revenue deficit = revenue expenditure – revenue receipts
- Fiscal deficit = total expenditure - total receipts except borrowings
- Primary deficit = Fiscal deficit – interest payments
- Effective revenue deficit = Revenue deficit – grants for the creation of capital assets
- Monetized fiscal deficit = that part of the fiscal deficit which is covered by borrowing from the central bank.

Deficit may refer to any one or more of the above versions in a description Thus, specification is always better for clarity. Using the first concept of budget deficit may especially be deceptive. Take for instance the following case of India on budget deficit. Notice that in Fig. 7.1 both revenue receipts and budget deficits are year-on-year change expressed in percentages. Changes are larger and sharper in deficits than variations in revenue receipts deficits have a sharp overall rise; in receipts, it is mildly downwards as the two curvatures show. The sum of the two in each block is the per cent change in expenditure.

Figure 7.1 illustrates how political considerations, especially around elections force deficit financing on governments. In the current Indian budget presented on 1 February 2019 the deficit rises despite a fall in estimated revenues for providing relief to the SMEs hit by demonetization and farmers agitating for loan waivers. Budgets tend to underplay deficits creating problems.

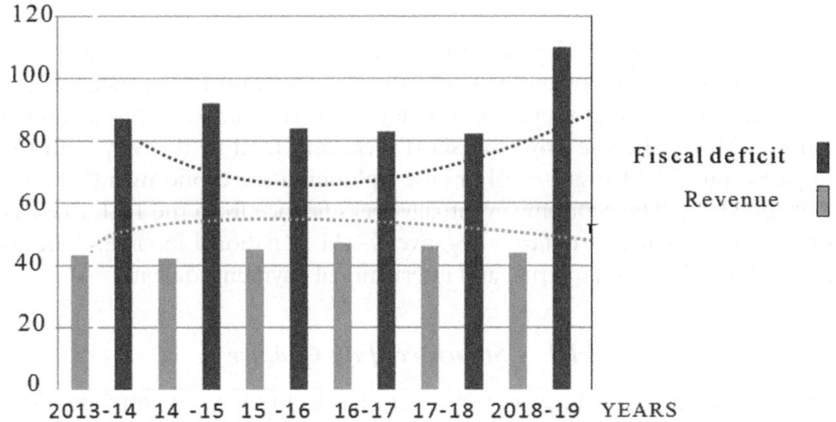

Fig. 7.1 Fiscal deficit of India from 2013–2014 to 2018–2019

A better and more revealing definition of the gap is provided by the *fiscal deficit*—total expenditure minus total receipt *excluding borrowings.* Thus, fiscal deficit represents government's loaning from the market and is the best measure of the budgetary health of a country.

The main factors that cause fiscal deficit are the negative difference between revenue receipts and public expenditure in an accounting sense. The shortfall has an external component too—the excess of goods and services imported (M) over their exports (X) usually expressed as (X − M). A negative (X − M) enhances fiscal deficit and signifies the balance of payments problem. The government can bridge the fiscal gap from three sources:

- Mobilizing domestic savings through financial instruments like bonds or saving certificates. However, as the domestic savings pool is the same for different users and is limited; if the government gets more, private enterprises will receive less. Aggregate mobilization and its impact on growth may be inconsequential.
- Printing of new currency notes is tempting and cheaper—unlike bonds no interest is payable. But its perils are no less than its attraction. It carries inflationary potential that may tend to get out of hand worsening income and wealth inequalities and depreciation of domestic currency.
- The third more commonly used source in the modern era is to borrow from abroad from friendly countries but mostly from international financial institutions, like the International Monetary Fund (IMF) as Pakistan is currently doing.

Rising corruption and governance inefficiencies tend to raise the cost of prestigious development projects over the years beyond the financial means of countries, pushing them to seek for, and encourage, external capital inflows. Much of these flows are short term and tend to fly away with the slightest signs of adversity—real or false—plunging the economy into a crisis that snowballs. The economy eventually seeks finance from the IMF to cover the yawning payments deficit—negative X − M in national income. A nexus is established between internal and international payments deficit.

7.1.1 Structure of the Chapter

This article is spread over four sections including the introduction. The following section explains how deficit financing is used as an instrument to mobilize physical resources for economic development, citing the experience of India's first two Five-Year Plans. The discussion is then raised to the global level showing that countries falling into non-manageable deficits to meet their financial obligations seek funds from the IMF as members to look back in hours of need. Here, the term 'conditionality' that has to be met for obtaining the needed assistance is explained. The nature of programmes falling under conditionality is discussed and evaluated in the light of the aid recipients' experiences. The discussion is then closed with a few concluding observations and suggestions.

7.2 Deficit Financing and Development Experience

Interestingly, deficit finance can be used, as it was, for example, in India, to mobilize resources for development during the 1950s. The financial resource estimate for the First Five-Year Plan (1951–1956) of the country from taxation and borrowings at the centre and state levels showed a substantial shortfall from the requirements to meet the planned growth targets. This brought under consideration the possible use of a third source—deficit financing. The measure was the direct addition to gross national expenditure through budget deficits on the revenue or capital account. In essence, the policy implied government spending in excess of revenues it collected from taxation, earnings of state enterprises, loans from the public, deposits and funds, and other miscellaneous sources. The government could cover the deficit either by running down its accumulated balances, or by borrowing from the banking system—mainly from the Reserve Bank of India (RBI), the central bank of the country; thus creating money as Fig. 7.2 demonstrates. Deficit finance at Rupees 2900 million provided 7.5% of overall financial outlay (14% of the public sector) for the plan over the five-year period.

To keep in check the inflationary potential of deficit financing (Sect. 7.3 of Fig. 7.2), operations like taxation and saving schemes were launched for mopping up extra money generated. Price control and rationing of essential goods were put in place. Nature was merciful with monsoon rains for three consecutive years. Crops were good thereby putting a tab on the prices of food grains and raw materials. The plan achieved its targets beyond expectations. The economy became stable and kicking.

The First Five-Year Plan was designated largely to agriculture irrigation and pre-partition projects' consolidation; the second (1956–1961) aimed at industrialization and transportation, though agriculture got

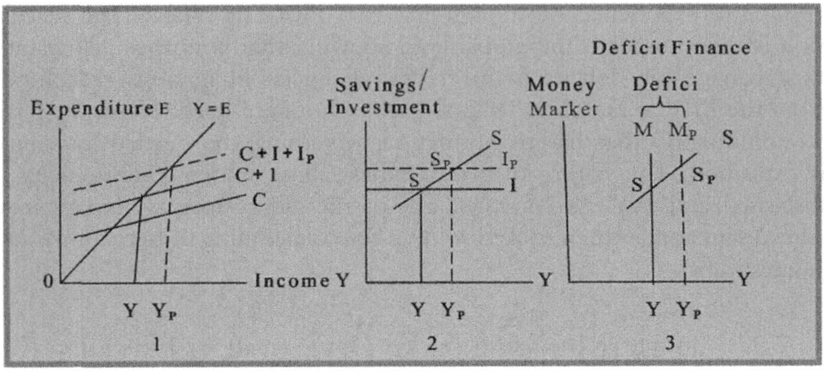

Fig. 7.2 Macroeconomic savings gap covered by deficit financing

its due share. Emphasis on expanding the public sector continued in view of the declared objective of establishing a socialistic social order. Emboldened by the success of the First Five-Year Plan, the size of the Second Five-Year Plan in outlay terms was raised to Rupees 480 billion of which no less than Rupees 120 billion or 25% was to be the deficit finance component.

The two plans raised the GDP of the country at constant prices by 42% and per capita income by 18% despite rapid increases in population. 30 years were also added to the life expectancy of an average Indian. These were laudable achievements wherein deficit financing contributed significantly as a tool for resource mobilization.

However, this merry march could not continue due to massive diversion of resources from development to defence after the 1962 Chinese attack across the North-Eastern border of the country.

7.2.1 *Deficit Finance and Inflation*

Deficit finance is a double-edged weapon that cuts both ways. If it facilitates resource mobilization, say for development, it can initiate and fuel inflation as well. Deficit finance adds to money supply and if the saleable output increases at a slower rate additional money is not fully absorbed and must result in inflationary pressures via an increase in effective demand. The situation aggravates if money adds to speculative activity. To ward off such possibilities effort is made to pull back the created money into savings through a well-managed system of price controls and rationing of wage goods. But such systems seldom remain clean; they more often than not give rise to corruption and black markets. Inflation beyond a limit alters the relative price structures to the disadvantage of weaker social groups; it perpetuates income and wealth inequalities generating social unrest. Thus, deficit finance has to be used, if at all, with utmost caution. India was lucky to contain inflation by good management and a bit of good luck during the 1950s. Things thereafter drastically changed for the worse on the price front during the Third Five-Year Plan and beyond.

7.3 Crisis Management

Microunits can and do indulge in deficit financing but it essentially is a macroeconomic phenomenon strictly falling in the fiscal policy domain. Keynes (1936) vigorously advocated using deficit financing as an anti-crisis measure when the 1930s Great Depression peaked, wage rigidity for downward adjustment becoming the obstacle in the way of remedial action.

In that crisis deficit finance was needed to revive the falling demand to cheer the gloomy markets; it was to create what Keynes termed as 'effective demand'. To this end, he advocated to employ people even to dig holes in the ground to put money in their pockets as wage and to employ them again to fill the same holes if needed. Thus, it was deficit financing mostly via printing money and was internal to governance. It was endogenous to the country's macroeconomic system.

This changed drastically in the great turmoil during the subprime crisis of 2007 unleashed across countries for years. The locus for deficit finance shifted from revival of aggregate demand to the bailout of failing giant financial institutions, notably banks, insurance companies and funds. The need was *external* to the macroeconomic systems. The economy was no longer the recipient; it was the giver to the players of the financial markets to save them from total annihilation of their own creation; of their greed and irrational exuberance. Institutions like insurance companies and funds—were running into huge deficits to meet their liabilities. This deficit was met by public funds.

A study by the Government Accountability Office (GAO) puts the 2008 financial crisis cost to the US economy at more than US$22 trillion (Melendez 2015). It further observes that the crisis was associated with not only a steep decline in output but also with the most severe economic downturn since the Great Depression of the 1930s. The Agency said the financial crisis toll on economic output may be as much as US$13 trillion—an entire year's gross domestic product of the US economy. Furthermore, paper wealth lost by US homeowners totalled US$9.1 billion while economic losses associated with increased mortgage foreclosures and higher unemployment since 2008 need to be considered as additional costs (Melendez 2015).

How the crisis affected the Islamic financial institutions is a moot point even as an IMF survey (2015) lauds Islamic banks as being 'More Resilient to Crisis'. Indeed, the literature is full of praises for Islamic finance on that count ascribing the achievement to two factors: Islamic finance maintains its links with real economic activities and is based on the principle of risk sharing. The claim of observed immunity might have elements of truth but it probably is being overstretched. It has been shown elsewhere that some Islamic banks and financial institutions did come to grief during the crisis and that the crisis overtook them indirectly through its depressing impact on macroeconomic variables—savings, investment, and output—across countries (Hasan 2016). Thus, one must take the superiority claims with a grain of salt.

7.4 Deficit Country Bailout

So far we have discussed the use of deficit finance by a country between its government and economic entities for development or for crisis management. However, a much bigger drama of deficit finance is staged between a country and the international community operating through the IMF which has been established for helping member countries out of financial deficits, if they land in, by granting loans under a programme governed by the terms contained in what is popularly known as *conditionality*. Earlier, it has been shown that the need for borrowing is linked to the rising costs of monumental projects and the ballooning funds the crisis management needs. Both costs are largely self-inflicted, natural calamities occasionally contributing.

Whatever be the reason, in essence the country is not able to escape default on its external commitments and liabilities unless helped to overcome the impasse. The last source for succour in such cases is the IMF. The help seekers are usually the developing countries while the funds the IMF provides to bridge the deficit come from the developed countries, the institution acting as their collective *mahajan*. IMF bailout loans are no charity; they are to be reimbursed in the common pool so that others in need could be helped.

The conditions IMF imposes are tight. So tight at times that they may make the patient bleed white. The IMF Greece bailout is a case in point. The pending case is of Pakistan who has approached the Fund for help under compelling economic circumstance. The country is neck-deep in foreign debt substantially related to China Pakistan Economic Corridor (CPEC) involving US$60 billion of Chinese investment. Political economy seems clouding the matter. The IMF has asked Pakistan to be transparent in revealing the details of the Chinese (and other) debt before Pakistan's application to bridge the deficit could be considered to which the country has agreed. Interestingly, China insists that the term of their debt to Pakistan must be fairly evaluated. Politics apart, let us have a brief look at the manner the IMF conducts its bailout business and what repercussions it has on the borrowing nation, if experience is a guide.

7.4.1 The IMF Conditionality

When a country approaches the IMF for help, its government agrees to adjust its economic policies to overcome the problems that led it to seek financial assistance from the international community. The terms on which the IMF agrees to financially help a country in trouble are collectively called the IMF conditionality.

The IMF conditionality broadly consists of two parts: (i) the design of its support programmes and (ii) the tools for monitoring the progress of programme implementation. In principle, the programmes are designed in consultation with the country seeking help. They essentially aim at resolving the balance of payment deficit problems of the country avoiding measures harmful to national or international prosperity. The monitoring measures at the same time oversee that the resources the IMF commits to help the country remain safe. The essence of conditionality is to help resolve the country's problems such that it is in a position to repay the IMF loan.

To reiterate, the member country seeking help has primary responsibility for selecting, designing, and implementing the policies that will make the IMF-supported programme successful. The programme is described in a letter of intent (which often has a memorandum of economic and financial policies attached to it). The programme's objectives and policies depend on the country's circumstances. But the overarching goal is always to restore and maintain the balance of payments' viability and macroeconomic stability while setting the stage for sustained, high-quality growth and, in low-income countries, for reducing poverty.

For ensuring progress in programme implementation and to mitigate risk to the IMF' provided resources, the loan granted is released in instalments linked to demonstrable policy pursuit. The progress is reported to the IMF Executive Board for review to see if the programme is on course or modifications are needed for achieving the prescribed objectives. The review approvals are based on various policy commitments agreed with the country authorities.

7.4.2 Programme Evaluation

A typical IMF programme focuses on correcting the balance of payment problems of a country seeking a bailout. Its main components are devaluation of domestic currency, liberalization of trade, and expansion of the private sector. The three elements are assumed as mutually compatible and each supportive of others.

Currencies of developing countries are mostly over-valued relative to the IMF based parities. The depreciating currencies of help-seeking countries bear testimony to this statement. The assumptions supportive of devaluation are that the act would make domestic goods cheaper for the foreigners boosting exports, and imports costlier reducing their inflows. This combined with liberal trade policy would help correct the adverse balance of payments the borrowing countries suffer from. Since public enterprises lack motivation, are prone to corruption and slow to act, encouragement to privatization of the economy may be an added advantage for programme implementation. The question is how valid are these assumptions?

The catch in this argumentation is that it ignores the issue of export and import elasticity. Most developing economies are exporters of primary products where price elasticity is generally less than one. To get the same revenue as before, the country must export more in physical terms than before. This apart, would they always have an exportable surplus ready at hand? Imports of these countries are even less price elastic. They import food grains to feed the teaming millions, machinery and spares for their upcoming industries and technical knowhow. They cannot cut down much on such survival needs. Devaluation for them, ipso facto means—continue imports at the same, even increased, level and pay more. Debt servicing also becomes costlier. Corruption is not the monopoly of the public sector. The private sector across the globe is showing itself no less corrupt, if not more; what caused the 2007 sub-prime debacle and what followed in its wake is evidence. Thus, the IMF bailout programmes may not always or entirely prove conducive or helpful to the seekers.

In the year 1966, the currencies of 34 countries, mostly developing, went down on their knees under the IMF programmes. The Indian rupee was one of them; 35% being the devaluation. The University Grants Commission (UGC) the same year organized, probably under government instructions, a seminar at Meerut entitled 'Foreign Aid in our Plans'. One of the specified topics was devaluation and foreign aid. The above arguments were then outlined by the author in his paper on the topic. Later developments vindicated the position taken. Foodgrains imports created payment problems as the Americans expressed their inability to export wheat to India and the USSR had to help the country out of the predicament with a wheat loan.

The episode also brought to the fore another danger of the devaluation-led bailout. Many developing countries start manufacturing products such as automobiles having a certain percentage of imported components. This percentage is gradually substituted with local makes until one looks back with satisfaction that a tiny fraction of the product is now imported. Many such industries find them at the sea, as India experienced, if that crucial fraction becomes unavailable due to the IMF programme or its cost becomes prohibitive due to devaluation. Billions worth of plant investment stands still, rather hostage to foreign dictates.

More recent is the story of two countries dealing with the financial crisis of 1997–1998—instructive and interesting. It was the massive short-term Western capital flights from South East Asia that had then hit the flourishing economies of the region. Originating from Thailand, the contagion spread fast to other nations including Malaysia even as her economic fundamentals—contrary to the IMF assessment—were sound. Anyway, Thailand sought relief from the IMF while Malaysia eventually took a different route—it resorted to the imposition of exchange controls (Hasan 2002, 2003).

In a small open economy like Malaysia, the flight of short-term capital during the 1997–1998 crisis led to a sequence of events involving the selling of shares by foreigners in the stock market and taking the sale proceeds to the currency market for buying US dollars to be taken out, the process leading to a downturn in both the markets as Fig. 7.3 demonstrates.

The run on the Ringgit, the Malaysian currency, led to a rapid depreciation (35%) in its value vis-à-vis the US dollar in months. Action had to be taken to stem the rot. For some time the country experimented with raising the interest rates to arrest capital flight but it did not work. Eventually, Mahathir Muhammad, the astute Prime Minister of Malaysia who knew that there was nothing wrong with the country's economy, took the monumental decision to impose exchange controls rather than go to the IMF for a bailout, despite internal dissensions.

The exchange rate was stabilized at RM3.8 to US$1. The events unfolding in subsequent months vindicated the validity of his decision.

Malaysia came out of the turmoil unscathed and faster than others in the region. The Economic and Social Survey of Asia and the Pacific of the UN (2011) declared: '*The experience of Malaysia suggests that capital controls can help stabilize an otherwise difficult situation*'. The IMF now envisages imposing fewer conditions on loans granted to developing countries so that they may have greater freedom to design their recovery plans in the future. The IMF made this announcement later in March 2013.

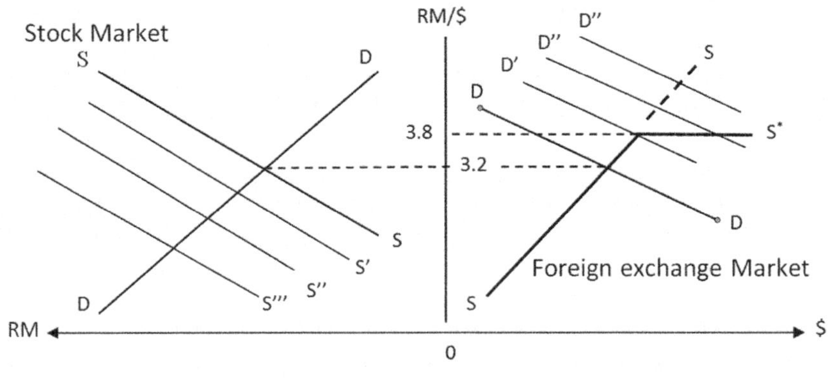

Fig. 7.3 Stock and foreign exchange markets interaction in Malaysia, 1997–1998

In contrast, after paying the last instalment of the IMF loan in 2013 the Thailand Prime Minister vowed to never seek IMF bailout in future. The lament of the prime minister was not without reason. The IMF conditionality framework has some inbuilt difficulties for the borrowers. The important ones are as follows.

- Reduce borrowing, increase taxes, and cut expenditure.
- Raise interest rate to stabilize the currency.
- Let failing firms liquidate.
- Initiate structural changes including increased privatization, deregulation and reduction in corruption as well as in official delays in decision-making.

The difficulty is that these conditions not only betray an ideological bias, the insistence on structural adjustment and the macroeconomic interventions they require often make the situation worse, not better, for the recipient country. This was the experience not only of Thailand but also of Indonesia and other aid receivers during the 1997/1998 crisis. As a result of enforcing tight monetary regimes pursuant to the IMF conditions purportedly meant to reduce budget deficit and stabilize currency, problems aggravated. Contrary to their objectives the enforcement tended to slow down growth and spread unemployment in the aided countries. What happened on the exchange rate front? Even as the IMF aid programmes' conditions have not understandably remained unchanged over time and space the departure in the case of Kenya concerning the rate of exchange during the 1990s is of interest. The IMF made the central bank of the country remove all restrictions to allow a free flow of capital in or out of the country. The critics validly argue that the decision went against the country as it allowed the politicians to take their ill-gotten money out of the country.

7.4.3 Demonstration Effect and Arms Race

The vital question is: why do developing economies fall into external debt traps? Some reasons are obvious. There is a demonstration effect. Expanding means of transportation and communication, especially internet resources and global advertising, have really converted the planet earth into a global village. The living standards and material affluence of the West coming into observation of people and leaders in developing

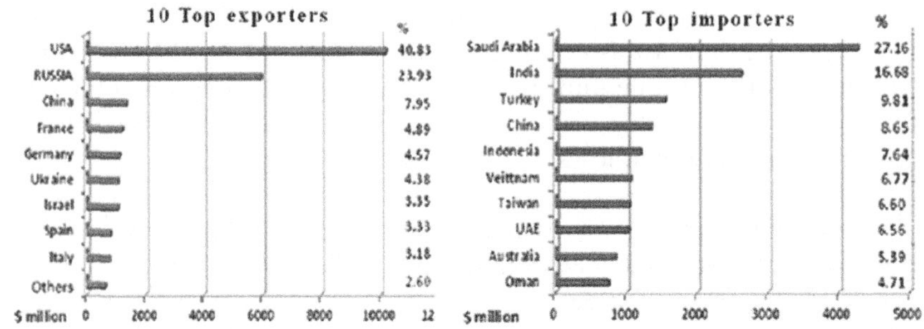

Fig. 7.4 Leading exporters and importers of arms in 2015

economies awaken in them the urge to copy. In their eagerness to imitate, the society is more and more divided into haves and have-nots. A sizeable and expanding upper class is created through corrupt and exploitative practices to finance lavish living. Foreign loans taken in the name of development projects in part land in Swiss or Panama accounts of leaders and the affluent. Can this all be stopped so that money is spent where it is meant to be spent? Imran Khan the new Prime Minister of Pakistan is trying to do it for building a Muslim country of his vision. Either he will soon give up or will achieve a miracle over time.

There is a wider and more sinister angle to the developed and developing economies divide in the world—the bloody wars—there is a chain from Vietnam to Afghanistan.

Flourishing economies have been destroyed on the whims and imaginary fears of the powerful to attain more power. The arms trade is the most lucrative of all businesses; it values profit, not blood. A mere look at Fig. 7.4 will make one understand the economics of war vis-à-vis peace.

Modern warfare is also a major contributor to international pollution. As per estimates released by the Council on Foreign Relations (CFR), in 2016 alone the US administration rained at least 26,171 bombs on seven different countries, averaging three an hour every day, every month, over the year. The figures, says the report, are relatively conservative, meaning the number of bombs dropped in 2016 could have been much higher. The report concludes that there was no legal validity for this action save stretching the interpretation of an old authorization for the

7.5 Concluding Remarks

Ann Pettifor in a brilliant article (2019) projects her views on deficit financing in a Keynesian/monetarist framework. However, her writeup does not cover the various aspects of deficit financing relevant to *developing* economies characterized with the imperfections of markets, especially financial. Her theoretical prescriptions are not being applied or delivering even in the developed mature economies of the West, their relevance to emerging economies is all the more limited. In the present paper, we have argued that a full scale and focused discussion on deficit financing *contextual* to developing economies must cover as discussed above the following three areas:

- Growth fueled inflationary potential could be kept under control.
- Use of deficit financing to fight recession in the Keynesian vein where rigidity of wages to downward adjustment and fear psychosis of entrepreneurs is the hindrance.

IMF bailouts: The country is heavily indebted to outsiders, its balance of payments position is precarious and no internal solution is available as is presently the case of Pakistan. In such situations, the country seeks succour from outside, especially through the borrowings from the IMF and what it brings in its train.

In the first two cases the solution via deficit financing is internal to the domestic economic system; in the last it is external.

Islamic economists naturally want to look at modern developments from an Islamic perspective. Deficit financing is no exception. Thus, Ahmad (2019, 79) argues that from a religious viewpoint deficit financing must be avoided both in the normal functioning of the government and during recessions. In either case, he advocates reliance on Zakah payments and taxation to meet current expenditure deficiencies and on *sukuk*—the Islamic bonds—to cover capital shortfalls. He does not touch upon the adequacy or operability of either measure in relation to the current economic realities that obtain in most Muslim countries especially in Indonesia, Pakistan, and Bangladesh due to meagre savings; deficit could arise despite Zakah and *sukuk* may not fill the bill due to insufficiency of savings. What looks possible may not be feasible. The Qur'ān in Surah Yusuf (12:43–48) calls for saving of the current surplus crop to fallback to meet the deficit as forecast for the years ahead. Beyond this there is nothing in our knowledge that can be related to current practice of deficit financing. There is a need to impart realism in the interpretation and application of the *Shari'ah* law (Hamoudi 2007). We may accept the benefits of deficit financing and guard against its ills until it is convincingly shown going against the Islamic law or custom, in the same way as we have accepted not a few things in Islamic finance and insurance avoiding interest, indeterminacy, and speculation. Foreign currency though money can be bought and sold as a different commodity presumably treating interest as a markup or rental?

Case Study: IMF Bailout

Between the Sea and the Mountain

Pakistan climbs up signing the Staff-Level Agreement on Economic Policies with the IMF for a Three-Year Extended Fund Facility

Current Account deficit in Pakistan averaged $721.14 million a year from 1976 to 2019 resulting in its external debt accumulation of around 32–33 billion US dollars. Rising inflation and sagging growth further complicated the economic situation. The Imran Khan government that came to power in 2018 tried to pre-empt the impending economic catastrophe through borrowing from some friendly countries. However, Pakistan could muster no more than $9.1billion from that source for the fiscal 2018–2019. The amount fell far short of her immediate requirement. Perforce, the country had to seek succour from the IMF that it initially wanted to avoid. After months of informal talks, an IMF team, at last, landed in Pakistan on Monday, 30 April 2019, to hold *technical* discussions for a bailout package, the 14th Pakistan was seeking during the past 30 years to sail out of severe domestic and external imbalances gripping the economy.

The negotiations with the IMF took a tortuous course because Western countries that financed the IMF loans were susceptible of a sizeable portion of the Chinese debt in Pakistan's external liabilities largely related to investments in the China Pakistan Economic Corridor (CPEC). They feared a diversion of the IMF support funds to pay off the Chinese. Thus, the Fund asked Pakistan to reveal the details of the Chinese debt related to the project before the country's bailout application could be considered. China insisted that the terms of their debt to Pakistan must be fairly evaluated.

Eventually, these problems have been sorted out in negotiations going on since October 2018 and Pakistan is reported to have reached May 12, 2019 a Staff-Level Agreement on Economic Policies with the IMF for a Three-Year Extended Fund Facility to receive $6 billion over the period subject to ratification by the Board of its Directors. The amount is $2 billion short of what the country had asked for as it still owes $5.8 billion from the past bailouts. The main provisions of the settlement are reportedly as follows:

- The Extended Fund Facility arrangement aims to support the authorities' strategy for stronger and more inclusive growth by reducing domestic and external imbalances, removing impediments to growth, increasing transparency including on terror funding, and strengthening societal spending.
- An ambitious structural reform agenda to supplement economic policies to rekindle economic growth and improve living standards.
- Financing support from Pakistan's international partners to critically help the authorities' adjustment efforts and ensure that the medium-term programme objectives would be achieved.

This all looks cozy on the surface but the ideological system that underlines these mutually agreed programmes mostly operates in conflict with the recipient countries' socio-economic interests and existing environs. They must adhere to the financial openness, trade liberalization, and privatization—the ideological pillars of the West. Their adoption will need cutting expenditure on social welfare schemes like health, education and insurance, minimum wages, crop support, oil subsidies, and rationing all woven into the social existence fabric of developing economies.

Source *Journal of Islamic Banking and Finance*, Karachi (April–June 2019).

Test Questions

Q.1 Define deficit financing giving its various forms. Examine the various uses of deficit finance and what are their likely consequences?

Q.2 State the most commonly used version of deficit financing. Explain the efficacy of different sources to meet the deficit.

Q.3 What is devaluation of currency? How does it differ from currency depreciation? Explain when can devaluation succeed in correcting an adverse balance of payments.

Q.4 'IMF loaning conditions are too stringent for the help seekers'. Do you agree? Argue your case.

Q.5 Write notes on

i. Fiscal deficit
ii. Balance of payments
iii. IMF conditionality

What Next?

We have mentioned the use of printing new currency for deficit financing here. In the next chapter we discuss about money in some detail—its origin, evolution forms, and functions and also policies regarding its management in a market economy.

References

Ahmad, H. (2019, January). Fiscal Policy and Deficit Financing: Islamic Perspectives. *Journal of King Abdul Aziz University, Islamic Economics, 32*(1), 79–86.

Hasan, Z. (2002, March). The 1997–98 Financial Crisis in Malaysia: Causes, Response, and Results. *Islamic Economic Studies, 9*(2).

Hasan, Z. (2003, March). The 1997–98 Financial Crisis in Malaysia: Causes, Response, and Results—Rejoinder. *Islamic Economic Studies, 10*(2).

Hasan, Z. (2016). Risk Sharing: The Sole Basis of Islamic Finance? Time for a Serious Rethink. *KAU Journal: Islamic Economics, 19*(2), 30–31, Section 5.

Hamoudi, H. A. (2007). Jurisprudential Schizophrenia: On Form and Function in Islamic finance. *Chicago Journal of International Law.*

Jose, T. (2016). *What is Deficit Financing? What Are the Different Types of Deficit in the Budget?* https://www.indianeconomy.net/splclassroom/what-is-deficit-financing-what-are-the-different-types-of-deficits-in-the-budget/.

Keynes, J. M. (1936). *The General Theory of Employment, Interest and Money.* UK: Cambridge University Press.

IMF Survey. (2015). https://www.imf.org/en/News/Articles/2015/09/28/04/53/sores100410a I. On line.

Melendez, E. D. (2015). *On Governmental Wealth Cost of Crisis Huff Post US.* https://www.huffingtonpost.in/entry/financial-crisis-cost-ao_n_2687553.

Pettifor. (2019). *How to Transform an Economic System That Has Driven Us to Disaster* (A Green New Deal Report). https://www.annpettifor.com/2019/09/how-to-transform-an-economic-system-that-has-driven-us-to-disaster/.

UN. (2011). *The Economic and Social Survey of Asia and the Pacific, UN Library.* https://www.un-ilibrary.org/economic-and-social-development/economic-and-social-survey-of-asia-and-the-pacific-2001_1c046692-en.

CHAPTER 8

Money: Evolution, Forms, and Expansion

Preview

This chapter deals with familiar facts in the evolution of money, with some unfamiliar conclusions. It argues that it is not factual to regard legal tender money and bank credit as being of different genus: they work in tandem to the same ends in an economy, conventional or Islamic. Also, it does not matter what serves as money—solid gold, flimsy paper, or just a notion like bitcoin—in the context of keeping its value stable. Only the blind would argue that a staff is indispensable for walking. Money is just an instrument; it was never, nor can it ever be, classified into Islamic and non-Islamic. What it does, good or bad, depends on how we use it. Money does not generate crises; its mismanagement does. It follows that the refuge the world is searching for today from recurring financial crises does not lie in money substance. History testifies that national economies could not remain turmoil-free during the centuries the yellow metal held sway over the monetary scene. The chapter concludes that it is the human factor that has been the source of good or evil for mankind in every walk of life, including in money matters. And only true religion can improve the quality of the human factor: rationality without the guidance of faith is a rudderless ship wandering on high seas. The chapter closes by talking briefly about crypto money: its nature, *modus operandi*, benefits, and dangers.

Z. Hasan, *Leading Issues in Islamic Economics and Finance*,
https://doi.org/10.1007/978-981-15-6515-1_8

Learning Outcomes
The study of this chapter is expected to enable readers:

- To understand how various commodities evolved to serve as money over time and space as an artificial social convention.
- To know why the state had to intervene in the evolutionary process of money and to what effect.
- To explain what brought paper money onto the scene and gave rise to central banks as regulators of money supply in society.
- To learn about the value of money its measurement and the importance of the stability in its value.
- To appreciate the role of a central bank in ensuring stability in the internal and external value of money and the efficacy of methods to achieve stability.
- To understand the role of commercial banks in financing trade, industry, and commerce through creating credit money and the need to keep a tab on the credit creation power of banks.
- To see the linkage between monetary and fiscal policies of the government and the possible consequences of their interface.

8.1 Introduction

At the dawn of societal living, economies were run by a system known as barter: a person exchanged whatever good or service he had with the goods or services others produced or possessed. Barter required a *double coincidence of wants*—B should not only have what A wanted but must also be in need of what A could offer in exchange. This was restrictive of transactions that could be made, consumed more time, and curtailed specialization. The frustrations barter imposed upon human ambitions led people to sense money. One can define money by what it does, i.e. by its *functions* or by identifying the *substance* that performed those functions. The temporal uniformity of money concept lies in the functional approach to its definition, because the substance that performed those functions over time and space is a welter of things, approaching infinity. But herein we find the romance of money. From hides and skins via cowrie shells, salt, spices, and precious metals, to promises to pay working as money, the story of money has been a fascinating journey of human ingenuity.

The functional approach to the definition of money sees its significance in serving as a medium of exchange, as a measure of value and its possible storing. Money also works as a unit of account. In essence, these functions help tear apart the two sides of the barter coin—sale and purchase. We can sell what we have for money, keep that money with us, and buy at will what and when we may want.. The eventual exchange is between real goods and services at both ends; money working just as a go-between. If paper, plastic, or book entry can perform the functions of money efficiently, why use more useful things as money. For, if roads could be built in the air, will that not release land for growing more food? Money derives its significance from its ***general acceptability***, and that acceptability stems from its value remaining reasonably stable, not from the value of what it is made of. We do not print cinema tickets on chocolate so that people can eat them in case they miss, or decide not to go for the movie.

Why then are there suggestions today for a return to gold as the fulcrum for restructuring the international monetary system?[1] To me, psychology, haplessness, loss of direction, and presumably some vested interests are among the major factors. The search for an answer takes us back to the history of the evolution of money. This we see in the following Sect. 8.2. In Sect. 8.3, we shall argue that it is not the monetary system failure, but the demise of human integrity that has so often pushed the world to the brink of disaster. In Sect. 8.4, we summarize the argument and present a few monetary policy prescriptions.

8.2 Evolution of Money

8.2.1 A Social Convention

Money was not invented; it evolved as a social convention and took numerous forms over time and space. This lent precedence to money substance over its function in discussions on the subject. The importance of what works as money was reinforced by the fact that in the process of measuring the value (price) of other goods and services, money assumed a value for itself that fluctuated inversely with variations in the general

[1] The suggestion, that surprised many, came from a person of no less stature than World Bank governor Bob Zeollick (in December 2010). Interestingly, it gave a boost to the clamour for a return to gold dinars and several articles on the subject made their appearance on the heels of Zeollick's statement, including by Kazmi (2010), KFH Research (2011), and Zein (2010).

price levels over time. In that, money was a different sort of measure compared to others that we used in our daily lives. The value of money—even when made of, or linked to, something having value in use such as gold or silver—would fluctuate inversely with those of other goods and services. The stability in the internal value of money thus required the controlling of fluctuations in the domestic price level. Also, what worked as money in various countries was not identical. This gave rise to issues relating to the termination of the values of different monies in terms of each other, or foreign exchange rates, for promoting internation trade.

The rising tide of international trade with the passage of time demanded something tangible that could help domestic monies enable their mutual convertibility. This need added to the significance of substance for the role money played in an economy. Bronze and copper were the first to be converted into coins, but it did not take much for gold and silver to replace them. Gold and silver coins were made in Lydian (modern Turkey) as early as around 560 BC and could well be regarded as the earliest forms of metallic coins.

However, these coins were too soft to withstand the wear and tear during circulation or to resist dishonest clippings, resulting in their weight falling below the initial measure. Gold and silver had to be mixed with alloy to make coins adequately hard. This demanded standardization of the alloy proportion in the coins to ensure their authenticity and uniformity in terms of their precious metal content. The work was done by informal private agencies for most of the 2500 years of sway the metals, yellow especially, had over monetary matters across the world. Touchstones were used to verify the purity of coins in terms of their fineness. The convention continued even beyond the publication of Smith's *Wealth of Nations* in 1776. Indeed, the author was much impressed by the spontaneous evolution of such beneficent social institutions as money, division of labour, and capital accumulation that played such a vital role in promoting growth in the *wealth of nations*.[2] Note that the gold standard in England was established by an Act of Parliament only in 1860 and in the United States much later, in 1900.

[2] See Gide and Rist (1953) for an excellent analysis of this influence under the subtitle: *The naturalism and optimism of Smith*, pp. 85–109. One would not, presumably, come across such a detailed and graphic description of the subject in other books on the history of economic thought.

8.2.2 *The State Entry*

In the private manufacture of coins, the standardization process required that gold be pre-alloyed and coins were weighted before they went into circulation. As long as people knew the manufacturer and had trust in him, no touchstones were needed. At the time when Islam made its appearance on the scene, the gold coins in circulation were made in Rome (not of Italy) and carried the stamp of pagan idols. The fact that the Prophet (Peace be upon him) allowed their remaining in circulation implies that the faith did not divide money into Islamic and non-Islamic. However, to continue with the thread, the governments soon began stamping the coins with an emblem to strengthen the process of standardization.

The emblem was a guarantee of the weight of the coin, its degree of purity, and its value. The facility gave people the satisfaction of carrying value *within* their money, but it could not prevent the loss of precious metal in the circulation process and more than that, through the clipping of coins for recycling. Carrying money in pockets and over space involved both cost and risk. Governments of all shades soon discovered that coins derived their value essentially from the emblem; rulers often debased the coins to lower their precious metal content. To that extent, coins became no better than notes printed on metal. This led Gresham to postulate during the Victorian era that bad (debased) money drove good (full-bodied) money out of circulation.[3] Finally, the joint circulation of coins made of gold, silver, and copper in many places, especially in Europe, led merchants to place a premium on gold and distort the relative price of the metal.

[3]Could that be the reason for the *Qur'an* to condemn the hoarding of gold and silver (9:34–35)? Some claim gold and silver are Islamic money and their hoarding will reduce the quantity of money in circulation, to the disadvantage of the economy. Thus the condemnation of the hoarding of these metals. I have a different interpretation. The reference in the two verses is explicitly to the stock of metals for which *zakah* has not been paid. Even after *zakah* has been paid, it may not be desirable to retain money just for the sake of the pleasure of seeing and touching it at will. However, this may not be punishable in the way the verses state.

8.3 From Metal to Paper

To overcome the above-mentioned difficulties of commodity money—the coins—banks began to issue paper receipts to depositors stating that the receipt was redeemable for the precious metals stored with them. Soon the receipts started circulating as money because everyone began taking them to be as good as gold. They were representative of the yellow metal. The suggestion of enforcing a 100% reserve requirement today, especially in Islamic economics, derives its inspiration from the policy of that era. But much water has since flowed into the oceans around the World.

It soon became apparent that spending money and toil on digging the glittering metal out from the bowels of the earth, only to lock it back into the dark vaults of banks as currency reserves, was an avoidable folly. To the relief of pretty ladies everywhere, representative money proved just a small step in ushering in the practice of banking based on a fractional reserve system. Banks were soon printing receipts above and beyond the amount of yellow metal deposited with them. It benefited traders and enriched the bankers. Paper notes appeared in China as early as AD 806—soon after the advent of Islam—and dominated the scene until the middle of the fifteenth century. China stopped using paper notes in 1455 because their overproduction led to high inflation. But the fractional reserve system being an easy and effortless way for self-enrichment, the banks could not curb the temptation to overissue notes.

Intermittent bouts of inflation became rampant across the world. If the linkage of money to gold at its zenith could not stop the emergence of that malady, on what basis can the advocates for its revival convince one that the resuscitation of gold can ensure it today? Inflation could not, as it cannot, sustain itself for long because it carries *within* its folds the weapons for its own demise. Eventually, it must turn tail upward and nosedive. The slump that the bursting of the bubble generates is found to be much more problematic and damaging. We shall return to the issue in some detail later. Presently, we turn to the two interesting developments in monetary history that the non-sustainability of inflation triggered.

The first was the emergence of the state as a monopolist for the conversion of gold into coins, and of coins into gold, at the official mint. Initially, this service to people was rendered free of cost but later on, a small fraction of the gold (or silver) brought to the official mint for coinage was taken out to cover manufacturing costs. The deduction was known as the *seignorage*—the right of the king/lord over the possessions of the commoners. Thus, free coinage did not mean free of cost. It meant that people were free to bring the indicated precious metals—gold or silver—for conversion into coins at the mint.[4] The main reason for acquiring a monopoly power over coin-making was its profit-churning potential. The need to keep a tab on money supply to curb inflation and keep it commensurate with the overall needs of the economy was of smaller significance. Thus, money creation could not be left entirely to private discretion. And this brings us to the second major development in monetary history.

Expanding international trade and the resultant complexity of foreign exchange issues added further to growing governmental interest in monetary affairs. Even as the authorities were attracted to money creation for a variety of reasons, especially the profit it was sure to bring in, they did not consider it expedient to put their fingers into the business directly; they chose to raise a facade—the central bank.

8.4 The Rise of Central Banks

The process of the government taking over the creation of money proceeded at a slow pace. First to come in were the regulations limiting the credit creation power of banks. Banks had to cope with organizational restrictions including the continuation of the partners' liability as unlimited for far longer than in other businesses. But at the same time, the risks bankers took were sought to be reduced through severe penal provisions, including even capital punishment for defaulters in some places. Recall the sixteenth-century drama, *The Merchant of Venice* by William Shakespeare.

[4]Coins were divided into two types: standard and token. The standard coin was full-bodied money. Its face value and intrinsic value (the pure gold content at market price) were the same. It was the unit of account, unlimited legal tender, and a standard for deferred payments. Minting was free only for standard coins. Token coins were multiples of standard coin and their face value was more than their intrinsic value. Token coins were legal tender only up to a limit, after which one could refuse to accept them in receiving payments or discharging debts. Token coins were made of base metals like copper and did not enjoy the facility of free coinage.

Table 8.1 Growth of central banks over time

Year	*1950*	*1990*	*2000*
Number of central banks	20	59	161

But governmental objectives for intervention as stated above were different. Bank failures during the second half of the nineteenth century created the opportunity for intervention and a large number of banks collapsing like a house of cards during the interwar period only helped hasten the process. Central banks came into existence as a response to the inability of banks themselves to cope with panic (Goodhart 2010). The process took the semblance of a natural evolution as initially some private banks were asked to operate as government banks (Gorton and Hung 2001).[5] These authors provide some interesting information on the rising number of central banks over time. This we reproduce in Table 8.1. Many of them were allowed to take up the 'Lender of last resort' function much later.

8.4.1 Central Banks and Economic Stability

The declared objective of establishing a central bank in a country was to have an institution devoted to keeping the value of its currency stable, both internally and externally. For performing this function, central banks were given several privileges: *inter alia*, they were to serve as bankers to the government, were given the sole right to issue currency notes, had to adopt measures to control the creation of credit by commercial banks, and had to operate for them as the lender of last resort. Central banks could not compete with ordinary commercial banks for business in the market. They had to guide and help the latter with a view towards achieving stability in the value of money. Since coins of gold were already in circulation in many countries, central banks were to streamline the system for the issuance of currency as linked to the yellow metal. The rules for such streamlining were embodied in what came to

[5] Prior to the establishment of the Reserve Bank of India, the Imperial Bank was entrusted to work for the government. Later it was converted into the State Bank of India and then nationalized. Even today in some matters, it works as an agent of the RBI where the latter has no branches of its own. The State Bank of Pakistan is an offshoot of the same development.

Table 8.2 Exchange rates 1US$ value in German Marks

January 1918	5.21	March 1923	21,190.00
January 1919	8.20	April 1923	24,475.00
January 1920	64.80	May 1923	47,670.00
January 1921	64.91	June 1923	109,966.00
January 1922	191.81	July 1923	353,412.00
April 1922	291.00	August 1923	4,620,455.00
July 1922	493.22	September 1923	98,860,000.00
October 1922	3180.96	October 1923	25.260,000,000.00
January 1923	17,972.00	November 1923	2.193,600,000,000.00
February 1923	27,918	December 1923	4,200,000,000,000.00

Source Ask.com//School History—The rise of Hitler. 10.1.2011

$$\text{For country B}: \frac{10x\frac{9}{10}}{3.2727273x\frac{11}{12}} = 3 \text{ units of its currencyfor one unit ofA}$$

Fig. 8.1 Determination of relative exchange rates

be known as the gold standard, described below. Table 8.2 shows how currency exchange rates were determined with reference to their pure gold contents (Fig. 8.1).

Monetary authorities had to keep the price of gold stable in the country to invoke public confidence. To that end, the central bank had—as a first step—to buy and sell gold at a fixed price. This was the essence of what was called in the literature as the *domestic* gold standard. But the gold standard as described above did not in fact ensure price stability. For the gold standard did not stabilize price levels, it merely stabilized the relationship between the volume of gold and the volume of currency. Even if the price of gold remained unchanged, fluctuations in the *volume* of gold made the *volume* of currency vary, forcing variations in the general price level. Thus, instead of stabilizing, the domestic gold standard forced prices to fluctuate.[6] It failed to curb inflation or to prevent

[6]A reduction in the volume of *currency* may cause a reduction in the quantity of money or it may not. The two can, on occasion, run divergent courses. See Crowther (1948, p. 297) where he also mentions several historical examples of such diversions with reasons.

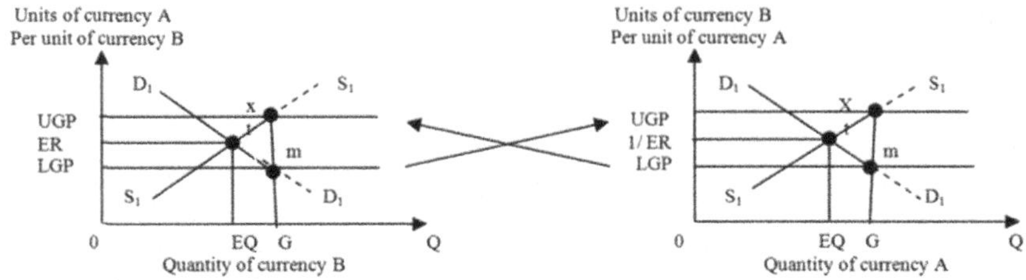

Fig. 8.2 The gold standard mechanism

depression. The domestic gold standard was part of the evolution of money—not the result of the invention—and its extension to external transactions was part of the same process.

For example, when gold coins constituted most of the money supply in two countries there was little room for variations in their exchange rate. So long as the two currencies A and B were freely convertible into gold at fixed prices, their rate of exchange could not vary from their *mint parity* by more than a small margin within what were called the *gold points.* Any demand for foreign currencies that could not be met in the foreign exchange market at a rate within, say, 0.5% on either side of the *mint par* was shunted out to the gold market. Thus, the demand for any currency in the foreign exchange market always equalled its supply. The gap was covered by the gold movement between the two countries. Figure 8.2 explains the automatic nature of the balancing mechanism between the two countries.

If the demand for currency B begins rising relative to its supply in country A—the balance of payments moves against A—the exchange rate in its market will start rising.[7] However, it cannot cross UGP[8] as it will become cheaper for importers to buy gold in the market and export it to country B. D_1 will cease shifting upward; excess of demand will move out from the currency market to that of gold, allowing only a tiny (tx) departure from ER. In contrast, if the balance of payments becomes

[7] For a real world illustration, see Halm (1965, pp. 176–177). He explains how the exchange rate between the US dollar and the pound sterling was settled when both countries were on the gold standard during the interwar period.

[8] It may be noted, as shown in Figure 7.2, that the gold export point of one country becomes the gold import point of the other country, and vice versa.

increasingly favourable to country A, raising the supply of currency B relative to its demand in her exchange market, ER will start falling; currency A will become more expensive in country B.

But the process cannot go on unabated. As soon as the rate crosses the upper gold point that would be the same as LGP in A—again a small divergence (tm) from ER—the importers in country B will find it cheaper to ship gold to country A, rather than buy currency in the exchange market. Under the gold standard, no country can stop either the export of gold or its import. The gold standard works on the assumption that at gold points, the demand or supply of the metal is kept perfectly elastic. The assumption holds only if countries, or some international authority, are willing to buy and sell gold at a fixed price.

The stability of exchange rates is desirable, rather necessary, in the present era of globalization to promote free trade and liberalization, but only the naïve or those with vested interests will insist on a return to gold. Let us explain very briefly the reasons why such a return is neither desirable nor practicable. The issue of internal stability, we have already touched upon. Under the strict rules of the game, it is realistic to assume that the central bank of country A just keeps the obligatory amount of gold in reserve, say, worth 40% of notes in circulation, to ensure their convertibility. Suppose now that there is an inflow of gold worth $1 million. This moves into the reserves of the central bank. If it does not, as it cannot, build a buffer stock of gold, it must put additional notes worth $2.5 million in circulation. And if the banking system is to maintain a 10% reserve for credit creation, the economy would become awash with a monetary expansion of $25 million. This multiple expansion of money supply may impose inflationary pressures on an otherwise stable economy. We may work out the deflationary potential of gold outflow of a similar magnitude. In fact, gold standard inherently carries a deflationary bias; a country losing gold must contract credit, but one receiving it is under no compulsion to expand credit.

The gold standard can work smoothly if prices—wages in particular—are reasonably flexible, there are no structural rigidities in the economy, and public authorities are willing to surrender their discretion and independence to the automatic requirements of the gold standard mechanism. The suspension of the gold standard under adverse circumstances in the past was proof of the unwillingness of policymakers to accept such surrender.[9]

This unwillingness has only become stronger with the passage of time. This stubbornness was one of the reasons why the original designers of the International Monetary Fund (IMF) scheme rejected a return to the gold standard, so as to impart a measure of flexibility in the arrangement. The amendments of 1978 in the rules of the institution ended the gold–money link for good. Until the beginning of the last century, the measure of money requirements was the amount of the work money had to do, largely as a medium of exchange. Given the velocity V of money circulation, the measure was in close harmony with the level of real output. For the medium of exchange function, the quantity of money required could initially be managed; but gold supplies soon fell short of the monetary demand of expanding outputs and currency notes with partial metal coverage soon appeared on the scene to fill the gap that coins left. Compare this situation with the current scenario.

During the second half of the last century, the real output the world produced was more than what it could during its entire existence before 1950. Where is the gold to support money expansion to match the increase? The growing volume of financial transactions knows no bounds. More than a trillion US dollars goes around in the world foreign exchange markets alone every 24 hours in speculative trading. It is estimated that the volume of money involved in their spot transactions alone is 70 times the money value of the world's annual real output. The supply of money tied to gold would fail to meet the money requirements of the modern age. One may be fond of daydreaming, but a return to gold is not even worth that dream. Today, financial transactions are an ocean, wherein real transactions are just tiny islands. A return to gold (dinar) is not possible (Hasan 2008). Since the last semblance of national currencies being linked together via gold disappeared 40 years ago, all countries have been running their economies entirely with fiat money: money that is not backed by reserves of any

[9]For a detailed explanation of monetary expansion and contraction processes under the gold standard, and their repercussions, see Halm (1965, Chapter 12, Section 4, pp. 189–192).

real commodity. Legal tender laws alone are the legs on which it stands. To us, it is true money. It is not the moon drawing its light from the sun (the reserves). It is the sun itself.[10]

8.4.2 *Creation of Money*

Undergraduate textbooks on money and banking invariably make a distinction between legal tender money, as issued by the central bank of a country, and credit or bank money that is generated by commercial banks through the granting of loans to borrowers. They also teach us that the fiscal policy of a country falls within the ambit of the government, while monetary policy is autonomously designed and operated by the central bank. All such lessons deserve to be obliterated from our memories. The early central banks were established during the mercantilist era. They were brought into existence by powerful businessmen controlling politics to serve their own nefarious ends (Di Lorenzo 2008). Ownership structures and the role of central banks have since witnessed many changes over time and space, but their basic functions have virtually remained unaltered (Goodhart 2010).[11] Three of their main functions are: (i) working as bankers to the government; (ii) being the sole issuer of currency notes; and (iii) controlling the volume of credit the commercial banks create. These functions unfold the linkage between the fiscal and monetary policies of a country and the extent of a central bank's autonomy. We shall revert to this topic in the following chapter.

[10]It will be wrong to believe that we have fiat money for the first time now. In fact, even during the era of commodity money, there were legal tender laws in operation to strengthen the monetary system. These laws legally relieved the debtors of their obligations if they offered to pay the debt using what the government declared as money. In some cases, refusal to accept this form of payment was illegal and could at times attract even the death penalty. Ancient Rome and post-revolution France are cited as examples (Cobb 2010). Why Cobb (p. 12) calls it a major breakthrough in the history of money is not clear. In the past, the existence of fiat money was an exception; today its non-existence is an exception.

[11]However, there is a strong case for scrutinizing the power structure in the central banks, especially the ones operating in the area of Islamic banking. This can bring to light forces influencing their workings.

8.4.3 The Fiscal Policy and Money Supply Interface

The function of the central bank to work as the banker to the government opens wide a window for the latter to tinker with the supply of currency, or *base* money, in a country. Even as the central banks have the sole right to issue currency notes, this right has not always been absolute. For example, in India, the one rupee note, which is unlimited legal tender, was issued by the government of India, not by the Reserve Bank of India (RBI). The government could always exchange these notes for bigger denominations with the latter. In addition, the government could always borrow currency from the RBI through the creation of treasury bills that the latter could sell in the money market. The conversion of government securities into legal tender money at the RBI against the accumulating pound sterling balances was used by the British to unleash unprecedented inflationary pressures on the Indian economy, to their own advantage.[12]

Another example, a revelation, comes from the German economy during the 1920s. After their victory in the First World War, the Allied powers imposed such heavy reparation on the vanquished that the payments devastated the economy of the country as never before in modern history. The annual national income plus the liquidation of the accumulated wealth of the Germans was not sufficient to maintain the payment schedule. On one side of the road, the central bank was printing notes day and night so that the government could purchase goods from the market for export to meet the dates, while on the other side, the Germans ran with basketfuls of currency to beat the spiralling inflation. In one year alone prices rose 10^{13} times. Inflation ran high exponentially.

[12] In short, the story was as follows. When England returned to the gold standard after the First World War in the 1920s, the Indian rupee was tied to it at a fixed rate, to enjoy the prestige of being on the gold (exchange) standard via the sterling. In 1931, England went off the gold standard, but the Indian rupee remained bound to the pound sterling, minus the prestige. The linkage enabled the British to finance their huge balance of payments deficits with the country during the Second World War by making the RBI issue Indian currency against the accumulating sterling debt, paper just replacing paper. Real goods and services moving to the theatre of war and money supply expanding within led to high inflation in India. It is interesting to note that the inflation rate in England during the war averaged not more than 7% a year from 1940 to 1945. Domestic inflation was largely transferred to India (and other colonies).

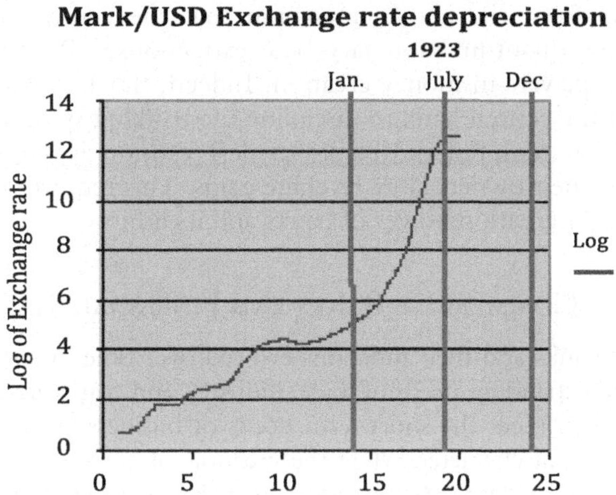

Fig. 8.3 Exponential depreciation of German Mark/$ (1923)

Figure 8.3 is constructed using Table 7.2 data on a semi-logarithmic scale to keep its size manageable. We did not place the actual dates on the x-axis to avoid congestion.

A recent illustration is of Pakistan. The central bank of the country is struggling to find ways of liquidating the huge debt the government owes it as a consequence of the deficit-generating fiscal policies of successive governments (Waheed 2006, Table 2.1). On 31 January 2011, the central government of the country owed a net amount of 1273 billion Pakistan rupees to the State Bank of Pakistan and the amount is on the rise.[13] The borrowing did not result in a corresponding rise in output. The result was a continual depreciation of the local currency inside and outside the country. The domestic debt is almost half of the country's GDP and fourfold its annual tax revenue. It is simply unsustainable.

[13]The latest position is as follows: the government's domestic debt increased from Rs. 3.861 billion or 30.3% of the GDP in FY09 to Rs. 4.652 billion or 31.7% of the GDP in FY10. The Pakistan Stock Exchange's (PSE) domestic debt increased from Rs. 290 billion in FY09 to Rs. 374.9 billion in FY10. The external debt increased from Rs. 4.155 trillion in FY09 to Rs. 4.658 trillion in FY10. At the current run rate, based on the first quarter data, the fiscal deficit could reach 6.0% of GDP. M2 growth during the first quarter of the current fiscal year has risen by Rs. 360.3 billion or 6.2% as compared to Rs. 237 billion.

It follows from the above discussion that the central bank cannot determine the quantum monetary base exogenously. Public authorities are the main players in money creation. Indeed, this fact has eroded the capability of the central bank to discipline the banking system and money markets. It has tempted the banks to defy caution in credit creation, which brings their owners large leverage gains. This requires us to understand the credit creation power of banks and its limits.

8.5 Commercial Banks and Financial Stability

Commercial banks and their functions evolved over time in response to the changing and expanding needs of trade, industry, and commerce. Eventually, they emerged to meet the short-term needs of business. These needs have been of a seasonal character, while the creation of currency was geared to the more enduring demands for money to serve as a medium of exchange and a store of value. Credit creation is meant to keep the growth of currency or base money smooth over time. This development left untouched the financing modes in the Muslim lands. Islamic finance emerged on the scene very late for a variety of reasons. Innocuously, it chose to follow in the footsteps of the same system that it rose to replace. To me, Islamic banks have little option in the matter of credit creation; their methods and precautions could, of course, be different. The real problem in fact is on the control side: what would, or could, replace the bank rate as a control weapon in the hands of the central bank? Even in the case of conventional banks, the policy has failed to deliver. Long-run profit expectations tend to run much higher above the schedules of interest rates after the Second World War. The rising leverage ratios and commissions must be curbed. Perhaps, there exists a case for taxation of leverage gains with steep progression.

There have been claims that Islamic banks withstood the 2007–2008 financial crisis better than their mainstream counterparts. But such claims have been disputed as well. A working paper by Hasan and Dridi (2010) exemplifies the state of confusion on this point. We will postpone the discussion on this claim to Chapter 10.

8.5.1 Cryptocurrency—The Virtual Money

Cryptocurrency is a medium of exchange. Currently, it is unattractive in developing economies, as common people there do not understand what it is and how it works. However, governments, banks, and many companies everywhere are well aware of its form, *modus operandi*, and importance. It is considered to be the money of the future. The day is not far off when one would hardly find a major bank, a big accounting firm, a prominent software company, or a government not occupied with this mode of payment, and academicians not publishing research papers on it. Cryptocurrency uses cryptography for security reasons: it is difficult to counterfeit. The greatest attraction is its organic nature: it is not issued by any central authority. Thus, in theory, it is immune to government interference or manipulation.

The first popular cryptocurrency was Bitcoin, launched in 2009 by an individual or group under the pseudonym 'Satoshi Nakamoto'. As of September 2015, there were over 14.6 million bitcoins in circulation with a total market value of US$3.4 billion. Bitcoin's success has spawned a number of competing cryptocurrencies.

As cryptocurrencies are virtual money and need have no central repository, a digital cryptocurrency balance can be wiped out by a computer crash if a backup copy of the *holdings* is not saved. Since prices are based on supply and demand, the rate at which a cryptocurrency can be exchanged for another currency can fluctuate widely. The Islamic position on cryptocurrency is unclear. Presumably, it cannot be allowed, as its supply cannot be regulated and it has great potential to work against ethical and moral norms of the faith.

8.6 Concluding Remarks

This chapter set out to discuss some familiar ideas in the area of money creation and control in modern societies from an Islamic viewpoint but arrived at some unfamiliar conclusions. The main ones are as follows:

1. Money evolved as a social convention. Its essence lies in what it does, not in what it is made of.
   Its significance follows from the fact that it tears apart the two sides of the barter exchange, into sale and purchase. Money has no religious content. It was never, nor can it ever be, divided into Islamic and non-Islamic.
2. The gold standard was established by the erstwhile imperial powers to exploit their colonies to obtain raw material and other inputs for their growing industries, and to open their vast markets to sell their products. It sacrificed the internal stability of an economy at the altar of external stability, i.e. of the foreign exchange rate. The gold standard never ensured that no one would stumble; it

only ensured that all would stumble together and that hurt the developing nations. The world should never, and can never, return to gold. Presently, IMF rules bar the linking of any currency to gold. The dinarists are travelling on a dead-end road.

3. The autonomy of central banks is illusory. Governments have always been the prime movers in the matter of money supply. Fiscal policies have frequently been the undoing of monetary policies initiated by central banks. Governors of central banks are, after all, appointed by the government; they have to be watchful of authoritative eyes. They tend to miss the train and often underkill to avoid the charge of overkilling.

We believe that any system can deliver if the human element is virtuous. Human beings are the greatest source of instability in the world—political, economic, and social. A president in South East Asia retired after remaining in power for decades and only then did it become public knowledge that he had bankrupted the nation for self-enrichment to the tune of no less than US$40 billion. After the riotous change of regime in Tunisia, the populous Arab state is now on fire; the thirty-year rule of its president is crumbling. In an interview with the British Broadcasting Corporation (BBC), an expert said that 60% of the country's wealth belongs to the besieged president and his son. Corruption, conspiracies, and injustice rule the world, presently on ascendency in India. Powerful armies have marched for non-existent reasons into flourishing countries and destroyed them completely. And for all that, they escaped consequences by merely saying sorry. Entire nations have gone bankrupt because of the misdeeds of their rulers—democratic or despotic. Greece and Ireland are recent illustrations. Today, if banks are too big to fail, nations are many times bigger. All reforms must fail to deliver unless human beings are reformed. Rational morality has failed; faith alone gives hope.

Test Questions

Q.1 Explain the meaning and significance of the following statements:

a. 'Money is what money does'
b. 'Money is accepted because money is accepted'

Q.2 What gave rise to the establishment of central banks in national economies? Explain their main functions. Comment on the autonomy of these banks in modern economies.

Q.3 Examine the various forms of the gold standard. How does the system work? Explain.

Q.4 'The gold standard is a fair weather friend'. Critically examine this statement, explaining the reasons why the gold standard no longer exists.

Q.5 Write explanatory notes on the following:

a. Difficulties of the barter system
b. Circuitry theory of money
c. Current IMF mechanism for exchange rate stability
d. Cryptocurrency—its merits and dangers

What Next?

In modern economies, base money or legal tender is a small fraction of the total money supply. Money created by banks constitutes the bulk of it. The next chapter deals with money creation and monetary policy.

References

Cobb, S. (2010). The History and Evolution of Money, UNT Center for Economic Education, Downloaded from (www.wikipedia.org/wiki/History_of_Money), downloaded on January 7, 2011.

Crowther, G. (1948). *An Outline of Money* (2nd ed., Chapter IX, pp. 277–335). London: Thomas Nelson & Sons.

Di Lorenzo, T. J. (2008, November). *The Corrupt Origin of Central Banking, Mises Daily.* Austria: Ludwig Von Mises Institute.

Gide, C., & Rist, C. (1953). *History of Economic Doctrines.* New Delhi: George, Harrap and co.

Goodhart, C. A. E. (2010, November). *The Challenging Role of Central Banks* (BIS Working paper No. 326), Monetary and Economic Department, Bank for International Settlements.

Gorton, G., & Huang, L. (2001). *Banking Panics and the Origin of Central Banking* (Working paper, pp. 1–10), The Wharton School, University of Pennsylvania and NBER. gtnews.com (16 December 2008): Commentary – The credit crisis timeline. www.gtnews.com.

Halm, G. N.(1965). *Monetary Theory: A Modern Treatment of the Essentials of Money and Banking* (Chapter 12, pp. 171–209). Bombay: Asia publishing House.

Hasan, Z. (2008). Credit Creation and Control: An Unresolved Issue in Islamic Banking. *International Journal of Islamic and Middle Eastern Finance and Management, 1*(1), 69–81.

Hasan, M., & Dridi, J. (2010). *The Effect of Global Crisis on Islamic and Conventional Banks: A Comparative Study* (IMF Working Paper WP/10/201).

Kazmi, M. Z. (2010, October). *Islamic Dinar Reloaded.* Odalisque: Islamic finance Intelligence (Issue 12–13).

KFH Research. (2011). *Gold Dinar: Time to return? Monograph* (pp. 1–21) Kuwait Finance House Research Ltd.

Waheed, A. (2006, January). *Sustainability and Determinants of Domestic Public Debt of Pakistan, NAGOYA 464-8601* (JAPAN Discussion Paper No. 137).

Zein, M. (2010). *Islamic Dinar Revisited.* Opalesque: Islamic Finance Intelligence (Issue 14–15). INCEIF Digital Library.

CHAPTER 9

Monetary Policy: Credit Creation and Control

Preview

The preceding chapter dealt essentially with the creation and management of the legal tender or base money and the role of the central bank in ensuring the stability in the internal and external value of currency. This chapter deals with the credit money creation by the commercial banks and its regulation bringing in Islamic considerations.

Islam banishes interest. This raises two questions contextual to credit creation and control. First, can Islamic banks create credit like the conventional? We shall argue that Islamic banks cannot avoid credit creation; an imperative for staying in the market where they operate in competition with their conventional rivals. Evidently, the interest rate policy would not be applicable to them as a control measure. This leads us to the second question: What could possibly replace the interest rate for Islamic banks? In reply, the chapter suggests what it calls a leverage control rate (LCR) as an addition to central banks' credit control arsenal. The proposed rate is derived from the sharing of profit ratio in Islamic banking. It is contended that the new measure has an edge over the old fashioned interest rate instrument which it can in fact replace with advantage. It can possibly be a common measure in a dual system where mainstream and Islamic banks operate in a competitive setting.

Z. Hasan, *Leading Issues in Islamic Economics and Finance*,
https://doi.org/10.1007/978-981-15-6515-1_9

Learning Outcomes
This chapter is expected to enable the reader understand and explain the following.

- What is credit money, why its creation is necessary and how it is created by banks.
- As Islam banishes interest, how return on investment is determined and how it is linked to interest.
- How a new measure—leverage control rate (LCR) can be designed and used as a credit control instrument in conjunction with other measures the central bank uses for the purpose.
- How the fiscal policy of a country does affects its monetary policy and how effective remain the credit control measures in achieving the monetary policy goals targeting specific variables.

9.1 Introduction

We deal here with an aspect of monetary policy in a dual financial system where Islamic and mainstream banking institutions operate side by side in a competitive setting. This policy addresses a number of objectives, including the mobilization of resources for development, promotion of distributional equity, and maintaining stability in the internal and external value of domestic currency. This we discussed in the preceding chapter. Presently we shall be looking at monetary policy contextual to the credit creation process and the control measures a central bank employs to mitigate volatility in macroeconomic variables. Such volatility often promotes proclivity to crises that snowball to inflict severe damage on national economies across the globe. The 2007–2010 turmoil is a recent example. In this process, the credit money that banks generate plays a crucial role.

In the following section, we briefly explain the process of credit money creation. In Sect. 9.3 we explain how Islam rewards capital in the absence of interest payments. How the profit sharing operates between the parties. Section 9.4 proposes a new instrument for controlling credit creation, explains and illustrates its operation as well as its linkage with the rate of interest and its relationship with other measures in the following section. Section 9.5 elaborates on the interface between the monetary and fiscal policies and its ramifications. It also discusses monetary policy objectives and targets. Finally, Sect. 9.6 concludes the arguments of the chapter.

9.2 Money Creation by Banks

There are multiple sources for obtaining credit (debt), for example, the government, cooperative societies, mutual funds, and individual money lenders, but most of the credit in modern times comes from commercial banks.

We have already made a distinction in the preceding chapter between (i) currency or legal tender money and (ii) credit or bank money. The two together constitute the M1 version of money supply. The relationship between them lies at the heart of the credit creation process that commercial banks utilize. The volume of (i), i.e. currency in an economy, serves as the *base* for generating (ii), the credit money. Part of the base money (currency) always remains *inside* the central bank while the remaining part is held *outside* by the public.[1] People deposit a part of the *outside* money with them in commercial banks as demand or time deposits that together constitute the *cash* deposits of the banking system. The banks have to keep with them a portion of deposits, say 10%, as a statutory reserve to meet the daily withdrawal needs of the depositors. The remaining they can lend on interest or invest in Islamic profit-earning schemes. In conventional banks, the sum loaned is credited to the account of the borrower. Thus, loans generate what we call *credit* deposits. These loans and deposits appear as contra entries in bank balance sheets. The banks make no distinction between the two sorts of deposits—cash or credit—in their lending operations. This enables banks to generate more loans that the cash people deposit with them. The process is as follows.

The bank knows by experience that normally withdrawals on a day are no more than a fraction of deposits. By keeping a safe margin to

[1] The classification of currency into outside and inside money is of recent origin and some economists have found it a useful explanatory tool in their discussions of the credit creation process of commercial banks.

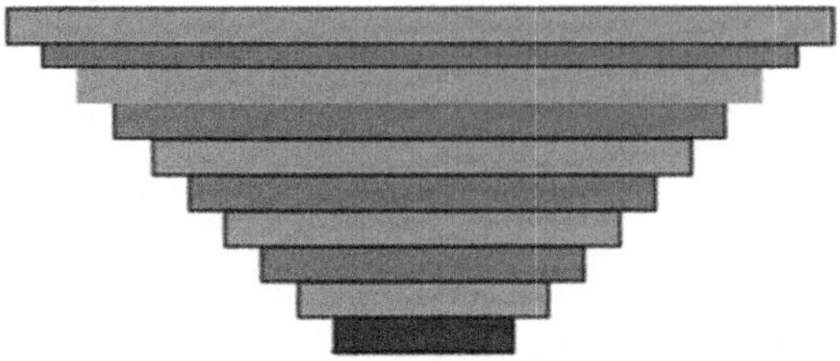

Fig. 9.1 Inverted credit money pyramid $F = 1/10$ and $R = 1/20$ giving $k = 9.5$

meet normal withdrawals the bank can lend the remaining cash to borrowers for interest income. Suppose each bank retains, on an average, $F = 0.1$ fraction of cash deposits as a reserve to meet daily withdrawals, while the central bank of the country wants banks to maintain with it a minimum fraction $R = 0.05$ of their deposits (cash +credit) in the form of cash. How much credit can a bank create given these constraints? The credit multiplier k provides the answer. Ignoring proof, k can be calculated as:

$$k = \frac{1 - R}{F} \tag{9.1}$$

Placing the values we have assumed in the formula, we obtain the multiplier $k = 9.5$. Thus, the cash available to the bank being $50 million it can support deposits worth 50*9.5 = $475 million. This would be the total deposits in the bank, composed of $50 million in cash + $425 million credit the bank can create as credit-on-credit. Figure 9.1 shows how the process develops: an inverted money pyramid tottering on a narrow tip, making the economy prone to turmoil.

Banking is thus an exceedingly lucrative business. Maturity transformation via renewals converts short-term funding into long-term. Leverage gains tend to make businesses over-adventurous. Rising

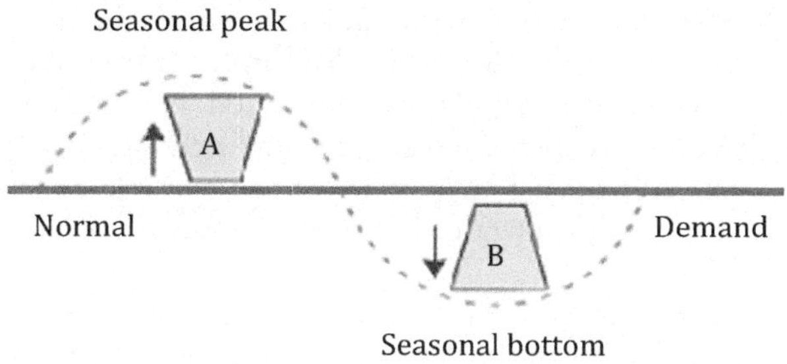

Fig. 9.2 Normal money demand and seasonal variations

profit margins lure banks[2] to continue pumping in air until the balloon bursts; banks tend to collapse. The economies roll down the hill. Unemployment becomes rampant. Rising leverage gains fuel greed and have largely been the cause of frequent financial turmoil like the one world faced after 2007.

The solution is seen in raising the capital coverage of borrowings to restrain credit expansion beyond the limits of safety. Standard capital adequacy ratios are being developed under what are known as the Basel Accords. However, evidence is mounting to show that minimum capital requirements such as the capital adequacy ratios are having little success in reducing the risk of bank failures (Nowak 2011, p. 3).

One compelling reason for allowing banks to operate on the fractional reserve basis is that the act facilitates the adjusting of money supply to seasonal demand variations. Figure 9.2 shows how credit creation keeps demand for money commensurate with normal base money supply in the economy.

Thus, credit creation is an economic imperative and Islamic banks should not be denied the option to promote their survival. Anyway,

[2] Non-performing assets pile up in banks via credit deposits and have eventually paid off by public money injections into the system. For instance, non-performing bank loans in India are on the rise and stood at 150.2 billion US dollars by end March 2018 and the government is in the midst of a massive rescue programme. Data source: ET Markets News www.etmarkets.com. Accessed August 29, 2018.

they have had to fall in line with global practices here also, as elsewhere. Monetary authorities in various Muslim countries and the Islamic Financial Services Board (IFSB) are captivated by the issue: the regulatory frameworks are being revamped and new standards are being designed. Credit control has to be part of the exercise as Islamic banks replace interest with a profit rate. Let us see how such a rate comes into existence.

In view of the absence of a precise price like the rate of interest in conventional financing, the Islamic money market remains underdeveloped. And so is the case with contractual relationships between the Islamic system and the central bank that reduces refinancing facilities for the Islamic banks. Until these weaknesses are overcome, credit creation and its advantages to the Islamic segment of the dual system must stay below par. Indeed, surplus liquidity anywhere in the Islamic system may tend to flow into conventional banking.

These limitations and possibilities need to be addressed. Contextually, one must note that for refinancing connectivity across countries, a corporate facility—the International Islamic Liquidity Management Corporation (IILM)—has already been in operation in Kuala Lumpur since October 2010. It was founded by a diverse group of shareholders, including central banks and monetary agencies as well as a multilateral institution, the Islamic Corporation for the Development of the Private Sector (ICD), from Turkey. The issuance of short duration *sukuk* at low profit rates in international markets is the essential source that the IILM uses for raising funds.[3]

9.3 Profit Sharing and Return on Capital

Participatory finance is regarded as the high point of Islamic finance, where losses are shared in the same ratios as the capital contributions of the parties. However, the sharing of profit arrangement is not the same. The interesting question then is how their sharing of profit ratio is determined. Of course, it is settled by negotiations between the parties. But there have to be some factors guiding the negotiations. *Mudharabah* is a contract in which a financier, say a bank, provides funds to an

[3] See IILM website at iilm.com.

entrepreneur (a firm) to invest in a business venture to share profits in an agreed proportion, losses falling on capital alone.[4]

This view implies what we may call a ***pure mudharabah*** model, where the financier is assumed to provide the *entire* capital to an empty-handed entrepreneur. The model is very beneficial, even today, to small partnership businesses to enable them to undertake specific projects. But the modern economic scene is dominated by large corporations that have long eclipsed small proprietary businesses in size and significance. Likewise, banks have almost completely replaced the personal financing of earlier eras with institutional arrangements. What realistically fits the present situation is a model of what we can term ***mixed mudharabah***, where the bank is an outside financier providing funds to running businesses on a profit-sharing basis. Corporations operate mostly with their (owners') shareholders' money, supplemented by bank finance, if need be. Banks mainly use customer deposits to provide finance to various sorts of borrowers—individuals, firms, and public institutions.

Islamic banks generally employ a two-tier *mudharabah* model to work as financial intermediaries. On the one hand, they obtain deposits from clients under profit/loss sharing arrangements; on the other hand, they finance clients using these deposits plus their own money under the same sort of profit-(loss-)sharing contracts. It is obvious that the profit-sharing ratio with the depositors would be less than the profit-sharing ratio with the borrowers, the difference being the ***banks' margin***. The profit-sharing ratio is a function of the rate or return on investment, the leverage ratio, the rate of interest, and the risk premium (Hasan 1985, 2010, 2014). We shall show that the profit-sharing ratio with the depositors can be used as a credit control measure by central banks.[5]

[4] Paraphrasing Bank Negara Malaysia, *mudharabah* is an agreement made between a party who provides the capital and another—an entrepreneur—who is thus enabled to carry out business projects on the basis of sharing profits in pre-agreed ratios. However, losses, if any, are borne solely by the provider of funds (Bank Negara Malaysia, http://www.bnm.gov.my/index.php?ch=174&pg=469&ac=383).

[5] Central banking made its appearance on the scene in a big way after the Great Depression of the 1930s, to regulate the working of commercial banks, especially their credit creation power, to keep the economy stable. Many books and articles on central banking appeared in due course of time. But the subject disappeared from the literature during the last 40 years. One comes across some good articles on the web, and the online book by Faure (2015) has a good coverage on the functions and policies of central banks. Islamic finance is of more recent origin and not much is available on the subject; Uzair (1982) and Zaidi (1987) may be casually referred to.

If γ is assumed to be the ratio of overall profit P going to the bank, λ the proportion of its contribution to total investment K in business, r_i the market rate of interest, α the risk premium or economic return needed, and π the expected rate of profit on K, then it can be shown that (Hasan 1985):

$$\gamma = \frac{\lambda}{\pi}(r_i + \alpha) < 1 \tag{9.2}$$

This derivation shows that the profit-sharing ratio γ for the bank is a function of four variables, i.e. the expected rate of profit π on capital K, the proportion of borrowings λ in K, the market rate of interest r_i, and the risk premium or economic profit α.[6] This derivation of γ allows, we shall see, the treatment of the ratio issue at the macro level in monetary policy analyses.

Equation (9.2) provides us with a common sense and useful link between the profit-sharing ratio of the banks and the rate of interest in a dual monetary system. It follows from Eq. (9.2) that in a competitive setting, the sharing ratio γ for the bank at the macro level varies inversely with profit expectation rate π and positively with the other determinants λ, r_i, and α.

The same sort of profit-sharing negotiations between the bank, on the one hand, and the depositors, on the other, would constitute the second tier of the *mudharabah* contract. For the purpose of narration and to keep it distinct from the tier one explanation, symbols for some of the variables in Eq. (9.2) need to be changed to avoid confusion. We assume that the contribution of the depositors and the bank to λK has been in the ratios ϑ and $(1 - \vartheta)$, respectively. Of the profit $\gamma \lambda P$ the bank receives from the firm on its contribution to investment K, ϑ fraction would accrue to the depositors and $(1 - \vartheta)$ to the bank. Profit that accrues to thee depositors has to be shared with the bank. Suppose this sharing ratio we fix for convenience at fifty-fifty $= y^*$. Further we keep y^* the same as in tier 1. Under our assumption the bank and the depositors would each get 0.5 of $\gamma \lambda P$. In other words, in tier 2 *mudharabah* the bank would receive $(1 - \vartheta)\, y^* \lambda P$ and the depositors $\vartheta\, \lambda P$ profit share for providing the depositors with entrepreneurial services to help them earn a return on their savings. For a detailed explanation. See Table 9.1 in the Appendix.

[6]As $\alpha > 0$, the expected rate of profit is greater than the interest rate of market.

Box 9.1: Islamic finance performance

- The Islamic banking sector retained its dominance in the global IFSI. The domestic market share for Islamic banking in relation to the total banking sector continued to increase in at least 19 countries, remained constant in six, and declined in 11 jurisdictions among the 36 jurisdictions covered in the IFSI Stability Report 2019.
- The Islamic banking sector's performance grew by a mere 0.9% in 2018, compared to 4.3% in 2017, and as at 2Q18 accounts for 72% (76% in 2017) of the total value of IFSI assets mainly due to the depreciation of local currencies in terms of the USD, especially in some emerging economies with a significant Islamic banking presence.
- The ICM sector as at end of 2018 accounts for 27% of the global IFSI assets on the back of a positive performance due to the sovereign and multilateral *sukuk* issuances in key Islamic finance markets to support respective budgetary expenditures as well as number market debuts of sovereign issuances, including green sovereign *sukuk* to finance eco-friendly environment projects.
- The share of global *takaful* industry in the global IFSI remains unchanged at 1.3%. Global *takaful* contributions grew by 4.3% (y-o-y and in nominal terms) in 2017, with a six-year (2012–2017) compound average growth rate of almost 6.9%. As at the end of 2017, an estimated 306 *takaful* institutions, including *retakaful* and *takaful* windows, now offer *takaful* products in at least 45 countries globally.
- Source IFDI Stability Report 2019

9.4 Credit Control: A Proposal

From the above groundwork, we may combine the relevant variables to set up the rate of return R_B on banks' investment in mixed *mudharabah* financing. To keep matters simple, we have kept y^* the same for both the tiers. We set up for bank profit P_B as follows:

$$P_{B}=(1 - \vartheta)y * \lambda P+(\vartheta y * \lambda P)y *$$

which reduces to:

$$P_{B}=y * \lambda P\left[1 - \vartheta(1 - y*)\right]$$

This gives

$$\begin{aligned} R_{B} &= \frac{\gamma * \lambda P\left[1 - \vartheta(1 - \gamma *)\right]}{(1 - \vartheta)\lambda K} \\ &= \frac{\gamma\pi\left[1 - \vartheta(1 - \gamma *)\right]}{(1 - \vartheta)\lambda}, \gamma = \gamma * \lambda \end{aligned} \tag{9.3}$$

This return is constrained to be no more than π β; thus we may set up:

$$= \frac{\gamma\pi\left[1 - \vartheta(1 - \gamma *)\right]}{(1 - \vartheta)\lambda} \leq \pi + \beta \tag{9.4}$$

The left-hand side part of Eq. (9.4) may be called the profit multiplier m for the bank. For Illustration 2 it works at 1.25. The profit rate π on total investment being 0.2 and $R_{B} = 25\%$. The merit of Illustration 2 is that here Eq. (9.4) captures all the variables relevant to the operation of LCR. The control variable β may force changes in one or more of the equation, allowing greater flexibility to the system with lesser ramifications compared to the interest rate mechanism.

Thus, β can be a cost-free policy variable that the central bank of a country can use for mandatory *ex post* adjustment of the PSR in Islamic finance to enforce fairness in the distribution of profits between the banks and the depositors.

The use of the instrument would also force banks to adjust their leverage ratios of Eq. (9.2) via to harmonize with changes in β, and the sharing ratio will also adjust accordingly. For, the introduction of β as the control variable into the picture would by definition affect α in Eq. (9.2) impacting in the process the size of the banks' profit-sharing ratio with businesses that is by making credit costlier or cheaper.

Let us put as any constant. We now have a linear equation where μ being a constant with T as the slope. It sets up a positive relationship between profit-sharing ratio and the rate of interest plus α as shown in Fig. 9.3. It follows that for the same the profit-sharing ratio may fluctuate with changes in leverage ratio λ or profit expectation or α the risk premium. But it could also remain constant, if changes in λ and take place in the same direction such that μ remains unchanged. We can now depict the equilibrium value for the profit-sharing ratio and its relationship with its determinants as in Fig. 9.3. An implicit assumption here is that risk premium α remains constant.

The use of β—the LCR—as a credit control measure in a dual financial system has several advantages over the traditional bank rate policy. Bank rate policy operates through the manipulation of the money-use price which conflicts with the Islamic ban on interest. In contrast, β leaves interest rate untouched; it operates directly on profit margins of both the financiers and the borrowing businesses having a better psychological impact. Interest rate is a blanket measure. It affects borrowings for all purposes in equal measure—relatively more urgent and socially desirable or frivolous. Possibly, using β would prove more amicable to pursue discretionary credit allocation policies, i.e. for selective control of investment channels.

Finally, changes in interest rate affect the entire financing system—all purposes, all modes, and all security markets restricting the frequency of using it. It forces upon the central bank a loss inflicting open market operations regime. β can be more flexible and selective; unlike the open market operations, it does not impose costs on the central bank (Hasan 2010).

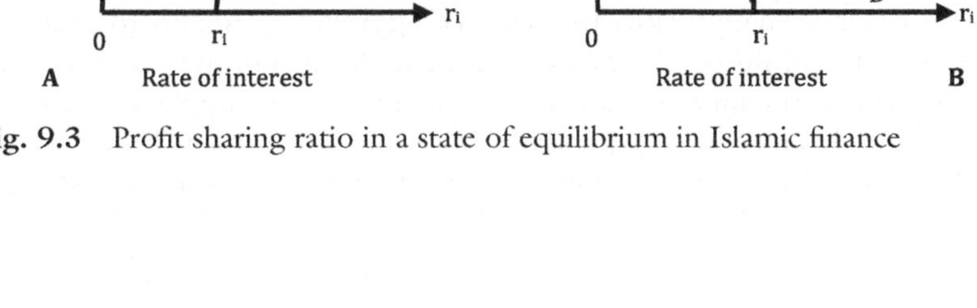

Fig. 9.3 Profit sharing ratio in a state of equilibrium in Islamic finance

9.4.1 LCR and Other Control Measures

It is clear from Eq. (9.3) that ceteris paribus the profit-sharing ratio! for the banks varies directly with β the LCR in a linear relationship. And Fig. 9.3 shows that rate of interest r_i and! too move in the same direction. Thus, a change in the LCR will tend to move the market interest rate to have similar results. The reverse is also true. Of the other credit control measures central banks use the various serve ratios are important. For example, all banking institutions—Islamic or conventional—have to maintain a Statutory Reserve Account with the central bank of the country. They have to keep a minimum proportion of their eligible deposits all the time in this account. This proportion is called the Statutory Reserve Ratio or the SRR. Lowering (raising) this ratio enables the central banks to expand (contract) credit in the economy. The measure is *Shari'ah* neutral. So is the case with statutory cash ratios that banks are required to maintain against time and current deposits. Moral persuasion too poses no problem. The difficulty arises in the case of 'open market operations' as a measure for credit control. The central bank has to sell securities to mop up liquidity during inflation when prices of securities in stock with it are falling and has to buy them during the downturn when their prices are relatively high. Thus, in either case, the central bank's ability to control credit would depend on how much loss it is willing to absorb. The LCR we have suggested helps avoid this dilemma.

9.5 Monetary Versus Fiscal Policy

A country uses two policy sets—fiscal and monetary—to guide its economy and to achieve the desired goals. Fiscal policy consists of the government using its expenditure and revenue collection instruments to promote social welfare and distributive equity. Monetary policy, on the other hand, is designed by the central bank of a country to control the supply of money, often targeting a rate of interest oriented to the promotion of growth and stability of the economy. The objectives of both overlap, the distinction being in relative emphasis and the instruments used.

Fiscal policy manipulates the level of aggregate demand to maintain price stability, full employment and growth un-bumpy. central bank uses various monetary measures influencing money supply towards the same ends. Taxation and expenditure allocation to various heads are the main tools of fiscal policy while monetary policy relies on Interest rates;

reserve requirements; currency peg; discount window; quantitative easing; and open market operations.

The two policies must supplement each other. Pure monetary policy makes no sense, nor does a pure fiscal policy. However, the two policies, on ground, are seen working more in conflict than in harmony. For example, while the government would like to encourage savings through tax reliefs, the cheap money policy of the central banks would tend to neutralize the effort. While public authorities may want to boost employment through deficit financing, the central bank may resist it as neutralizing its anti-inflation curbs. In such clashes governments invariably have the last say; they appoint the central bank governors, can dismiss the non-compliers or refuse to extend their terms in office. Islamic economics has little to say about the two policy sets save the abolition of interest as a monetary tool and adding *zakah* to the fiscal.

9.5.1 Monetary Policy Tools[7]

There are several ways in which one can approach monetary policy. One is to narrate history, tracing the origin and evolution of the present central bank in a country and the actions it has taken in various years. The other is to focus on an evaluation of monetary policy discussing its goals and the efficacy of the instruments employed to meet them in a broad stabilization programme. Given the space constraint here we take the second route.

In recent writings on monetary economics a distinction is often made between its goals and targets of policy as follows.

Goals

- Growth rate acceleration to achieve high performance levels.
- Keep price level firm, working for optimal inflation.
- Improvement in the distribution of income and wealth in society.
- Sound management of the country's balance of payments.

Targets

- Money supply
- Bank credit
- Interest rates

[7]This Section uses material from author's book: *Economics with Islamic Orientation* (pp. 553–560). Oxford University Press (2015).

Change in the magnitude and direction—increase or decrease—of the targeted goal is the measure of policy success or failure. Of the listed targets, monetary policy mainly focuses on the credit creation power of the commercial banks. We have briefly referred to the two—interest rate and open operations—policies in Section 9.4. Let us discuss them in more detail along with others to complete the picture.

9.5.1.1 Interest Rate Policy

It is the rate of interest at which commercial banks can borrow money from the central bank and can also rediscount their first-class trade bills with it at the same rate. The rate also impacts the foreign exchange rate of the domestic currency.

Bank rate targets the *price* of loan as the market loan rates structure varies directly with the bank rate. Thus, the raising of the bank rate is expected to make finance costly for the business firms increasing the cost of production. This is likely to decrease profit margins and dampens investment and may help curb inflation. The sequence of events reverses if Bank Rate is reduced. Firms may borrow and invest more. Production and employment would look up. However, Bank rate policy may not help if profit rates continue running ahead of interest rates or banks already have sufficient funds during inflation not needing the central bank for funds. The failure of the policy is more likely during the downturn of the cycle when businesses are generally suffering losses. Cheap funding may not allay the fears. One can take the horse to water but cannot make him drink if he does not. Finally, the Bank Rate policy is a blanket measure, does not discriminate between urgent and frivolous credit needs of the economy.

9.5.1.2 Statuary Reserve Ratio

Commercial banks are required to maintain a minimal ratio of their deposits, including credit, in the form of cash with them for safety reasons. In addition, they also have to keep a faction each of their demand and time deposits with the central bank as a reserve. These latter ratios it uses to control credit. Unlike the Bank Rate policy, this measure targets not the *price* but the *volume* of credit the banks have the ability to generate. The central bank can raise or lower these ratios simultaneously or separately. In case these ratios are raised, there, credit must reduce much in a downward anti-inflation multiplier spiral. The opposite will happen if the ratios are lowered during deflation. This is a costless effective measure of credit control compared to others.

9.5.1.3 Open Market Operations

Normally, the central bank of a country does not enter the money market. But occasionally it uses the right for operation to encourage the expansion or contraction of credit through impacting the credit creation base of a commercial bank. This is possible as it always carries a stock of first-class treasury and commercial securities. Open market operations can increase or decrease the cash base of commercial banks and thus their credit creation ability.

When an economy is climbing up, the money incomes expand faster than real output. Prices rise and the economy soon finds itself in the grip of inflation. To reduce the cash base with the commercial banks, the central bank starts selling securities in the market, competing with other sellers. The people purchasing these securities withdraw cash from their banks. Thus cash moves out of commercial banks into the confines of central bank. The credit multiplier works in the reverse direction reducing power of banks to create credit. This has a dampening effect on rising prices. The policy is reversed if the economy changes direction and plunges downward. The central bank enters the market to buy securities. Securities move in and cash goes out to banks in increased public deposits. But if an increase in the banks' cash base would enhance credit creation investment and revival of the economy is uncertain. Borrowings are not availability elastic; they are expectations elastic. Thus, it is relatively easier to control inflation than to cure depression. That apart, open market operations have some serious limitations as a method of credit control.

During inflation, the prices of fixed return securities—mainstream or Islamic—because higher return possibilities in competing avenues for free funds. Thus, in all probability, the central bank would sell securities at lower prices than their acquisition cost. In the same way, it must purchase securities during recession at a price higher than competing new investments. How much of a loss the central bank can take in each case and justify it is the question.

9.5.1.4 Moral Suasion

As a central bank has special privileges and power, especially as the lender of the last resort, it is said to act as a philosopher, friend, and guide to all commercial banks, rather the entire financial system of the country. Banks are supposed to listen to its advice. Sometimes a circular issued by it to the banks concerning credit management may have the desired impact. Thus, moral suasion is counted among the credit control measures of the system.

9.6 Conclusion

We have examined the measures central banks can use to regulate credit creation from Islamic perspective and have suggested a new instrument based on the Islamic profit-sharing norm. Its merit is that it can impact both categories of banks—Islamic and conventional—in the same direction without imposing costs on the central banks. The year 2009 was a critical one for Islamic Finance as the downturn tested the resilience of the institutions and financing structures that endeavour to comply with the ethical and moral investment guidelines that form the core of the *Shari'ah* law. The crisis, however, showed that the sector has not been without its casualties, with high-profile Islamic names such as Tamweel, Amlak, and The Investment Dar falling foul of the credit crunch (Howladar 2010). Thus, the industry is likely to face increasing challenge in the future. Diversification, product innovation, and the standardization of norms along with the harmonization of regulations across countries can go a long way to help Islamic finance industry face the impeding challenge.

Risk sharing in finance is not an exclusive principle for Islamic finance. Fixed return rate on the stochastic earnings contracts is permitted as in *Murabahah* models based on moral and religious behaviour. On ground, such models are much more in use than the sharing contracts. In fact their role in promoting growth and stability is dominant.

Islam stands for freedom of the individual and the markets but not at the cost of social well-being and fair play. The religion is not anti-rich and grants all protection to private earnings and wealth. But its norms of legitimacy are not a matter for market arbitration. State regulation of market behaviour and practices carries undisputed evidence over time and space in history. Islamic requirements for the fulfilment of basic needs, removal of poverty, reduction in inequities, and keeping the balances straight in all spheres of life presupposes a substantial state intervention in the economic life of the community with discretion. Government intervention in economic activities is to be a source of stability, not of chaotic fluctuations under Islamic dispensation.

However, to pronounce ethical norms is one thing; to see them operate on ground is another. It would be far from truth to opine that conventional financial settings are devoid of ethical norms of behaviour; the lament is that it is the blatant and continual violation of these norms that has dragged the world to the brink of disaster in recent years.

Appendix

Illustration 1

From Eq. (9.3) we get the maximum possible equilibrium value for the profit-sharing ratio. It is obvious that for any given values of and λ the profit-sharing ratio would vary directly with β. The relationship allows the central bank to use as a cost-free instrument for credit control.

It is easy to see that the central bank of a country can lower β to increase the rate of return to the depositors leading to a reduction in bank margins. To keep their margins intact the banks are expected to demand higher profit-sharing ratio from the borrowing firms reducing the leverage lure for profits. Thus, β can be an effective control measure in the hands of a central bank to curb inflation. During recession an increase in β could boost the sagging business morale through brightening profit expectations. Demand for investment funds may look up and credit creation may fill up the possible gaps.

We can find out in a given situation the leverage gain that is β by inserting the relevant values in Eq. (9.3). If the central bank finds the margin too high, it may fix a lower β as a control measure to dampen the leverage lure.

Test Questions

Q.1 Explain the process banks use to create credit money. Illustrate the power of banks in this regard using the multiplier concept. Is this power unlimited? Give reasons for your answer.

Q.2 Distinguish between risk and uncertainty. It is contended that 'while Islamic banks are only risk takers, the conventional banks transfers risk to others'. Comment on the statement.

Q.3 Explain clearly the concept of a leverage control rate. Do you think the proposal is theoretically sound and practically workable? Argue your case.

Table 9.1 Profit sharing in a two-tier *mudharabah*

Total Capital Employed K = 10,000		
Firm's Equity $(1-\lambda)\ K = 6000$ Where $\lambda = 0.4$	Rate of Profit π =20% Agrees sharing ratio 50:50	Bank's contribution = $\lambda K = 4000$
Firm arns: $(1-\lambda)\ P + y^{*}\ \lambda P = 1200 + 400 = 1600$ or 26.67%	Profit P earned on K = 3000 (10,000 * 0.20)	The Bank gets Ap or 2000 * 0.4 800 – 400 Bank's share = 400
Tier 1 Division of Profit		
Tier 2 Division of Profit Assumptions: The contribution ratio of the bank to λK is $(1-\vartheta)$ and of Depositors ϑ Where $\vartheta = 0.75$ However they share profit received 50:30		
Bank's contribution to $\lambda K\ (1-\vartheta)\ \lambda K$ or 4000 *0.25 = 1000 Bank's Profit 400 * 0.25 + (400 – 100) 0.5 = 250 25%	$\lambda K = 10{,}000 * 0.4 = 4000$ composed of Bank and Depositors shares 1000 + 3000 Distributable Profit: $y^{*}\ \lambda P = 400$ Rate of return 10%	Depositors' contribution $(1-\vartheta)\ \lambda K$ or 4000 * 0.75 = 3000 Depositors' Profit (400 – 100) 0.5 = 150 5%

Q.4 In Table 9.1 assume that the firm's equity is 4000 and the contribution of the bank 6000 and rework the whole table, other things remaining unchanged. Compare your results with the table and comment on the differences.

Q.5 What is a cryptocurrency? Explain its merits and demerits for monetary policy.

Q.6 Write critical notes on the following
  a. Inverted pyramid of credit
  b. Credit multiplier
  c. Leverage gains.

What Next?

The fading effectiveness of central banks in monetary management and lax credit controls have led economies across the globe fall victim to more frequent and devastating financial crises as the turmoil that started with the mortgage debacle of United States in 2007. Even as the world was seized with concerns about the damage such upheavals cause to global economies as the history of Basel Accords testifies the 2007 shock awakened the world to the fragility of the current financial system and let Basel put afresh in sharp focus. The following chapter takes a critical look at these Accords and evaluates their efficacy for Islamic finance.

References

Faure, A. P. (2015). *Central Banking and Monetary Policy: An Introduction.* bookboon.com.

Hasan, Z. (1985). Determination of Profit and Loss Sharing Ratios in Interest-Free Business Finance. *Journal of Research in Islamic Economics, 3*(1), 13–27.

Hasan, Z. (2010). Profit Sharing Ratios in Mudarabah Contract Revisited. *International Journal of Islamic Banking and Finance, 7*(1), 1–17.

Hasan, Z. (2014, June). Basel Accords Financial Turmoil and Islamic Banking. *ISRA International Journal of Islamic Banking and Finance, 6*(1).

Howladar, K. (2010). *Shariah Risk: Understanding Recent Compliance Issues in Islamic Finance* (Moody's Investor Service Report, p. 1).

Nowak, R. A. (2011). *How Effective Is Global Financial Regulation? The Basel Accords' Role in Mitigating Banking Crises.* econ.duke.edu/uploads/assets/NowakRobert.pdf.

Uzair, M. (1982). Central Banking Operations in an Interest-Free Banking System. In M. Ariff (Ed.), *Monetary and Fiscal Economics of Islam*. Jeddah: Centre for Research in Islamic Economics, King Abdul-Aziz University.

Zaidi, N. A. (1987). Profit Rates Policy for PLS Depositors. *Journal of Islamic Banking and Finance*, *4*(4), 35–46.

CHAPTER 10

The Basel Accords and Islamic Banks

Preview

The primary cause of the colossal failure of financial institutions worldwide—banks in particular—in the wake of the 2007–2008 turmoil has been the heightened lure of leverage gains that led them to expand credit beyond what the volume and quality of their capital assets warranted. The devastation led to a major policy shift in finance at the national and international levels, with a focus on capital adequacy that financial institutions must observe for their own safety as well as for the wider social interest. It was felt that a stringent and regular watch was needed to make adequacy norms work. The Basel Committee on Banking Supervision developed what are known as Accords (agreements) defining capital and its adequacy for banks to limit the risks they can take within reasonable confines. Ironically, the world has since February 2018 facing the possibility of a major shock, the tremors are getting stronger with the passage of time.

It is worth noting that Malaysia has in a sense been pre-emptive of the danger revamping its own regulatory framework. Also, the Islamic Financial Services Board (IFSB) has been quick in announcing several new standards that Islamic banks are to observe. This chapter briefly takes stock of these developments for seeing how far the Basel Accords the Bank for International Settlements has announced are relevant to Islamic banks in view of the arrangements already in place in Muslim countries.

Z. Hasan, *Leading Issues in Islamic Economics and Finance*,
https://doi.org/10.1007/978-981-15-6515-1_10

Learning Outcomes
It is expected that the study of this chapter will help the reader to understand and appreciate:

- What leads banks to overshoot credit expansion beyond the safety limits their assets can support—the leverage gains lure.
- How this lure has led banks into bankruptcy and imposed huge bailout costs on public authorities to help them survive.
- What the Bank for International Settlements is and how it works for the maintenance of the stability of global banking systems within and across countries.
- What capital adequacy is contextual to risk coverage, and how the Basel regulatory Accords, if implemented, can improve the security of banks.
- How the Basel Accords have evolved over time from I to III and beyond, and to what extent they are relevant to Islamic banks in view of *Shari'ah* academies and the Islamic Financial Services Board developing and issuing their own standards.

10.1 Introduction

Banks normally expand their credit levels within the limits of safety, but lured by leverage gains, they have, over recent decades, done so beyond what the volume and quality of their capital assets has warranted. They initially restrained expansion in credit levels, but eventually proceeded unabated, resulting in the massive failures of a number of banks amid the 2007–2008 financial crises. The Basel Committee on Banking Supervision (BCBS, or the Committee) has developed, since late 1980s, what are known as Accords (agreements) to define capital adequacy levels of banks, so that the risks they take can remain within reasonable confines. These Accords have progressed from Basel I (1988) through Basel II (2004) and Basel III (2010–2011) to IV growing more AND MORE stringent in their adequacy terms.

10.1.1 Leverage Gains Lure

We have discussed this topic at length in Chapter 8. Let us recall briefly that in an economy, the entities that save money out of their current incomes are largely not the same as those needing money for a variety of uses, especially for business. Financial institutions, predominantly banks, operate as intermediaries between the savers and the users of money. They collect large and small amounts from savers in the form of deposits and advance the same as loans to those who need financing. The revenues banks earn from their lending operations, minus what they pay to attract cash deposits constitutes gross bank margins. From such margins, banks take out their operating expenses to arrive at the net profit for their owners. Collectively, these profits are the cost that society has to pay to the banking system for performing the mediation function so vital for wealth creation and distribution.

In their lending activities, the banks do not only use the cash deposited with them; they also create credit-on-credit that the conventional fractional reserve system so liberally facilitates. Credit deposits equal the cash holdings of a bank multiplied by the reciprocal of the reserve ratio, minus the cash base of credit creation.[1] This base is enhanced by the technique known as maturity transformation.[2]

Not only banks, but their business clients too, gain by multiple credit expansion. Businesses with access to credit enhance profits for their stakeholders through leveraging on equity, as long as the schedule of expected profits runs above the schedule of interest rates (that is, until the bubble bursts). Thus seen, credit expansion is extra-attractive to both parties: the banks and their business clients. For the same reason, however, bank margins become extra-risk ventures. The profit lure has frequently led to an over-expansion of credit, coupled with reckless speculative borrowing, the process eventually culminating in financial crashes, big or small.

[1] If R is the risk-free rate of interest and α the risk premium, the rate of interest charged on loans R_L will be determined as follows: $R_L = (R + \alpha)$. Likewise, if the risk discount rate β is the rate of interest R_D on deposits, it would be expressed as $R_D = (R - \beta)$. The formulations will yield gross bank margins as equal to $R_L - R_D = (R + \alpha) - (R - \beta) = (\alpha + \beta)$, where α need not be equal to β $[(\alpha + \beta)/\text{total assets}]$ gives the margin coefficient for inter-bank profitability comparisons. However, in the Islamic profit and loss sharing system, why R should be discounted is tenuous.

[2] Maturity transformation is the bank practice of borrowing on shorter time durations and transforming these short-term funds into loans of longer maturity. This is possible due to the fractional reserve banking system where banks hold reserves less than the amount of their customers' deposits. This concept is applicable to businesses as well, which tend to transform the short-term loans that they borrow from commercial banks into long-term ones through a renewal or rollover process, which benefits banks as well.

Certain developments initiated by the liberalization movement during the decades before the turn of the century pushed the leveraging lure persistently beyond sustainable limits. Credit expansion and borrowing both gave way to adventurism that ended in the onset of the 2007–2010 financial turmoil the like of which the world had seldom experienced before. The turmoil continues unabated in a unique go-halt-go mode: today, there is high elation on stock markets tomorrow a deepening gloom.

The failure of banks, insurance companies, and investment houses across the globe have been immense: the devastation wild and wide, the chaos and despair unparalleled.[3] Indeed, the experience has caused a distinct paradigm shift in financial economics. Yesteryears' advocates of liberalization and privatization have turned almost overnight into vocal pleaders for raising safety walls to protect the stakeholders, especially the depositors.[4]

The existing conventional regulations of financial institutions are being tightened at the local and international levels via what are known as the Basel Accords. The measures they contain focus on strengthening the balance sheet structures of financial institutions. They specify capital adequacy norms relative to credit volume these institutions, banks especially, generate. There is insistence on the observance of the norms with a view to improving their resistance to future crises, especially in times of runs on bank deposits. Interestingly, the Accords maintain silence on credit creation and control measures. Since this chapter is meant to look at the Basel Accords from the viewpoint of Islamic banks, a few preliminary observations may not be out of place.

To begin with, Islamic banking is a tiny fraction of the gigantic world financial system; Islamic banks held less than 1.2% of global banking

[3]The falling US housing prices and rising delinquencies on the residential mortgage market could lead to losses of US$565 billion. When combining these factors with losses from other categories of loans originating, and securities issued, in the United States related to commercial real estate, potential losses were put at about US$945 billion. The US$945 billion estimate of losses represents approximately US$142 per person worldwide and 4% of the US$23.21 trillion credit markets. Global banks are likely to carry about half of these losses. The loss figure of US$945 billion is just an estimate; the actual amount may even be higher (IMF Global Financial Stability Report, 2008).

[4]Under the Basel Accords, in the event of a winding-up, depositors' funds rank in priority before capital, so depositors would only lose money if the bank makes a loss that exceeds the amount of capital it has.

assets by the end of 2017. Their areas of operation, socio-economic environment, trading modes, and instruments used are much different from the Basel Accords' underpinnings. Again, these Accords are structured to protect conventional banks in the future against possible damage of the type the current turmoil has inflicted on them. It is widely claimed that the impact of the crisis on Islamic banks was negligible due to the inbuilt strength of the system, especially the firm linkage between money and real values. We shall soon comments on this claim, but if it is true, to what extent would Islamic banks need to implement the Basel Accords? Finally, Islamic banks have to meet *Shari'ah* obligations that restrict indulgence in overly risky transactions. Why then place an additional burden of observing the Accords on them?

To ponder on such questions and search for answers, a brief background of the Basel Accords and what they seek to do may be helpful.

10.2 The Basel Accords

To reiterate, chronic capital insufficiency to cover mounting debt default risks has increasingly been cited as the primary source of agony that the world frequently passes through because of recurrent financial crises. The predicament has led to a focus on defining capital more precisely and fixing the levels of its adequacy individual financial institutions must scrupulously observe for their own safety as well as for the wider societal interest. In the fast-changing world of finance, a regular watch over systemic liquidity situation is needed to enable the security concepts to work effectively, without impairing economic dynamism.

The Basel Committee on Banking Supervision (BCBS), an organ of the Bank for International Settlements (BIS), has long been made responsible for keeping the all important watch. The Committee is a group of eleven developed countries—G10 + Spain.[5] The work of the Committee is to harmonize banking standards and regulations within and between countries, especially to see that no foreign banking institutions of the group could avoid or evade supervision. Thus, the Committee was an exclusivist organization in its very origin and so it continues to remain.

[5]The group includes France, Germany, Italy, Japan, the Netherlands, Sweden, Switzerland, the UK, the US, and Luxembourg (G-10) in addition to Spain.

To promote the related objectives, the Basel Committee has developed the concept of a capital adequacy requirement for banks.[6] Each bank has to fulfil the requirements that the Committee defines specifically for it. Individualization of institutions enhances not only the exclusivity of the Committee but may also place its transparency in the treatment of different banks under the scanner. If the scope of the Committee's operations has truly been internationalized, the possibility of discriminatory treatment must be eliminated. Globalization demands participation of more countries in the Committee deliberations to ensure fair dealing. The present Accords do grant ample discretionary latitude to non-members, but the range and content of their recommendations may not be uniformly conducive to all. There is room for oligarchic decision structures to eventually become a *fait accompli*, applicable without distinction. Indeed, some writings seem to imply that the process is already underway (Carroll 2014).

The Committee has issued three Accords on capital adequacy since 1988. These Accords contain minimal standards expressed as ratios that individual banks have to maintain across the globe. The focus of attention in developing these standards has understandably been the eagerness to impart stability to the financial systems.

10.2.1 Capital Needed to Cover Risk

As explained above, the primary objective of the Basel Accords is to ensure adequate liquidity available in each bank to face abnormal cash withdrawals at critical times. This needs expeditious asset management. Assets are classified according to the difference in the degree of risk (loss in value) they carry; that degree determines the comparative quality status of each class. This degree varies with the ease and speed with which one asset can be converted into another, particularly cash. The assets that carry a low degree of risk in this sense are of high quality, and those that carry high risk are of low quality. Holding cash carries zero risk, and

[6] Capital inadequacy refers to the possibility of a financial institution being hurt by an unexpected loss. To ward off such an eventuality, Basel I categorizes the assets of these institutions with reference to such a risk into five categories (0, 10, 20, 50, and 100%). Banks that operate internationally are required to have capital adequacy—a minimum of capital—that would keep the weight of such risk at 8% or less. Basel II modified the categorisation.

the same is almost the case with government securities; thus, both are regarded as high-quality assets. In contrast, assets like residential mortgages carry higher risk; their asset quality (liquidity) is low. Similarly, assets such as debentures (corporate bonds for long-term financing) are assigned a higher weight and are included in lower-class assets. Thus, risk weight varies inversely with asset quality. We take the risk-weighted aggregate of all bank assets as a measure of a bank's overall risk exposure. We check if a bank has capital (liquidity) at least equal to this aggregate. For this purpose, the Basel Accords define four capital categories called 'Tiers'.[7] Here, we will focus on Tier 1 capital and Tier 2 capital. The capital adequacy ratio (CAR) is calculated for each bank as follows:

$$\text{CAR} = \frac{\text{Tier 1 capital} + \text{Tier 2 capital}}{\text{Aggregate risk weighted assets}} \quad \text{CAR must be } \geq 1$$

Tier 1 capital is that which is permanently and freely available to absorb losses without causing the bank to cease operating. For example, it includes ordinary share capital (equity) of the bank, excluding revaluation reserves. Tier 1 capital is important because it protects both the survival of the bank and the stability of the financial system.

Tier 2 capital has items that generally absorb losses only in the event of bank liquidation; it thus provides a low level of protection for depositors and other creditors. It is available only when the bank has lost Tier 1 capital. Tier 2 capital generally includes items like revaluation reserves and other provisions. Tier 2 capitals are divided into upper and lower components. The former have no fixed maturity, while the latter have a limited life span, making them less effective as a buffer against losses. Also, there are some restrictions on Tier 2 capital; its upper part cannot be more than 100%, and the lower part more than 50%, of Tier 1 capital.

The Basel Accords also provide for Tier 3 capital that consists of short-term low-priority (subordinated) debt. It can be used to cover market risk losses which Tier 1 and Tier 2 capital are insufficient to meet. Here, we shall restrict our discussion to Tiers 1 and 2 capitals only.

[7]The tiers are regulatory capital types defined in the Basel Accords for estimating capital adequacy levels for banks. Tier 1 is the core capital or basic equity. Tier 2 is supplementary capital. Tier 3 consists of short-term subordinated debt covering market risk, while Tier 4 refers to a variety of hybrid debts. The increase in tiers makes regulation progressively more stringent.

It is prescribed that the CAR should not be less than 4% for Tier 1 capital and not less than 8% for both Tier 1 and Tier 2 combined. It may be noted that capital adequacy ratios, even if higher than the minimum prescribed, do not necessarily make the bank safe. They primarily deal only with credit risks, to the exclusion of other risk types. For example, risks of loss due to moral hazards or *Shari'ah* non-compliance remain uncovered in the CAR calculation. Even so, the ratio approach is commendable for the following reasons:

- It provides an easier way of comparing banks across different jurisdictions;
- Off-balance-sheet exposures can be easily included in capital adequacy estimates;
- Banks are free to carry low-risk liquid assets in their accounting books.

While one need not find difficulty with the efficacy of the weighting system, the CAR calculation sidesteps a crucial fact by focusing on the appropriate adjustment of the numerator—the capital requirement to maintain the ratio—thus paying little attention to the denominator, the *ipso facto* root of the trouble. The leverage lure leads to mounting credit-on-credit expansion, and all receivables appear on the asset side of the balance sheet, magnifying the denominator. Banks cannot keep increasing the capital (numerator) to match the credit expansion to hold the ratio level intact. Instead, the pressure may lead to 'watering' the stocks or reducing the asset volume through undervaluation or excessive depreciation.

To counter this criticism, one can possibly argue that faced by the pressure of maintaining the ratio-imposed capital adequacy, banks would have to restrict credit expansion. However, such a restriction carries the potential of affecting the economy adversely on the growth and employment fronts. It might unwittingly trigger the same sort of crises it was intended to stop. The Basel Accords neglect this side of the story. The solution to the problem lies in directly curbing the leverage lure. This demands a review of the traditional instruments central banks use for credit control to limit leverage gains.[8] This lends credence to the new

[8]Chapter 8 has reviewed current measures used for credit control and proposes a technique for limiting the leverage gains in a dual banking framework.

instrument for credit control LCR we have mooted in the preceding chapter. Also, the review must focus on the fast-growing adverse impact of public policy on monetary practice. The collapse of powerful banks and the spread of state bankruptcies in the wake of the recent turmoil are not accidental; the public policy dimension is quite visible. The autonomy of central banks is being fast eroded.

With the foregoing background developments, we may proceed to examine the basic provisions of the various Basel Accords in order to understand their content, thrust, and implications in the context of Islamic banks operating in a dual financial system.

10.2.2 Basel I (1988)

Soon after the formation of the Basel Committee, its members began to discuss the contours of a formal standard regarding the appropriate capitalization of internationally active banks. They noted that some of these banks took advantage of jurisdictional differences to escape the regulators; they even moved their activities to locations where the rules were not so stringent. The petrodollar boom had virtually ended, and the financial sector was in the grip of the resultant crises of the 1980s. These circumstances pushed the issue of banks' capitalization to the top of the Committee's programme priorities. Lengthy negotiations among the members led to the announcement of the first Basel Accord in 1988.

This Accord was simple and straightforward, as it was essentially an agreement between the Basel Committee members and was initially applicable only to those banks that were operating at the international level outside the parent country. The Accord received prompt acceptance not only from the banks in the Basel Committee member countries, but also from other global institutions. Basel I divided the capital of banks into two tiers on the basis of differences in the quality of their underlying assets, as already discussed above. Each of the two tiers was assigned a 4% risk weight that considered only credit risk, leaving out others, thus making the overall CAR equal to 8%. As this ratio was intended to define the minimum, not the optimal, capital requirement for a bank, it was assumed that well-capitalized banks would go in for higher ratios in order to cover the market and operational risks or currency exchange risks that the Accord had left out. It also did not cover the banks that were not operating outside the member countries.

One oft-mentioned aspect of Basel I is the four pillars on which it stands. The first pillar is the *Constituents of Capital*—Tier 1 and Tier 2—that we have already explained. The second pillar is the *Risk-Weighting System* that constitutes a comprehensive process of assigning weights to various bank assets. It mentions five risk categories that cover all assets on the balance sheet of a bank over a 0–5 point range. The specification for an asset depends on the discretion of a country's central bank. It seeks to take advantage of the close proximity between a bank's capital and the risk exposure of its assets.

The third pillar is a *Target Standard Ratio*. It ties together the first and second pillars of the Accord. It sets a universal standard, stipulating that 8% of a bank's risk-weighted assets must be covered by Tier 1 and Tier 2 capital reserves. Additionally, Tier 1 capital must cover 4% of a bank's risk-weighted assets. This ratio is taken as specifying the minimum safety limit for a bank. Finally, the fourth pillar—*Transitional and Implementing Agreements*—sets the stage for putting the Basel Accords into operation. It requires the central bank of each country to ensure that the Basel Accords are implemented. The central banks of all countries are requested to erect a strong surveillance and enforcement system to ensure that the Basel Accords are observed and that the transitional weights are provided to the Committee so that it can adopt the same over a four-year period, in place of the Accord standards.

10.2.2.1 Criticism

By the year 1999, all countries, including China, Russia, and India, had adopted the Accord provisions. Even so, the Basel I Accord has attracted much criticism. The main points raised are as follows.

- First, Basel I focused its attention only on credit risk, to the exclusion of other types of risks that are no less important, and it restricted the application of its recommendations to the G10 countries. Also, it did not cover all local banks, only those that were also operating outside their own country.
- Second, due to the haste that the Committee displayed in the implementation of its recommendations, banks were not always able to translate them into language easily understood by their wide-ranging clientele. This hindered the popularization of the recommendations.

- Third, even though the G10 countries already had in place, for the purpose of long-term growth, most of the basics that Basel I required, the national regulators deemed the Basel I recommendations excessive and a form of discrimination against their mega private banks; they began to demand extension of the Accord across the globe, including to emerging markets.
- Finally, the Accord provided leeway for banks to apparently maintain a low-risk profile while actually being able to indulge in much higher risks. To illustrate, the gap between short-term and long-term debt weighting was in the 1:5 ratio and the banks could easily convert short-term debt into long-term debt through the technique of maturity transformation. The weighting system in implementation also contained an incentive for banks to shuffle the geographical locations of their operations.

We shall see that subsequent Basel Accords did take notice of such criticisms and that changes were made to plug the loopholes.

10.2.3 Basel II (2004)

The limitations of the Basel I Accord surfaced over the years, and the criticism of its recommendations led the Basel Committee to revise the standards of capital adequacy for internationally active banks. The Basel II Accord was published in June 2004 and was titled *International Convergence of Capital Measurement and Capital Standards: A Revised Framework*. The framework was further amended in July 2005. Basel II greatly expands the range, depth, and technical aspects of the original Accord. This was essentially done by revising and revamping its pillars.

Taking note of the criticisms of Basel I regarding the first pillar, Basel II makes the measurement of a bank's risk-weighted assets more sensitive and candid, closing the loophole the earlier Accord contained. A bank cannot now conceal risk-taking through a transfer of assets to subsidiaries or by combining branch assets into a composite whole for the bank. Changes have also been made in the weighting scheme, incorporating the rating agencies' evaluation of assets into the picture. For example, A+ to BB+ debt is weighted at 50% while all debt rated below B− is risk weighted at 150%. Pillar 1 now covers not only credit risk but other types of risks as well. The Accord now provides risk weightings for all other market-based assets. Its strategy covers stocks, commodities, currencies, and mixed instruments, where weight assignment is based on a separate set of methodologies.

A special feature of Pillar 1 relates to the provision of protection against operational risks; it requires the creation of reserve pool out of profits. Of the three methods proposed for the purpose, the *Standardized Approach* appears simpler and easier to operate. The method identifies the business lines of a bank and the percentage that each line's profit should contribute to the reserve in cash form. The following is a brief description of the nature and role of each pillar:

1. Pillar 1 seeks to quantify the reserve that banks would need to cover market risk arising due to fluctuations in asset prices. For this, it makes a distinction between fixed-income assets like bonds and other sources, such as equity, commodities, and currencies, where income could be fluctuating. Implicitly, it separates the two components of the overall market risk: interest rate risk and volatility risk.
   a. For fixed-income assets, the risk evaluation is the 'value at risk' estimation (VAR). It is a complicated technique. Therefore, for banks that do not want to implement the VAR, Pillar 1 recommends the creation of a reserve tied to the asset maturities, to protect their fixed-income assets against interest rate variations.
2. Compared to Pillar 1 of the Basel II Accord, Pillars 2 and 3 are much less complicated. Pillar 2 essentially deals with regulator–bank relations. Regulators have the right to supervise the banks; they can even liquidate a bank if needed. They have the power to oversee the internal risk evaluation procedures, thus implementing the provisions that Pillar 1 specifies. They also have the discretion to change or amend these provisions in light of local requirements, especially if they find that a bank cannot manage its credit, market, and operational risks.
   a. Pillar 2 has indeed enhanced the regulatory power considerably. Regulators are now allowed to create a 'buffer' capital facility in addition to the minimum capital requirement if banks are found attempting to avoid Pillar 1 provisions. The regulators are allowed to take appropriate action to pre-empt oncoming crises in countries like China and Korea if capital reserves tend to fall below the minimum.

3. Pillar 3 seeks to improve market discipline within a country's banking sector. In this regard, the Accord makes a rather revolutionary proposal: to make available for public gaze some of the information regarding the banking structure and performance that was until then available only to the regulators.

10.2.3.1 The 2016 Revision

The 2007–2008 period of severe market stress exposed weaknesses in the framework for capitalizing risks from trading activities. In 2009, the Committee introduced a set of revisions to the Basel II market risk framework to address the most pressing deficiencies.[9] More improvements followed in subsequent years, but 2016 witnessed a substantive revision to the market risk framework. This was to ensure that internal model approaches to market risk deliver credible capital adequacy outcomes and promote consistent implementation of the standards across jurisdictions. The demarcation between trading and banking transactions was refined. The key features of the revised framework include:

- The internal models approach for market risk was revised to remove ambiguities;
- The standardized approach for market risk was revised to improve understanding;
- A shift was made from value at risk to an expected shortfall measure of risk under stress;
- The incorporation of the risk of market illiquidity was initiated.

10.2.4 Basel III (2010–2011)

Building on and carrying forward the Basel II framework, the Committee made public its third Accord, popularly known as Basel III, during 2010–2011. The Accord was scheduled for implementation over the period 1 April 2013 to 31 March 2018 (now extended to 31 March

[9]Losses in most banks during the financial crisis had been significantly higher than the minimum capital requirements under the former Pillar 1 market risk rules. A key point of the 2009 amendment was an additional response to the crisis, requiring banks to calculate a 'stressed value at risk' relating to significant losses.

The revised market risk framework comes into effect on 1 January 2019.

The revised market risk frame work has come into operation since 1 January 2019.

2019). The Basel III Report is a comprehensive document focusing on the consistency of risk weightings for banking assets. The salient features of the Accord are briefly as follows:

- **Capital requirements**: In addition to raising the capital requirement ratios for Tier 1 and Tier 2, Basel III introduces two more capital buffers:
  - A 2.5% capital conservation obligatory buffer; and
  - A countercyclical buffer, which would allow national regulators to require up to another 2.5% of capital during periods of high credit growth. The adoption of this proposal is not compulsory.
- **Leverage ratio**: Basel III introduces a minimum leverage ratio that is calculated by dividing Tier 1 capital by the bank's average total assets. The banks are expected to maintain a leverage ratio in excess of 3%. In July 2013, the US Federal Reserve Bank announced that the minimum leverage ratio would be 6% for eight system important financial institutions (SIFIs) and 5% for their bank holding companies. A SIFI could be a bank, an insurance company, or some other financial institution whose failure could trigger a financial crisis.
- **Liquidity requirements**: Basel III introduced two obligatory liquidity ratios. One is the *liquidity coverage ratio* that requires a bank to hold sufficient high-quality liquid assets to cover its total net cash outflows over 30 days. The other is the *net stable funding ratio* that requires the available amount of stable funding to exceed the amount needed to cover a one-year period of extended stress, i.e., the exposure of bank capital levels to turbulent economic and financial scenarios. Thus, Basel III tightens the leverage ratio framework and disclosure requirements of banks and other financial institutions to enforce discipline in the wavering financial markets.

Basel III was designed for staggered implementation over time. The span gave it flexibility and space for adjusting to changing needs and circumstances. Another welcome feature was that countries could adjust capital adequacy requirements to suit local conditions.

Unfortunately, Basel III has arrived on the scene when costs are rising and returns on capital falling. Critics have been quick to argue that the step would hinder growth rates, ignoring the fact that bumpy rides may also cause slower rates. In Europe, regulators, ignoring such apprehensions, are insistent on implementing the Basel Accords. Smaller banks are likely to gain. Indeed, part of the criticism emanate from ideological commitment to free markets.

10.3 The Basel Accords and Islamic Banks

Islamic finance operates as an integral part of the global financial system. As such, Islamic banks have to fall in line with international regulations as and when enforced. This adds to a unidirectional convergence of the systems (Hasan 2011). The Basel Committee Accords on capital adequacy measures have forced the pace of such convergence. Basel I was narrowly focused on the banks of the Committee's member countries and was of little consequence for Islamic banks. Basel III recommendations are in the process of being implemented over a time span. Thus, it is the Basel II standards that demand consideration in the present context. These standards have a blanket reach, covering banks across the globe. Islamic bankers and jurists found some of the prescriptions of the Accord incompatible with the nature of Islamic bank portfolios. For instance, the equity estimation for Islamic banks must include not only the bank owners' stake but also the investment deposits involved in participatory contracts.

Since the aim of these Accords is to have an adequate level of capital available in a bank for risk management, the following discussion is contextual to the risk-weighting of assets. It is also important to mention that in the calculation of risk weights, banks have the choice of either adopting the Basel II framework for the bank's calculation of capital adequacy or the internally set standards.

For Islamic financial institutions, various sorts of standards are set by two autonomous international institutions: the Accounting and Auditing Organization for Islamic Financial Institutions (AAOIFI) and the Islamic Financial Services Board (IFSB). The AAOIFI sets the *Shari'ah*-compliance standards for entering the Islamic financial markets, while the IFSB issues global prudential standards and guiding principles for the Islamic financial services industry in order to promote and enhance its soundness and stability. Overall, the objective is to build the confidence of the populace in Islamic finance by ensuring the transparency of transactions and protection of depositors' interests.

The following discusses the aspect of Islamic bank regulation both from the perspective of a local jurisdiction—the case of Malaysia is used as illustration—and from an international perspective. Specifically, we mention the regulations set in place by Bank Negara Malaysia—the central bank of the country—that harmonize with the Basel Accords. We also briefly look at the standards issued by IFSB to strengthen the regulation of Islamic banks at the global level, in line with the Basel Accords.

10.3.1 Pre-emption Bid

Malaysia was quick to see the Basel Accords coming and initiated measures (Table 9.1) in advance compliance, thanks to the foresight of Bank Negara Malaysia (BNM). The regulatory framework and supervisory structure for financial management had already evolved over time at a rather brisk pace, characteristically remaining focused on preventive actions aimed at stability and growth of the sector. Arrangements were made to enforce responsible business conduct, curb financial waywardness, ensure *Shari'ah* compliance of contracts, keep financial markets orderly, and payment systems sound, in addition to having tools ready to deal with crises when needed.

There is neither the need nor the space here to discuss in detail the provisions or the implications of the listed laws for Islamic banking in Table 10.1. Suffice it to say that they harmonize well with the intention and thrust of the Basel Accords. Their existence verifies that BNM is not merely the central bank but is the *bank* of Malaysia. It has acted with expedience and faster than most central banks in developing countries have done in testing situations. BNM has been able to harmonize national interests with global demands, especially in the tumultuous years since the turn of the century. It has kept *Shari'ah* scholars, academicians, and industry players continually engaged in meaningful deliberations on various issues relating to the industry.

Consensual decisions have emerged to become the basis of several reforms, culminating in the recent introduction of the Shari'ah

Table 10.1 Malaysia's laws for regulating the Islamic finance industry

CBA	Central Bank of Malaysia Act 2009
IFSA	Islamic Financial Services Act 2013
FSA	Financial Services Act 2013
DFIA	Development Financial Institutions Act 2002
AMLATFA	Anti-Money Laundering and Anti-Terrorism Financing Act 2001

Governance Framework (in 2011). As a result, practices such as the ongoing imitation of conventional products resulting in the erosion of their *Shari'ah* compatibility, is now frowned upon, and a December 2012 ruling intends to phase out the buy-back (*'inah*) sale and replace it with commodity *murabaḥah* (*tawarruq*). Most important is the rationalization that the Shari'ah Governance Framework has executed in the organization and role of *Shari'ah* committees: the number of their members has been raised from three to five, the frequency of their meetings has been increased, the scope of their participation in management has been enhanced, and they have been given greater operational independence. It is suggested that the voting and non-voting distinction among the members may also be abolished.

The supervisory role of the Shari'ah Advisory Council (SAC) of BNM has been expanded, making it the apex authority for the ascertainment of applied *Shari'ah* in Islamic banking and finance. The central bank has already demonstrated the value of the 2009 Central Bank of Malaysia Act. This was followed by the introduction of the Islamic Financial Services Act 2013, which is probably the most comprehensive legislation the industry has ever seen, worldwide. Supervision, audit, and research have all been revamped. The Shari'ah Governance Framework not only introduced the two tiers for capital adequacy but also initiated measures aimed at ensuring a robust risk management control process and internal research capacity. In this context, the International Islamic Liquidity Management Corporation (IILM) was established in 2010.[10] The Corporation not only provides *Shari'ah*-based short-term cross-border liquidity facilities to Islamic financial institutions, but also facilitates cross-country linkages and investment flows that promote stability. In sum, it is working to create international *Shari'ah*-compliant financial markets.

[10]Although the Corporation's headquarters is located in Kuala Lumpur, it has been established by central banks, monetary authorities, and some multilateral organizations to create and issue *Shari'ah*-compliant short-term financial instruments to facilitate effective cross-border Islamic liquidity management. The IILM Governing Board comprises the Islamic Development Bank Group, Bank of Indonesia, Central Bank of Kuwait, Banque Centrale du Luxembourg, Bank Negara Malaysia, Bank of Mauritius, Central Bank of Nigeria, Qatar Central Bank, Central Bank of the Republic of Turkey, and the Central Bank of the United Arab Emirates.

10.3.2 The IFSB Stance

In the same vein as Malaysia, the IFSB has recently announced IFSB-15 (2013) for Islamic financial institutions to strengthen the regulation of Islamic banks at the global level. IFSB-15 has revised capital adequacy for institutions offering Islamic financial services (IIFS), excluding the *takaful* institutions and Islamic collective investment schemes. The revision has enhanced the versions of two previous standards, namely IFSB-2 (2005) and IFSB-7 (2009), dealing with requirements for *sukuk*, securitizations, and real estate investments. It is worth noting that IFBS-15 also adopts Basel III proposals on capital components and macro-prudential tools for the IIFS. The standard will help implement a capital adequacy framework that will ensure the effective coverage of risk exposures of IIFS and allocation of appropriate capital to cover these risks.

For this purpose, IFSB-15 provides guidance on the features and criteria of high-quality regulatory capital components, including Additional Tier 1 and Tier 2, to comply with *Shari'ah* rules and principles. Similarly, the standard also provides new guidance on macro-policy tools, such as capital buffers, leverage ratios, and important local banks, which will facilitate supervisory authorities in achieving the goal of protecting the banking system and the real economy from system-wide shocks. Supervisory authorities among the IFSB member countries were expected to begin the implementation of IFSB-15 in their respective jurisdictions by January 2015.

Overall, we find that, at the Malaysian level, considerable measures have already been set in place by BNM to ensure proper regulation and to promote the stability of Islamic banks. Equally, at the global level, the IFSB has taken the necessary steps to incorporate measures proposed by the Basel Accords to ensure proper regulation of Islamic banks worldwide. The question posed is: to what extent are the Accords needed for Islamic banks in view of the arrangements that are already in place?

10.4 Concluding Remarks

This chapter has attempted to improve the general understanding of the Basel Accords, their objectives, and implications. We find that the Basel Accords need not create any special difficulty for adoption in the Islamic institutions of the global finance sector because these Accords largely aim at achieving liquidity risk mitigation and stability—objectives that *Shari'ah* also aims at and supports. Furthermore, the Accords contain flexibility to meet local and Islamic norms, and the greater role the Accords grant to regulators must be taken as a boon for the financial industry, including its Islamic segment.

However, the Basel Accords are lopsided to the extent that they exclusively focus on the numerator—the capital (and its tiers)—in calculating the adequacy ratios. But the denominator that includes receivables resulting from the creation of credit-on-credit seems to be the main culprit in crisis generation. Based on the fractional reserve principle, the credit creation power of the banking system as a whole is indeed vast. It is the major source that fuels speculation and fans the lure of leveraging, the impact of which is devastating. Insistence on capital adequacy is welcome, but it may not deliver unless credit control measures are revamped and expanded to effectively curb the leverage gains. Islamic banking has an inbuilt safeguard against the danger, as maintaining linkages with the real economy in all its transactions is obligatory.

A general framework of *Shari'ah* governance has been developed in Malaysia It contains measures to strengthen Islamic finance at the national and international levels though their impact is not yet much visible. The 2013 Islamic Financial Services Industry Stability Report of the IFSB is also a well-placed consolidation of its position on standards.

Interestingly, the Report negates the much-cherished thought that Islamic finance has not been notably affected by the 2007 financial crisis. The following Fig. 10.1 is self-explanatory. Notice that in 2007, financing, and deposits—were almost equal was almost equal. In 2008, the industry was booming—financing was much higher than deposits. However, by 2009 the crisis had reversed the relationship—financing and assets were both at their lowest ebb, leaving much of deposits unutilized. The shrinkage of the Gross Domestic Product and trade was thus *the* conduit not much talked about in discussions on 'crisis and Islamic banks'.

The problem of Islamic finance is not the shortage of liquidity, the focal point of the Basel exercise. In contrast, it is the underutilization of available resources. Arguably, insistence on adherence to the Basel Accords could be more a trend than a need. The standards evolved by local institutions are sufficient to take care of Islamic finance.

The recent developments in Islamic finance operations seem to be progressively dissolving into the mainstream currents. There is a

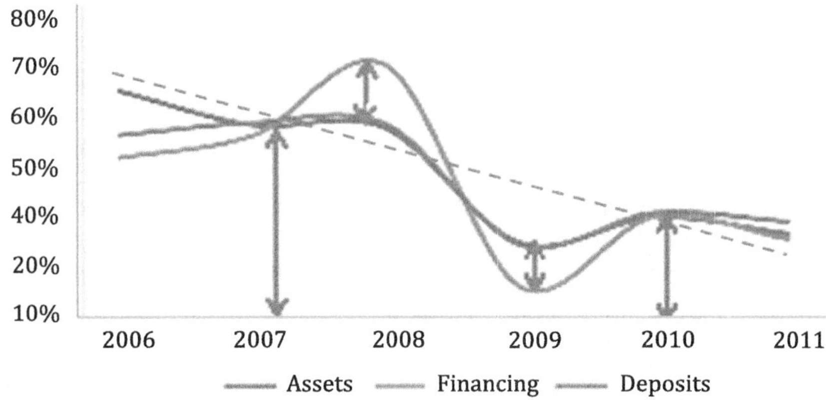

Fig. 10.1 Islamic finance variables behaviour during 2007 crisis (*Source* IFSB Services Report 2013 [Edited])

perception that its Islamic character is being eroded (Ahmad et al. 2014). Most of the Basel recommendations are so far welcome, but the situation may not remain so in the future. The composition of the Committee is exclusive in terms of its membership: the G10 plus Spain. The membership of the organization must be expanded to include members from the developing countries, including Muslim countries where Islamic finance is concentrated and is going to be dominant in the course of time.

Box 10.1: Bank for International Settlements

Consultative Document: Revisions to the minimum capital requirements for market risk

The Bank for International Settlements (BIS) was established in 1930 to promote global monetary and financial stability through international cooperation. The BIS operates as the bank of the world central bank. Its Committee on Banking Supervision (the Committee) is the primary global standard-setter for the regulation of banks and provides a forum for cooperation on banking supervisory matters. Its mandate is to strengthen the regulation, supervision, and practices of banks worldwide with the purpose of enhancing financial stability. The Committee reports to the Group of Central Bank Governors and Heads of Supervision and seeks their endorsement on major decisions. The Committee does not possess any formal supranational authority and its decisions do not have legal force. Rather, the Committee relies on its members' commitments to achieve its mandate.

The Committee continuously reviews its recommendations on regulatory standards with reference to capital adequacy ratios and revises them in light of members' feedback. The latest proposals were announced on 22 March 2018, for implementation next year.

In January 2016, the Committee published the standard 'Minimum capital requirements for market risk.' The proposals included in the consultative document are intended to address issues that the Committee had identified in the course of monitoring the implementation and impact of the standard. The proposed changes relate to the following aspects of the standard:

1. Changes to the measurement of the standardized approach to enhance its risk sensitivity;
2. Recalibration of the standardized approach risk weights for general interest risk, equity risk, and FX risk;
3. Revisions to the assessment process to determine whether a bank's internal risk management models appropriately reflect the risks of individual trading desks;
4. Clarifications to the requirements for identification of risk factors that are eligible for internal modelling; and
5. Clarifications to the scope of exposures that are subject to market risk capital requirements.

In addition, following the Committee's June 2017 consultation on proposals for a simplified alternative to the standardized approach, the consultative document *Revisions to the minimum capital requirements for market risk* proposes a recalibration of the Basel II standardized approach for use by banks with less material market risk exposures, to determine their capital requirements.

Source: Bank for International Settlements, https://www.bis.org/bcbs/publ/d436.htm, accessed 28 March 2018.

Basel III was initiated in the wake of the current turmoil that was blamed on chronic liquidity deficits. Thus, it focused on liquidity improvement and introduced to that end, two more ratios—the liquidity coverage ratio (LCR) and the net stable funding ratio (NSFR)—to strengthen the banks' ability to face crises. It is argued that compliance with the new requirements may be hard on Islamic banks (Ahmad et al. 2014). Islamic banks are yet very tiny compared to their conventional counterparts. One wonders if they need to follow the entire Basel paraphernalia, or would compliance with it be an unwanted and unnecessary burden on them? After all, Islamic banks do not create credit-on-credit, leverage gains do not play a dominant role in their profitability calculus, and the arrangements that are already in place seem sufficient to provide the required security.

In any case, no policy, irrespective of its form and content, is worth more than what its implementation achieves on the ground. Financing per se does not create perils; its mismanagement does. And successful management demands a minimal level of honesty, transparency, and equity to make policies work and achieve their goals. The critical minimum of these requirements is unfortunately missing. The recent turmoil (in February 2018), despite Basel, endorses the truth of the statement. The claim that Islam can do the trick may be valid, but can the present-day Muslim countries demonstrate the needed commitment to Islamic ethical norms and values? That is *the* question.

Case Study 10.1: Basel IV?

Released by the Financial Stability Board, Basel IV is a disputed term used to describe the changes to the Accords agreed in 2016 and 2017. It introduces changes that limit the reduction in capital that can result from banks' use of internal models under the internal ratings-based approach. These include:

- A standardized floor, so that the capital requirement will always be at least 72.5% of the requirement under the standardized approach;
- A simultaneous reduction in standardized *risk weights* for low-risk mortgage loans;
- Requiring banks to meet higher maximum leverage ratios (an initial leverage ratio maximum is likely to be set as part of the completion of the Basel III package);

- A higher leverage ratio for global systemically important banks, with the increase equal to 50% of the risk-adjusted capital ratio.
- More detailed disclosure of reserves and other financial statistics.

Test Questions

Q.1 Explain and illustrate how leverage gains lead to financial turmoil and may cause massive bank collapses via the piling up of non-performing loans.

Q.2 What is meant by capital adequacy under the Basel Accords? It is said the ratio that measures capital adequacy focuses on the denominator, ignoring the numerator management altogether. Do you agree? Give reasons for your answer.

Q.3 The directional approach to the Basel Accords was spelled out in 1988. Explain.

Q.4 Trace the evolution of Basel Accord III and critically examine its latest provisions.

Q.5 Write notes on the following:
  a. The Basel II pillars
  b. Capital adequacy ratio
  c. Risk-weighted assets.

What Next?

The two financial systems—Islamic and mainstream—are evidently moving closer in many ways. The next chapter explores the nature and causes of this growing affinity. More specifically, it examines whether the convergence is a boon or a bane for Islamic finance.

References

Ahmad, et al. (2014). Empowerment Through Microfinance: The Relation Between Loan Cycle and Level of Empowerment. *World Development, 62*(C), 75–87.

Carroll, J. H. (2014). *Hawser*. Grapnel Books.

Hasan, Z. (2011). Islamic Home Finance in the Social Mirror. *ISRA: International Journal of Islamic Finance, 3*(1), 7–24.

CHAPTER 11

Systems' Convergence: Boon or Bane?

Preview

This chapter examines if the convergence of the Islamic and conventional financial systems has been beneficial or cumbersome for faith-based economics. It finds that convergence has led to an initial structure-objective mismatch in the launching of Islamic finance. The abolition of interest and promotion of growth with equity were goals of the conceived system. These goals expressed a long-run vision to improve the condition of Muslim communities across the world. However, the organizational form adopted for Islamic finance, especially banking, was of the existing commercial institutions that provided essentially short-term loans on interest to trade, industry, and commerce.

The choice thus involved an intrinsic mismatch between the structure and objectives of Islamic finance. The choice did carry some advantages, but on a more important level, it exposed Islamic finance to commitments and influence that could not align well with the goals the pioneers of Islamic finance had in mind. Note that the intention here is not to suggest a reversal of the mismatch, but to guard against the stimuli that have led the nascent Islamic financial system into convergence and competition with the mature conventional counterpart the West dominates.

It is not the ground realities that are being adapted to *Shari'ah* norms; it is the norms that are being stretched to the limit in meeting the demands of the conventional system. Ordinary Muslims who hoped to benefit from Islamic financing remain unheeded. Thus, what Islamic finance can or cannot change will depend on where its ongoing

Z. Hasan, *Leading Issues in Islamic Economics and Finance*,
https://doi.org/10.1007/978-981-15-6515-1_11

integration with the conventional system leads it. Currently, most merits claimed for the Islamic system from convergence lack convincing evidence. The basic reforms financial systems require in the face of recurring crises are the control of credit, leverage lure, and speculation. Islamic finance is in principle, better equipped to achieve these ends. The impact of market-led changes has adversely affected academic pursuits.

Learning Outcomes
The study of this chapter is expected to make the reader understand the following facts and trends in Islamic finance that seek to arrest certain growth trajectories in its future development.

- The objective of launching Islamic finance was to shun interest, avoidable uncertainty, and speculation in the running of the system, with a view towards promoting the welfare of the common man.
- The stated objectives demanded more attention to long-term financing arrangements, but following in the footsteps of conventional banking caused more focus on the short-term financial needs of growing and expanding businesses.
- **The structural choice tends to encourage the imitation of conventional tools, but with** an Islamic veneer. Innovations are scanty.
- The convergence has made the Islamic system submit to the same norms of *modus operandi* as the conventional system and has forced market competition onto nascent Islamic finance to its disadvantage, when compared to the developed mature mainstream.

11.1 Introduction

The topic 'What Islamic finance does or does not change' was intelligently left vague at a 'Workshop on Islamic Finance' held at Strasburg, France 2008 where the author presented a paper on what he regarded as a structure-objective mismatch in Islamic banking. Islamic finance is of course a wider term than its banking constituent, but that being its most dominant and consequential part, we restrict here the use of the term as referring mostly to banking. Conventional (commercial) banks were, and mostly remain, the providers of short-term finance to trade, industry, and commerce, while some long-run communal (*ummatic*) goals, including promotion of growth, improvement in distributional equity, and alleviation of poverty were initially conceived to be the focal points of Islamic finance for resource allocation. However, Islamic banks adopted the conventional organizational forms when making their appearance on the scene.

These forms, in retrospect, have been found unsuitable for serving the objectives the early writers on Islamic finance implied they would. But the choice they in fact made was not without reason. Muslims had for long experienced commercial banks working around them as dealers in money. What these writers found unacceptable in their operations from the Islamic viewpoint was the use of interest as a price for loans the banks advanced, or the cost for deposits they obtained. If interest was expelled from the transactions of commercial banks, they were obviously the first institutions to attract attention as conforming to Islamic norms.[1] Participatory finance of the old days—*mudharabah* and *muskarakah*—based on profit/loss sharing could take, they thought, the place of interest as a return on funds committed to business or paid to depositors. The precept 'no risk no gain' was proposed and projected with little loss of time as the sole, inviolable, and departing principle for Islamic finance. The proponents missed the point that structures erected to meet short-term ends could rarely be efficient in achieving long-run goals. Islamic banking thus began with a structure-objective mismatch on its road to progress.

The removal of this mismatch is not the point of this chapter; its consequences are.[2] Even today, a large number of writings on Islamic finance continue adhering to the tradition and argue, rather innocuously, that the scheme of participatory finance is the answer to all the ills of modern finance. They do not care to find out why that mode of financing is not picking up pace: its share, despite the merits claimed, has not yet crossed the 10–20% mark in aggregate.[3] Any discussion on what Islamic finance does or does not change can hardly ignore without discomfiture of the form-objective mismatch and what it has led to. Indeed, the failure to

[1] These writers, in all fairness, did make it clear that the Islamic economic system is much more than merely capitalism plus *zakah*, minus interest. Nevertheless, they lacked the economic acumen to visualize the ramifications of choosing the nomenclature in conceiving banking without interest.

[2] Islamic finance has crossed the point of no return on this road, but there is scope for course modification and that is taking place in some measure.

[3] For hurdles in the way of participatory finance, see Hasan (2002).

realize this vital fact lies at the heart of the many divergent views on the convergence of the Islamic and mainstream financial systems.

On the one hand, we have those who argue that the convergence is imminent, although it might remain asymptotic.[4] This, of course was no discovery; one could have easily seen this coming as the logical consequence of the organizational forms Islamic finance had chosen. On the other hand—and this is more interesting—there are those who stress that the scope for convergent evolution of the two systems is very limited due to the narrow range of Islamic financial instruments, even if we ignore other reasons (see Honohan, July 2001).

It is worth noting that over the decades—especially during the past 10 years—Islamic finance has made great strides. The industry has experienced dramatic growth and transformation. Its reach, coverage, risk diversification, development of regulatory frameworks, professional education programmes, and international funds movement have all improved and kept up the pace in a fast-globalizing environment. Opportunities for Islamic finance are increasing, but so are challenges (Bank Negara Malaysia 2008). The total volume of Islamic assets held by banks—Islamic and conventional—was expected to cross

the US dollar one trillion mark by 2010. It is noteworthy that by the close of 2018 Islamic finance has already crossed US dollar 3.4 trillion mark.[5] But at the same time one must not be oblivious to the fact that conventional finance has also been expanding at no less a pace, if not faster. The result is that, on a conservative estimation, the shares of the two sectors in market assets worldwide remain almost steady at around 1:80. Islamic finance is as yet no more than a candle facing the sun. Are the two realistically comparable on any performance or achievement criteria, more so when the bulk of the business is with the Islamic windows or subsidiaries of the Western banks? The phenomenon is the result of the convergence of the systems being largely unidirectional; thus far, one sees the little impact of Islamic finance on its mainstream counterpart.

[4] See Askari et al. (2009). It echoes the same sort of realization that 'the search for an alternative to Capitalism is [now] fruitless ... Those who wish to reform the world should focus on the potential for change within capitalism.' (Ahmad 2007, IRTI).

[5] IFSB, https://www.islamicfinance.com/category/market-information/market-size-and-growt. Accessed 1 September 2018.

What Islamic finance can or cannot change in the near future would largely be determined by the facts stated above. On matters of product design, rules and regulations, fixing of standards, benchmarking, risk management, and rating procedures, Islamic finance has already been drawn in by the mainstream whirlpool; follow the leader has been the underlying truth of the story. Hopefully, Islamic finance may have some impact on the moral, ethical, regulatory, and social responsibility aspects of the global financial architecture in due course of time, for reasons we shall have occasion to mention later.

This chapter is spread over five sections, including the present one. In Sect. 11.2, we shall discuss in some detail the reality with reference to the much talked about convergence of the Islamic and conventional systems. Section 11.3 is devoted to some problems internal to Islamic banking itself, especially relating to the divergent interpretations of Islamic injunctions across countries. In Sect. 11.4, we elaborate on several problems that threaten the future of the world financial systems, irrespective of their types, especially the impact of the current turmoil on financial institutions. We shall evaluate in particular the claims Islamic finance scholars make in that context. Section 11.5 evaluates the impact of financial convergence on teaching and learning in academic institutions. Finally, Sect. 11.6 contains some concluding observations.

11.2 Convergence: Nature and Consequence

Convergence has been an increasingly used term in the more recent literature on Islamic finance. Interestingly, most of the writings that talk of convergence emanates from the West, more so from the economists working with international financial institutions: the World Bank or the IMF.[6] Even so, the nature and implications of convergence remain largely unexplained. Convergence means the movement of two objects from opposite directions such that the gap between them steadily tends to become narrower. This movement would be rather fast if both objects approach each other with the same speed, but convergence

[6]The Arab Financial Forum (AFF) at Harvard University in 2006 focused its yearly discussion on convergence issues. A paper by Hasan (2004), dealing with sustainable development and Islam, was also included in the proceedings, because it was seen as implying that finance and environment were areas bearing promise in promoting *positive* convergence of the two systems.

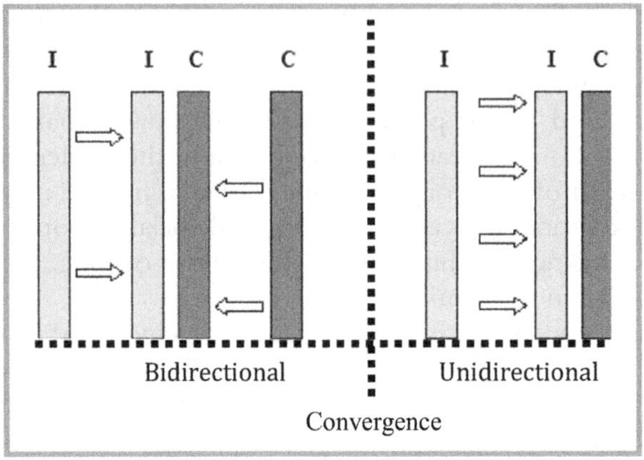

Fig. 11.1 Convergence types between Islamic (I) and conventional (C) financial systems

is still possible if one object remains stationary while the other alone moves. Differences in these two processes—bidirectional and unidirectional, as depicted in Fig. 11.1—may not have the same message or consequence.

Convergence has benefited Islamic finance and has contributed to its rapid growth in many ways. The literature had evaluated critically the role and character of interest finance and found how the institution is a hindrance to achieving growth, equity, and stability in modern economies. Convergence helped avoid isolation of Islamic finance from the global structures; dealings with international organizations like the World Bank, the IMF, and the World Trade Organization (WTO) remained intact. More importantly, product designs were found ready at hand for modifications to make them meet *Shari'ah* requirements. Not a few see as a great facilitating advantage. In fact, a jurist friends who sit on the *Shari'ah* boards of a couple of banks informed in response to a question that scholars on such boards invariably avoid initiating new products. Instead, they prefer to ask the bank managers the details of the conventional product for which they need to have an Islamic counterpart. For it is much easier, he said, to place on a product an Islamic veneer, rather than to structure an entirely new one. Imitation is, of course, easier than innovation and abounds, but this need not imply that

Islamic finance has completely been devoid of innovation. In fact, there have been many and varied innovations, some even novels.[7] However, the advantages of convergence have not been an unmixed blessing.

The fast expansion in the volume of Islamic finance in recent years has led many to see a clear functional parallelism between most modern Islamic and conventional financing instruments to the extent of postulating—rather overconfidently—that Islamic finance, in most areas of economic activity, is at par with mainstream capabilities. In any case, the expansion has led to a convergence that essentially is unidirectional. The conventional system, because of its size, age, and maturity, has had a tremendous magnetic pull that the nascent Islamic system could hardly resist. Islamic products are, and will increasingly be, structured for the global marketplace, thus hastening convergence to universally accepted mainstream norms. Policymakers for Islamic finance are relentlessly pushing the system to that destination. The governor of the State Bank of Pakistan was candid on the point when she observed:

> Practically, the Islamic industry currently is bank-based. Product diversification, albeit slow, is emerging but returns are *engineered* to ensure conformity and convergence with conventional industry.[8] (Emphasis added)

The convergence of Islamic finance and the mainstream positions has resulted in Islamic instruments being seen as a subset of those available in conventional finance. The pressure to make products simpler, more appealing to customers, and more diversified, and to conform to mainstream standards, is being insisted upon in order to be more competitive. Is it not strange that countries have so often advanced and used the infant industry argument to protect their manufactures, insurance, and shipping, for example, but initiators of Islamic finance ventured to challenge the giant from day one? Clearly, the sort of convergence that is being forged must serve the interests of developed countries more than others in two ways:

[7] See Honohan (2001) op. cit. for some interesting examples from Iran, the Sudan, Malaysia, and Pakistan.

[8] Shamshad Akhtar (April 2008). Note that the Seventh Harvard University Forum on Islamic Finance (April 2006) was entitled 'Integrating Islamic Finance in the Mainstream: Regulation, Standardization, and Transparency'.

1. Conventional banks that dominate and control the global financial system can achieve in the Islamic finance area what they cannot in the conventional system. To illustrate, in the mainstream system, the rate of interest must observe the central banks' ceiling. There are as yet no such restrictions on markups used in Islamic transactions. In participatory finance, using the interest rate for benchmarking the return to depositors enhances leverage benefits for bank owners. Islamic finance is potentially more profitable for them.
2. urrently, there is much liquidity in Muslim countries, especially in the Middle East, because of high (and rising) oil prices. Most of this money comes from developed countries. Islamic finance promises to enhance the possibility of a larger flow of this money back to where it came from. Western countries eye an effective control over the use of this wealth.[9] (This observation can be an important topic for research.)

The compulsions for unidirectional convergence have put experts and scholars alike under pressure to make *Shari'ah* norms somehow adaptable to the demands of modern finance and its increasingly wilful mechanisms. Islamic finance now operates more as a supplement to the conventional system, rather than in parallel as a competitor. This has made public opinion in the Muslim world turn to another presumably more potent issue: the convergence between the instruments Islamic finance has been using, and their compliance with *Shari'ah* norms. In Malaysia, both the governor of Bank Negara, and the chairperson of the Securities Commission (SC), has voiced this concern. Then-Governor Zeti Akhtar Aziz, drawing attention to the ongoing development of mechanisms for risk mitigation and liquidity management, made a significant observation: Of importance are the solutions needed to converge the market requirements and the *Shari'ah* compliance.[10]

[9] Islamic Finance Report (2009). The report concludes: 'Islamic finance has moved beyond uncertain experiment during its embryonic life. Teething problems remain but with the right tools, collaboration between regions and greater transparency, convergence towards Western conventional markets and a greater share of investors' portfolios is well within reach'. (Project Finance International, Tuesday, 9 February 2010).

[10] See Zeti Akhtar Aziz (2008a): A global growth opportunity amidst a challenging environment, Governor's Keynote Address delivered on 8 October at State Street Islamic

Zarina Anwar, then the SC chief, candidly stated that Islamic finance products must be strictly *Shari'ah* compliant, but she believed that convergence to law could have spatial differences to internationalize Islamic finance. Her more significant observation we feel is that:

> There is always the need to explore how Islamic finance can help the Muslim community (the *ummah*).[11]

This is a point we referred to in the Introduction above. And this brings us to our next section on the issue of *Shari'ah* compliance of Islamic financial instruments.

11.3 Divergent Views on Compliance

In recent years Islamic finance has seen the appearance of some serious differences in what instruments and practices have or have not been *Shari'ah* compliant. Most of the controversy has centred on the activities of banks which hold the bulk of Islamic assets, followed by *sukuk* (bond) issue, investment funds, and *takaful*.[12] The modes of business these banks use mostly involve *murabahah* transactions and the issuance of *sukuk*. Both have run into difficulties on the issue of *Shari'ah* compliance in recent years.

Commodity *murabahah* has so far been the most widely used financing instrument in Islamic banking. But of late, some court decisions have gone against Islamic banks in Malaysia on *murabahah* contracts, and have placed people in a quandary. It is being increasingly asked if commodity *murabahah* defies Islamic requirements. Evidently, in principle it does not. Commodity *murabahah* falls in the same generic category of *uqud al-mu'awadhat*, or exchange contracts, that cover all the types

Finance Congress, 2008, Boston U.S.A. The observation is bit cryptic on the nature of convergence she implied.

[11] Zarina Anwar in an interview with Anna Maria, August/September 2008, downloaded from the Securities Commission website at https://www.sc.com.my/.

[12] Of the total global assets of Islamic finance, estimated at US$951 billion for the year 2008, commercial banks accounted for about US$704 billion or 74%. For investment funds, *sukuk*, other funds, and *takaful*, the percentages were 10, 10, 5, and 1, respectively (IFSL Research, January 2010).

of transactions that Islam allows. In exchange contracts, a given quantity of one commodity is traded for a given quantity of another commodity, including money. The money value of a commodity is called its price. The delivery of a commodity and the payment of price may be simultaneous, i.e. on the spot, or the obligation of one of the parties may be deferred to a future date. Contracts involving commodity *murabahah* belong to the deference of obligations group. A client may, for example, request a bank to purchase a car for him on a cost-plus basis. The arrangement per se does not contain any element of interest. Markup pricing is allowed on the ground that 'time has a share in price' (*lil zamani zun fil thaman*). Indeed, it is this juristic pronouncement that constitutes the justification for allowing the deferring of obligations in Islamic contracts. It was not the principle but the structuring of the contracts[13] that went wrong in the cases mentioned. The reasons for the current disquiet are to be sought elsewhere.

Commodity *murabahah* contracts may not defy the *Shari'ah* norms if viewed on a case-by-case basis, i.e. in a microframe of analysis, but their overwhelming use at the aggregative or macro level is working against the *Shari'ah* spirit.[14] Debt transactions dominate the scene to the cost of the real economy. The use of deferred contracts seems to have already been carried too far. Even Zeti, the former governor of Bank Negara Malaysia, had to advise Islamic banks to curb the use of fixed return transactions. Presumably, it is time to apply the principle of *saad-al-dharai* that closes the potential avenues for circumventing the *Shari'ah*; more so its objectives and spirit. It is not the permissibility

[13]Opinions also differ considerably on the structuring of contracts. A significant example is the commonly upheld prohibition of multiple contracts in a single sales transaction. But Nizam Yaqubi argues that the prohibition refers to specific instances where the combination of contracts is used as a legal device to permit or facilitate *riba*, or where the combination leads to any other textual prohibition (e.g. *gharar*). He supports the view that the strict rules of combining contracts can be relaxed in certain cases to facilitate Islamic finance contracts. *Ijara*, *murabahah*, and *musharakah*, are, to him, the clear examples (Harvard University Forum on Islamic Finance, April 2006). Eyebrows may be raised on this interpretation of the *Hadith*.

[14]*Shari'ah* scholars tend to miss the point: what may look perfectly permissible at the micro level may become violative of the spirit of the law at the macro level. On this, see Mahmoud A. El-Gamal (2009). Macro vs. micro considerations in Islamic financial *ijtihad*, Lecture, IIFF, Istanbul.

of ***murabahah*** contracts per se but their defective structuring and indiscreet use that is fuelling the perception that Islamic bankers are covering up the taking of interest through the back door. Debt sales, ***inah***, and ***tawarruq*** have deeply divided juristic opinions within and across countries. Malaysia and the Middle East stand poles apart on the issue of their permissibility. Here, two observations may not be out of place:

- The Islamic economic system has social implications related to economic development, especially for the fulfilment of basic needs and achieving distributional equity. Islamic banking operations are not contributing to these goals; they are essentially guided by profit considerations. Admittedly, profit is important, or rather imperative, for Islamic banks too, as for any other business, but it cannot be the sole criterion in evaluating their performance. Econometric models on the performance of Islamic banks invariably consider profit, cost, or size as determinants of efficiency. Their structural blemishes apart, no social welfare measure appears in such models, presumably because quantification is not possible on a uniform basis.
- Islamic banks are also diverting—like their conventional cousins—the savings of those in the lower rungs of the society to the upper classes, aggravating income inequalities. In addition the distribution of earnings between the owners of banks on the one hand, and their depositors on the other, is greatly skewed in favour of the former. The combined GDP of 57 Muslim counties is estimated at more than one trillion US dollars, but the question of how *Shari'ah*-compliant Islamic finance benefits him is the sort of question the man in the street is still asking.
- Islamic ***sukuk*** is mostly based on commodity ***murabahah*** and is one Islamic instrument that has recently been getting all the attention. Broadly speaking, ***sukuk*** are asset-backed, ***Shari'ah*** compliant, trust certificates. They are generally used in conjunction with two types of contracts:
  a. The ***ijara*** structure where the lease rental provides an income (profit) to the holder; or
  b. The ***musharakah*** structure where profit share becomes the holder's income.

The juridical validity of *sukuk* has been suspect since the time Sheikh Taqi Usmani cast doubts on its *Shari'ah* compatibility in 2008.[15] His reasons for declaring 85% of *sukuk* as non-compliant of the law were briefly as follows:

- There have been cases where the assets in the *sukuk* were the shares of companies that did not confer true ownership, but that merely offered to *sukuk* holders a right to returns.
- Most *sukuk* issued today are identical to conventional bonds with regard to the distribution of profits from their enterprises at fixed percentages benchmarked on interest rates. The legal presumption regarding *sukuk* is that no fixed rate of profit or refund of capital can be guaranteed. And this brings us to the third point.
- Virtually all *sukuk* issued today guarantees the return of the principal to holders at maturity—just as in conventional bonds—through a binding promise from either the issuer or the manager to repurchase the assets at the stated price, regardless of their true or market value at maturity.

However, in one of his recent writings, Taqi Usmani does not touch on the issue. Rather, he appears to quote with approval an Associated Press business writer where she says: '*Sukuk* are the equivalent of bonds, but instead of selling a debt, the issuer sells a portion of an asset which the buyer is allowed to rent'. In that aspect, *sukuk* avoids causing a mismatch between pure money and real transactions.

As if anticipating such positions, Islamic economists have argued from the very beginning that the sharing of profit (or loss) is the basic distinguishing feature of interest-free finance. Indeed, they claim participatory finance to be the alchemy responsible for numerous ills in the conventional financial system.[16] Of late, this claim has been getting louder. It is being vociferously stated that one of the most serious gaps in Islamic finance is the reluctance of market players to promote risk-sharing equity-styled financing and investment. Thus, the promotion of institutions supporting risk-sharing partnerships is vital to realizing the full potential of an Islamic financial

[15] Harbhajan Singh, '*Sukuk* debate rages—*Shar'iah* compliance questioned', News Analysis: Islamic Finance, *The Malaysian Reserve*, 11 February 2008, p. 5.

[16] This argument implies the need to research the evolution of the capital structures of modern corporations as we find them today, and nullify the arguments against having equity shares alone as the source of funding.

Table 11.1 Oligarchic concentration of advisory positions in Islamic financial institutions

No. of advisory board positions	*Total number of scholars*	*Occupancy per scholar (minimum)*	*Occupancy per scholar (mean)*
467	94	2	5.0
400	38	4	10.5
339	20	6	16.9
253	10	15	25.3

Source Constructed using data provided in the report "Top Shari'ah Scholars in GCC: Funds @Works 18.09.09"[24]

system. On this, economists, jurists, and central bankers are all seemingly in agreement. However, claims do not win conviction, evidence does. And despite all efforts, participatory funds currently do not constitute more than 10–15% of Islamic financing worldwide.

What blocks the way is again the structuring of Islamic banking on the conventional pattern. Mainstream banks could bring long-term investment financing under their umbrella by introducing what is known as universal banking, although they still remain short-term credit providers. Islamic banks, because of their infancy, small size, and lack of adequate funds, in addition to a dearth of managerial skills, may find it difficult to go universal. Western banks running Islamic windows or subsidiaries are in a different category in this context.

Finally, the mismatch is a complicating factor in interpreting the law, in that it has also been in some measure a contributory factor, causing the regulatory regimes of Islamic financial institutions (IFIs) to vary across countries. The variations may possibly widen as Islamic financial centres gain strength within a conventional banking environment in places like London, Singapore, Hong Kong, and now, France. Some differences may be accommodated, but narrowing them down is always advisable. International organizations have been established to set standards that are expected to strengthen and eventually harmonize prudential regulations as they apply to IFIs.[17] It is hoped that evolving regulatory

[17] Dahlia El-Hawary, Wafik Grais, and Zamir Iqbal, 'Diversity in the regulation of Islamic Financial Institutions', *The Quarterly Review of Economics and Finance*, vol. 46, no. 5, 2007, pp. 778–800. See Table 11.1 in footnote 17, although it is based on 2000–2001 data. The situation may have since changed substantially.

Table 11.2 *Shari'ah* advisory distribution in gulf cooperation countries (GCC) 2013

Rank	*Name of the scholar*	*Countries*							*Total*
		Bahrain	*Dubai*	*Kuwait*	*Qatar*	*Saudi Arabia*	*Abu Dhabi*	*Others*	
1	Shwik Nizam M. S. Yaqubi—(8)	19	4	6	2	1	3	11	46
2	Sheik Dr. A. S. A. Ghuddah—(S)	9	5	11	2	4	1	13	45
3	Dr. Muhammad Eid. Elgari—(S)	7	3	9	1	7	0	8	31
4a	Dr. A. Khalifa Al Qassar—(K)	2	0	18	0	0	1	1	22
4b	Sheik Dr. Mohd. Daud Bakar—(M)	6	4	2	1	0	0	9	22
6	Sheikh Sulaiman Al Manear—(S)	7	2	0	0	9	1	1	20
7	Sheikh Dr. H Hamid Hasan—(D)	6	6	0	0	0	3	4	19
8	Sheikh Dr. M. E. Qaradaghi—(S)	4	5	2	3	0	0	3	17
9	Dr. Essa Zaki Essa—(K)	1	0	15	0	0	0	1	17
10	Sheikh I. Jasimi Al Nashimi—(K)	4	4	5	0	0	1	1	15
Total		65	33	64	9	11	10	52	254

Source Funds @ work (2018)

frameworks will entail convergence of the practices of Islamic financial intermediation with its conceptual foundations, rather than being led by convenience-inspired imperatives.

One possible reason of divergent interpretations of Islamic law could be the dearth of qualified jurists, giving rise to oligarchic competition among them. A recent study, *Shariah Scholars in the GCC—A Network Analytic Perspective*, finds that 94 scholars from 19 countries sit on 467 advisory boards with five positions per head. This seems reasonable, but the distribution of positions among scholars is far from being uniform as Table 11.1 in footnote 17 so clearly brings out. Some doubt that most *Shari'ah* scholars tend to work in unity to promote mutual interests. It is intriguing, if true.

The study provides valuable insights into the engagements of jurists in financial institutions in the Gulf Cooperation Council (GCC). It finds that scholars from just five countries hold 254 advisory board positions, averaging more than 25 positions per head.[18] This seems oligarchic (Table 11.2).

11.4 Islamic Banks and Financial Turmoil

The 2007–2008 turmoil originated in conventional finance for a variety of reasons. The main ones were the race for credit creation in the banking system, the corporate leverage lure, the expansion of secondary markets, heightened speculation, and reckless fiscal policies of the US administration, all being the results of incorrect market incentives. A detailed analysis of the causes of the current global meltdown falls outside the scope of our discussion here. Two characteristics of conventional financing systems that often tend to bring them to their knees, as recently happened, are however worth noting: the avaricious credit expansion and reckless speculation, especially in the volatile derivative markets.

We have shown in Chapter 7 how conventional banks create an inherently unsteady inverted pyramid of credit on a narrow cash base and how the leverage gains' lure makes the system additionally prone to instability. Islamic banking has won much praise from bankers, foreign professionals, scholars, and jurists for staying resilient and stable during the current

[18] A comparable survey revealed a similar sort of concentration in 2009 for Islamic banks across the globe (Hasan 2009).

global crisis. We are of the view that the praise has been overdone; the claim ignores the relative position of the two systems. Arguably, Islamic finance, being risk averse and liquidity-oriented, has not yet developed enough to catch the affliction. In a storm, it is the oaks that are uprooted, not the reeds. Even so, Naveed Mohammed wrote:

> Islamic financial commerce co-exists within the wider economy and as such is not a safe haven bubble despite often being labeled as such. During the global financial crisis of 2008, initially the market was not affected as the 'toxic assets' built up on the balance sheets of American banks were not shari'ah compliant hence Islamic banks were not impacted. However following the collapse of Lehman Brothers Islamic institutions were impacted from drops in valuation of real estate and private equity as these sectors tend to be heavily invested by Islamic firms.[19]

Indeed, some Islamic banks did go down because of the turmoil. For example, The Investment Dar in Kuwait, Amlak and Tanweer in Dubai, Islamic Bank in Qatar, Gulf Finance House in Bahrain, and Emirates Islamic Bank all came to grief in 2009 in one way or another. Please refer back to Fig. 10.1 of the preceding chapter and the accompanying narration.

The lack of connectivity of Islamic banking with the global financial system only changed the route of the turmoil in reaching Islamic banking. It came via the shrinkage of the economies during the turmoil, changing the relationships between the crucial macroeconomic variables, as Fig. 9.1 of the preceding chapter illustrates. Going back, notice that around the year 2007, the assets, financing, and deposits of Islamic banks were in a state of harmony. Then, 2008 saw an expansion in the excess of deposits over financing, a situation that reversed in 2009, but as part of an overall downward drift of all variables. A few individual banks in the Middle East did come to grief, and in Kuwait, some banks in trouble were denied a bailout. The evidence detracts much from the claim of Islamic banks coming out of the crisis unscathed (Hasan 2016). Thus, we find that it is unwittingly the same linkage between the financial and real sectors of the economy, which is claimed as imparting relative stability to the Islamic system, which may, in a way, tend to work in the opposite direction.

[19] Naveed Mohammed, 'Islamic and Conventional Banking Comparison', IslamicFinance.com. Accessed 28 March 2018.

Banks, businesses, and society all suffer in a crisis, irrespective of systemic differences. Governments tend to become hostage to big business. Large banks cannot be allowed to fail; rescue packages and bailouts involving trillions of dollars have become the order of the day. For instance, Barry Ritholtz, in his forthcoming book *Bailout Nation*, estimates US rescuing costs until now at US$4.6165 trillion. He calls the figure conservative, even as the current credit crisis bailout, he notes, is the largest outlay in American history (Hasan 2008). This seems to lay bare the latest axiom of capitalism: *profits are private, losses public*. Islamic banks are not yet part of the story because they do not indulge in multiple credit expansion the way their conventional counterparts do.

Unabated credit expansion and its consequences, as explained above, bring us to another point. Mounting loans during the current crisis have fuelled the expansion of the derivative markets and in turn, have received a boost from that expansion. The risks of the rise in loans were covered by complex derivatives, but those exotic instruments only generated an unending 'cover-risk-cover' chain fuelled by traders' greed for enhanced commissions and short-term capital gains (Stieglitz 2009b). US derivatives in 2016 stood at more than 20 times the world GDP and over 10 times global stocks and bonds!

Initially, some jurists—Hashim Kamali (2002) in particular—claimed that there is scope in law for the creation of derivatives in the area of Islamic finance as well; a few were in fact launched. However, currently, it is being argued that derivatives are unIslamic for a variety of reasons, especially because they are no more than bets on bets on debts on debts. One opinion is that: '… regulations and prosecutions are needed to punish and deter present and future self-paid corporate crooks looting and draining other peoples' pensions and savings'.

Box 11.1: Immitation vs compliance

It is frequently argued that Islamic banks imitate conventional financial products but must at the same time operate in accordance with the rules of *Shari'ah*. This imposes on them additional jurists' and lawyers' fees for *each* product they sell. Add to these costs similar expenditure on title deeds and on erecting special purpose vehicles. Thus, Islamic financing tends to cost more than the conventional, reducing their comparative efficiency, and therefore profitability. Voluminous empirical evidence has been marshalled in support of this contention.

One need not question the actuality of this line of argument; it contains elements of truth. However, it stops short of answering a few questions. The argument implies a *ceteris paribus* assumption. Comparing Islamic financial institutions, with their tiny size and minimal infrastructural facilities, with the gigantic, mature, centuries-old conventional systems is like standing an earthen lamp before the sun. The mismatch between the objectives and the structuring choice has contributed to competitive disadvantages. Then, where is the committed to faith clientele? Is it the assumption of the critics that relative profitability is, or should alone be, the deciding factor in choosing the mode of finance for Muslims? If so, why have Islamic finance at all? Which is better: letting savings lie idle or earning a return, although smaller, in Islamic finance? Author

11.5 Academic Problems

Islam is the only religion whose scripture opens to mankind with an instruction to read. The *Qur'an* tells us that Allah was the first teacher of man and is the source of all knowledge. He releases it to those who seek little by little, so that pride and arrogance may not overtake humans. History tells us that so long as Muslims followed this instruction and gathered knowledge from wherever they could and improved upon it, they led the world in various fields: sociology, ethics, philosophy, astrology, medicine, mathematics, and crafts. Until the early decades of the nineteenth century, there was hardly any university in Europe worth the name that did not have a translation department converting Arabic works into Latin and thence into the vernacular.

So long as Muslims led the world in various fields of knowledge, they dominated in political expansion and prosperity, reaching their zenith in the middle of the thirteenth century. But the pursuit of wealth converted the teachers into traders and with that began the decay of their glory. It was completed with the colonial occupation of their lands. After the Second World War, the lands became independent but intellect remained subjugated. The process and consequence of this subjugation have to be understood.

11.5.1 *Approach and Direction*

Broadly, two streams of thought guiding, at least implicitly, the writings on Islamic economics, including finance, are discernible. First, is what we may call the puritan or all-or-nothing approach that focuses mostly on Islamic requirements to define or mould reality. It essentially relies on *negative filters*. Thus, we find scathing criticism of mainstream economic order to establish over it the superiority of the Islamic system. The stance promotes divergence and confrontation. The second is what we may call a gradual step-by-step approach. Writers in the areas of Islamic economics and finance during the past two decades or so have increasingly taken this route. It works on the principle that what is conducive to human welfare and cannot be shown, with or without modification, to violate *Shari'ah* norms, is acceptable as Islamic. The approach promotes *positive filtering*; it assimilates all that is useful in the growing stock of knowledge in mainstream economics. The approach is accommodative and friendly. The teaching and learning of mainstream economics cannot be, if at all, done away with abruptly. However, this approach is fraught with difficulties. Some of these faced by the discipline are briefly as follows:

- ***Rise of finance:*** The type of knowledge and skills the market seeks largely determine the form, content, and level of instructions for various academic disciplines. Education has to follow the market. In the present context, financial markets have become dominant in Muslim countries. We have discussed above why and how the unidirectional convergence of the Islamic financial system and the conventional tends to move it away from *Shari'ah* norms and requirements. The rise of financial markets has paled the rest of Islamic economics into insignificance; it is fighting for survival (Khan 2013).
- ***Course structures:*** Islamic economics programmes contain diverging course structures at various levels of instruction in institutions of higher learning across the globe, in the sense that they contain a couple of exclusive types of course modules dealing with Islamic economics and finance, fitted into an otherwise mainstream programme. They do not attempt the inclusion of Islamic content or modification of the conventional material, even where it is appropriate and feasible. The level of demarcation is mostly hazy; the undergraduate and graduate courses tend to overlap. Structural changes are too frequent, and are at times ill conceived.

- ***Reading material:*** Present-day Muslims are not generally in the habit of reading and writing. We do not have many world-class economists among us, even as in not a few countries the bulk of university academics received their higher-level degrees from Western universities. A perusal of the readings recommended in the course outlines finds that most of the entries are from Western sources. Regrettably, there are no textbooks available on *Islamic economics* that have won recognition, let alone acceptance. A committee was formed in 2004 at the Islamic Research and Training Institute (IRTI) to write one; it has yet to finalize the table of contents for the book. ISRA has taken up the challenge and may soon publish a textbook on Islamic economics for which they have commissioned contributions from individuals.
- ***Dearth of journals:*** There are few good journals on Islamic economics and finance published in Muslim countries and for two reasons. First, there are not many writers who can make publishable contributions to Islamic economics, although finance has an edge. Second, Western degrees carry a premium in developing economies, including Muslim. Western education sharpens rational thinking and analytical skills, supported by an advanced toolkit. The disadvantage is that it is ethics-neutral in its positivist stance. It conditions the thought process to Western values and modes of thinking. There is an insistence on publication in the Western journals for professional acclaim and promotion. This has assumed the proportions of a lucrative business. Journals of all sorts are mushrooming in the Western countries. Marketing is on the rise for fast and frequent—even monthly—*listed* publications. Handsome publication fees have to be paid, empirical modelling is an imperative. Students receive concessional rates. We have examined a few articles published in such journals and have evidence of low quality and erroneous language.[20]

[20]In recent years there has been an alarming rise in predatory publishing in social sciences. Education in Islamic economics and finance has not remained unaffected by the contagion. A recent work has explored its reasons and unwelcome consequences for the nascent discipline. It argues that the proclivity needs curbing (Hasan 2018).

In courses on Islamic economics and finance, teachers and students mainly rely on journal articles, monographs, and books that often do not meet the requirements in terms of analytical depth or coverage for college-level students. IRTI, the Islamic Foundation in the UK, the International Institute of Islamic Thought, and the Islamic Economics Research Centre at King Abdulaziz University have all done laudable work in publishing useful reading material. Of late, international Islamic universities in Islamabad and Kuala Lumpur are adding to this effort. Indeed, it is these institutions that give shape and stature to the subject so as to enable it to win worldwide recognition as an upcoming academic discipline. However, their publications have by and large failed to attract referencing in course modules at institutions of higher learning, broadly for three reasons:

i. Most of the books are not cohesive and their authors tend to sidetrack the contributions of other writers, unless the same are in line with the older stream of thought. They often attempt to cover vast and varied topics in the same volume. The result is that most authors are found hopping from one topic to another without coming to grips with any.
ii. At times, the writings suffer from serious internal inconsistencies and erroneous formulations. Their reviews published in academic journals have been rather prosaic, not evaluative. Even when weaker areas of any work were sometimes highlighted, the subsequent literature took little notice of the comments, however valid. One must know that nobody of knowledge can develop on the right course in the absence of constructive evaluations and the cognizance of what they are worth. The response from authors to the comments in the literature on Islamic economics is almost non-existent.
iii. Many of the publications treated as e-books by their authors and publishers are at best no more than extended papers on specific topics. Individually, they seldom bear the format of a reading text for students. Publications from IRTI, especially, tend to fall in this category. They are useful, but are generally more informative than analytical or evaluative. For graduate-level students, their value is especially limited.

Box 11.2: Islamic finance performance

- The Islamic banking sector retained its dominance in the global IFSI. The domestic market share for Islamic banking in relation to the total banking sector continued to increase in at least 19 countries, remained constant in six, and declined in 11 jurisdictions among the 36 jurisdictions covered in the IFSI Stability Report 2019.
- The Islamic banking sector's performance grew by a mere 0.9% in 2018, compared to 4.3% in 2017, and as at 2018 accounts for 72% (76% in 2017) of the total value of IFSI assets mainly due to the depreciation of local currencies in terms of the USD, especially in some emerging economies with a significant Islamic banking presence.
- The ICM sector as at end of 2018 accounts for 27% of the global IFSI assets on the back of a positive performance due to the sovereign and multilateral *sukuk* issuances in key Islamic finance markets to support respective budgetary expenditures as well as number market debuts of sovereign issuances, including green sovereign *sukuk* to finance eco-friendly environment projects.
- The share of global *takaful* industry in the global IFSI remains unchanged at 1.3%. Global *takaful* contributions grew by 4.3% (y-o-y and in nominal terms) in 2017, with a six-year (2012–17) compound average growth rate of almost 6.9%. As at the end of 2017, an estimated 306 *takaful* institutions, including *retakaful* and *takaful* windows, now offer *takaful* products in at least 45 countries globally.

Source IFDI Stability Report 2019.

11.6 Concluding Remarks

It is neither expedient nor possible to indulge now in substantive structural changes in Islamic finance, but it is still not too late to initiate some sideward diversions. Even remaining within the existing framework, there is much that can be done to make Islamic finance meet the ends it was initially meant to serve. Indeed, some policy measures have already been initiated in this direction. However, the decisive question still remains: for whom does the Islamic finance bell toll?[21] Our stand is that Islamic finance was conceived to serve the *ummatic* interests and that objective need not be sacrificed at the altar of globalization. Others can, of course, benefit from the system if they so desire, following Islamic norms. It is with this perception that we venture below some observations for the consideration of scholars and the policymakers:

- One reform the Islamic system calls for is the separation of short-term financing from the long term. Experience shows that the two are difficult to handle efficiently under the same organization. Non-Western Islamic banks attempted, for instance, to diversify their activities by introducing various types of funds in their ambit, but the overall progress in the area has not been encouraging. The money flows into Islamic funds from Muslim countries are disappointing. It is reported that there is a very small number of Islamic funds—just 500 plus—and they held assets under their management in 2008 valued at a meagre amount, about US$25 billion, even as the private wealth in the GCC alone was estimated at US$1800 billion. Participatory (profit and loss sharing) finance too, as indicated above, is not making much headway. Universal banking is not the answer for reasons explained earlier. What is required is the expansion of well-managed and cost-effective specialized institutions like unit trusts, investment houses, and multipurpose cooperative societies.
- Industrial/commercial units in Muslim countries are, on average, of much smaller size than in the West. The promotion of micro-financing institutions can do wonders in alleviating the grinding poverty in many of the economies. What rural (*grameen*) banks have done in Bangladesh is an eye-opener not only for what they have achieved, but for the method they used. Note that it was the much-maligned interest-based financing, not the exalted banking without interest, which won the day.[22] Presumably, that was *the*

[21] One argument advanced for a speedy convergence of Islamic finance and mainstream requirements is that the system is not for Muslims alone. Others can, and are, taking advantage of it. The rules of the game must be even handed.

[22] Public sector banks in India too, are handsomely contributing to the transformation of the rural economy. The State Bank of India has sponsored 3000 poor girls in and around Chandigarh in their education (see *Mail Daily*, March 2010, p. 11).

message implied in conferring the Nobel Prize on Prof. Yunius, interestingly, not for economics but for peace!

- Another matter that is hanging fire in Islamic finance is regulatory rules, procedures, and authority allocation. Much laudable work has been done in this area, but regulation will always remain an issue in finance, for both economic and ideological reasons (Stieglitz 2009a). The question in principle is: how much regulation do financial systems require? There is a clash between market freedom and policy intervention. The problem is to find a balance between the two and maintain it under the volatile economic conditions and social aspirations of today. The answer in fact depends on who commits the mistake of crossing the perceived limits. In the current crisis, it is plainly market misconduct that brought in the devastation. Naturally, the regulators have their tails up.[23] In Islamic finance, the regulators have the opportunity to streamline, *inter alia*, the legal advice system. The task may, for example, be centralized as in Malaysia. Again, finance is not without economics. To keep the bigger picture in view and to make implications of proposed regulations clearer, well-qualified economists must be associated with such advice as full members at all levels.
- In Islamic finance, one needs sound governance, resistance to the conventional forms, and sophistication, so that this may result in avoidable complications and costs for a yet tiny segment of the global system. It is not necessary to imitate each and every little thing just to have the elation of being at par with the conventional system.
- It is futile to think of Islamic finance as being in competition with the mainstream institutions in sharing the market. In contrast, a favourable terrain for competing is transparency in contracts, promotion of information equality, avoidance of the detachment of finance from the real economy, and eschewing the temptation of shady dealings. There is a need to tighten and streamline the documentation of contracts. It is the moral high ground where Islamic finance can lead the conventional system by example. The current meltdown has shaken the conventional system to its foundations and its proponents are realizing the value of being virtuous; they are searching for appropriate ethical norms to pursue.

[23] A. Greenspan, 'Section IV.1. Principles of Reform', in *The Crisis* (Second Draft, 9 March 2010), pp. 19–37. Available at: http://csinvesting.org/wpcontent/uploads/2015/12/BURRY_The_Crisis_By_Alan_Greenspan-3-9-10.pdf.

- With the fast growth of Islamic finance, there has also been an increase in the expectations gap between Islamic finance practitioners and civil society members on the role that IFIs should play in society. There is a growing feeling that speed is no advantage if things tend to move off course. The recently released AAOIFI standards cover 13 aspects of social responsibility, such as client engagement, employee welfare, charity, environment, investment quotas, and more. On these criteria, the overall response of the IFIs to social responsibility is quite encouraging, even as performance varies widely between institutions' social responsibility.[24] More has to be done until the man in the street feels that something is indeed being done for him. Of the 57 Muslim countries, 25, or almost half, are among the least developed economies in the world.
- Islamic finance is no more than a highway under construction in a vast roadmap of economies intended to develop with Islamic orientation.[25] Related issues have to be attended to simultaneously if Islamic finance is to deliver. Political will alone is the key that can unlock the doors to prosperity along the right path. And remember, no public policy, however well designed, is worth more than what it is in practice. Governments in various countries—irrespective of their formal shades—have to demonstrate that Islamic norms can well be converted into ground realities to become a way of life.
- The impact of market-driven systemic convergence on academic organization and activities cannot be ignored; course correction is an imperative.

Finally, if Islamic finance was restricted to Muslims, the words of Allah alone would have been enough to shun interest and set the community on the road to progress and prosperity. But because others were invited to benefit from its advantages, a rationale had to be provided. The conflict eventually led to an objective-structure mismatch.

[24]Survey Report (2009) on Social Responsibility: Trends in Islamic Financial Institutions.

[25]Anwar Ibrahim, delivering his keynote address at the Seventh Harvard University Forum on Islamic Finance (April 2006), reminded the audience of the larger framework within which Islamic finance functions—the *Shari'ah*. Specifically, he stated that there was a need for an expanded discourse with global relevance and impact. It was appropriate, he argued, that we strive not only to be contractually *Shari'ah* compliant, but also to attempt achieving the main goals of the *Shari'ah*.

Test Questions

Q.1 Explain the nature of convergence of financial systems—mainstream and Islamic. Comment on the merits and demerits of such convergence.

Q.2 Verse 3:130 in the *Qur'an* terms the 'doubling and quadrupling' of the sum lent as *riba* but as there is no further clarification of the verse, either in the scripture or in the prophetic sayings, is it valid to define *riba* as *any* addition over and above the sum lent? Argue your case.

Q.3 Of the world market share of Islamic banking, over 70% is the share of six Gulf countries—Saudi Arabia, UAE, Kuwait, Qatar, and Bahrain. How would you account for this concentration?

Q.4 It is claimed that some defining characteristics of Islamic finance kept Islamic banks unaffected during the 2007–2008 global turmoil. Would you support this claim? Give reasons for your answer.

Q.5 Write notes on the following:

a. System convergence versus independence
b. Academic consequences of convergence
c. Fast, imitative, expansion of products vs. slow but compliant growth

What Next?

An important characteristic of Islamic finance is that it seeks to encourage the use of risk-sharing products in financing activities. However, risk sharing is vigorously being presented as the sole principle of Islamic finance. Chapter 12 evaluates the proposition.

References

Ahmad, K. (2007). *Capitalism. Socialism and Welfare State.* IRTI Jeddah Power Point Slides.

Akhtar, S. (2008, April). *Speech at a Securities Commission Forum on Islamic Finance.* Malaysia.

Anwar, Z. (2010). An interview with Anna Maria August/September 2008 downloaded from SC web site. IFSL Research Report on Islamic finance.

Askari, Iqbal, & Mirakhor. (2009). *Globalization and Islamic Finance: Convergence, Prospects, and Challenges*. Singapore: John Wiley & Sons (Asia) Pte Ltd.

Bank Negara Malaysia. (2008, October). *Governor's Keynote Address Islamic Finance: A Global Growth Opportunity Amidst a Challenging Environment*. State Street Islamic Finance Congress 2008, Boston.

El-Hawary, D., Grais, W., & Iqbal, Z. (2007). Diversity in the regulation of Islamic Financial Institutions. *The Quarterly Review of Economics and Finance, 46*(5), 778–800.

El-Gamal, M. A. (2009). *Macro vs. Micro- Considerations in Islamic Financial Ijtihad*. Lecture IIFF Istanbul.

FDI Stability Report. (2019). *UNCTAD*.

Finance Congress. (2008). Boston, U.S.A.

Greenspan. (2010, March 9). Section IV.1. Principles of Reform. In *The Crisis* (pp. 19–37). Second Draft. http://csinvesting.org/wpcontent/uploads/2015/12/BURRY_The_Crisis_By_Alan_Greenspan-3-9-10.pdf.

Harvard University Forum on Islamic Finance. (2006, April).

Hasan, Z. (2002). Mudarabah as a Mode of Financing in Islamic Banking: Theory, Practice, and Problems. *Middle East Business and Economic Review, 14*(2), 41–53. Sydney, Australia.

Hasan, Z. (2004). *The New World Order, Muslim Predicament, and the Way Out* (MPRA Paper 3009). University Library of Munich, Germany.

Hasan, Z. (2008). Credit Creation and Control: An Unresolved Issue in Islamic Banking. *International Journal of Islamic and Middle Eastern Finance and Management, 1*(1), 69–81. UK, (Emerald).

Hasan, Z. (2009). Islamic Banking: Commodity Murabahah Remains in a Lurch – Note. *International Journal of Islamic and Middle-Eastern Finance and Management, 2*(1), 77–79. Emerald.

Hasan, Z. (2016). Risk-Sharing: The Sole Basis of Islamic Finance? Time fora Serious Rethink. *Journal of King Abdulaziz University: Islamic Economics, 29*(2), 23–36.

Hasan, Z. (2018, June). Academic Sociology: The Alarming Rise in Predatory Publishing and Its Consequences for Islamic Economics and Finance. *ISRA International Journal of Islamic Finance, 10*(1), 6–18.

Honohan, P. (2001, July). *Islamic Financial Intermediation: Economic and Prudential Considerations*. Development Research Group of Financial Sector Strategy and Policy Department, World Bank.

IFSL Research. (2010, January). London.

Kamali, M. H. (2002). *Islamic Commercial Law: An Analysis of Futures and Options*. Selangor: Ilmah Publications.

Khan, M. A. (2013). *What Is Wrong with Islamic Economics*. Northampton, MA: Edward Elgar.

Mail Daily. (2010, March 10).

Mohammed, N. (2018). *Islamic and Conventional Banking Comparison*. IslamicFinance.com. Accessed 28 March 2018.

Napier, C. (2009). *Survey Report (2009) on Social Responsibility: Trends in Islamic Financial Institutions*. www.researchgate.net/publication/4737506_Social_reporting_by_Islamic_Bank.

Stieglitz, J. (2009a). *Capitalist Fools*.

Stieglitz, J. (2009b). *Freefall: Markets and the Sinking of the Global Economy*. London: Allen Lane.

The Malaysian Reserve, 11 February 2008. https://www.vanityfair.com/news/2009/01/stiglitz200901-2.

Zeti, A. A. (2008a). *A Global Growth Opportunity Amidst a Challenging Environment*. Governor's Keynote Address delivered on 8 October at State Street Islamic Finance Congress, Boston, MA.

Zeti, A. A. (2008b). *Keynote Address Delivered on 8 October at State Street Islamic Finance Congress, 2008*. Boston, U.S.A.

CHAPTER 12

Risk and Islamic Finance: Correction of a Misconception

Preview

The discussions on risk—its meaning, bearing, sharing, or transfer—have recently assumed prominence in Islamic finance literature in the wake of devastations the 2007–2008 financial crises unleashed across nations. Islamic scholars were quick to claim that there was no impact of the crisis on Islamic banks because they worked on a risk-sharing principle. In contrast, mainstream institutions suffered, they thought, because they worked on a different plank—the transference of risk to counter parties.

This chapter argues that neither the current practice of Islamic banking supports risk sharing as its sole principle nor does its future prospects depend on it. The proposition only seeks to put Islamic finance on a non-existent trajectory. The author clarifies confusion regarding the proposition and some of its corollaries. Contextually, it deals with measurement of risk, its relationship with return to capital and its distributional equitability. The focus of the chapter is rather restricted. It does not deal with various types of risks the banks face in their financing activities or with issues in risk management.

Z. Hasan, *Leading Issues in Islamic Economics and Finance*,
https://doi.org/10.1007/978-981-15-6515-1_12

Learning Outcomes
The study of this chapter is expected to help the readers understand the following.

- Risk referring to the possibility of the future outcome of an economic decision being unfavourable (loss) has two components (i) measurable and (ii) unmeasurable.
- Measurable component can be insured against and the premium can be included in the cost of production reducing reported profits. The real risk of business resides in the unmeasurable part of risk called *uncertainty* in the literature.
- Realized or ex post profit is historical data. It can be one of the factors that influence profit expectations but other factors are usually dominant. Thus uncertainty and profit influencing business decisions are both futuristic or ex ante concepts.
- No one-on-one relationship can be established between the two ex ante concepts that justice would demand.
- Risk or uncertainty is not a tradable commodity in Islam. The principle of sharing profit does not include sharing of loss that in any case falls on capital owners, not the entrepreneur. Risk sharing is a result of profit sharing, not its cause.

12.1 Introduction

Islam prohibits giving or taking of interest in finance. Instead, it allows financing contracts broadly of two sorts. First is the financing on a participatory or profit and loss sharing basis. The contract may assume the form of ***mudharabah*** or ***musharakah***. The second is what are called the deferment contracts wherein the obligation of the party to make payment or of the party to deliver the effects is postponed to an agreed future date. The generic form of this latter arrangement is known as murabahah or the cost-plus system. The plus part is known as the 'markup' and derives its permission from an Islamic maxim that allows a time value for money in deferred price payments (Laldin et al. 2013, pp. 30–36). However, the early Islamic scholars swayed by some distinctive features of the participatory models regrettably put a rather restrictive interpretation on the maxim deriving from it a 'no risk, no gain' precept which, they thought, makes risk sharing the exclusive principle of Islamic finance.

The fact is that the maxim covers both sorts of contracts we have mentioned. The choice of one or the other category is discretionary; no preference whatsoever is indicated. Interestingly, the proponents of the 'no risk, no gain' precept accept this much. For example, see Chapra (2014) and Osman and Mirakhor, of the same year for such acknowledgement without realizing that the acceptance conflicts with the 'sole principle' tag they stick to risk sharing; it becomes irrelevant, rather misleading. Instead, the proponents of the precept continue to parade their exclusivist approach without any let up. Their insistence on sharing of risk being the absolute and paradigmatic imperative of the Islamic financial system remains unrelenting.[1]

The world's financial system is inherently prone to instability and financial crises since it works solely through the transferring of risks, not through their sharing; It is instructive to recall how all this confusion started. The early Islamic scholars, eager to showing Islamic finance sans interest as superior to and distinct from the conventional, saw the departure point in its participatory modes based on the sharing of profit and loss in financing and hastened to deduce that risk sharing was an Islamic imperative for claiming any share in profit. The view led to the coinage of the precept—no risk, no gain (Chapra 1986, pp. 64, 166).

The precept lay dormant in the literature, save some occasional mention until it was challenged in the literature (see, for example, Hasan 1983, 2005). However, the devastation that 2007—2008 financial turmoil inflicted on the global economy provided the proponents of Islamic finance with a fresh impetus to highlight the fallibility of the conventional system and push the divine one, as they understand it, to the fore as a replacement.

The reason for the turmoil was, they argued, the interest-based conventional finance which subsists on transferring risks to counterparties. In contrast, Islamic finance, they believed, promotes risk sharing that ensures stability and equity in the growth process. The distinction led to the retrieval of the 'no risk, no gain' precept from the literature. The task of reloading it back on the pedestal is led, rather religiously, by Prof Abbas Mirakhor the First Chair Holder of Islamic Finance at the

[1]For deferment contracts are like interest-bearing debt contracts; ṣukūk are known as Islamic bonds. Indeed, the proponents of the principle themselves lament this being the position in Islamic finance. (See quotation from Mirakhor below in the text.) Take note also of the very title of Mirakhor (2015).

renowned INCEIF. Risk sharing has been a major theme in most of his recent lectures including YouTube-tube uploads, and publications he has co-authored with others. Some researches he supervises also focus on the same theme. He states his position as follows.

Practitioners grounded in conventional finance, however, were interested in developing ways and means of finance that, while *Shari'ah* compliant, were familiar to and accepted by market players in conventional finance Scholars emphasized risk sharing while practitioners focused on traditional methods of conventional finance based on risk transfer and risk shifting. In doing so, instruments of conventional finance were replicated, reverse engineered, or retrofitted for *Shari'ah* compatibility, a somewhat regrettable process. (Mirakhor 2014, p. 107).

The observations along with supportive statements in other writings of Professor Mirakhor on the topic may be put below as his basic convictions, without being unfair to him, we suppose.

- The world's financial system is inherently prone to instability and financial crises since it works solely through the transferring of risks, not through their sharing;
- Islamic finance which allows only sharing of risks, not their transfer can alone pull the world back from the brink of disaster. It is the replacement for the faulty crisis-prone conventional system.

The contentions coming from a senior academician and practitioner carry far-reaching implications for Islamic finance, its substance, character, and direction. That the interest-based conventional system of finance is fragile and unstable is an established fact. That equity is better than debt as a source of finance is also not in dispute. The difficulty with the contentions of Professor Mirakhor essentially is with their 'solely' and 'only' aspects. These aspects need a litmus test to find whether his thesis has legs to stand on or tends to collapse under its own weight. This chapter is a humble attempt in that direction.

To that end, Sect. 12.2 briefly explores the relationship between risk and return to capital. Section 12.3 examines the proposition that Islam allows only the sharing of risk as the basis of financing. Section 12.4 extends the critical appraisal of the risk-sharing rule in its exclusivist frame. A number of empirical studies—Mirakhor (2015) being the latest in the series—claim that Islamic banks have faced the current turmoil better than the conventional. The proponents of the precept cite these empirics as the evidence in support of their claim to the relative superiority of Islamic finance to project it as a replacement for the conventional system. Section 12.5 comments on the efficacy of this evidence. Finally, Sect. 12.6 concludes the argument of the chapter with a few additional observations.

12.2 Risk and Return to Capital

The adage 'no risk, no gain' presumes an unbreakable linkage between risk and return to capital. Is this presumption valid? Historically, the association of risk with return on capital emerged to justify the charging of interest on loans largely taken to meet basic survival needs or to perform social rituals (Rubin 2011, p. 1313). The flow of money was mostly from the rich to the poor in society. The rates of interest were exploitative as borrowings usually did not create the means for their own repayment. In default, the transfer of tangible assets from the poor to the rich was a common occurrence. The emergence of grinding poverty and abhorrent distributional inequalities of wealth and incomes were the consequence.

However, commercial lending grew rapidly with the passage of time and the bulk of the loans in Arabia were indeed for commercial purposes when Islam made its advent on the scene (Chapra 1986, p. 64). But during the early decades of industrial expansion (1775–1825), people normally used their own capital in dominant industries, hiring labour and renting land and tools from others. The managerial function centred on the capitalist, and competition was moderate. Thus, Marshall in the first edition of his Principles of Economics (1890) could see an industry dotted with tiny owner-operated firms, rising and falling on their own while the industry continues to expand just as trees do in a forest which itself continues to grow. The analogy implied that the issue of profit appropriation was then of little consequence, with entrepreneurship and management forming a single functional entity.

During this early era of industry, the income of the owner–manager naturally got linked up with capital in all the classical writings, the word 'profit' is found to be used in this sense (Ormerod 2010). However, this association gave rise to much confusion in economic theory as interest also was attributed to the owners of capital. Early classical writers could not provide a basis to separate the two or justify their attribution to the same functionary, the capitalist (Knight 1921, p. 23). The latter-day economists created the distinction between interest and profit by linking profit to risk (Hawley 1893), albeit they still saw an element of risk remaining associated with interest (Knight 1921). Importantly, however, Knight nullified all theories tying profit to risk. He did so with a simple argument which briefly runs as follows. Under perfect competition participants in production have, by assumption, complete information of the market and enjoy perfect mobility, economic profit must be zero; for normal profit that the firms get is treated as an element of cost.

Dynamic change that cannot be foreseen, however, makes competition imperfect, and business ventures become risky—money invested could shrink. This fear of losing money divides society into two sorts of people. Most people prefer to have assured incomes rather than face uncertain fluctuations. Such assurance is available if they are willing to work for others. For, there are also people in society who are willing by temperament to derive their income by engaging in businesses wherein they expect to earn higher incomes as profits. Accordingly, risk divides society into the hired and un-hired factors of production, the latter being called the entrepreneurs. They are the risk-takers and earn profit. Others like the workers seek to join the production process for secure fixed incomes. Thus came into being the residual claimant theory of profit (Hawley 1893).

Knight (1921) regarded the possession of capital as a necessary condition for entrepreneurship; for, in his view, an empty-handed person could not guarantee contractual payments to the hired factors of production.[2] He divides risk into two parts—measureable risks and unmeasureable risks which he labels, respectively, as 'risk proper' and uncertainty, the division difficult though (NYU.edu 2014). Measurable risks can be insured at a cost; thus they pose no threat to business and being cost. And yet, Knight did not see any connection between profit and capital. He considered profit to be a reward for entrepreneurial services. The proposition must be discomforting for the 'no risk, no gain' proponents in Islamic finance. For, they do not regard the possession of capital as a prerequisite for entrepreneurship. On the contrary, their *mudarib* is an

[2] Possession of capital being a necessary condition for entrepreneurship, Knight raises the question: Is it really the mental attitude to risk-taking or lack of means to face uncertainty that plays the dominant role in dividing people into the hired and un-hired production factors? To me the question looks more as belonging to income and wealth distribution than a matter of temperamental differences.

empty-handed worker possession of capital being a necessary condition for entrepreneurship in Knight puts a question mark on this proposition. However, more damaging to the 'no risk, no gain' proposition is Knight's treatment of risk in his work.

Knight divides risk into two parts—measureable risks and unmeasureable risks—which he labels, respectively, as 'risk proper' and uncertainty (NYU.edu 2014). Measurable risks can be insured at a cost; thus they pose no threat to business and being cost, cannot be a part of profit. The premium paid to the insurer is a charge against revenues like wages or rent the businesses pay. It is uncertainty, the unmeasurable risk, that forces one to peep into the future but what he could see would depend purely on luck or chance. The bifurcation is of far-reaching consequence for Islamic finance where gharar or uncertainty has to be avoided. The injunction implies reference only to uncertainty that can be measured, i.e. to 'risk proper' as defined above.

Unless one is able to refute the logic of the uncertainty bifurcation, risk-management discussions in modern finance—Islamic or conventional—must lose much in content and significance. For, measurable risk must be insured; the unmeasurable ones or uncertainty, we have no means to guard against. Beyond what can be insured at a cost, *tawakkul*—welcoming what Allah may grant, profit or loss—is alone the best risk-management tool for Islamic finance. Indeed, present-day risk management does not, as it cannot, measure total risk due to an unmeasurable mix. Risk managers measure probable (insurable) loss, and to avoid it incur an internal cost possibly higher than the insurance premium.[3] Also, the risk-profit linkage we referred to above cannot be shown delivering justice, one of the top priorities of Islamic finance; for, no one-on-one correspondence can be established between risk and profit because of uncertainty affecting both. Furthermore, the risk-profit linkage is but ex ante whereas, the negotiated sharing applies to a division of ex post profit; no risk is involved. Islam allows sharing of profit (loss) of which risk sharing is a consequence, not the cause.

The contribution of Knight's contextualization to Islamic finance is twofold. First, he provides a precise definition of what risk is and what

[3]There is a fundamental difference between the reward for taking a known risk and that for assuming a risk whose value itself is not known. Risk managers can measure only the mathematical probability of loss—the known risk—but a known risk will not lead to any reward or special payment at all (Knight 1921, p. 38).

it is not. In contrast, the proponents of basing Islamic finance solely on risk sharing never clarified what they meant by risk or what distinction they make between risk sharing and risk transfer? And, in what situation one of the two would hold well against the other?[4] Is sharing or transfer of risk to be within the capitalist class or other factors in production should also be participating in sharing? It is such sort of issues that we shall address in the following sections.

Second, Knight took note of the rise to dominance of modern corporations that has characteristically changed the risk-profit equation in businesses; especially finance. Capital, organization, and entrepreneurship have become distinctly separate entities with reference to their rewards. The bond between profit and risk-taking has much loosened. The appropriation of profit has long become non-functional, not governed by any theory; power is the arbiter. The proponents of risk sharing do not seem to have imbibed the ramifications of this change and its impact on the risk-reward equation.

Box 12.1: Risk and Risk Management

Risk is a psychic concept, i.e. it is 'perceived'. It is difficult to measure. All risk cannot be measured. Components that can be measured have to be identified. These components, along with their probability measures and weightings have to be settled. If enough data on them can be gathered, it can form the basis of risk measurement framework. Still, technical risk analytics requires assumptions about underlying preferences—typically expressed through a utility function. Such analysis is usually used to:

- Rationalize behaviour we observe
- Provide guidance/control over our own behaviour

Once utility comes into the picture, measurement is not possible unless based on somebody's preferences; for, we need preference ordering. Whose preferences would matter must be identified. The problem

[4]The fact that both conventional and Islamic banks use exactly the same formula to make provisions for loan.

does not end with such identification. There are a host of risk-management models. Model selection poses a different set of risks and problems related to manage them. It is suggested that:

> Model risk should be managed like other types of risk. Banks should identify the sources of risk and assess the magnitude… Banks should consider risk from individual models and in the aggregate.

Thus viewed, risk measurement is a hazardous affair; still, risks must anyway be measured.

Based on:

Hsiu-Mei Chang, FCAS AIG, Risk Management Director. (2016, October). *Model Risk Management*. http://www.casact.org/education/caserm/2016/presentations/CS6_2.pdf. 29 March 2018.

12.3 Risk Sharing and Islamic Finance

The claim 'no risk, no gain' is based on a rather restrictive interpretation of a leading Islamic maxim derived from a Prophetic tradition; it says: 'benefit goes with liability'.[5] The problem is with the interpretation of the word 'liability' in the expression as the bearing of risk in financial transactions.[6] Islam allows profit and loss sharing contracts among financing modes but not to the exclusion of others considered equally valid. Risk bearing is a consequence—not the cause—of such contracts. To put it straight, there is no such thing in Islam as a risk-sharing contract which, when entered into, would result in the sharing of profit or loss. Liability in the maxim focuses on compensation, not on risk; for risk is not a tradable commodity in financing. Risk-taking per se cannot

[5] For a detailed discussion on the maxim, see Laldin et al. (2013, pp. 156–160).

[6] Presumably, putting the maxim as 'benefit goes with liability (to compensate)'—would be more explicable of its intent and import. It would also be commensurate with another Islamic maxim—legal permission negates liability. Candidly, the liability to bear loss in business cannot be abolished; it would go against the Islamic ban on interest. For details on the quoted maxim, see Laldin et al. (2013, pp. 164–166).

contribute to production; ownership of useful things including capital does. Equity of a profit share can be better judged with reference to capital investment, not with reference to risk. There has to be a compensation for receiving a gain. Thus, for a claim to profit, the financier is liable to bear ex post loss, not the ex ante risk (Baqir al-Sadr 1984).

Conventional finance is of course dominated by interest-based transactions, but it is far from the truth that it entails no risk sharing. Equity holders share risk and equity dominates in long-term financing. Even when loans are advanced on interest, banks do face the risk of default and of adverse movements in the prices of bonds and collateral. If there is a difference between equity and debt with reference to risk, it is of degree, not of kind. That conventional banks collapsed in the crises is evidence enough to see that interest-based finance is not always or entirely risk free (see Appendix). And, there is not, nor can there ever be, any worthwhile estimate of the risk transfers to serve as a policy guide.

What capital faces in deferred payment Islamic contracts is not much different from the risks conventional banks face; mortgages providing cover in both cases. Islamic banks transfer risk via hedging contracts. They also take collateral to cover default risk. The bulk of the transactions *Shari'ah* supervisors approve are debt based; participatory finance, despite all efforts and pleadings, is still not popular. The valid distinction between Islamic and conventional banking is then not that one is entirely risk sharing and the other is entirely risk transferring; what matters, in either case, is the proportion of the two in the mix.[7] It is a myth that interest-banking is entirely free of risk-taking while Islamic banks are entirely free of risk transfer.

The Islamic ban on interest needs not to imply that the ban automatically blocks risk transfer. It is a matter of interpretation. Indeed, there is an argument that in pure classical muḍārabah where the worker entrepreneur is empty-handed, the financier transfers a part of his risk to the worker. The financier does not make any payment to him in the case of loss. He reduces his own loss equal to the worker's wage which he now does not pay.

[7]It is interesting to note that some writers find Islamic finance inherently more risk averse and thus hold back the pace of economic development in Muslim countries; they produce empirical evidence to support this view (see, for example, Suzanna and Ola 2013). In contrast, those who argue that it is, in principle, based on risk sharing have nothing to show as testimony.

Furthermore, risk sharing need is not always equitable. Indeed, it may rarely be so. Risk being an ex ante entity has no cardinal measure. The sharing ratio is a crude proxy for the division of profit. No one can demonstrate a one-on-one correspondence between the profit share of the parties and their respective risk exposures. Justice and fair play is the first requirement for calling something 'Islamic'. The difficulty is that substantial juristic writings analyzing contract forms provide little help to determine whether or not there is injustice in an exchange contract. Arbitrariness is the rule.[8]

The present resurgence of risk sharing is no more than the echo of the 'no risk, no gain' adage which is ingrained in the literature as the sole principle for organizing Islamic finance as noted earlier. The present author provides a detailed discussion on the precept much earlier (Hasan 2005, pp. 16–18). Interestingly, reiteration of the precept tends to rely essentially on evidence extracted from mainstream sources rather than from earlier Islamic finance literature. The mainstream writings in economics are growing fast and the literature is so vast that evidence can often be marshalled on either side in a debate, including risk sharing, with impressive documentation.[9] Important, however, is to examine the logic behind theoretical formulation.

At times, the proponents of risk sharing switch from a narrower argument to the cosmopolitan plane in their explorations without notice and without forging a link with narrower business-oriented discussions (Askari et al. 2012).[10] They unwittingly voice concern over market capitalism in restricting their focus to the risk of losing money and material,

[8]Contextual to footnote no. 4 the profit which the owner of a commodity obtains through its sale is based not on the risk involved but on the basis of the commodity proprietorship, even if the price (and profit) increases due to his transferring it to the market for ready availability to the consumers, for he continues to remain its owner (Baqir al-Sadr 1984, p. 76).

[9]Classification of notes and references in one such study in the references confirms the generous borrowings from mainstream sources; some even from the heterodox literature. The bibliography contains 325 entries. Only 75 of these are from Islamic writers. Of the 75, no less than 40 belong to writers of the book itself. Thus, for criticism of the mainstream positions too our scholarship essentially draws on the mainstream!

[10]For a neat summary of the content of this work see Islahi (2010). Sticking scrupulously to the norms, a book reviewer must observe, one finds Islahi more on the explanatory side; for the analytical and evaluative content of the review, one has to read more between the lines.

while the risk that human beings face working in various sorts of production lines are ignored; even as such risks could be, and usually are, more persistent and fatal to limbs and life compared to the loss of money in business.

Men, women, and children working in coal mines, glass blowing, cement factories, cotton ginning, on oil platforms in open seas, on nuclear reactors, or even controlling traffic at the crowded road crossings, face hazards no amount of money can compensate. During cyclical ups and downs who suffer more—capital or workers—it depends on the terms of contracts that govern their employment. Acute is becoming the case of victims of war, epidemics, and natural calamities. Thus, if there is a case for risk (and profit) sharing among the providers of capital, there is one million times stronger case for such sharing between labour and capital, especially from an Islamic viewpoint (Hasan 1975, 1983).

Finally, another distinction the proponents make relates to fixity versus variation of payments with regard to interest and profit. It is argued that fixed return to capital is not allowed in Islam; even its use as a benchmark is questionable in some forums. However, this is only partially true. Islam does allow a time value to money as part of the price in deferred payment contracts based on murābaḥah (cost plus—an agreed fixed margin financing mode). Deferred payment sales involving markups are debt-based transactions (Hasan 2014, pp. 14–15, 96, 105). We are not aware of any juridical preference between contracts involving profit sharing on the one hand and those stipulating predetermined returns on the other if both meet the stipulated *Shari'ah* requirements.

12.4 Some More Comments

Knight (1921) was categorical that profit is not a return to capital; it is a reward for entrepreneurial services—primarily relating to the direction and coordination of business. But by the time he was writing the preface to the fourth edition of his Risk, Uncertainty, and Profit in 1957, the corporate form of business organization had risen to dominance, the personality of the classical entrepreneur, as alluded to earlier, had disintegrated; decision-making had become scattered throughout the managerial hierarchy of firms and competition had become increasingly intense. What remained intact of Knight's work was the distinction between risk and uncertainty and its implications for economic theory and practice. The distinction shows that risk-taking cannot be planned to produce desired results.[11] It could be a personality trait but cannot be measured, and no economic value could be put on it. Thus, risk is a specific mental state that instils in a person the fear of adverse consequences of an action; for example, the fear of losing capital as an investor. Two options are open to such a person; for example:

1. The capital owner is free to desist from the action if he cannot overcome the fear of adversity, i.e. of losing money; no one would penalize him if he does; or,
2. He must conquer his fear to act and accept whatever be the consequence. Risk-taking is purely discretionary for humans. For that reason, Islam neither promises a reward to a risk-taker nor refuses a reward unless the risk is taken. Consider the following examples as evidence:
   (i) Risk-free earnings: One can earn a profit in spot transactions without facing any risk. The post-price risk one takes is out of one's own sweet will; it does not arise in the course of the spot sale and purchase transaction. Pecuniary gains arise, devoid of risk, in the form of wages or rent for contributing to the permitted productive effort.
   (ii) Abolition of interest: One justification capitalism advances for charging interest is the element of risk involved in lending. Thus, the lender has a right to compensation in the form of interest. No Islamic economist can deny that loans carry risk; why does then Islam ban interest? Simply, for the reason that interest is not the result of any productive exertion undertaken by the lender to earn it.
   (iii) Ban on gambling: Like interest, Islam prohibits gambling and earnings based on it, albeit gamblers take great risks and are even ruined at times. The reason again is that labour in gambling is unproductive of real goods. The ban on gambling also extends to the sharing of a pool of individual earnings. To illustrate, the *Shari'ah* would not allow two doctors entering into a partnership to take patients separately but pool their

[11] Knight's uncertainty theory was reduced to a windfall profit/loss case of little significance as probability-based instruments cannot predict or measure them (Hasan 1975, 1983).

earnings to be shared in a pre-agreed ratio. This is to avoid the risk of any one of the two not getting the just reward for his work due to the possibility of a plus or minus element brought in by the sharing of risk (Baqir al-Sadr 1984, p. 78).

(iv) Tools of production: The tools of production are not allowed to have a share in the profits of a venture even though they too are exposed to risk in the production process. But tool owners are not denied a return; they gain in the form of fixed returns (rentals). However, the Ḥanafis do allow the tools as part of capital contribution provided their monetary value is agreed upon at the start of production (Baqir al-Sadr 1984).

(v) Some other earnings involving risk are disallowed: certain sources of income (gain) like magic, witchcraft, fortune telling, or jugglery are not allowed in Islam even if risk is involved because they do not contribute to socially useful production.

All these and the like are ways of illegitimately consuming one another's wealth as no trade with mutual consent is involved (Qur'ān, 2:188; 4:29). Even though risk may be involved, gain/profit may not be legal. The permissible way of generating a profit and its sharing is allowed in all cases where participants can be shown as contributing to socially useful production. Consequently, Baqir al-Sadr (1984, p. 76) laments as follows:

> Many have fallen into error influenced by capitalist thought which has a tendency to explain the point and its defense on the basis of risk. They say or have said that the profit allowed to the owner of the stock-in-trade (cash capital or commodity) in the muḍārabah contract is theoretically based on risk because even though the owner of the stock-in-trade does not do any work yet he bears the burden of the risk and exposes himself to loss over his cash or commodity to the agent trafficking with it; so it is the duty of the agent to make proportionate percentage of compensation against the ventured risk out of the profit agreed upon in the *muḍārabah* contract between them.

But the fact has been made fully clear in the previous discussion that the profit which the owner of the cash or commodity obtains as a result of the agent's trafficking of it is not based on the risk but receives its justification on the basis of proprietorship of the owner of the cash or commodity with which the agent traffics.

If one wants to make risk sharing the fulcrum of Islamic finance to the exclusion of other permissible modes of financing, one must take an extended view of risk and show its applicability in various socio-economic conditions as harmonizing with the Islamic norms of justice. An attempt to do so has to be comprehensive and complete to avoid raising insoluble problems. This would be a palpably horrendous task not worth the effort.

12.5 Islamic Banks and the Crisis

The crisis that originated in the 2007 sub-prime crash in the United States is considered the most devastating since the 1930s Great Depression. 'It swept away around 8 million jobs and led to the foreclosure of 4 million homes. It took around 18 trillion dollars or more than 30 percent of the world gross output' (Chapra 1986, p. 1) The widespread devastation economies suffered across the globe set the world looking for reasons and measures to pre-empt the recurrence of such turmoil in the future. Most economists—mainstream and Islamic—broadly agree on the causes but not so much on remedial action. Islamic economists contend that abolition of interest and risk-sharing schemes can alone be the source of deliverance. As proof, they cite the evidence of Islamic banks facing the crisis better than the conventional.

We have already discussed this issue in the preceding chapter; suffice here some more observations as under:

1. Islamic banks are still too small to attract contagion because of their tiny existence; the ratio of Islamic banks' asset to conventional was just 1:118 in 2011. It improved for a few years but has recently been falling. It stood at 1:112 in 2014 but touched 1:10.7 in June 2015.[12]
2. Islamic banks have not yet developed enough connectivity with the mainstream system for the transmission of contagion. Even then, it is not true that all Islamic banks have been unaffected by the crisis. It is on record that several banks plus Nakheel in the UAE landed in trouble and the state had to bail them out (Hasan 2010).

[12] The ratio is based on the volume of global bank assets being \$16 trillion and Islamic banking assets \$1.496 trillion for the year 2015 (WB: Financial Report and IFSB Financial Report both for 2016).

3. Most comparisons employ econometric models where sample designs are dubious and the reliability of data, especially their homogeneity, over time, and space, is questionable. Contagion within the banking system is a smaller matter than the overall effect of the turmoil on the totality of the economic phenomena. The injury to banks is not the result of financial market chaos; it is just its reflection. Economic damage is the consequence of wide and volatilities in key variables such as savings, investment, and wages that cause national income to shrink.

12.6 Concluding Remarks

This chapter aimed at examining the logic and tenability of an old precept whose revival in Islamic finance is recently being discussed vociferously. The precept is claimed to mean that Islam permits no gain unless risk is involved in its earning. It is further argued that risk sharing alone is commensurate with Islamic norms of financing. The supporters of this view blame the increasing recurrence of financial crises on interest-based finance because it promotes, they say, only the shifting of risks in financing, not their sharing. This critique has highlighted the unacceptability of this line of argument on both the juridical and feasibility fronts.

We showed that the three Islamic maxims—benefit goes with liability, liability accompanies gain, and deferment constitutes a part in price—read together lead us to only one conclusion that the right to receive any permissible benefit carries in Islam a counter liability to compensate the benefactor unless there is a legal waiver. The law remains neutral towards the exogenous consequences of meeting such liability, be it the risk to money, limb, or life.

One must also note that interest-based financing is not altogether devoid of risk nor all transactions in Islamic finance need to be based on risk sharing in the same way as in the case of equity. It is interesting that the Kuala Lumpur Declaration of 1 October 2012, on risk sharing as an alternative to interest-based finance by-passed the proposal.[13] to say only this much:

[13] It must be noted that it was the chapter of Professor Abbas pleading for risk sharing as the sole basis of Islamic finance that formed the basis of discussion at that high powered seminar. And his views can be attributed to INCEIF where he works.

> Governments should endeavor to move away from interest-based systems towards enhancing risk sharing systems by leveling the playing field between equity and debt.[14]

It is contended that the 'no risk, no gain' precept cannot be defended as an exclusive principle of Islamic finance. Risk is not a tradable commodity; nor is it an act in itself contributing to the value of output. Many transactions involving risk are not allowed while many transactions not involving it are the principle of sharing of profit and loss is valid, but its basis is not the existence or absence of risk.

In evaluating a situation and its causes, the moral and ethical dimension invariably escape our attention. Principles of economics are essentially principles of economic policy, and no policy is worth more than what it is in execution. An Islamic Development Bank (IDB) publication aptly says:

> At its heart, Islamic finance is a moral system of finance. It emphasizes the balance between forprofit activities, or the market, and not-for-profit activities, including social and philanthropic activities. No economy can enjoy sustainable prosperity without the two domains in healthy equilibrium. Just as a bird cannot fly smoothly without the two wings properly functioning in tandem, an economy cannot "fly" without the two domains properly operating and serving the common good of the society. (Al-Suwailem 2014)

Most of the writings in the area of Islamic economics and finance are oblivious to the fact that the spiritual/moral wing of the bird today is utterly nonfunctional, if not broken; for, it is the moral stimuli ingrained in human nature that inspires people to undertake 'not-for-profit' activities to help others.

They present their postulates on the tacit assumption that people are reasonably committed to moral and ethical norms, which is unfortunately not the case. When confronted with the choice of reaping economic benefits or obeying religious imperatives, worldly concerns tend to outweigh hereafter considerations. For making risk sharing the sole

[14]The KL Declaration is provided as an Appendix for a ready reference to the readers. The content is too brief and deficient in explanation. Some of the statements it contains are open-ended. To us, it accords no status to profit sharing as an exclusive principle of Islamic finance.

basis of Islamic finance, the proponents should re-evaluate the *Shari'ah* basis of their argument. They should as well reexamine the feasibility of their suggestions.

It may be noted that risk-taking is not the same thing as risk sharing or risk transfer; it is fuzzy as to what variables could capture each of these expressions. In any case, such models cannot deal with the totality of risk that banks face; they only deal with its measurable truncated part. And, where variables are stocked with morality norms, the use of non-parametric methods seems to have an edge over the probability-based explorations now so fashionable in Islamic finance research.

Finally, this chapter is neither opposed to sharing of risk nor does it seek to mitigate the need for risk management. It is just an attempt to arrest the perilous tilt the emphasis on a non-existent 'solely and only' character of Islamic finance in the current literature has the proclivity of providing to its future growth.

Appendix

Kuala Lumpur Declaration (Emphasis added) The Second Strategic Roundtable Discussion, jointly organized by the International Shari'ah Research Academy for Islamic Finance (ISRA), the Islamic Research and Training Institute (IRTI) and Durham University, met on 20 September 2012 in Lanai Kijang, Kuala Lumpur.

After lengthy deliberations on the issue of risk sharing, the participants acknowledged that the financial crisis which started in 2008 highlighted the fact that the most salient feature of the dominant conventional financial system is the transfer of risks away from financial institutions onto customers, governments and the public at large. Islamic finance is in a unique position to offer an alternative to the present interest-based debt financing regime that has brought the whole world to the edge of collapse. Bearing this in mind, the second annual ISRA-IRTI-Durham Strategic Roundtable Discussion (2012) agreed on the following:

- The *Shari'ah* emphasizes risk sharing as a salient characteristic of Islamic financial transactions. This is not only exemplified in equity-based contracts, like *mushārakah* and *muḍārabah*, but even in exchange contracts, such as sales and leasing, whereby risk is shared by virtue of possession.

- Risk transfer and risk shifting in exchange contracts violate the *Shari'ah* principle that liability is inseparable from the right to profit.
- Sales must be genuine transactions in open market.
- Although the *Shari'ah* recognizes the permissibility of debt, it is acknowledged that excessive debt has detrimental effects on society.

The recommendations of the Roundtable Discussion are as follows:

1. Governments should endeavour to move away from interest-based systems towards enhancing risk-sharing systems by levelling the playing field between equity and debt.
2. Accordingly, governments should increase their use of fiscal and monetary policies based on risk sharing.
3. Governments could issue macro-market instruments that would provide their treasuries with a significant source of non-interest-rate-based financing while promoting risk sharing, provided that these securities meet three conditions:
   (i) They are of low denomination;
   (ii) Are sold on the retail market; and
   (iii) Come with strong governance oversight.
4. There is a need to broaden the organizational structures beyond traditional banking models to formats such as venture capital and Awqaaf to fulfill the social goals and risk-sharing features of Islamic finance.

Test Questions

Q.1 Why is the risk associated with capital alone in economics? Do you think that workers are not exposed to any risk on jobs?

Q.2 Distinguish between risk and uncertainty and elaborate the significance of the distinction for the return on capital.

Q.3 Distinguish between risk sharing and risk transfer. Will you agree that risk sharing is the *sole* principle of Islamic finance? Argue your case.

Q.4 Is it valid to claim that interest-based finance is based on risk transfer alone bearing no risks? Give reasons for your answer.

Q.5 It is argued that risk is not a tradable commodity; risk bearing is the *effect* of profit sharing not its *cause*. Comment.

Q.6 Write critical notes on:
(a) Measurement of risk
(b) Shari'ah maxims related to risk
(c) One-on-one correspondence between profit and risk
(d) Islam and risk management

What Next?

Chapter 13 deals with an important but controversial topic—a comparison of two models for home financing in Islamic banks.

References

Al-Suwailem, S. (2014). *Essence of Islamic Finance*. Jeddah: Islamic Development Bank (IDB).

Askari, H., Iqbal, Z., Krichene, N., & Mirakhor, A. (2012). *Risk Sharing in Finance: The Islamic Finance Alternative*. Singapore: Wiley.

Baqir al-Sadr. (1984). *Iqtisaduna* [Our Economy, Trans., Vol. 2]. Tehran, Iran: World Organization for Islamic Services (WOIS).

Chapra, M. U. (1986). *Towards a Just Monetary System*. Leicester and London, UK: Islamic Foundation.

Chapra, M. U. (2014). *Morality and Justice in Islamic Economics and Finance*. UK: Edward Elgar Publishing.

Hasan, Z. (1975). *Theory of Profit*. New Delhi: Vikas Publishing House Pvt. Ltd.

Hasan, Z. (1983). Theory of Profit: The Islamic Viewpoint. *Journal of Research in Islamic Economics, KAAU 1*(1), 1–17.

Hasan, Z. (2005). Islamic Banking at the Crossroads: Theory Versus Practice. In R. Wilson & M. Iqbal (Eds.), *Islamic Perspectives on Wealth Creation* (pp. 11–25). Edinburg, UK: Edinburg University Press.

Hasan, Z. (2010). Dubai Turmoil Before and After the Bailout. *International Journal of Islamic Banking & Finance*, Karachi.

Hasan, Z. (2014). *Scarcity Self-Interest and Maximization from Islamic Angle*. IDB Prize Winning Lecture, Jeddah.

Hawley, F. B. (1893). The Risk Theory of Profit. *The Quarterly Journal of Economics, 7*(4), 459–479.

Islahi, A. A. (2010). Four Generations of Islamic Economists. *Journal of King Abdulaziz University: Islamic Economics, 23*(1), 165–170.

Knight, F. H. (1921). *Risk, Uncertainty and Profit*. Boston: Houghton Mifflin.

Laldin, A., et al. (2013). *Islamic Legal Maxims and Their Application in Islamic Finance*. Kuala Lumpur, Malaysia: ISRA.

Mirakhor, A. (2014). Foundations of Risk-Sharing Finance: An Islamic View. In K. Lewis, M. Ariff, & S. Mohamad (Eds.), *Risk and Regulation of Islamic Banking*. London: Edward Elgar.

Mirakhor, A. (2015, July 8). *Issues in Islamic Finance: Risk Sharing – An Economic Revolution*. INCEIF: The Global University of Islamic Finance on YouTube. Accessed on 16 October 2015.

NYU.edu. (2014). Chapter 4: How Do we Measure Risk? Retrieved from http://people.stern.nyu.edu/adamodar/pdfiles/valrisk/ch4.pdf.

Ormerod, P. (2010). Risk, Recessions and the Resilience of the Capitalist Economies. *Risk Management, 12*, 83–99.

Rubin, J. (2011). Institutions, the Rise of Commerce and the Persistence of Laws: Interest Restrictions in Islam and Christianity. *Economic Journal, 121*, 1310–1339.

Suzanna, E. M., & Ola, A.-S. (2013). Risk Aversion and Islamic Finance: An Experimental Approach. *International Journal of Information Technology and Business Management, 16*(1), 49–77.

CHAPTER 13

Home Financing Models: On Their Shari'ah Compliance

Preview

Enabling people to own their homes has emerged as a disquieting concern across the globe. The issue tends to assume alarming proportions in all countries, developed or developing. All sorts of agencies, national regional and international, public and private are seized with the problem. Housing is ranked second only to food in the hierarchy of *basic needs* the provision of which for every national Islam makes obligatory eventually for the state.

Promotion of home ownership is a complex and multi-facet issue. All cannot be covered in the space available here. This chapter deals with a small but significant part of it: home financing and Islam. Here too, the discussion is further narrowed down to model comparison on two issues: return on capital and ownership transference to the buyer.

For financing consumer durables like computers, cars, and houses, conventional banks use models to determine what are called the equated monthly installment (EMI). EMI is the fixed payment a borrower makes to a lender to pay off both interest and part of the principal each month so that over an agreed number of years, the loan amount is cleared in full and the client becomes the absolute owner of the house.

Islamic banks have followed the practice; they determine the EMI using diminishing musharakah partnership model, popularly known as the MMP, following the abbreviation of its Arabic nomenclature. The defining character of this model is increasing amortization of capital the customer progressively buying-back the bank's equity under the

Z. Hasan, *Leading Issues in Islamic Economics and Finance*,
https://doi.org/10.1007/978-981-15-6515-1_13

agreement. This chapter shows that models of the sort, like the conventional, invariably involve compounding of return on capital, called profit, and pass the ownership of property to the client at a slower rate than capital repayment or amortization, until the contract is concluded. It puts forth an alternative model free of the indicated blemishes and having some additional advantages as well.

13.1 Introduction

In financing consumer durables, Islamic banks take care, as they must, to ensure that contracts they sign with their clients leave no room for *riba* (interest) to enter its structuring. One must recall that compounding is more vociferously condemned in the Qur'an (2: 275; 3: 130) than interest.[1] Otherwise also, to charge 'interest-on-interest' when servicing a loan should be avoided, because it seems unfair to the borrower, almost like kicking a person when he is down. Furthermore, fair play demands that the ownership of the asset financed must pass to the customer in the *same* ratio as the ratio loan cleared to the total at any point in time.[2]

Islamic banks have been using a number of models for home financing and literature bristles with their discussion. We do not intend to survey that literature through reference to some contribution would benefit. We look the home financing issue from a rather limited perspective: how far the models used are *Shari'ah* compliant in form and consequences? Even here we narrow the discussion to see if interest is being avoided and contracts are equitable from the viewpoint of the buyers? There is no harm in being anticipatory. Rather it may cut at time and space. We find that banks without exception are using a uniform installment payment system not only in housing but in financing most consumers' durables from smartphones to luxury cars. As the payment is usually monthly a formula

[1] Some academics are of the view that Islam associates compounding to *riba* alone and not to profit (or rent). Supporters of this view must provide conclusive evidence from Islamic sources of knowledge. Analogical reasoning seems to reject compounding of profit or rent as well (see Qur'an 26: 183).

[2] Both norms follow from the Islamic notion of justice. The Qur'an (44: 38–39) states: "*Allah has not created the earth and heavens in idle sport but with just ends*". Also, the scripture forbids withholding from people that which rightfully belong to them (Qur'an 7: 85; 11: 85 and 26: 83).

borrowed from the mainstream is used to determine the equal monthly installment (EMI).

We discover that the embedded in the EMI system is compounding of interest, rent, or profit whatever name one chooses to give to the rate of return on capital borrowed in a particular case. Even if this claim is disputed there are other faults in the system calling for its rejection from an Islamic perspective. If this rejection is convincing we venture to present a model for financing consumer durable, especially home purchase. This model we will demonstrate is not only fully *Shari'ah* compliant but has an edge over others in use. We shall take the diminishing balance method which derives its abbreviation MMP from its Arabic nomenclature: *musharkah mutanwshah partnership*.

The chapter is spread over five sections including the Introduction. In the following Sect. 13.2, we present an illustration and its relevant aspects that we shall use in the following sections review some selected writings on Islamic home financing contextual to our work Sect. 13.3 demonstrates how the popular MMP model Islamic banks invariably use across counters violates the *Shari'ah* requirements.

In section three we present the MMP model and show that in results it is identical with the conventional interest-based model. In Sect. 13.4 we present the outlines of the ZDNM mand compare its results with those of the MMP. The final section summarizes the argument and makes a few concluding observations.

13.2 Case Facts, Formula, and Implications

We start with a simple adequate enough to narrate our main contentions on *Shari'ah* compliance of models. Suppose there is one Mr. X who wants to purchase a house from a builder worth 80,000 in local currency. He has no money to invest though he is creditworthy being in a good employment. He wants to borrow 80,000 from a bank payable over a period of 10 years in semi-annual installments. He approaches an Islamic bank that agrees to finance the purchase of the house advancing with full amount needed on payment of a semi-annual installment under the MMP. He explains to Mr. X that he has to enter into contract with the bank for a joint ownership of house, whereby he must buy the ownership rights of the bank in semi-annual installments, the bank charging as profit 8% per annum (4% semi-annually) on the outstanding balance of loan. For this plus the buy-back of bank's share in the house Mr. X must pay 5887 semi-annual installment to fully own the house in ten years. The part of the installment in excess of the profit share would be towards the return of loan. Under the arrangement the loan of the bank will be cleared in ten years and Mr. X will be the owner of the house. It was not necessary for Mr. X to understand; he agreed to sign the contract as he thought that paying 5887 every six months was not burdensome.

However, we must understand how this all falls into a neat pattern. There is a formula from the interest calculation family that is readily available to determine the EMI or similar periodic installments if sufficient data to feed in is available and forms part of Excel programming. The formula is as follows:

$$A = P_0 \frac{r(1+r)^n}{(1+r)^n - 1} \tag{13.1}$$

where A is the desired installment amount, P_0 is the principal loan amount, r is the chargeable rate of interest, and n is the number of time units involved. These values in our case are 80,000, 0.04, and 20. Feeding the values in the formula we get $A = 5886.54$. As semi-annual installment. The formula involves exponential, that raises the query if compounding of interest is embedded in the system? For, if it does, its use in the MMP is violative Islamic norms. We believe it does. Consider the following argumentation.

The standard compound interest formula is:

$$P_n = P_0(1+r)^n \tag{13.2}$$

Thus, inserting our case values for our illustration: $P_0 = 80{,}000$, $r = 0.04$, and $n = 20$ in the above formula we get:

$$P_n = 80,000(1 + 0.04)^{20} = 175,290 \tag{13.3}$$

We can discount back the amount using the formula $P_0 = P_n / (1+r)^n$ we would arrive at the loan amount, 80,000. To find the actual rate charged, let us set up for end value $P_n = A \times n$ as follows:

$$5886.54 \times 20 = 80,000(1+r)^n$$

Dividing through by 20, we get $5887 = 4000(1+r)^{20}$
Using log conversion we get

$$ln\,(5887) = ln\,(4000) + 20\,ln\,(1+r)$$

Table 13.1 Installment period and interest rare relationship

Periodicity →	*Monthly*	*Quarterly*	*Semi-annual*
Installment ($)	971	2924	5887
Effective rates (%)	4.56	4.62	4.72
Nominal rates (%)	0.67	2.00	4.00

$$3.7699 = 3.60205 + 20\,ln\,(1 + r)$$

$= 0.0083925$

$$(1 + r) = 10^{0.00839} = 1.01951 \quad (13.4)$$

Thus, r=0.01951 that yields 1.951% semi-annual or 3.9% annual compounding rate.

Verification:

$$P_n = 80,000(1 + 0.01951)^{20}$$

$$= 80,000 \times 1.47174$$

$= 117{,}739$, same as 5887×20

$$\text{Return on capital} = 117,739 - 80,000 = 37,739 \quad (13.5)$$

The IRR or the effective semi-annual rate of return is 117,739/80,000=4.72% [same as before]. We have estimated in the same way the monthly and quarterly effective rates (IRRs) shown in Table 13.1.

The installment payment need not necessarily be monthly; it may be quarterly, semi-annual, or yearly. Only the values of r and n in the formula would appropriately change. The impact of compounding decreases as the periodicity of installment payment increases. Table 13.1 is based on the above illustration and verifies the statement. The Table provides one more test of compounding in the uniform installment regime. Notice that the effective interest rates run higher than the nominal interest rates. The gap between the two rates narrows down with an increase in the periodicity.

13.3 MMP at Work

Applied to our case the MMP in operation will stand as in Table 13.2.

It is easy to find the effective rate of return payable on the borrowing. Column *C* of the Table shows us the total payment to the bank at 37,740 money units in 10 years, i.e. 3774 a year. Installment payments are semi-annual. One can get the IRR (effective rate) as 3774/80,000, i.e. equal to 4.72%, same as in Table 13.1. The client does not discover how the effective rate he pays becomes more than the rate of return 4.0% semi-annual shown in his contract. The mechanism is inbuilt in the formula used for installment determination. One can find the concealed rate enhancement from the facts of the case. Let us show that *C* has

Table 13.2 The results of borrowing on interest or via MMP are identical

n	*Balance outstanding*	*Return of capital* R *on* C	*Return on capital* a × *0.04*	*Installment* b +c
	a	b	c	d
1	80,000	2687	3200	5887
2	77,313	2794	3093	5887
3	74,408	2905	2981	5887
4	71,624	3027	2860	5887
5	68,597	3143	2744	5887
6	65,454	3269	2618	5887
7	62,185	3400	2487	5887
8	58,785	3536	2351	5887
9	55,249	3677	2210	5887
10	51,572	3824	2063	5887
11	47,748	3977	1910	5887
12	43,771	4136	1751	5887
13	39,633	4302	1585	5887
14	35,331	4474	1413	5887
15	30,857	4653	1234	5887
16	26,204	4839	1048	5887
17	21,365	5032	855	5887
18	16,333	5234	653	5887
19	11,099	5443	444	5887
20	5656	5685	226	5887
Total	942,764	80,000	37,740	117,740
Variables →	Funding deposits	*R* of *C*	*R* on *C*	Cash flows

ipso facto paid a rate more than 8% a year as R on C. Let B denotes the excess. We can set up for an yearly charge as under:

$$80,000(0.08 + B) = 11774. \text{ Solving we get } B = 0.0672\%. \quad (13.6)$$

Adding this capital redemption factor as it is called, to the nominal rate 0.08, the bank gets its total revenue flow from the installments (80,00 0 × 0.1472 × 10) = 117,760. The semi-annual capital redemption factor[3] would make the rate 0.04 + 0.0336 = 0.0736. The effective rate is reduced to 4.72% as before, the return being calculated on the diminishing balance of capital.

13.3.1 Compounding of (R on C)

The presence of the terms with exponentials in Eq. (13.1) implied a compounding process in the determination of periodic installment, the fact which Islamic bankers and many academicians dispute. Equation (13.4) identified for our illustration the rate underpinning that process but it does not isolate the compounding involved in the installment determination; this demonstration now follows.

Let us take the semi-annual case of Table 13.1 to build up our argument. Let us break the uniform installment approximately 5887 into 4000 for capital redemption and 1887 for return on capital. The bifurcation is logical because 4000 × 20 = 80,000 and 1887 × 20 = 37,740 as the summations of columns *b* and *c*, respectively, provide in Table 13.2. This means that each time the return on capital is not calculated on diminished balance. It is added back to (R on C) each time for the purpose; it is being compounded. The compounding element would add up to 1887 × 0.04 × 20 = 1510 over the 10 year period. There is a way to verify this result.

[3]Given the nominal rate and the time units, one can find the capital redemption factor from readymade tables available for the purpose. The capital redemption factors for the monthly and quarterly installment cases work out at 0.0056 and 0.0168, respectively.

Interesting it is that in the illustration of their MMP, called the 'Lease to purchase model or the LTP' for home financing once the American Finance House—La-riba, circulated on line, the capital redemption factor thy used was found to be 3.47%. The AFH to it in their document as the imputed or implied interest rate they are under obligation to report to authorities but did not reveal in their contracts (Hasan 2012, 3–4).

Table 13.3 Compounding of return on capital (*R* on *C*) in the MMP

n	*Balance* (n)	*Return on capital*	A+B	*C − 5887 Balance* (n − *1*)	*Compound interest*
	T	B=A × *0.04*	C	D	E=B × *0.04*
1	80,000	3200	83,200	77,313	128.00
2	77,313	3093	80,405	74,518	123.72
3	74,518	2981	77,499	71,612	119.24
–	–	–	–	–	–
18	16,333	653	16,986	11,099	26.12
19	11,099	444	11,543	5656	17.76
20	5656	226	5882	–	9.04
Total	942,764	37,740	990,504	862,764	1510

The balance outstanding at the end of any period n can be calculated as follows:

$$\text{Balance } n = \text{Balance } (n - 1) + \text{Return on capital } n - \text{Installment.} \quad (13.7)$$

For example, for period n − 2 in our illustration the outstanding balance would be 80,000 + 3200 − 5887 = 77,313. The process goes on until the end of the contract. Thus, the preceding year return on capital is subjected to charge in the current year. Table 13.3 shows the isolation of compounding in the MMP which is the same as it would be in the interest-based conventional finance.

We can add columns *A* and *B* and deduct installment to get *D*. *E* we get as $B \times (0.04)$. We can get column *E* directly as $T \times (0.04)^2$ confirming compounding. The squared rate of return thus confirms the compounding underlying the MMP process as in the conventional. Figure 13.1 shows the process.

Nabil (2013) in a lengthy conceptual paper has convincingly established that Islamic home financing models in current use—MMP included—involve compounding of return on capital—interest, rent, or markup—if the EMI formula IS used for the determination of uniform periodic installment payments. Figure 13.1 isolates the compounding in the return on capital in the MMP and the conventional models of home financing alike. Figure 13.1 separates the relevant entities.

Figure 13.2 separates the compounding element imbedded in the uniform installment payments. Balance due and the compound element

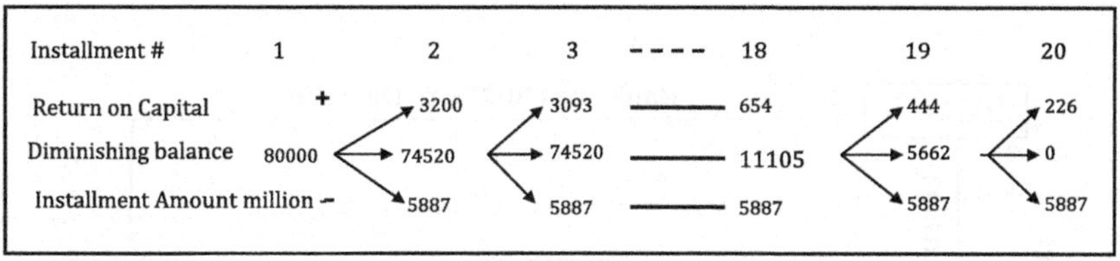

Fig. 13.1 Compounding infests all uniform installments model as the MMP

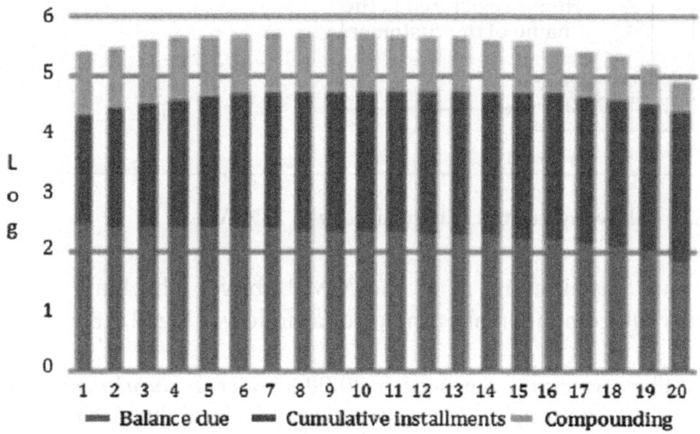

Fig. 13.2 Cumulative installments, balances due, and compounding in the MMP/Interest-based models

values from Table 13.3 expansion. Cumulating the uniform installment was easy. We have used the logarithm of their values to keep the diagram manageable.

13.4 ZDBM: The Alternative

We present the Zubair Diminishing Balance Model (ZDBM) as an alternative to the MMP. There has been much discussion on the model in the literature on Islamic home financing. Therefore, we present it here and the related argument briefly. The customer in the semi-annual payments regime of our illustration approaches an Islamic bank to find details for obtaining the 80,000 money units payable in 10 years spread over 20

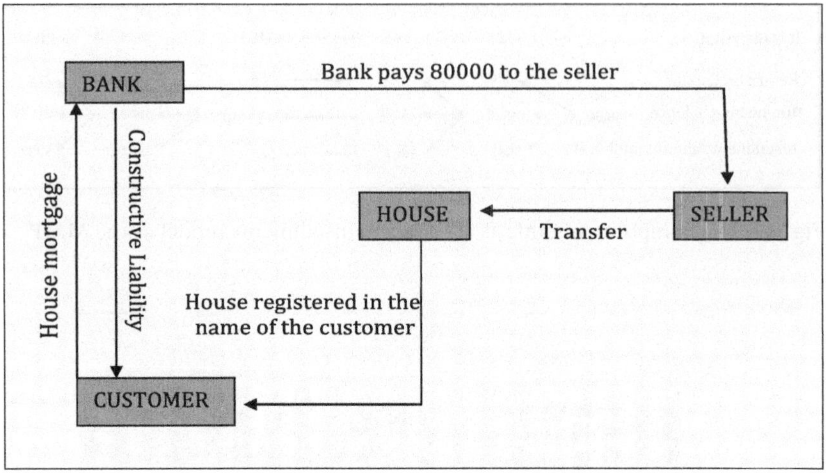

Fig. 13.3 Showing contractual details of the ZDBM

semi-annual installments as in the MMP above. The bank agreeing to meet his requirements makes the offer as follows (Fig. 13.3):

> We shall provide you the needed 80,000 under a *murabahah* contract[4] with a yearly mark-up of 8% to acquire proprietary rights in the house via a *constructive possession* clause in favor of the bank (Brain 2011, 49).[5] For getting back our investment in 20 installments spread over ten years, you will pay $4000 each six months to clear the loan. In addition, at any point in time; the mark-up amount (return on capital) will be calculated on the diminishing balance of the loan. That would reduce your *constructive liability* to the bank proportionate to the passage of time until perodic installments – amortization + return on balance remaining due - are all cleared.

[4]In earlier chapters we had explained the ZDBM in the form of MMP structure. Here we have used *murabahah* modelling for explanation because it covers the use of the instrument over a wider range where identical problems with reference to compounding and ownership transfer arise. However, related details and consequences remain the same.

[5]The item for sale—the house in this case—should, in principle, be under ownership of the seller and in his corporeal possession at the time of contracting its sale. However, both common civil law and Islamic Shai'ah allow what is known *constructive possession* as valid in a deferred sale. It means that the asset financed will be deemed as the property of the financier until the buyer clears his financial liability in full under the contract (see also Craig 2012).

Table 13.4 ZDBM in operation

n	*Return of capital*	*Balance outstanding*	*Return on capital*	*Installments*
	A	*B*	*C*= *B*× *0.04*	*A*+*C*
1	4000	80,000	3200	7200
2	4000	76,000	3040	7040
3	4000	72,000	2880	6880
4	4000	68,000	2720	6720
5	4000	64,000	2560	6560
6	4000	60,000	2400	6400
7	4000	56,000	2240	6240
8	4000	52,000	2080	6080
9	4000	48,000	1920	5920
10	4000	44,000	1760	5760
11	4000	40,000	1600	5600
12	4000	36,000	1440	5440
13	4000	32,000	1280	5280
14	4000	28,000	1120	5120
15	4000	24,000	960	4960
16	4000	20,000	800	4800
17	4000	16,000	640	4640
18	4000	12,000	480	4480
19	4000	8,000	320	4320
20	4000	4,000	160	4160
Total	80,000	840,000	33,600	113,600

The client agrees to the terms offered and the deal is signed involving the following set of contracts between the bank, the customer, and the seller.

a. A sale contract between the seller and the customer with registration in the latter's name but conditional with constructive responsibility.
b. A contract between the seller and the bank to pay in installments or lump sum 80,000 to the former.

Table 13.4 contains the details of such semi-annual payments—return of capital plus return on capital—for our illustration.

Based on the data of the above Tables, Fig. 13.4 compares the installment character of the two modes of home financing—ZDBM and the MMP model.

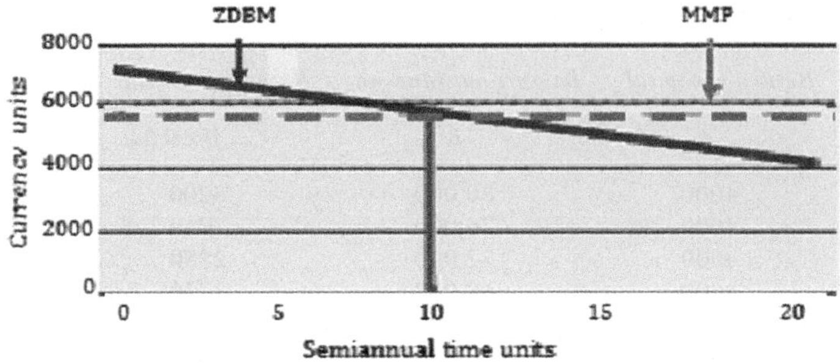

Fig. 13.4 Periodic installment paid under the ZDBM and the MMP models

The bankers invariably show their preference for the MMP claiming the uniformity of installment payments as the main advantage of the programme. The customer does not have to readjust his budget every time as the upfront payment is the same. This payment not only remains uniform but is lower than in ZDBM for the early periods thus making it easier for young people to seek house financing even when they are at the lower rungs of the income ladder. But even if one concedes the advantage for a moment, it is questioned whether meeting the Islamic imperatives can be sacrificed for that gain. The criteria for acceding to house financing do not always or entirely dependent, on age. It is well to note that periodic payments in the ZDBM, though not constant, are regular in the sense that they decrease by a constant amount. The payments are of course on the higher side to start with, but they become increasingly lower halfway through. Figure 13.4 vividly brings out these facts. Which side of the divider one would consider more advantageous cannot be determined a priori; individuals' circumstances would matter. Furthermore, families where both husband and wife work are becoming increasingly common. The trend causes the life-cycle theory to pale into insignificance.

On a sober note, larger initial payments tapering off with the passage of time are likely to be helpful to the young with no or small family to start with. Diminishing installments would certainly be welcome at a time when the family is expanding and expenditures are peaking in the middle of the age-income cycle. Furthermore, the cases of both husband and wife working in modern couples are on the rise softening the rigours of life. The provision of shelter for all is obligatory in Islam; eventually a state responsibility. Public authorities may subsidize home financing for the poorer sections of the society as is presently the case in India for rural housing. In fact, this is being done now in many other developing economies also. For example, in China and Malaysia subsidized home financing is being used as part of their poverty alleviation programmes.

13.4.1 Cost and Efficiency

Notice that the ZDBM is not only free of compounding return on capital (R on C); it turns out to be cheaper for the customer due to a faster repayment of capital plan. Notice the gain in our illustration measured by the difference in the return on capital, C columns show in Tables 13.2 and 13.4: (37,740 – 33,600=4140).

Significantly, the customer does not gain at the cost of the banker. Notice that the sum of outstanding balance, the proxy for funding deposits, is proportionate to the reduction in the returns on capital in Eq. (13.8). For this reason the margin on funding deposits remains the same in both cases, i.e. 4%. ZDBM is thus a win–win position for both the parties: The cost of the house is reduced for the client. Islamic banks get an edge over their conventional rivals without losing on profit margin. This means that ZDBM is a more efficient model than the MMP; It absorbs less funding.

$$\begin{array}{ccccccc} \text{Model} & & \text{Funding Desposits} & & \text{Return on capital} & & \\ \frac{\text{ZBDM}}{\text{MMP}} & = & \frac{840{,}000}{942{,}764} & = & \frac{33{,}600}{37{,}731} & = & 0.891 \end{array} \tag{13.8}$$

13.4.2 Some More Merits

- Researches show that constant amortization programmes, as in the ZDBM, are more equitable than other schemes in operation (Chambers et al. 2007). In our illustration, halfway down the time scale 50% ownership passes to the customer as compared to 40% under the MMP as we shall presently see. Thus, for the customer and society the fixity of amortization—not the fixity of installment payments—is more important and just.
- In the case of default, the ZDBM is more equitable to the parties. Suppose, in our illustration the default takes place halfway, after 10 installments have been paid in each case (see Table 13.5). Under the ZDBM, the buyer's liability reduces proportionately to 50%

Table 13.5 Transfer of ownership to the client—MMP vs. ZDBM

Time units		*MMP*		*ZDBM*	
n	*Time ratio [n/20] 100*	*Return of capital*	*Ownership transfer ratio [c/80,000] 1000*	*Return of capital*	*Ownership r transfer ratio [e/80,000] 1000*
	%	R *of* C	%	R *of* C	%
a	b	c	d	e	f
1	5	2687	3.359	4000	5
2	10	5481	6.857	8000	10
3	15	8386	10.483	12,000	15
4	20	11,413	14.266	16,000	20
5	25	14,556	18.195	20,000	25
6	30	17,825	22.281	24,000	30
7	35	21,225	26.531	28,000	35
8	40	24,761	30.951	32,000	40
8	45	28,398	35.497	36,000	45
10	50	32,222	40.277	40,000	50
11	55	36,199	45.249	44,000	55
12	60	40,335	50.419	48,000	60
13	65	44,637	55.796	52,000	65
14	70	49,114	61.392	56,000	70
15	75	53,767	67.209	60,000	75
16	80	58,606	73.257	64,000	80
17	85	63,638	79.548	68,000	85
18	90	68,872	79.547	72,000	90
19	95	74,315	92.894	76,000	95
20	100	80,000	100.000	80,000	100

Note Columns *c* and *e* contain cumulative values of the *R* of *C*

while under the MMP he will still have to pay almost 60% of the debt, i.e. 47,745.

- The condition of the customer in default may not be comfortable under the MMP for another reason. A few banks have insisted that not only the balance of capital remaining outstanding but also the return on it for the remaining period must be treated as an unpaid liability of the client to meet the banks' commitment to their depositors. Hundreds of cases are reported pending in courts pertaining to such disputes in Malaysia.

- Home financing usually being of a long-term duration, there may arise disputes as in the MMP on the revision of rental, the value of the property, and the amount of liability remaining unpaid once default takes place. In the ZDBM model matters are clearer. The return on capital stops at once in case of default. The house remains under charge only for any outstanding balance on capital account.
- The MMP also requires the creation of three transactions: (i) creation of joint ownership in property; (ii) the financier leases his share in the house to the customer on rent; and (iii) the customer undertakes to purchase different units of the financier's share until the ownership is completely transferred to the former. Taken singly, the jurists regard the three transactions valid if certain conditions are fulfilled. However, it is strongly doubted if their combination in a single contract can be allowed (see Taqi Usmani 2010).
- Scholars are divided on the issue of whether the undertaking of the customer to purchase the financier's share in the property would be enforceable in a court of law because it is just promise without counter consideration.
- The shares are not divided into uniform units and the mechanism of determining the fair value of each share is not in place. What is done is to treat the rent portion accruing to the client as both the price and the market value of the share—the client never sees a penny of the rent he earns. He has no option but to agree to this arrangement.
- Some scholars provide implicit support to the MMP structure on the plea that the interest rate serves as a benchmark. The statement is misleading. A benchmark is the reference point to measure the efficacy of the actual value. If it is used in place of the value itself, it no longer remains a benchmark. Sea level is used as the benchmark for heights of existing or future structures from the geographic viewpoint; structures are not be built at that level. The reservation on the point is further strengthened by the recent disclosure of the manipulation of LIBOR by the 'too big to fail' Western banks. It is noteworthy that the Islamic Development Bank (IDB) is confronted with the problem of developing a benchmark for Islamic financial institutions.
- Meera (2012) uses the fact of the internal rate of return (IRR) equality in the three models—interest based. MMP and the ZDBM—to raise two interesting queries. The first is why the bank

for that reason would not be indifferent to a choice between them. Possibly a more relevant question to ask would be why would the bank not be attracted to the ZDBM model to please the customers with lower payments without incurring any loss or additional costs; would it not give Islamic banks a competitive edge over their conventional rivals?

The second question is: from where and how is the 8% rental rate for the ZDBM model derived? The question looks frivolous in the present context. Using the *same* rate, whatever it be, is a methodological tool for model comparisons, not an operational reality. In the illustration, La-riba also fixes the rate at 8% a year. This helped us discover that they too are using the Excel formula. Meera and Razak (2009) himself uses 8% for all models in his critique for comparing results.

- Some have argued that the formulas discussed above are applicable to savings, not to capital amortization. But is not capital is accumulated savings? Banks are intermediaries. They collect savings from scattered entities and convert them into investable funds. Thus the formulas are as much applicable to investments as to savings.

In sum, we have established that the use of Excel formula for installment payments in home financing violates both the Islamic norms: It is based on the compounding of interest principle and is iniquitous failing to transfer ownership of the house to the buyer commensurate with the periodic payments he makes. One wishing to refute the above contentions on the academic front has to provide cogent proof that slower payment in the present case would not violate Islamic norms. Classical jurists never faced such eventualities which characterize the modern age.

13.4.3 Ownership Transfer

Nabil (2013) agrees, as alluded to earlier, that there is compounding of the return on capital in the MMP model while ZDBM is free of the blemish. However, he contends that it too fails to transfer the ownership of the house pro rata over the contract period. This is incorrect. The criterion for pro rata transference is that at each time point the percentage

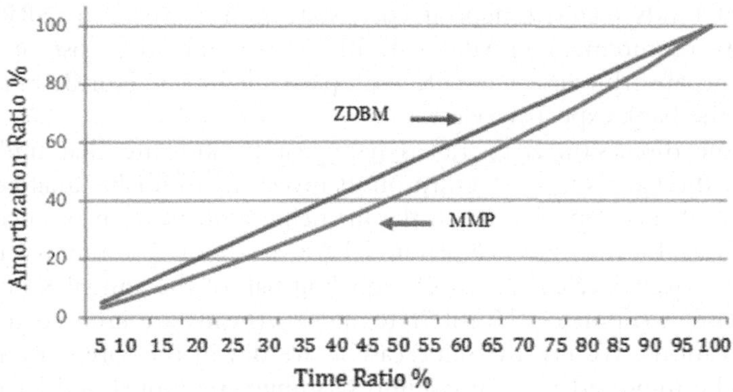

Fig. 13.5 Ownership transfer to client: ZDBM VS MMP

of capital amortization must be the same as of time covered. In other words the following equation must hold good.

$$\frac{\%\text{ of capital amortization}}{\%\text{ of time elapsed}} = 1 \tag{13.9}$$

Based on the data of the Table 13.5, Fig. 13.5 provides a graphic depiction of the ownership transfer to the client under the MMP model and the ZDBM.

13.4.4 *Cost of Capital*

Even though ZDBM is cheaper for the customer than the MMP under identical circumstances, he does not gain at the cost of the banker. For, the funding deposits as represented by the sum of outstanding balances, are proportionately reduced (Eq. 13.3). For this reason the margin on funding deposits remains the same in both cases, i.e. 4% semi-annual. ZDBM is thus a win–win position for both the parties: The cost of the house is reduced for the client while Islamic banks get an edge over their conventional rivals without losing on profit margin. This means that ZDBM is relatively more efficient; it absorbs less funding than the MMP. In our illustration, the model absorbs funds 10.9% less compared with the MMP/Conventional structures. This can be verified by calculating the price of funds as under.

$$\text{Price of funds} = \text{Cost of funds} + \text{Risk factor} + \text{Hurdle costs} + \text{Overhead costs}$$

Cost of funds includes deposit cost, statuary reserve ratio (SRR), and liquidity requirement (LAR) cost. Risk factor includes cost of capital charge to absorb market, credit, and operational risks. Hurdle rate is the return the bank expects to earn.[6]

As the discussion is restricted here just to showing that under the ZDBM the bank's rate of return on its investment remains unaffected, it is assumed that deposits match the financing amortization balance. SRR is taken at 4% with zero return and LAR at 2% on 1% minimal return. Capital charge is calculated at 4% equaling half of the annual 8% markup the contract stipulates. Hurdle rate and overheads are ignored to avoid complications. We use the same case as we did in the foregoing discussion. The indicated rates in column headings are annual and have been *halved* in each case to get their semi-annual values. Below are the worksheets for both the ZDBM and MMP cases. They reveal that the de facto rate of return in the two models is the same. The Tables also narrate the happenings on both the assets and liabilities sides of a bank's balance sheet. Notice also that the return on investment is identical at 4.82% (0.41×20) in the two models (Column 12). However, the *funding deposits* are lower by 11% in the ZDBM than the MMP. Thus, the model is more efficient in managing funds and liquidity.

13.5 Shari'ah Compliance

With the rise of finance—banking in particular—to dominance in Islamic economics, ensuring the adherence of contracts to the letter and spirit of the of *Shari'ah* become a matter of paramount importance. With the fast growth of the sector, the dearth of scholars competent to serve as *Shari'ah* advisors became apparent.[7] As demand ran ahead of supply,

[6]A numerical illustration compares *capital* costing and risk coverage in the two cases—ZDBM and the MMP—using monthly installments is available in Hasan (2012) for ready reference.

[7]A Shari'ah advisor is a person or institution, deemed acceptable in Islamic financial services industry to advise on Islamic legal and wider Shari'ah matters related with structuring of Islamic financial products and contracts. Additionally, Shari'ah scholars engage in halal food certification, product development, document verification, portfolio consultancy, Shari'ah audit and research. They are also involves in the verification Global Investment Performance Standards (GIPS). They have established an Association of Shariah Advisors in Islamic Finance—ASAS to coordinate their activities and look after their interests. Interestingly, they advertise advisory jobs as well. Shari'ah advisement on financial matters varies from country to country on details of the duties, responsibilities, and modus operandi of the boards.

money was seen in the advisory work. *Shari'ah* scholars became scarcer—the most sought after of professionals, in the non-Muslim countries as well that saw Islamic finance as a juicy business, Middle East being awash with petrodollars.

The abrupt rise in demand for advisors made their fees rocketed up fast, especially of those at the top rungs of the ladder. It brought in their mushrooming; numerous half-backed ones claiming 'expertise' and getting placements as well. The development led to an oligarchic proclivity and qualitative delivery in the profession. The incumbents sorely lacked knowledge of economics, especially of macro complications and mathematical modelling. To make up for the deficiencies in the advisement they could not resist the entry of economists to the boards but denied voting rights to them.

In conferences and across the table discussions, they often argue that the role of the jurists starts only after the client has given his consent to the terms of the contract with the bank. What process or formula is used to arrive at the uniform installment payments are none of their business to investigate; they only examine the various parts of the contract to ensure that there is no violation of the Islamic norms and this is what their signatures on the document certify. The Appendix provides specimen of such a certificate. It is brief and silent on issues we have raised on MMP FINANCING. This patently is unfair. They must in addition investigate the possible consequences of the contract until its fruition. It is the dereliction of this responsibility on the part of the jurists decorating bank advisory boards that has seen thousands of cases relating to home financing pending in courts across countries.

Central banks in many countries have of late felt the need for streamlining the constitution and working of the *Shari'ah* advisement in the financial sector. For example, Malaysia introduced a regulatory framework dealing with the qualifications training and responsibilities of the advisors overcoming the resistance from the scholars (Lee 2012).

13.6 Concluding Remarks

Most Islamic banks have been shifting to the MMP for home financing. We have shown that Islamic banks that use an interest-based formula of uniform installment in that model violate Islamic norms in that the return on money borrowed from the bank follows compounding and the ownership of the house passes to the buyer at a slower rate than payments made. Islamic efficacy of the MMP, or any other financing mode for that matter, must be evaluate before its selection for use, not thereafter. We have not stopped at indicating the non-Islamic character of the MMP but have also provided an alternative model for replacing it. The alternative—the ZDBM—is not only free of blemishes the MMP has, but it is also cheaper for the customer without any reduction in the margin of profit for the banks as it absorbs proportionately less funds. It is also much better on some related issues like costs, efficiency, liquidity, and equity compared to models Islamic banks presently use for home financing. To us, the life-cycle concerns of the MMP proponents are trivial in the face of these gains. The fixity of upfront payments for ease of remembrance cannot condone their *Shari'ah* non-compliance.

Also, the initial higher payments in the ZDBM would curb the instinctive urge to go in for houses bigger than the means can probably afford. This was incidentally one of the main causes that led to the sub-prime crisis of 2007 in the United States eventually plunging the world into one of the worst-ever financial turmoil.

Once the ZDBM model is recognized for its simplicity, efficiency, and freedom from blemishes other models have, *Shari'ah* scholars may, if need be, fine-tune the model for better *Shari'ah* compliance. The time is opportune to give ZDBM a trial as housing projects are being promoted en mass in the developed and developing countries alike. In Africa and Asia special attention is being paid to rural housing. The Islamic Development Bank has taken initiative to support large projects in Central Asia. National governments are also seized with the housing issues.

Finally, there is a case for improving the *Shari'ah* advisement in Islamic finance. The certification of educational qualifications of the advisors, they are on job training in economics including mathematics and modelling, regulation of their duties, responsibilities, and remuneration are called for. The steps taken in Malaysia are laudable and must be reinforced.

Appendix

(From the) Declining Balance Co-ownership Home Acquisition Program

Fatwa

We, the Shariah Supervisory Board of Guidance Financial Group, LLC (Guidance) have examined the documents of the Declining

Balance Co-Ownership Home Acquisition Programs, inclusive of the Co-Ownership Agreement, Security Instrument, Consumer's Obligation to pay, and Assignment of Agreements, all of which are required for each programme. We have reviewed these documents and the purposes for which they have been designed, namely:

1. to assist Muslims and others residing in the United States to acquire their homes in compliance with *Shari'ah*,
2. to enjoy the tax benefits accorded by the federal government to homeowners,
3. and for the investors to securitize their ownership investment in homes. The basic concept behind these contracts and documents is that the property is purchased in joint ownership between an affiliate of Guidance (the Co-Owner) and the person who requires finance (the Consumer). The Consumer makes monthly payments which are comprised of Profit Payments and Acquisition Payments. Profit Payments represent the Consumer payments for the enjoyment and use of the whole property, while Acquisition Payments represent the Consumer's payments for his acquiring the Co-Owner's interest in the property. It has been ascertained by the Shari'ah Supervisory Board that the documents comply with the *Shari'ah* requirement for a valid 'Diminishing *Musharakah*' arrangement, and that both parties benefit and bear the risks of their respective shares in the property throughout the contractual arrangement. The documents designed for 'Replacement' are meant for a situation where a person has already acquired a property and wishes to enter into a *Shari'ah*-compliant arrangement. In this case, he will sell a share of his property to the Co-Owner, and then both parties will have the same arrangement of 'Diminishing *Musharakah*' as detailed above. Since the units of property will be purchased by the consumer—2—under this arrangement at cost, and without increase, there is no element of*'ina* in this arrangement. After reviewing the mechanism as well as the agreements and documents, and after suggesting amendments that have been incorporated, the Shariah Supervisory Board is of the view that given the circumstances prevailing in the United States, this arrangement conforms to the rules and principles of *Shari'ah*; and therefore, Muslims may avail themselves of this opportunity to acquire homes and properties by means of this method. Agreed this on 21 October 2002.

Six leading *Shari'ah* scholars have appended their signatures to this certificate of approval as can be seen on the website of the Guidance Bank. United States.

Test Question

Q.1 Housing problem is aggravating across all countries—developed and developing; only the nature of problems is different in the two cases. Comment on the statement.

Q.2 State and explain the formula used for determining the periodic installment payments in home financing by banks. Do you think that the payment involves an element of compounding? Demonstrate the validity of your position.

Q.3 The current use of the MMP in Islamic finance is flawed on *Shari'ah* requirements. Do you agree? Justify your answer.

Q.4 Compare the MMP with the ZDBM as models for home financing. Which one will you support and why? Elaborate.

Q.5 Write explanatory notes on the following.

- IRR and nominal rate of return
- Constructive ownership
- Merit of the ZDBM

What Next

The following Chapter 14 deals with a rising lament that the reason for the unsatisfactory state of Islamic economics is the use of wrong methodology for its development or its neglect. This chapter examines this contention and poses a question: Does the subject really need a methodology in the philosophical sense as in the mainstream?

References

Chambers, M. S., Garage, C., & Sehlagehauf, D. (2007). *Mortgage Contracts and Housing Tenure Decisions* (Working Paper). Federal Reserve Bank of St. Louis. Research Division.

Craig, N. (2012). *Islamic Finance: Law and Practice* (D. Eisenberg, Ed.). Oxford: Oxford University Press.

Hasan, Z. (2012). Money Creation and Control from Islamic Perspective. *Journal of Islamic Banking & Finance, 29*(1), 70–75.

Lee, W. S. (2012). What is Inquiry-Guided Learning? https://doi.org/10.1002/tl.20002.

Meera, A. K. (2012). A Critique of Diminishing Balance Method of Islamic Home Financing. *ISRA International Journal of Islamic Finance, 4*(2), 7–23.

Meera, A. K. M., & Razak, D. A. (2009). Home Financing Through the Musharakah Mutanaqisah Contracts: Some Practical Issues. *JKAU: Islamic Economics, 22*(1), 3–25.

Nabil, B. M. A. M. (2013). Conceptual Analysis of Islamic Home Financing Models. *ISRA International Journal of Islamic Finance, 5*(1), 29–88.

Usmani, T. (2010). Musharaka and Mudaraba as Modes of Financing. *Journal of Islamic Banking and Finance, 27*(3), 57–76.

CHAPTER 14

Methodology and Islamic Economics: Efficacy of Discussion

Preview

There is a marked concern among Islamic economists about the slow, rather inconsequential, growth of the subject over the recent decades Some influential voices lament that use of wrong methodology or its neglect is responsible for the present muddled state of the subject. The number of articles, books, seminars joining such concerns is on the rise. There is insistence that putting the subject back on a growth trajectory push from the methodology end. This chapter takes a look at this insistence.

The word methodology has several usages. Here, we shall use it to denote its two uses. First, it is the subject that fixed targets for economics to achieve and supervises the discipline from outside to see how far those targets have been achieved with the passage of time. In this sense, methodology is a branch of the theory of knowledge with philosophical import. In this sense, the discussions on methodology in Islamic economics are fruitless and misleading. Second, methodology as a part of economics helps design research and its supervision. In this sense, the methods used in Islamic economics are unduly loaded with Western approach and techniques and call for reform. The controversy and confusion on the issues involved have been lingering for long but has of late assumed disquieting proportions. The paper discusses the subject in the

The author is grateful to Dr. Salma Sairally who went through an earlier draft and suggested some improvement.

Z. Hasan, *Leading Issues in Islamic Economics and Finance*,
https://doi.org/10.1007/978-981-15-6515-1_14

light of the prevalent puritan versus pragmatic approach to the study of Islamic economics. Indeed, their confrontation threatens the very survival of the subject as a distinct academic discipline. The paper suggests a way out of the predicament evaluating the efficacy of the rising concerns and focus on the subject.

Learning Outcomes
The reading of this chapter is expected to help the readers to:

- Make them understand what methodology is about and what led to its rise and fall in mainstream economics?
- Realize that methodology has seldom been a major issue in Islamic economics once the subject freed itself of the classical juristic hold. The literature on the subject is scanty and immature. There is no full book integrative work since 2008 of Addas the IIUM published.
- Know that unlike the mainstream, law in Islam follows interpretation of its sources and is not flexible proportionate to human will; methodological exploration more than that applications to change economics are limited.
- Appreciate that the methodology of Islamic economics is limited to the application of *Shari'ah* norms of conduct to economic activities.

14.1 Introduction

In common law, law is made first, interpretations follow. Parliament enacts laws through debate and majority vote. Courts interpret what is so enacted. Interestingly, in Islam interpretation comes first, the law follows. What is interpreted are the sources of law—the holy *Qur'an*, Sunnah (prophetic traditions), *ijma* (Jurists' agreement), *qiyas* (Analytical reasoning), *urf* (customary practices), *maslahah* (public interest), and *fiqhi* (*juridical*) opinion. And, who interpret these sources: the jurists. Thus, Islamic laws are not divine, as is commonly believed, in the strict sense of the term; they are *jurist-given*. The jurists stand between Allah (swt) and the community for guidance. It is the juristic origin of Islamic laws that there are four major schools of Sunni jurisprudence, each with interpretive differences *within* as well. The Shiite schools are additional. A Muslim is free to choose any from the corpus. As the juristic scholars are the law givers in Islam, they occupy a place of utmost reverence and responsibility in Muslim societies. Islamic economists, like the present author, cannot replace or dare counter them. The society grants the jurists, as it must, the final say in religious matters.

However, social phenomena are dynamic and the dynamism is on a sharp ascend. Juristic interpretations of sources too cannot remain static or sticky. Indeed, Islamic jurisprudence has never been entirely devoid of temporal changes. However, juristic dynamism has of necessity been slower as pace can be risky; frets with pitfall.[1] Still, the Jurists have to keep pace with expanding frontiers of knowledge with a socially adjustable perspective. For example, jurists cannot get away merely by looking at the legal permissibility of contractual structuring; they remain answerable for anything discovered against the tenets of Islam later during the operation of a contract. Errors could, for example, creep in because of technical jargon used or mathematical formulations forming part of the document they certify. Most contemporary jurists, especially at the top, do not have the time or age to learn newer things in a fast-changing world. Advisably, they may better have adequately qualified professionals to work with them to check technicalities.

Finally, all modern states, Muslim included, operate within a *constitutional framework* overseeing their *legal systems* in content and operation. In developing countries constitutional laws are inspired by, rather patterned on, those of their erstwhile colonial rulers. Constitutions embody socially agreed value systems. Modern societies are multi-religious and have to meet global commitments on human rights. National constitutions tend to remain neutral between different faiths their residents follow. They are books of civic rights, not the faith scriptures. In view of the rising religiosity in the Eastern countries, including Muslim, Islamic economists must see that their theoretical stance and constructs are general enough to remain workable despite constitutional differences across

[1]An interesting illustration of sticky nature of juristic pronouncements is that of the five edicts issued against Sir Ahmad Khan for his efforts to establish the MOA College in 1875 (converted into Aligarh Muslim University in 1920) the severest was from the Imam of Makka which said: 'This man is erring and causes people to err. He is rather an agent of the devil and wants to mislead Muslims. It is a sin to support the College. May God damn the founder! And if this college has been founded, it must be demolished and its founder and his supporters thrown out of the fold of Islam', The Fatwa has not been withdrawn even to this day (*Source* Prof. M. Faizan in Indian Express, 17 October 2017).

countries. This applies in particular to a puritan stance some Islamic scholars take on various economic issues

Thus, one speaking on methodology of Islamic economics must first make explicit which of the juristic schools underpins his narrative. He must further clarify whether his proposals match the constitutional provisions of his country or there is a political will to make the needed changes. For, Islam does not believe in philosophical hair-splitting, or idle theorizing. It is a way of life; its road to salvation does not loop around the worldly pursuits; it passes through their turmoil. Islamic economics that one may visualize to build must deliver on the ground. The superiority for Islamic economics over the conventional, in finance especially, is claimed because of its linkage with ground realities. One cannot, as one should not, propose something hanging in the air violative of this claim. Thus, a discussion on worldview does not seem as important as the *actualization* of a basic needs fulfilment programme. Debate on substance versus form looks less significant than sharing of profit with labour. Diminishing balance partnership may be declared *Shari'ah* compliant but equally vital is whether the contract remains *just* to both the parties throughout the course of its fruition.

Structure of the chapter

Methodology as a term mainly has two uses. First, it may refer to the subject that oversees the performance of economics from *outside*. In this sense, methodology is a branch of *epistemology*—the theory of knowledge—and stands on philosophical bearings. It seeks to evaluate if and to what extent economic theory has been developing in the direction to realizing in the real world the goals methodology sets for it. To lay down the criteria and rules for such evaluation is also the task of methodology (Hausman 1984, Chapter 1). In the following Sect. 14.2, we shall limit the discussion on methodology contextual to mainstream economics in this sense. In the process, we shall also examine the comparative position in Islamic economics on some of the issues. The two economic disciplines are doubtless much different; nevertheless, it is the mainstream discussions on methodology that have provided the motivation and the basic inputs for debates on the subject in Islamic economics.

Second, methodology is conceived of as operating *within* economics. In this sense, the rudiments of methodology help economists design research projects and fix their goals. This view of methodology is particularly important for Islamic economics. We shall discuss its theoretical elements in Sect. 14.3. In Sect. 14.4 we examine research methods popularized in academic institutions and the impact of Western norms and methods on research done in the area. The last Sect. 14.5 would be devoted to summarize the discussion and conclude with an answer to the poser in the title of the paper.

14.2 Nature of Mainstream Methodology

Methodology attracted much attention in economics during the interwar period as the era witnessed extremes of cyclical devastations—the 1923 galloping inflation in Germany followed by the Great Depression of the 1930s. However, the interest in the subject faded away by the close of the century. Confusion and controversy ultimately reduced methodology to a puritan sort of philosophy for ivory tower thinkers. In many universities, the subject was shunted out from departments of economics to find refuge in departments of philosophy. Any survey of the voluminous mainstream literature on the subject would here be out of place.[2] Important is that the time was opportune for the subject for reception in the nascent Islamic economics that took off as an academic discipline during the mid-1970s.

Discussions on methodology in Islamic economics usually derive their inspiration and content from what is termed as the worldview of a society, a popular subject in the Islamic studies in the Islamic social sciences.[3] Differences in the defining features of economic systems—mainstream and Islamic—are attributed to their worldview differences. Worldview refers to the collective perception of a community about the purpose of creation, the place of humans therein, their relations with the Creator and with fellow human beings including the principles shaping and regulating them. The concept of worldview is architectonic and evolutive with reference to time and space.

The Islamic worldview is seen as God ordained; it is shaped and conditioned by moral and ethical codes of conduct for the individuals and groups in various spheres of life including economics. It has juristic

[2] Readers interested in such a survey would find Daniel Hausman (1984) and Mark Blaugh (1992) useful references on the subject.

[3] See, for instance, the seminal work of Professor Naqib Al-Attas 1993 on the subject.

foundations allowing interpretive flexibility but cannot be diluted or replaced by human will. In contrast, the West has developed what it calls a 'scientific worldview' based on rational empiricism and changeable by social agreement.[4]

14.2.1 Impact of Worldview Differences

The basic distinctions the worldview differences create between Islamic and mainstream versions of economics, broadly include the 'is-ought' controversy, reason–revelation relationship, and the doctrine–reality relationship. We discuss them below.

a. ***The 'is–ought' controversy***: The secular worldview expelled all transcendental ideas from the purview of economics on the plea that science is concerned only with 'what is'. 'What ought to be' was admissible only if supported by empirical logic. Mainstream economics continue to hold this view as an article of faith.[5] Thus, Marshall (1924) could conceive of economics only as catering to 'material requisites of well-being', while Robbins (1932) declared it 'neutral towards the ends'. On the contrary, the Islamic view is that the absence of hereafter and accountability to any superior being makes one feel only existing because he exists. He sees no difference in an act of suicide and a feat of sacrifice; for, he faces no system of reward and punishment in the hereafter. Value-neutral material progress, has been phenomenal but at an incalculable cost to humanity in terms of environmental damage and other sufferings, especially in the form of abject poverty and vulgar inequalities in the distribution of wealth and opportunity. Islam makes one see matter–spirit interlocks in self urging him/her to follow the prescribed ethical path.

[4] For a detailed discussion on the two worldview differences and their impact on Islamic versus mainstream economics, see Hasan (2017).

[5] See for instance these two definitions: Science is science and ethics is ethics; it takes both to make a whole man; but only confusion, misunderstanding, and discord can come from not keeping them separate and distinct, from trying to impose the absolutes of ethics on the relatives of science (Friedman 1955, p. 409). Morality, it could be argued, represents the way that people would like the world to work—whereas economics represent how it actually does work (Levitt and Dubner, *Freakonomics*, 2005, p. 13).

b. ***Reason–revelation relationship***: One may look at this relationship in two ways. First, reasoning operates as a tool of analysis *within* discussions on revelation. Second, reason confronts and questions revelation from *outside* the confines of religion. Contextual to methodology, the first way of looking at the relationship is Islamic, the second mainstream. The meanings and argument are not the same in the two cases.

The monistic view of Islam includes both reason and sapience—intuitive wisdom—in the ambit of rationality; mainstream methodology leaves sapience out (Al-Attas 1995, 18, 35; Hasan 1995, 59). For distinction, we shall treat reason with its Islamic import as intellect meaning 'reason plus sapience', leaving the term reason for usage as it is in the mainstream.

Now, 'intellect' is the faculty that transcends the realm of understanding and provides preclusive principles for human guidance in worldly affairs. It makes comprehensible to human mind the metaphysics of the visible and invisible and of their mutual linkage, thus enabling one to imbibe a holistic and integrated vision of life. Unlike secular rationalism, Islam does not see nature as a material physical object meant for human exploitation and use; it accords nature an additional and deeper significance. The Qur'an upholds nature[6] as an open book which *intellect* alone can help read, understand, and interpret. Intellect makes one feel and grasp the cosmic purpose and relevance of nature. It must be revered as it contains symbols and signs bearing testimony to the existence of Allah (swt) and His lordship over the universe.

c. ***Doctrine–reality circuitry:*** An economy invariably has an underlying doctrine that shapes its institutions and prescribes goals to achieve; it helps design policies and gives content and direction to ground realities. Thus, economies have an operable doctrine–reality circuitry. For example, in mainstream economic

[6]The following two verses from Surah Al-Fatir sum up all possible branches of knowledge or that could ever be taught or learnt in any school; covering solids, liquids, plants, animals as well as the varieties of the human race: Do you not see that Allah sends down rain from the sky, and We produce thereby fruits of varying colours? And in the mountains are tracts, white and red of varying shades and [some] extremely black (27). And among people and moving creatures and grazing livestock are various colours similarly. Only those fear Allah, from among His servants, who have knowledge (28).

> systems—capitalism or socialism—the doctrines resulted from the formalization of realities on the ground. For instance, Adam Smith observed the accumulation of capital, technological breakthroughs, division of labour and monetary institutions maturing in Britain—he could foresee the industrial revolution coming to make his country the leading colonial power of the world. In his '*Wealth of Nations*' Smith crafted the foundation stones for capitalism from observed realities. He was the system builder. Likewise, Karl Marx saw the dark side of capitalism—exploitation and alienation of the working class, capitalism eventually spreading mass poverty, deprivation, and denial. Based on what he observed, Marx succeeded to provide the initial design for socialism. The commonality between capitalism and socialism that resulted is that in both cases the glide has been *from reality to doctrine*. What about Islam?

Islam has had neither a Smith nor a Marx. Colonization of Muslim lands did not allow them to grow out of the late mercantilist era in economic thought. Thus, Ibn Khaldun's Introduction (The ***Muqqadima***, 1406) could hardly go beyond discussing the causes that accounted for the rise and fall of nations along an inverted parabolic path; he could not draw the contours of an Islamic economic system because he did not observe it operating candidly on the ground. By the dawn of independence around the mid-1950s, Muslim economies had already gone far on the road of capitalism their colonizers had charted for them. Some Islamic economists see methodology as the tool for the reversal. They assume that methodology can make ground *realities* change to match the doctrinal structures of the religion. To convince people, they highlight the maladies of the mainstream systems now in practice and show how Islam, if followed, would convert the existing hell into paradise ahead. One does not come across a greater naivety that has caused so much of avoidable controversy and confusion in Islamic economics. Methodological enthusiasts violate a basic principle of valid comparisons: likes cannot be compared with un-likes—the apples with oranges, chalk with cheese, or parrots with crows. Since no economic system on ground following the Islamic prescriptions operates anywhere even on a miniature scale, Islamic economists exhibit a proclivity to comparing a system painted on Islamic ideals with the one as capitalism operating on ground divergent to its doctrinal norms. No value judgement can be valid one way or the other based on such comparisons.

Given the nature of Islamic economics, methodology as an evaluator to supervise the performance of Islamic economics parallel to mainstream is not possible. Methodology of Islamic economics is what principles of jurisprudence are to jurisprudence. Islamic methodology can only be the application of juristic norms to economic practice (Addas 2008). Let us now turn to the second usage of the term methodology which is significant from a practical viewpoint. We find that it carries a deep *linkage* with the philosophical approach to methodology discussed above in that research in economics has increasingly become dominated with empiricism—the use of mathematics and econometric modelling.

Box 14.1

Until the 1980s *Methodology of Economics* did not have many texts and had philosophical overtones mostly discussing old disputes with historical perspective. There was a pronounced proclivity of associating it with positivist tones with emphasis on theory testing against objective facts and insisting on making a distinction between the normative and positive statements, associating economics with the latter alone, especially to fulfill its predictive role—role which was much disputed.

Views on methodological issues underwent a defining change with the publication of Mark Blaugh's authoritative work *The Methodology of Economics*. The publication aroused tremendous interest in the subject. An international Network was erected for *Economic methodology* with its online Journal of Methodology. The literature on the subject swelled in no time; Methodology of economics emerged as an independent subject. Confusion and controversy heightened involving Friedman, Samuelson, Kaldor, and many others; the subject shifted to the Departments of Philosophy in many institutions of higher learning. One could feel the change coming in 1992 preface of Blaugh.

The growth of the field still emphasizes the need for a deeper understanding of the old debates but the range of topics that methodology now covers is much wider. In the twenty-first century, Methodology has no role in the construction of mainstream economics, only methodology as an explanatory tool has. Can *Methodology* rebuild Islamic economics?

Z. Hasan (2020)

14.3 Methodology for Research

14.3.1 Historical Sway

Higher education facilities in terms of infrastructural provisions and quality of teaching had been limited in developing countries during the centuries of colonial rule. Universities and colleges, when established, followed the curricula patterns, course contents, and reading materials prescribed in the ruling countries.[7] Sometimes, even teachers were imported. Those from the richer classes of the country went out to obtain degrees abroad that carried high premium in the local employment markets. In course of time, the process put a psyche discounting of what was local. Thus, even when lands had become free, intellect remained occupied.

That psyche continues dominating the education policies in the developing world unabated. It has created some additional problems in Muslim countries as education expanded in social sciences, especially economics. The freedom movements in most of these countries were led by the clerics who fed mass aspirations on hopes of erecting a social paradise of Islamic vintage once the foreigners left. However, the colonial rulers transferred political power at the dawn of independence to the secular elite, not to the movement leaders. For instance, in Pakistan, it was Jinnah & Co. who succeeded the British, not the Maulana Maududi's legion of Jamaat-e Islami. This had unsavoury consequences. The community got divided horizontally between the so-called *modernist* and the *orthodox* groupings, engaged in acrimony. In the ensuing chaos and instability, orthodoxy lost the race; it could extract only some marginal concessions from the ruling elite; especially in the field of education. The sequence of events was not much different elsewhere in the Muslim world

The clerics leading the freedom movements across countries had already launched a comprehensive global programme for looking at knowledge from an Islamic prism. For brevity of expression, they called

[7]To illustrate, in the 2017 syllabi for the prestigious BA (Honours) in Economics Course (University of Delhi), one finds that almost all the required readings are from foreign writers; the courses on Indian economy being an exception. It is an irony that none but few among the over 6000 faculty in the colleges of the university plus that of the reputed Delhi Schools of Economics could not write textbooks for their students.

it *the Islamization of knowledge programme*, albeit a misnomer. Arabs in the Middle East, Jammat-e-Islami in the Indian subcontinent and Malays in the South East Asia, for example, led the programme that received massive support for public funding.

After the mid-1970s, Islamic economics emerged as the centre-piece of this programme, when, following a well known 1976 conference in Jeddah; the subject was launched as a formal academic discipline across the world. Educational institutions, scholarly journals, research work, and funding arrangements, emerged fast on the scene in various countries. The control and regulation of the developments understandably remained with the movement people who had already done substantive pioneering work in the area. However, this control had to unwind with the expansion of economic studies and research over time. Doors had to be opened for academics and support staff from the mainstream secular discipline. Not all of the newcomers had knowledge of Islamic jurisprudence. Most of the teachers were educated in the Western tradition at universities, local or abroad and had a rationalistic, value-neutral view of economics. Their tool kit was full of mathematical and econometric techniques. This group gained added ascendancy with finance fast eclipsing other areas in Islamic economics. This was a divisive development.

Reasons noted above apart, the control of the movements over the education system started weakening with the expansion of the financial segment in Muslim economies. The increasing technical complexities of business and the pace of change added to the difficulties. Of course, there were jurists who were well equipped for adapting to the change. In fact, they found the expansion quite lucrative as the demand for *Shari'ah* advisement in financial institutions ran far ahead of supply. However, most Islamic economists working in higher education institutions across countries could not extract much advantage from the change.

14.3.2 The Bifurcation

The ascendancy of Islamic finance left vast areas like public economics, distributive justice, economic development monetary issues, and social welfare problems almost unexplored. This has led to some sharp divisions among Islamic economists, the broad bifurcation being between the old guards and their followers imbued with the classical *puritan* tradition and the later day entrants from the modern economics stream, who mainly handled finance. The traditionalists chose to attack the modernists for infesting Islamic economics with mainstream pollutants.[8] Theirs is an effort to pull the subject back into its historical tracts.[9]

For restoring the old edifice, they plead for opening the discussion from the methodology end as, in their view; it is the use of an inappropriate methodology that has brought Islamic economics to its present impasse. The contention is a frivolous escapade. Methodology is a receding subject in mainstream economics itself.[10] A digression here on methodology in its philosophical attire is not warranted. Relevant to the present context is the methodology that has almost exclusively occupied the dissertation writing at the graduate level as a mark of quality in prestigious institutions of higher education in Muslim class oppress their subordinate class to advantage and strengthen itself.

14.4 Research Methods[11]

Predatory publishing in Islamic economics owes its emergence and proliferation to the increasing entrance in the Islamic higher education institutions of teachers who had studied and worked in foreign universities. Their conditioning in the mainstream thought processes has convinced them that the way to raising academic standards to global levels in Islamic economics was to imitate the Western structures and methods in teaching and research.[12] The conviction has proved misleading; especially the penchant for mathematical/empirical formalization is misplaced.

[8] See the writings of Masudul Alam Chuodhury, Assad Zaman (2012b), and Syed Nasr as illustrations of insistence on the adoption of this approach to rehabilitate Islamic economics. However, the problem with the puritan insistence of the group is that the resultant economic order they paint has not yet been shown operating even on a miniature scale anywhere in the Muslim world while Islamic finance ironically claims an edge over the mainstream for being firmly linked to the economy on the ground!

[9] For insistence on reverting to puritan classical methodology for developing Islamic economics see Nasr (1992), Choudhory (2009) and Zaman (2012b) as illustrations. They prefer to reside in ivory towers while Islamic economics claims its firm linkage to ground realities, especially in finance.

[10] The rising tendency of formalization in modern economics has paled empiricism adding to methodological confusion in the discipline (Blaugh 1992).

[11] This part of the paper is mainly based part of Hasan (2020).

[12] An inept consequence of such reviewing is notable. Even the leading journals of Islamic economics prefer to get submissions received evaluated by mainstream scholars often working abroad. This practice has two limitations. First, all such reviewers are not adequately aware of Islamic position they are approached to comment on. More than

Arguably, mathematics helps fix ideas precisely, especially to spell out the optimization conditions for economic agents and entities under a variety of complex situations. The advantages led in the eighteenth century to the proliferation of formal economic modelling based on differential calculus that made optimization feasible. In the process, economics became increasingly mathematical during interwar period and the later coming in of new techniques, like the games theory, allowed wider generalizations. The use of newer tools became fashionable, a symbol of knowledge and scholarship. The developments promoted caustic divisions in the profession and accentuated the formalization of the subject.

However, the unwanted formalization of discipline could not go unchallenged. No one denied the utility of mathematics for economics but it did not take long for its ***overuse*** in the subject to awaken criticism. Some noted economists like J. M. Keynes, Robert Heilbroner, Friedrich Hayek, and others expressed *concern over* the increasing spread of mathematical models for exploring human behaviour. They were candid that some economic choices, especially involving moral and ethical norms, were irreducible to mathematical symbolism. Abstract models for explaining human behaviour do not meaningfully submit to mathematical manipulations, they argued. Furthermore, most political problems such as budgetary allocations, fighting over the tax structures, welfare reforms, international trade, or concern for the environment have economic aspects. Both the voters and the leaders they elect can fulfil their role more effectively if they have a fair understanding of the basic economics; mathematics would only confuse them. Still, there are well-known Islamic economists, who enjoy unleashing that confusion.

Also, one cannot ignore the fact that there is today a worldwide scare of mathematics among students.[13] Attention diverters are increasing fast; youngsters have neither the patience nor the time to struggle with the learning of mathematics. They are running away from economics especially because of its increasing orientation to mathematics.

that, they find contributions obsolete due to mainstream advances. The rejection deprives Islamic economics of knowledge on the subject where it may have never been touched upon. The point is what may be obsolete for the mainstream could useful for Islamic economics.

[13]A news paper report titled: France wants to conquer the fear of maths, informs that a commissioned survey describes the grades students obtained in the subject as 'catastrophic' and suggested raising them to improve the pass percentage (*Times of India* 14.01.18; 18).

14.4.1 *The Econometric Syndrome*

An advanced form of mathematical propagation in Islamic economics is the craving for the use of econometric modelling. Illustrative of the emphasis is the compulsive use of such modelling at the prestigious global institutions of Islamic finance. The following narrative is based on the personal experience of the author as a faculty member at an institution for years. Typical was the case of a student who the author supervised for her Master's project paper worth three credit hours with the title: ***Sukuk: definition, structures, and Malaysian experience.*** A high power Graduate Studies Committee with the supervisor as an invitee had to evaluate the work. The Committee appreciated the flawless language of the paper and its structuring. However, they expressed reservation to clear it as it did not use empirical modelling. The supervisor had to plead for quite sometime in defence of the student asking what model, if any, could the student have used in the definition or the structure sections of the work while in support of her position on Malaysian experience, she did produce appropriate and adequate supportive data in tabular form? On the insistence of the supervisor that the work was good enough for a pass as the rules required no grading, the Committee eventually relented to clear the work.

The obsession of the faculty with econometric modelling as an imperative for acceptable research, save in case of topics dealing with Islamic jurisprudence, was understandable as the teachers were largely foreign educated and what got sunk in most of them was the econometric culture of the Western institutions where they had studied. For such teachers using econometrics in doing and supervising research had advantages. Models of all sorts are readily available in the mainstream literature to choose from; even foreign collaboration could be garnered. Thus, research becomes relatively easy. Feed the relevant information in a computer program and torture the data until they yield what is required. Bulk of the manuscript, save the interpretations, the machine generates. Numerous impulse impact graphs in the work towards the close of manuscript the authors do not explain, nor do the readers care to look at, let alone understand. One rarely comes across a genuinely original model formulation in Islamic economics and finance.

14.4.2 The Devastation

The above observations are not to deny the significance of empirical methods in research work. Econometric modelling has analytical grandeur and utility; it can undo age-long convictions.

> No doubt, there are many reasons for believing that demand curves are negatively inclined but there is little doubt that if the statistical evidence repeatedly ran the other way, none of these reasons would suffice to make economists believe in the law of demand.
>
> Blaugh 1992, Preface (p. XX)

This is true in principle and reinforces the significance of falsification in improving theoretical generalizations. However, empirical research has not mostly been refutative and has rarely thrown up conclusions independent of time and space. Econometric work in Islamic economics has been confirmative without exceptions; not adding an iota to its theoretical corpus. On the contrary, it has fueled a dangerous proclivity in Islamic economics, encouraging what can be termed as *academic predation*. The term refers to the publishing of articles with little merit in dubious open access journals against prior payment.

A group of writers in a paper published in the prestigious science journal *Nature* voiced grave concern at the explosive proliferation of predatory publishing, the number of journals promoting it shot up to over 10,000 in few years (Kolata 2017). Predatory journals tend to mushroom in natural sciences but social disciplines like economics are not free of increasing incursions.[14] Fake journals make imitative writings look original.

The Western-educated elite in developing countries imposed the *perish or publish* culture in higher education for academic appointment and promotion. Local journals for publishing research were few and seldom won recognition as meritorious on undefined standards. The norm for quality soon became publishing abroad in some refereed reputable journal. With the spread of education in Islamic economics more and more publication was sought abroad where empiricism has won the day in academic research. Thus, research methodology in Islamic economics

[14] See Hasan (2020) for a detailed discussion on academic predation and its impact on research in Islamic economics, especially finance.

got geared to econometrics. As the research was mostly imitative and less acceptable for publication in the reputable journals, the Say's law of market reversed—demand created its own supply. Predatory publishing became a flourishing business. Fake journals are mushrooming fast; the author receives at least one call daily for submitting a paper for fast publication with payment on acceptance (POA) basis.

Econometric-oriented research for payment publishing has become a flourishing business. It is inflicting incalculable harm on Islamic economics and finance. Students come to reputed institutions from numerous academic disciplines having divergent academic backgrounds ranging from philosophy to medicine. They do not all have the same taste or ability to absorb even the minimal of econometric shock they receive after admission. Admittedly, it cannot be a case of the same size fitting all feet.

The majority of academics are not at home with empirical methods. Data quality is often suspect and availability scanty. Variables were chosen mostly lack the needed Islamic import.[15] Bulk of students and staff remains tense and pressurized. Models employed are invariably picked up from the published mainstream sources. These limitations apart, improvement in the quality of research is sought by rejecting repeatedly what a student does, positive helpful guidance is rare. Supervisory contribution is minimal, appropriation of credit for sound work maximum. Data mining for the supervisors is commonly a duty of the students. Completion time knows no limit. Cases, where students leave without completion or shift to other institutions, are not rare. However, those who go abroad often discover that the ordeal is no different from what students faced at home. A case reported in Appendix is an eye-opener. It tells more than meets the eye. And, this is not a solitary case of Islamic economics students suffering abroad in frustration; there are several others in author's knowledge as they occasionally call for help.[16]

Econometric models have explanatory power but they are found weak, even misleading, on the prediction front. Their policy conclusions

[15] Most of the data used comes from the UN sources. Even the Islamic Development Bank (IDB) at Jeddah mostly reproduces data separated from the same Tables for the Organization of Islamic Cooperation (OIC) member countries. Data generation in size and quality expressive of Islamic essence is conspicuous by its very absence.

[16] A classic illustration of the potpourri of disjointed ideas and errors from the title to conclusion is the Yosuf et al. (2017) article published in a refereed and listed journal.

are rarely found guiding economic activity in the Muslim world. Most researchers fail to explain how their findings add to usable wisdom and can help improve economic performance; they just make sterile claims of filling knowledge gaps.

Interestingly, stochastic empiricism is on the decline even in the mainstream economics research: the use of non-parametric methods allowing multivariate analyses is on the rise. Unlike **parametric** models, **non-parametric** constructs do not require the researcher to make any assumptions about the distribution of the population, and are for that reason sometimes referred to as a distribution-free method.[17]

Econometric models for research keep students occupied with data exploration, the values of parametric variables, and the levels of their significance. This lets self-control go, leaving little time for creative out-of-the-box thinking. It kills initiative. ***Imitators cannot be innovators, followers, the leaders.*** Let intellect not remain shackled in free lands.

What useful purpose parametric research is serving?[18] Professor Assad Zaman (2012a) teaching econometrics at Islamabad makes a pertinent observation as follows.

> Econometric methodology is based on logical positivist principles. Since logical positivism has collapsed, it is necessary to re-think these foundations....positivist methodology has led econometricians to a meaningless search for patterns in the data. An alternative methodology which relates observed patterns to real causal structures is proposed.

There is time for a cost–benefit accounting. The reward apparent is the international recognition of merit even sought via predatory publications. The merit test for research articles must be the extent they promote the Islamic viewpoint and the number of people in the academic world reading and benefiting from them.

[17] For examples, many tests in parametric statics, such as the sample *t*-test, are derived under the assumption that the data come from normal population with unknown mean. In a non-parametric study the normality assumption is removed.

[18] This issue was discussed thread bare in an earlier paper: See Hasan (2005) and also the illuminating discussant Assad Zaman's comments on the paper in the Conference proceedings.

14.5 Concluding Remarks

The main points we have made in the above discussion are:

1. The term methodology has two usages in economics. First, as a philosophical subject where it belongs to epistemology, a branch of the theory of knowledge. In this garb, it evaluates the performance of economic theory to help achieve given objectives on the ground. Here we compared mainstream elements with Islamic norms on the basis of worldview differences—secular versus Islamic.
2. In the second usage methodology is intrinsic to economics, it is a part of the discipline dealing with and guiding designing, and methods for conducting research to expand the frontiers of knowledge in economics.

We have argued that there cannot be a methodology for Islamic economics on the same pattern as for mainstream economics, especially because there is no economy on the ground operating according to the Islamic norms and requirements: It is hard to go beyond building castles in the air. Here is just one illustration of advocacy for such norms having no impact on ground realities despite tall claims of Islamic economists having an egalitarian and altruistic approach helpful to reducing poverty and distributive injustice. Figure 14.1 A is revealing. Note that in the Islamic Middle East income inequalities are the highest while in secular Europe the lowest.

Section B testifies that it is not merely a point of time position but a long-run trend (1990–2016) also, though with a difference.[19] Overall, inequalities show a rising trend across the globe, sharpest in India and slowest in Sub-Saharan Africa. Pondering on such issues is urgent than spending time on methodology hair-splitting which is not needed. Here, let us endorse the saying 'anything goes, or let a thousand flowers bloom'. The nature of Islamic economics being what it is, methodology is just a continuous interpretation of sources of knowledge in view of social dynamism and seeing that *activities* on ground conform to revision

[19] The Figures are from the just published World Inequality Report 2018. They have been edited and juxtaposed here to facilitate comparisons.

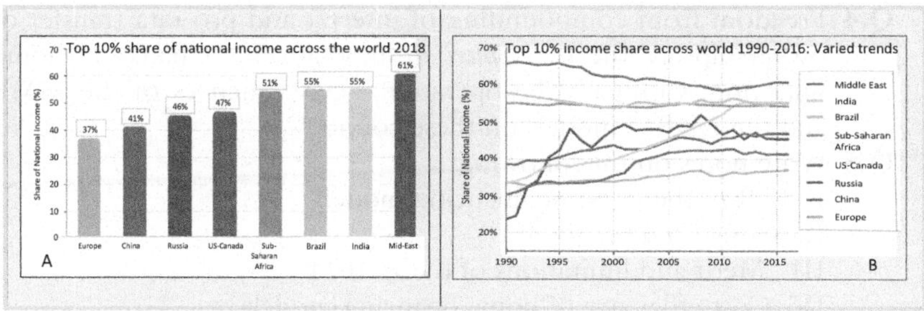

Fig. 14.1 Income inequalities—magnitude (World Bank 2018)

of norms if any. Harmony between *Shari'ah* and constitutional provision has to be ensured and maintained.

A *veil-ignorance approach* to the methodology in the first philosophical sense may push Islamic economics into unforeseeable future. Methodology in the second sense imbued with the first must eschew the injudicious use of mathematics and econometric modelling as an imperative to research, for a variety of reasons we have alluded to earlier, especially to shun temptation for predatory publishing. Testable propositions in economics from the Islamic viewpoint would be limited because of their *intention* orientation and data lacking the incorporation of this vital element in modelling. Thus, to us the answer to the question the title of this paper contains is negative: methodology of Islamic economics is not a subject worth discussing.

Test Questions

Q.1 Housing problem is fast aggravating across both developed and developing countries. Explain the nature and extent of this problem, with special reference to financing.

Q.2 State and explain the formula used for determining the periodic uniform return on capital. IS compounding embedded in the process? Argue your case.

Q.3 The MMP model is no better than the conventional interest-based model. Show if this claim is valid?

Q.4 Freedom from compounding of interest and pro rata transfer of ownership are the two *Shari'ah* imperatives for banks in home financing. Compare the operational consequences of the MMP and the ZDBM models on these counts.

Q.5 Write notes on the following:
I. IRR in the in home financing models
II. Constructive liability
III. Merit and limitations of the ZDBM
IV. Cost efficiency of home financing models

What Next?

One discussion usually missing in textbooks on Islamic economics and finance is on accounting issues. The final Chapter 15 of this book looks at some accounting issues that drive a wedge between the accountants and the economists. It makes no claims to original contribution in the mainstream vein but it does introduce issues new to Islamic disciplines.

Appendix

Students' predicament abroad illustrated:

A student, who had attended lectures of the author in Islamic Economics at INCEIF for her graduation, joined the PhD program at a well-known university abroad. She believed, like most locals, that foreign exposure and a foreign PhD would be valuable in career-building back home. Paraphrased, she narrated in an email message her predicament on that journey as under.

My supervisory team was not supportive at all. Many differences between them and me cropped up concerning research issues affecting my progress. I had requested the university to change the supervisory team, but they could not help as no one really understood my topic involving Sharīʿah compliance aspects. My principal supervisor was a Muslim but I could not feel that he or others in the team had any understanding of the Sharīʿah questions involved in my work; they showed no empathy either. On the contrary, I felt that they were just exploiting me. In fact, my principal supervisor had hijacked my work, publishing it in a top journal with a professor in Europe. I reported the matter to the Research Ethics and Integrity Committee of the university. They interviewed the supervisor and examined my documents. I was informed that the evidence I had produced was not strong enough to prove the allegations. Surprisingly, the Professor left the university abruptly and moved to the UK.

The student had since also shifted to another university.

References

Addas, W. A. J. (2008). Methodology—Secular Versus Islamic. Kuala Lumpur: Research Management Centre, International Islamic University of Malaysia (IIUM).

Al-Attas, S. M. N. (1995). *Prolegomena to the Metaphysics of Islam: An Exposition of the Fundamental Elements of Islamic Worldview*. Kuala Lumpur: Malaysian International Institute of Islamic Thought and Civilization.

Blaugh, M. (1992). *Methodology of Economics or How Economists Explain* (2nd ed.). Cambridge, UK: Cambridge University Press.

Choudhory, M. A. (2009). Islamic Critique and Alternative to Financial Engineering Issues. *Journal of King Abdulaziz University: Islamic Economics, 22*(2), 205–244.

Friedman, M. (1955). The Methodology of Positive Economics. In *Essays in Positive Economics* (pp. 3–43). Chicago: University of Chicago Press.

Hasan, Z. (1995). Economic Development in Islamic Perspective: Concept, Objectives and Some Issues. *IIUM Journal of Islamic Economics, 1*(1), 80–111.

Hasan, Z. (2005). Islamic Banking at the Cross-Roads: Theory Versus Practice. In R. Wilson & M. Iqbal (Eds.), *Islamic Perspectives on Wealth Creation* (pp. 11–25). Edinburg, UK: Edinburg University Press.

Hasan, Z. (2017, June). Academic Sociology: The Alarming Rise in Predatory Publishing and Its Consequences for Islamic Economics and Finance. *ISRA Journal of Islamic Finance, 10*(1), (Emerald).

Hasan, Z. (2020). Methodology of Islamic Economics: Is the Subject Worth Discussing? (Chapter 1). In *Methodology of Islamic Economics: Problems and Solutions*. Istanbul, Turkey: IKIM.

Hausman Daniel, M. (Ed.). (1984). *The Philosophy of Economics: An Anthology*. Cambridge, UK: Cambridge University Press.

Kolata, G. (2017, November). How Faux Journals Are Making Pseudo-Science Legit. *Times of India*.

Marshall, A. (1924). *Principles of Economics*. New York: Macmillan.

Nasr, S. V. R. (1992). *Islamization of Knowledge: A Critical Overview* (Occasional Paper No. 17). International Institute of Islamic Thought, Islamabad.

Robbins, L. (1932). *Nature and Significance of Economic Science*. London, UK: Macmillan.

Yosuf, R. M., Wahab, N. A., & Hamza, H. (2017). Does Home Financing Promote Affordability of Home Ownership in Malaysia? An Empirical Analysis Between Islamic and Conventional Banks. *International Journal of Economics, Management and Accounting, 25*(3), 601–627.

Zaman, A. (2012a). Crisis in Islamic Economics: Diagnosis and Prescriptions. *Journal of King Abdulaziz University: Islamic Economics, 25*(2), 227–250.

Zaman, A. (2012b). Methodological Mistakes and Econometric Consequences. *International Econometric Review (IER) Econometric Research Association, 4*(2), 99–122.

CHAPTER 15

Issues in Profit Measurement: Accountants Versus Economists

Preview
This Chapter discusses a topic rarely addressed in the literature on profit theory over the decades. In empirical work on subjects like growth, efficiency and welfare in economics—mainstream or Islamic—business profits at times appear as one of the variables. Such studies perforce use profit data reported in the business accounting records. This data is invariably at variance in important ways with the economists' theoretical view of profit. The cause of divergence is the cosmopolitan forward looking ex ante view of entrepreneurism the economists take as opposed to the narrow conservative ex post focus of the accountants needed to protect the interest of business proprietors who pay them for the job. There is a need to narrow this gap to improve the results of empirical explorations. This Chapter identifies some areas of divergence like maintenance of capital, evaluation of inventory and the impact of conservatism. It concludes that the economists are obliged more to take cognizance of accounting constraints than the other way round.

Learning Objectives

- This Chapter is expected to help accounting students look at certain issues from the economists viewpoint and students of economics to look at the same issues from the side of accountants so that they may understand the conceptual gaps between the two disciplines and attempt at narrowing them to bring the resultant statistics

Z. Hasan, *Leading Issues in Islamic Economics and Finance*,
https://doi.org/10.1007/978-981-15-6515-1_15

emanating from accounting records may better serve the ends of each discipline.

- To this end, it hopes to make both sides look at the ex post and ex ante notions of business earnings of maintaining capital in some real terms.
- As both the accountants and the economists must be interested in curbing cyclical fluctuations in the macroeconomic variables the Chapter may help students understand the inventory valuation systems contribute to magnify the cycles and evolve corrective mechanism to reduce that impact.

15.1 Introduction

The atomic analysis of profit at the theoretical level has caused great divergence of opinion on the subject among the economists and has, in addition, driven a wedge between their views on profit on the one hand and those of the accountants on the other. The accountants see the firm, not the waning entrepreneur like the economists, as the seat of profit. They take a wider 'catch-all' view including in profit implicit returns, windfalls, scarcity rents, and monopoly revenues which imparts realism to the concept. If the economists relax on their hair splitting analytics, the two approaches may promise a workable reconciliation. The narrowing down of the gap to the extent possible must be attempted. The accountants provide the techniques for the measurement of profit. The economists need the data thus generated for the testing of their hypotheses as also for business policy evaluations. Thus, they need a relook on their theoretical structures. But this does not mean that accountants have no responsibility, or cannot do anything, for reducing the conceptual gaps on profit between the two disciplines. However, there are reasons, we shall presently see, that put greater responsibility on the economists for initiating effort at reconciliation.

Even if the economists shift the locus of profit from the heuristic entrepreneur to the firm, and broaden reasonably their definition of profit, they would remain at odds with accounting practice on the issue measurement issue (Hasan 2016). Some of the main questions giving rise to disagreement for instance are: Should we have an ex post view of profit or ex ante? What is the meaning of capital? Why, and in what sense—nominal or real—should it be kept intact? How far can modern accounting be expected to eschew conservatism and become forward looking? Palpably, the answers to such sort of questions crucial to the measurement of a profit would depend mainly on the time dimension of a study, because it would be quite simple to measure profit for the entire life of a business firm. From the sum of amounts received will be deducted the amounts paid into or invested in the business during the firm's entire life. The difference thus obtained would be the profit or the loss. The results of such a calculation are not, however, of much significance except for purely financial concerns or business undertakings with extremely short lives. And though this method has the advantage of finality and precision—indeed it is the only method of profit computation that can conceivably be free of error but its insistence that profit determination must await the final liquidation of a business sharply limits its usefulness.

Businesses are not founded for liquidation but with the hope that they would prosper and continue for an indefinite time. The span of life of a business firm has been greatly lengthened with the advent of the modern corporation. The case of practical importance, as well as of theoretical interest, therefore, is that of the measurement of periodic profit of a going concern. The notion of periodicity here is arbitrary for, there is no logical basis to decide the relevant time dimension. Accounting has fixed the periods for profit measurement not as a matter of rule but according to the conventions of the line of industry in which the firm operates or the nature of the business. The element of arbitrariness in choosing the time dimension for the measurement does not, however, detract from its practical significance. The periodic measurement of the profits of a business firm is of vital importance from the points of view of its owners, management, workers, and creditors. The consumers and the government, the economists, and the politicians are all interested in the periodic measurement of business profits for reasons of their own.

The accountants had to feel, of necessity, greater impact than the economists of this concept of periodicity. The latter have not cared to forge their own tools for measuring profit and continue to rely on accounting records as the primary source of statistics for this purpose. Accounting is not yet a perfect art and the compulsions of his role in measuring profit do not leave much scope for the accountant to modify his methods to suit the needs of the economist. Thus viewed much of the criticism of the accountant and his methods by the economists, though understandable, is uncalled for. So long as accounting records remain the basic source of data for the measurement of profit, the economists have to go more than halfway to meet the accountant. It is only with this understanding that we can proceed in a useful way to reconcile the views of the economist and the accountant on the basic issues thrown up by the need of periodic measurement of profit.

Periodic measurement of profit requires one to distinguish and choose between ex post and ex ante concepts of profit. Conventional accounting is largely concerned with past events. Historical costs and historical revenues lie at the very foundation of accounting techniques. The profit that accountants measure is, therefore, essentially, ex post in nature and content. This accounting view of profit has been widely criticized by the economists. An evaluation of this criticism led us to conclude that the basic definition of profit should be ex post, even if ex ante profit is considered as a more proximate determinant of economic behaviour.

15.2 Concept of Capital

Issues in the measurement of profit stem from the going concern notion of a business enterprise. Periodicity lends meaning and significance to the organism of a firm. Both economic theory and accounting practice conceive of this organism in terms of the capital invested in the firm. The two approaches however differ from one another in an important way.

The definitional characteristic of capital for the economist is that it is something real in character. 'It consists of all those goods existing at a particular time which can be used in any way so as to satisfy wants during subsequent periods' (Hicks 1960, 75). The organism of the firm is nothing but an aggregation of assets devoted to the production of goods or service over a period of time. In other words, lands, buildings, plant and machinery, furniture and fixtures, stocks of raw materials, and of finished and semi-finished goods will broadly constitute the economic capital of a going concern (Bray 1952, 15). On the other hand, the accounting concept of a firm's capital has two versions (a) broad and descriptive, and (b) narrow and analytical.

15.2.1 Accounting Versions

15.2.1.1 The Broad View

The broad and descriptive version is based on the classification of business outgoings during a period into current and capital transactions. The distinction is essentially generic in character, and problems arise when an attempt is made to set the line of demarcation. To meet the situation accountants have directly associated capital expenditure with slow-moving outgoings made for the purpose of acquiring relatively durable assets which are held with the object of earning revenue and not for the purpose of sale in the ordinary course of business. Expenditures on the acquisition of lands, buildings, plant and machinery, furniture and fixtures, etc. easily fall into this category. Constitutional outgoings such as the preliminary and formation expenses incidental to joint stock companies and some deferred charges are taken into the same generic classification. However, it is not always easy to decide if an outgoing associated with an existing asset is necessarily a capital expenditure. One of the accounting tests for this purpose is based upon the influence such expenditure would have on the life and efficiency of the asset concerned. If it increases the life of the asset or promotes its productivity, the outgoing is a capital expenditure. On the other hand, if it has only maintained the asset in the working order, it is regarded as current expense, like that on fuel, light, wages, carriage, raw materials consumed etc. The former have relative stability in the balance sheet statement of assets, liabilities and proprietorship worth, while the latter find their place in the income, or profit and loss account. Accounting developed primarily as a tool of private business and accountants with a limited perspective. The centre of their attention has been the interests of the owners of business. Therefore, most often, they adopt a narrow view of capital wherein it is only regarded as proprietorship worth. They look upon the amount of money or money's worth coming in to start a business as its original capital and seek to adjust it in the light of later contributions and withdrawals, capital gains or losses, and retained profits. Although accountants maintain a clear distinction between proprietorship worth and the general pool of assets to which it lays claim, they 4 also insist on a close tie between the two. This is perhaps the main cause of the intimate association of accounting techniques with historical costs.[1]

[1] "... the preliminary record of a fixed asset in the books of an enterprise is always made at the amount of money for which it was bought" and even when "assets are revalued ... a balancing adjustment is always necessary to the monetary statement of proprietorship worth" (Bray 1952, 16).

15.2.1.2 The Narrow Version

The broader and descriptive view of capital in accounting usage has been largely responsible for the evolution of the design of accounts while the narrow analytical view has been an essential tool in measuring the profitability of the undertaking to its owners. In any case, accounting concept has tended to remain on the money end of things as opposed to the economists' real or physical view of capital. This distinction between economic theory and accounting tradition would have been only of academic value in a stationary state if only the value of money continued to remain fairly stable. This, however, assumes great importance, especially with reference to the problem of maintaining capital intact under dynamic conditions and rapidly changing price levels.

15.3 Maintenance of Capital

Although accountants, as well as economists, emphasize the need of maintaining capital intact to preserve the organism of a going concern, their approaches to the problem substantially differ. Consistent with his narrower view of capital, the accountant is concerned primarily with the maintenance of proprietorship worth of a business firm, expressed in money terms. When confronted with periodic measurement of profit his object is that the whole cost of output produced and sold, during the period must be recovered. A good part of the expenditure is directly allocable to the operations of the current period but there may be a considerable amount of money spent which cannot be so allocated and has to be spread over a series of short periods. Money spent on fixed assets and other deferred expenditures fall into this latter category. We shall, however, confine ourselves for the moment, to expenditure on fixed assets as this leads to the problem of capital maintenance, which accounting attempts to solve by providing for depreciation of these assets.

15.3.1 Depreciation in Money Terms

The conventional accounting approach regards depreciation as

> that part of a fixed asset to its owner which is not recoverable when the asset is finally put out of use by him. Provision against this loss of capital is an integral part of cost for conducting business during the effective commercial life of the asset and is not dependent on the profit earned. (Bray 1952, 66)

The amount of periodic depreciation (D_n) depends upon the acquisition cost of the asset (A_c), its probable scrap value (S_v) and the number of time units during which the asset is expected to be commercially useful to the undertaking (N_t). Symbolically:

$$D_n = \frac{(A_c - S_v)}{N_t} \tag{15.1}$$

Of the elements in the calculation of depreciation specified in the equation, A_c is known, S_v can generally be estimated only within fairly wide limits and N_t is highly susceptible to precise calculation. Thus, provisions for depreciations are mostly a matter of estimation based upon the available experience, knowledge, and assumptions rather than of precise determination. It is important to observe that to the extent the accountants have to estimate the depreciation chargeable to the revenues of particular periods, an ex ante element is included, as in economics, even in the accounting concept of profit.

15.3.2 *Depreciation in Real Terms*

In contrast to accounting view of depreciation based on the money values of assets, the economists have always insisted that the capital of a going concern should be maintained intact in some physical sense. For them the preservation of the firm has been more important than the money value of fixed assets. The firm, as a going concern, must end up the period with the same potential capacities, as it began with, before it can assess its disposable profit.[2] Thus for a continuing enterprise, the function for depreciation accounting should be to provide resources adequate enough for the maintenance of real assets. This requires the abandonment of original money costs of assets in favour of their replacement costs as a basis for calculating the amount of depreciation. Thus in each case, the sums of money allocated to depreciation from the current revenues of different period segments should ultimately accumulate to an amount which would be sufficient to enable the replacement of the asset

[2] "The purpose of income calculation in practical affairs is to give people an indication of the amount which they can consume without impoverishing themselves. Following out this idea it would seem that we should define a man's income as the maximum value which he can consume during a work and can still expect to be as well off at the end of the work as he was at the beginning" (Hicks 1946, 172).

in question when it becomes worn out or obsolete, by some reasonably equivalent asset.

There is not much to choose between the original value or the replacement cost basis of depreciation if the price of the asset remains unchanged over time. In fact, the original or historical cost concept of depreciation in accounting has been, by and large, a legacy from periods of stable prices. The war and interwar years of wide fluctuations in prices, however, brought out clearly the weakness of this concept and the economists put the accountant and his methods to close scrutiny and scathing criticism.[3] Depreciation calculated on the basis of original cost of assets falls too short of replacement requirement during periods of rising prices. The erosion of real capital became so obvious and alarming during war and post-war inflations that accountants themselves began to doubt if their traditional approach could be defended any longer.[4] A closer examination of the issues involved in the cyclical fluctuations contextual to the economic view of maintaining capital in real terms would, however, reveal that the day has not altogether been lost for the accountants.

The contention of the economists is that the purpose of depreciation in the case of a continuing enterprise can hardly be anything except to provide for the replacement of assets after the expiry of their useful life to the firm. One way of achieving this objective is to view both income and capital in some physical sense. Capital would be maintained intact so long as the initial capital stock remains absolutely unchanged in physical terms. The depreciation here would form that part of the income flow from selling goods and services which replaces the physical deficiency of the initial stock of capital goods.[5] Some inherent ambiguities of this approach apart, it makes, saves under very different circumstances, the comparison of the resultant profit of different firms extremely difficult because of the incommensurability of the physical unit of the

[3]"F. schimidt made the first formidable attempt as early as 1927 towards erecting the shortcomings of Accounting into a causative factor in business cycles", says Mountz (1951, 157).

[4]Revaluation Accounting developed and is now well-established as a tool of business management in recognition of these facts. The general accounting approach however continues along the traditional lines.

[5]Pigou (1932, 45–49) has been one of the main supporters of this viewpoint.

measurement involved. This difficulty is sought to be avoided by using the money prices at some point of time as weights. This brings us to the second, and more widely used, concept of 'real capital maintenance in money terms'.[6] Let us call it as the RCM concept.

15.3.2.1 The RCM Concept

To reiterate, according to the RCM concept depreciation has to be measured on the basis of replacement costs instead of original values. If we assume that the physical quantity (q_0) of a particular asset would become (q_i).[7] after its effective life measured by time interval $t_0 \ldots\ldots t_n$, the physical erosion of capital would be expressed by $q_0 - q_i$ or Δq. The accountant values this depreciation at the original price ($p_0 q$). If prices do change over time the economists insist that depreciation should take into account not only the physical depreciation of an asset but also the effect of change in its price. This may be called as the price component of depreciation. If p_0 becomes p_i at time t_n this price component would be $\Delta p\ \Delta q$. It will be positive if $p_i > p_0$ and negative if $p_i < p_0$ for a given Δq. The total depreciation (D) in money terms that could maintain capital in real sense may now be found out with the help of combining physical ($p_0 \Delta q$) and the price ($\Delta p\ \Delta q$) components in the following way:

$$D = (p_0 \Delta q) \pm (\Delta p \Delta q) - S_v \tag{15.2}$$

If the time span ($t_o \ldots\ldots t_i$) of the effective life of the asset is composed of Nt segments for the measurement of profit, the periodic depreciation (D_n) will be given by the following formula minus the scrap value of the asset:

$$D_n = \left[(p_0 \Delta q) \pm (\Delta p \Delta q) - S_v\right] / N_t \tag{15.3}$$

The basic requirements for finding depreciation using the above formulae are to know, or estimate, the time when the asset in question would be replaced (t_n), the price of an identical asset at that time (p_i) and the scrap value of the old asset at that time. All these estimates are, by and large, a matter of subjective considerations of entrepreneurs and make the resultant profit concept inherently imprecise and extremely difficult,

[6] For a lucid discussion of the various income concepts see George F. Break (1954, 48–62).

[7] To find qi we can divide the scrap value of the asset by the price (p_i) of an identical new asset at the time t_n.

if not impossible, to measure and interpret. Consider for example the problem of comparing the profits of a number of business firms, using identical assets, if their managements expect to replace that equipment in the future at different times when price levels would be different. This difficulty, it is suggested, maybe obviated if current costs are used in place of the replacement cost. Such a policy would require upward or downward adjustment of the original cost with every change in the prices of identical assets. This adjustment has to be made regardless of the date of replacement and even if no replacement takes place at all. Ex post profit is now independent of the entrepreneurial expectations and hence clearer to that extent. A number of practical difficulties, however, will have to be faced.

The Difficulties

1. If the price of the asset in question changes, erratically or the change is short-lived, it may play havoc with the measurement of profit. The suggestion of Bray (1952, 68) that we may circumvent this difficulty by having regard for the general trend of replacement costs rather than the cost known at the accounting date is not of much help. For, one must now face difficulties, both conceptual and computational, regarding the general trend of replacement costs.
2. A business will hardly replace its worn-out equipment with something which is exactly the same. In this age of fast technological changes and scientific inventions the firm will take up new, sometimes cheaper, forms of equipment to fulfil similar functions more efficiently. Under these circumstances there is hardly any relevance of the current cost of the old asset for purposes of replacement.
3. 'If replacement funds are set aside currently on the basis of the current market prices of the assets to be replaced, they may be excessive if prices fall or deficient if they rise'.*for example, while a particular asset is still held by a business enterprise, the price of an identical asset goes up and remains thereafter at that high level. The total depreciation allowance in this case—being the sum of a number of early deductions based on original cost and later provisions based on current price, will be less than the actual replacement cost of the asset in question. Just the opposite will happen if prices were high at the time of acquisition but fell to a constantly low level afterwards. This shows that past provisions accumulating

in the in the depreciation reserve should be brought uptodate by some adjustment. However, the price assessment of such an adjustment would be, by and large, a matter of judgement though the guiding considerations may often be clear. One method of avoiding this difficulty often advocated by modern accounting is to invest the depreciation fund out of business in some real assets. This would be helpful only if the price of the investment and the asset concerned move in the same direction, and by identical magnitude. This will rarely happen and the greater is the discrepancy in this movement on either count the lesser would be the advantage of not keeping the depreciation fund in business itself.

4. At times, the current prices of assets identical to those which are to be replaced are not available and have to be estimated through the use of price index numbers of the main group of capital goods. Apart from the limitations of index numbers which are well known, their use in this connection makes the RCM concept subsidiary and derivative.[8]
5. The basic aim of RCM concept is to maintain the same service stream as was provided by old assets when these were new.[9] This suggests that the firm should be able, in a broader sense, to replace not only its material and fixed assets but the non-material and current assets as well. It is obvious that the RCM concept would encounter a number of additional difficulties if extended to cover these assets also.

It thus comes about that the accounting approach to the problem of capital maintenance, based on the original money values of the assets, is more precise and clear than the economic view of maintaining capital in some real sense. It has great computational utility and is at once consistent with our view that the basic definition of profit must be ex post.

[8]"(Real value maintenance) RVM income is in fact is simply IVM (initial value maintenance) money income converted into real income through division by a Paasche type price index" Break (1954, 55).

[9]It is sometimes suggested that the income (profit) flow is more important rather vital to the existence of a firm than the output flow. Hence the former need be maintained unchanged while the latter may be allowed to fluctuate. This in brief is the Prospective Income Maintenance concept. However, it suffers from many more blemishes than the RCM concept of income.

This conclusion, however, need not make the insistence of the economist on maintaining capital in some real sense insignificant. It is difficult to understand as to how a going concern can continue to earn profit in the long run if it does not maintain its capital in real terms. For, a management oblivious of this need may be distributing the capital of the firm by way of dividends over periods of continuously rising prices. This may ultimately put the very existence of the firm in jeopardy.

The arguments advanced above are, therefore, meant only to emphasize that the RCM concept need not blur the basic definition of profit. When, however, the replacement cost of a fixed asset far exceeds its original cost by reason of a continuous rise in prices, this must engage our attention but must be treated as a separate and distinct problem from that of depreciation. Replacement considerations must be looked upon more as questions of policy relating to the utilization of profit earned rather than a matter pertinent to its measurement. Different sections of society are exposed to the effect of changes in the value of money in accordance with the respective price elasticity of their incomes. Tax legislation does not seek to counter the effect of price changes on different sections of society. This may be regarded as a defect of the present legislation but so long as we are governed by the law as it is, to allow the charging of depreciation at replacement cost of assets in business accounts in favour of the recipients of profits would clearly constitute an unjust discrimination.

The business practice of building up strong general reserves out of current profits is an effort to guard against future contingencies. It is difficult to understand why possible rise in the replacement cost of assets should not be treated as one of these contingencies. Or alternatively, why can we not build up a reserve called, say, the Fixed Block Real Value Maintenance Reserve like the Investment Fluctuation or Exchange Variation reserves. The creation of such a reserve out of periodic profits, facilitating adjustment of asset values and when their prices change, would help accountants meet the objections of the economists, and conform to the legal view of depreciation.

15.4 Inventory Valuation

A going concern not only requires a plant, equipment raw materials, and manpower in order to turn out goods and services, it must also carry a considerable quantity of commodities during a period of profit measurement, and often from one such period to another. Manufacturers keep a sufficient quantity of raw materials on hand in order to avoid interruptions to production. There must almost always be some goods-in-process as the cycle of manufacturing operations invariably takes time to complete. Again, many manufacturers carry the stocks of finished products with a view to avoiding delays in filling the customers' orders. Likewise, the main function of most wholesalers and retailers is to have an extensive stock of all sorts of goods ready at hand so as to provide purchasers with a wide range of choices. And finally, many firms may sometimes carry inventories much in excess of their normal requirements with a purely speculative motive.

Whatever be the need for and motive for carrying inventories, their existence is of great significance in the affairs of a going concern. On the one hand, they constitute an important element of the cost of goods sold, on the other, they form an integral part of the asset organism continuing enterprise; accounting techniques used for their valuation in each case are well known.

15.4.1 The FIFO System

The inventory of finished products becomes an expense when sold. This expense, according to accountants, should be measured by the acquisition cost of these products for finding out the profits of the period under review. As different lots of inventories are hardly purchased at identical prices, the estimation of their acquisition cost becomes the crux of the problem. Conventional accounting uses the first-in-first-out (Fifo) basis for arriving at this estimation on the assumption that physically materials move out of inventory on, more or less, a first-in-first-out basis. This is quite realistic; the oldest stocks are normally used up first. The selling price decisions of a business are, however, influenced more by current costs of inventories rather than by their historical values (Antony 1970, 231) The conventional Fifo system, therefore, results in the emergence of what economists call as 'inventory profits' during periods of rising prices and 'inventory losses' when prices are falling. In each case, the goods are sold at prices commensurate with current costs while the profit and loss account is charged with earlier (lower in inflation and higher in deflation) cost of these goods.

Thus viewed, part of the profit realized in sales is an 'inventory gain' when prices are rising and vice versa (Crum 1932, 231). The magnitude of this inventory gain (or loss) will depend upon the staying time of materials in inventory, the volume of conversation costs, if any, the degree of correlation between selling prices and current costs, and above all, the speed of the rise or the fall in prices. These realized inventory profits (and losses) apart, the Fifo system breeds purely paper profits (or losses) which may or may not be realized in subsequent periods. The source of these unrealized inventory differentials in the estimation of the excess in the value of inventory at the end of the period over that at the beginning of the period. For, if the excess is positive it acts as a partial offset against other items in the cost of goods sold, thus raising the reported profits; if the excess.

These realized inventory profits (and losses) apart, the Fifo system breeds purely paper profits (or losses) which may or may not be realized in subsequent periods. The source of these unrealized inventory differentials in the estimation of the excess in the value of inventory at the end of the period over that at the beginning of the period. For, if the excess is positive it acts as a partial offset against other items in the cost of goods sold, thus raising the reported profits; if the excess is negative it must lower the residual figure for profits. Under Fifo, and during inflation, the end period valuation of stock will be greater for identical physical volume of inventories in the opening stock reflecting the advance in prices over the period. The opposite will happen when prices are falling.[10] In case the firms obliged to carry large inventories to operate, and especially if inventory is comprised of commodities subject to wide price fluctuations, Fifo must result, on this score, in magnifying profits (or losses) in an illusory way. To the extent that the results of these accounting processes influence the decisions and actions of individuals and groups, they are important causative factor in trade cycles.[11] Further, to the extent that inventory profits are not realized corporate income taxes are assessed on illusory incomes.

[10] If the change in price over the period is quite sharp or the physical volume of inventories has not changed much over the period, the direction of excess in value may even fail to reveal the direction of physical excess in inventory stock.

[11] "The intensity of cyclical movements is magnified by inventory profits and losses and even the shape and timing of cyclical movements may be distorted in some degree for the same reason", says Crum (1932, 275).

15.4.2 The LIFO Method

Of the several proposals which have been advanced from time to time for dealing with these problems, accounting has granted recognition only to Lifo which stands for 'Last-in first-out'. 'In this method, inventory is costed as if the units most recently added to inventory (last in) were the first units sold (first out) even though this is in fact not the case. Ending inventory is assumed to consist of the oldest units and is measured at those oldest costs' (Antony 1970, 231). The Lifo method is a great accounting innovation. It seeks to squeeze out all water of inventory gains and losses from reported profits, and during periods of rising prices, tends to conserve funds for the firm to maintain a level of inventories commensurate with the scope and intensity of its operations as a going concern. There are, however, some serious objections—both on grounds of theory and feasibility—to its adoption as a universal accounting method. If there is a close correlation between the changes in selling prices and those in current costs reflecting a general change in the value of money in the economy, or the rate of inventory turnover is quite fast, Lifo has little advantage over the conventional Fifo system. On the other hand, if there has been a real change in the profit margins in a particular firm which have nothing to do with fluctuations in the price level, the use of Lifo may distort the picture by concealing such changes.

Lifo is obviously not applicable to every firm. It rests on the assumption that there is a definite relationship between the selling price and the current cost of inventories. This, however, is not always the case. The selling prices of many firms such as those in retail trade are related to the invoice cost of goods and not to their current cost. The use of Lifo in such cases would be illogical and misleading. 'Lifo is also not appropriate for companies which eliminate inventory profits or losses by the practice called 'hedging' nor for companies which are in the business of speculating on price changes, as are certain companies that trade in grain and other commodities' Antony (1970, 233).

It is easy to apply Lifo when the inventory consists of fungible products but cumbersome, if not impossible, when inventories consist of numerous, unlike items. A so-called Lifo money value method based on the use of price index numbers is in vogue in the United States to obviate this difficulty (Antony 1970, 233–236). Appropriate index numbers are not, however, constructed in every country for this purpose, and even if they are, the adjustments would at best be only approximations. Again, there can be several alternatives, in the application of the general idea of Lifo. These variations, most often, only increase confusion.

Furthermore, the cost of materials is just one ingredient of the total cost; reckoning it at current values while other elements like rent, interest, and even wages are charged at their historical values means adding up of non-homogeneous rupees. It is perhaps to remove such inconsistencies that studies sponsored by A.I.C.PA. and the American Accounting Association have evolved procedures for expressing each item in the profit and loss account and balance sheet in uniform dollars. These procedures are, however, advocated only as a supplement to, and not as a replacement of the conventional procedures (Antony 1970, 241–242).

If we pass on from the expense-view of inventory to its broader version, the asset-view, a few more dimensions are added to the problem of inventory valuation. Accounting practice in this context regards stock-in-trade essentially as current assets held for realization in future and insists on their valuation at lower of the cost or current price.[12] Economists, on the other hand, regard inventories, whatever be their stage of conversion, as an integral part of the real assets of a going-concern which, like the plant and other facilities, have to be kept intact. The question of the method being appropriate for the purpose apart; we have to decide first the quantum of inventories to be so maintained.

Many times business concerns may carry unusually large inventories from one accounting period to another either as a matter of policy or under the compulsions of the market conditions. No one would, therefore, insist that all the opening stock of goods should be maintained. Both the accountants and the economist make a distinction between normal and speculative components of inventory (Marshall 1946, 333, 338). The normal inventory level is what is necessary for a firm to continue its activity without interruption, and to avoid risks of seasonal shortages. The speculative component is referred to by Keynes (1930) as surplus stock which constituted the liquid capital composed of inventories over and above the normal quantities needed for production and

[12]It is interesting to note that this 'lower of the cost or current price rule' would give double advantage to the firms adopting the LIFO system. The American Income Tax laws do not, therefore, allow companies using LIFO to adjust their inventories at the end of their accounting year according to this rule.

distribution. It is suggested that only the normal component of inventories should be maintained in some real sense (Bray 1952, 76).

The problem, however, is how to ascertain the normal component of inventory. Clearly, this has something to do with the scale of output, but an objective and stable criterion can hardly be evolved for such ascertainment. Much will depend on each case of judgement. And as soon as we bring in subjective considerations in our estimates the normal, and surplus stocks begin to wear the garment of planned and unplanned inventories- terms which have gained currency in the literature on trade cycles. Economic theory has frequently assumed a constant inventory-sales ratio as a specific criterion for estimating planned and unplanned inventories; such as assumption, however, seems to be extremely arbitrary.

Even if it were possible to ascertain objectively the normal inventory requirements for a going concern, the effort to maintain inventories in some real sense can hardly ignore their speculative component if we want to deal effectively, and in a fuller way with the problem of inventory profit (or loss).

It is interesting to note that while LIFO is a close approximation of replacement costs for the purpose of profit measurement, it may impair the usefulness of the inventory figure for the balance sheet. For, under Lifo 'inventory is valued forever in terms of whatever the price level happened to be at the time Lifo was introduced. As time goes on and price levels change, the inventory figure under Lifo departs further and further from reality, becoming neither a reflection of actual purchase costs nor of current costs' (Antony 1970, 233).

It then comes about that from the viewpoints of theory as well as feasibility, considerations of replacement of inventory should be dealt with as questions relevant to the utilization of the profit rather than its measurement. While inventory valuation both for purposes of the profit and loss account and balance sheet may be continued according to the conventional accounting procedures, adjustments pertinent to replacement values may be given effect as an appropriation of profit through an Inventory Stabilization Account which would find its place in the balance sheet.

This way of dealing with inventory profits (of losses) has some distinct advantages. It leaves the basic concept of profit ex post. There is no need to demarcate between planned and unplanned inventories. The magnitude of and changes in the balance of this account from time to time may help business management formulate expectations with the correct prospective and to that extent may absolve accounting techniques from the charge of accentuating booms and depressions. And last, though not the least, the accountant may provide the economist with useful data on inventory profits without sacrificing much of his traditions and outlook.

15.5 Impact of Conservatism

We have seen that the gap between original values of fixed assets and inventories and their replacement costs can be easily taken note of within the existing framework of modern accounting. Unfortunately, it is not so much the historicity of accounting data that vitiates the measurement of profits as its strict adherence to conservatism. The narrow proprietorship point of view is at the root of this conservatism and has been further reinforced by the desire to play safe in the face of uncertainty about the future. Conservatism in accounting practice means 'the avoidance of overstatement of assets even at the risk of gross under-statement, the avoidance of under-statement of debts even at the risk of marked over-statement and the avoidance of over-statement of proprietory and periodic profit. That these objectives are often time inconsistent, and perhaps even contradictory, is widely recognized but nevertheless conservatism prevails as a rule of conduct' (Mountz 1951, 162).

An important influence of this conservatism has been the adoption of a narrow definition of costs in accounting. Based on some easily verifiable evidence, the term is restricted to include only the cash outlays related to the item in question in a fairly obvious way. Most overheads of indirect costs including interest do not enter into the cost of assets. Indeed, these indirect costs are considered current expenses. Further, certain important expenses such as proprietary capital are ordinarily omitted altogether because of the emphasis on explicit contractual costs. This restricted view of costs distorts the measurement of current profit in three ways (Mountz 1951, 161–163).

1. To the extent that investment and fixed assets are understated because of the restricted definition of cost used, reported profit will be understated during the period when investments are being made and will be exaggerated in subsequent periods when these understated assets are converted into receipts from customers. In

brief, profits will be shifted in the records from the earlier to the later periods.

2. Conservatism also requires that certain costs such as are incurred in developing future markets by means of advertising brand names and other promotional devices, or in developing improved operational methods by means of research and development work in general even though explicitly be denied status as an investment in assets. Instead, they are immediately classed as expenses and hence the recorded profit as well as the capital of the concern is understated.
3. Future receipts are not recorded until they assume the form of enforceable contracts with outsiders. Inventory items are, for instance, valued at acquisition or fabrication cost, narrowly conceived, until sold. At the point of sale, all the growth since acquisition is reflected, so that recoded revenues in the period of sale contain the value accretion properly assignable to earlier periods. If the rate of inventory turnover is high, this characteristic is not of serious consequence; however, if it is low the distorting effect of conservatism is quite pronounced. What is true of inventories is also true of the fixed assets.[13]

These distorting effects on profit measurement not only intensify cyclical phases but as the data from accounting records are the most important source for social accounting; it is advisable that the accountants should discard conservatism in favour of adherence to realities of the situation. They can remain unconcerned only if they refuse to recognize that their profession has any sense of mission or social responsibility.

There is, however, a limit to which accountants can be expected to modify and adapt their art to meet the requirements of the social and economic needs without impairing or making cumbersome the duties which are their primary concern. These limits have to be fully recognized by those enthusiasts who seek reform in accounting techniques

[13]The services of the fixed assets in particular may not be converted into receipts for many years. Meanwhile the accountant will reflect these services at cost, again narrowly defined There full growth and fruition will not be recognized until the period of the output into which these resources have been incorporated is over. As a consequence, we find a tendency for revenue to be exaggerated on the on hand by reflections in period of sale of all the growth accruing to the item sold and for revenues to be understated.

and procedures and would like the accountant to take care of all the needs of the economists. Accounting data will always be lacking in its form and details to satisfy these needs. The accountant, placed as he is, can hardly become interested in all the social and economic ramifications of trade, commerce, and industry. It is wiser to be content with reforms in accounts not so radical in nature as would vitiate the very object of accounting, and supplement and adjust the data provided by the accountant for social and economic purposes. The suggestions made in the foregoing pages should be viewed from this perspective.

Test Questions

Q.1 Accountants and economists look at business profits differently. Explain. Account for the reasons that cause the divergence. Do you think there is a need to reconcile their views? Give reasons for your answer.

Q.2 What is meant by keeping capital intact? Explain in what way and for what reasons the accounting view differs from that of economics. Which one would you endorse and why?

Q.3 Economists charge the accountants of their techniques magnifying trade cycle effects. Do you agree? Give reasons for your answer.

Q.4 Accountants adopt a conservative approach is reporting business profits. Explain why? Would you support their conservativeness in the matter? Argue your case.

Q.5 Write CRITICAL NOTES ON:

- Accountants help businesses avoid taxes.
- Lifo curbs inflation better than fifo during the upswing of a cycle.

References

Antony, B. N. (1970). *Management Accounting, Text and Cases.* Homewood: Richard D. Irwin.

Bray, F. S. (1952). *Measurement of Profit.* London, UK: Macmillan.

Break, G. F. (1954). *Capital Maintenance and the Concept of Income.* Berkeley: University of California Press.

Crum, W. L. (1932). *Corporate Size and Earning Power*. Harvard University Press.
Hasan, Z. (2016). Risk-Sharing: The Sole Basis of Islamic Finance? Time for a Serious Rethink. *Journal of King Abdulaziz University: Islamic Economics, 29*(2), 23–36.
Hicks, J. R. (1946). *Value and Capital*. Oxford: Crandon Press.
Hicks, J. R. (1960). *Social Framework*. Oxford: Crandon Press
Keynes, J. M. (1930). *A Treatise on Money*. UK: Cambridge.
Marshall, A. (1946). *Principles of Economics* (18th ed.). UK: Macmillan (print).
Mountz, M. (1951). The Valuation of Business Capital: An Accounting Analysis. *American Economic Review*.
Pigou, A. C. (1932). *Economics of Welfare*. UK: Macmillan.

Glossary

Bank for International Settlements: Established on 17 May 1930, the Bank for International Settlements (BIS) is an international financial organization owned by 60 member central banks, representing countries from around the world that together make up about 95% of world GDP. Its head office is in Basel, Switzerland, and it has two representative offices, in the Hong Kong Special Administrative Region of the People's Republic of China and in Mexico City.
The mission of the BIS is to serve central banks in their pursuit of monetary and financial stability, to foster international cooperation in those areas, and to act as a bank for central banks. Its recommendations are not mandatory; the member banks may or may not follow them. Still, concerns have been voiced that the BIS is an instrument of financial capitalism to subjugate the world financial architecture and to serve the interests of the powerful developed nations.

Capital consumption: Capital Consumption refers to the reduction in loss of the productive capacity of capital equipment due to depreciation that can take place due to the machines wearing out, getting lost, or breaking down. The equipment may face reduction in competitive efficiency becoming obsolete through advances in technology. In either case it may require repair or replacement for which accounting has to make provision out of the revenue follows from the production process.

Z. Hasan, *Leading Issues in Islamic Economics and Finance*,
https://doi.org/10.1007/978-981-15-6515-1

The concept of maintaining capital intact through charging depreciation to replace what has been consumed is not significant only for firms at the micro level but at the macro level too it must be deducted from the GDP of a country as capital consumption reflects the amount of investment necessary to replace worn-out material and as such does not indicate an increase in living standards. It may help to keep the money and physical parts of capital consumption during different phases of the cycle. As indicated in Chapter 15.

***Constructive liability*:** Constructive liability is a legal term used in various criminal and civil situations. The term is commonly used in business and accounting areas. It is also recognized in relation to home financing both in the mainstream and Islamic contracts. For example when a bank buys a house for a client, the registration is usually in the name of the client; the name of the bank does not appear on the deed although it is a co-owner with the client until the bank has received back the money lent and money due as the return on capital. The bank uses one or both contracts to safeguard its interests. The house is mortgaged with the bank as security. Second, the parties sign a contract defining the liabilities of the buyer and the rights of the bank relative to the property binding until the successful completion of the contract.

***Constructive liability*:** To avoid duplication registration charges, Islamic banks enjoy the waiver for one in some countries. Where such concession is not available, Islamic banks can insert a constructive liability clause in the loan contract whereby the client agrees to meet such conditions regarding the property as the bank would like to insert to safeguard his interests. The principle of constructive liability is well recognized in law both secular and Islamic.

***Consumerism*:** Consumerism refers to an obsession with shopping that feeds material ambitions. The term comes from the developed affluent societies of the West, where the problem of basic needs fulfilment is conspicuous by its very absence. In these societies, consumerism is fed by status consciousness and lifestyle competition. It is pre-emptive of supposed economic depression: it keeps demand in harmony with the supply that is created in the process of growth. Thus seen, consumerism is considered conducive to social welfare.

The story is different in developing countries, where per capita incomes are low, poverty rampant, and income inequalities are severe. Excessive spending on consumption is perceived among the narrow band of high-incomes, leading to allocation of meagre national resources in favour of luxuries, away from the production of goods and services for the poor masses to meet their minimal basic needs. The demonstration effect distorts the spending priorities of lower-income groups attempting to imitate the lifestyles of the rich. These psychological urges lead to a rise in corruption and crime in efforts to get rich. Consumerism by the rich lowers growth rates and widens economic inequalities. Morality stands at a discount. Muslim countries are no exception.

Credit multiplier: Cash with banks provides the base for providing loans. This allows more and more creation of credit. The process gets flexibility by treating credit advanced like cash deposits facilitated by maintaining a fractional cash reserve to meet average daily withdrawals. A multiple of cash with the bank supporting maximum deposits—cash + credit – is called the credit multiplier. In simple terms it is the reciprocal of cash reserve ratio. To illustrate, if for supporting each 100 of loan the bank must have 10 in cash, the reserve ratio for deposits would be $10/100 = 1/10$ the credit multiplier being its reciprocal, i.e. 10. This means that if the bank holds 1000 in cash it can expand deposits up to 10,000.

Cryptocurrency: Cryptocurrency is a notional name given to digital money. It is usually called virtual currency. Bitcoin and Ethereum are examples. The value of a cryptocurrency can be expressed in terms of legal tender money. For example a bitcoin equal to X Indian rupees or Y US dollars. The market value of a cryptocurrency in terms of any money would depend on the relative demand and supply of that currency. Cryptocurrency is digitally traded. It can be used for making payments and lends itself to maintenance of accounts. It can be created by public as well as by private agencies.

An inter-ministry committee (IMC) in India noted that the most appealing as well as the most dangerous features of a cryptocurrency is the absence of regulation by the central bank. Thus it advised the government not to allow private agencies deal in cryptocurrencies (The Indian Express, July 29, 2019, P. 11). The effect of the proposed ban would be that anyone who holds or trades in these currencies in India would go to jail. Some who see a few merits in their use, thus advocate against a blanket ban on them.

Deficit financing: Deficit financing may be defined as a practice wherein a government spends more money than it receives as revenue the difference being made up by borrowing or minting new money. It assumes several forms but the most common is *fiscal deficit* conceived as excess of total governmental expenditure on its total revenue excluding borrowings. Deficit can arise due to a variety of reasons—internal and external. It could be deliberate, e.g. for mobilizing resources to finance development but has to be used with caution because of its potential to create problems; it is inherently inflationary. Deficit can be covered by borrowing from the market at home or abroad and including the printing of more currency. Its reckless use can land a country in deep indebtedness requiring painful international bailout.

***Definition of economics*:** Given the fact that resources available to mankind from the inexhaustible provisions of nature are scarce relative to the multiplicity of human wants, the definition and scope of Islamic economics cannot be entirely different from its mainstream counterpart. Thus, one can argue that Islamic economics is the subject that studies human behaviour in relation to the multiplicity of wants and scarcity of resources, having alternative uses, to maximize *falah*, that is, human well-being, both in the present world and in the hereafter.

***Definition of money*:** Money evolved as an artificial social convention to overcome the difficulties of barter. Thus, it won recognition as the commodity that served as money. But these commodities changed quickly over time and space. From hides and skins to promises to pay, innumerable items served as money. Evidently, a definition of money with reference to what served as money could not give it a universal definition. What remained unchanged from day one were the basic functions of money—as a medium of exchange, a measure of value, a standard for deferred payments, and a store of value. Eventually, a functional definition was considered as most appropriate: *money is what money does.*

***Derivatives and Islamic finance*:** Islamic bankers are anxious not to miss any opportunity to match conventional products in a competitive change sweeping the industry. Why then should they not have derivatives to improve the risk factor of their products, especially when learned jurists find supportive content in the literature? The result is a house divided. There are two ways of looking at the debate—the theoretical extended permissibility, and the practical experience. Not everyone is competent to participate in the juridical debate on the point, but many would oppose the introduction of derivatives in

Islamic finance. This is due to their potential to go far beyond the legal controls and degenerate into promoters of heightened speculation as in the mainstream markets—something that is repugnant to Islam. The overextension of derivatives has triggered many devastating turmoil. The introduction of derivatives will lead to a further submersion of the Islamic system into the mainstream, detracting from its definitional identity.

***Devaluation*:** One source of trouble causing adverse and persistent balance of payments difficulties for the country seeking help the IMF sees in the overvaluation of its currency. Thus in most cases, it urges the applicant for help to devalue its currency to the extent it deems necessary to normalize the exchange rate quoted as units of domestic currency for a unit of foreign currency, the US Dollar. Devaluation is the *official* reduction in the value of domestic currency (less dollars for a domestic unit of currency).The argument is that devaluation could make imports costlier and exports of the country cheaper in trading thus help correct the adverse balance of payments. This is too simplistic. It ignores the fact that in most cases the exports and imports of the borrowing country are not sufficiently elastic to have the claimed result.

Distributive justice: The term refers to the sharing of wealth and income within or across countries over time and space, conforming to some rational or faith-based standards like Islamic justice norms. It is essentially a socially perceptive concept lacking objectivity. Usually, it implies notions of ceilings and floors as limiting rent and interest rates, or defining minimum wages and poverty lines. The levelling measures include taxation of the rich and expenditures to benefit the poor. Income transfer may be voluntary, as via charities, donations, trusts, etc.

***Economic development*:** From the Islamic perspective, it is the development of human personality that calls for growth commensurate with the fulfilment of basic needs—food, clothing, shelter, education, and health care—and is concerned with environmental demands and distributive equity on the mundane front. At the same time, it inculcates in humans the spiritual urges of creativity, justice, patience, compassion, and cooperation.

***Economic system*:** An economic system refers to the structuring and operation of economic activity in accordance with its theoretical constructs. The main points on which various economic systems differ from one another include foundational axioms, property rights, value selections, motivational bases, and social priorities. An important role of methodology in each discipline is to examine the divergence between theory and system operation as well as how and to what extent this divergence can be resolved.

***Expenditure on advertising*:** The expenditure of many multinational corporations is more than the annual budget of the government of India. Most of this expenditure is self-cancelling, for example, hostile neighbours spending money on armaments. In developing economies, advertising encourages the neglect of the basic needs of the poor in favour of investing resources in cars, smartphones, and designer clothing. The demonstration effect leads to crime and corruption to obtain what honest means cannot provide. This urge for newer varieties leads to discard things that are still usable and which the rich internationals attempt to sell to poor countries.

***Global warming*:** Global warming, also referred to as climate change, is used to describe a gradual increase in the earth's average ground and atmospheric temperatures across the whole planet. The following graph illustrates the change in global surface temperature relative to 1951–1980 average temperatures. The phenomenon has been attributed to the use of harmful chemicals and the elimination of trees. Other causes include volcanic eruptions, plate tectonics, solar radiation, and biotic processes. The atmospheric concentration of carbon dioxide has increased by more than 30% since pre-industrial times, trapping more heat in the lower atmosphere. Human activities such as the burning of fossil fuel and deforestation cause rises in the surface temperature. The climate changes are also due to the variations in the earth's orbit, affecting the way sunlight reaches the surface of the earth.

Global warming is a serious issue and not an isolated one. A number of environmental problems revolve around global warming. The resulting changes in the global climate bring a range of risks to health, from deaths in extreme high temperatures to changing patterns of infectious diseases. In fact, it threatens all life forms on Earth.

***Gold and oil*:** International gold standard had two major weaknesses. First, it compromised domestic price level stability in maintaining exchange rate stability. Second, even exchange rate stability could not be maintained in cases of major turmoil. Thus, the gold standard was abandoned passing through several phases and we eventually have the freely fluctuating exchange rate regime since 1979.

Opposition to this regime surfaced in Islamic economics where gold is considered the basic money. With gold standard out of the way, real goods were being sold goods in international trade for fiat money printed on paper. The dissatisfaction gave rise to pleas for the revival of gold currency (*dinar*). This was not found feasible for a variety of reasons. Oil being the main wealth and export commodity of the Muslim world, the idea that oil prices must be quoted in gold equivalent was mooted. This alarmed the United States and most of the developed nations of the Wes, US dollar constituting the dominant reserve currency of the world. The implementation of the idea meant that oil buyers the world over would want gold for dollars (and other currencies) to pay for oil imports. Gold from the United States that held its large stock and other parts of the world would have flowed to the oil-exporting countries. Iraq was the first to show the intention for gold pricing of oil; Libya was the second. Both had to pay dearly for the act. Iran could be the next in line.

***IMF loaning conditions*:** For a country deep in external debt and nowhere to go, the International Monetary Fund of which it is a member works as a lender of the last resort. The Fund uses the money of other member countries for the purpose. Thus, as their custodian, it has to ensure that the money it lends remains safe and the borrowing country follows voluntarily the economic programmes it designs in consultation and with the approval of the Fund such that it overcomes its financial difficulties ensuring at the same time the return of the loaned money. The various schemes' programmes and procedures involved are complicated and stringent and form part of what is technically called the IMF *conditionality*.

***Impact on investment*:** In a macroeconomic framework, the impact of redistributive measures in favour of the poor is uncertain. To the extent increase in consumption improves labour productivity; it works as though investment-boosting growth has been augmented. Furthermore, the inequality-reducing income transfer from the rich to the poor is a double-edged sword that can cut either way. If the rich reduce their consumption to maintain the savings level intact, growth may not be affected. However, if they choose to maintain consumption levels, savings and investment would fall, reducing the rate of growth.

***Income layers and consumption*:** Until recently, Islamic economists mainly treated consumption as a microeconomic phenomenon, even as macro considerations were not entirely missing. However, a 2016 article brings into focus the writings of an Iraqi jurist named Shibani who classified human wants into necessities, comforts, and luxuries, through income layers—high, medium, and low—with reference to the major allocation of income spending on the three categories of wants in the given order.

***Inventory valuation*:** In accounting, any way to estimate and report how much a firm's inventory—closing stock consisting of raw materials, finished and semi-finished goods, and stores—is worth in money terms at the closing of accounts date. There are two primary ways of estimating this value. The first in, first out technique treats inventory acquired first as if items were issued in the historical order and are charged at their purchase price of the oldest inventory, even if the physical goods are not the same. The other technique *last in, first out* does the opposite: it records issues against the purchase *price* of the most recently acquired inventory. The choice depends on which of the techniques would estimate the value of inventory in a way that would reduce the firm's tax liability keeping intact the book value of its assets.

***Maximizing behaviour*:** Resource scarcity imposes a maximizing of results behaviour in human beings, both as consumers and producers, leading to efficiency. With the results of economic activities being in the future, maximization becomes a heuristic directional concept. It is value-neutral; what is maximized, how it is maximized, and to what end, decide whether the effort is desirable or damaging. Islamic economics cannot discard this analytical tool to construct theories or assess performance. Maximization can be carried on within ethical-religious confines.

***Methods of economics*:** These refer to the rules and procedures to establish economic generalizations and their verification: induction and deduction. There has been much debate and controversy in literature as to which of the two serves the purpose better eventually leading to the acceptance of both. It is possible to use the two in the same inquiry at different stages; such combining known as the 'scientific methods'.

***Monetary circuit theory*:** The monetary circuit theory is part of financial economics. It contends that money is created endogenously by the banking sector, rather than exogenously by central bank lending. The circuitry model attempts to explain how credit money originates in the banking sector to part-finance business firms; circulates from the firms to wage earners; and flows back via the firms to the banking sector, where it is extinguished. The theory is not part of mainstream economics. It looks at the role of money in an economy from the supply side and can possibly help in the better understanding of trade cycles, presenting new approaches to deal with their ill consequences.

***Nature of Islamic law*:** Prof. Faizan Mustafa, a leading luminary of law emphasized in a recent TV talk a distinction of significance between the common and Islamic laws—civil or criminal. In the former case, he pointed out; law comes into existence first through a legislative process its interoperation by the professionals follows. In Islam, the process is the other way round. The law follows interoperation—interoperation of its various sources that the men of religion the learned jurists undertake. In principle, these laws are not open to legislative review for a change without juristic concurrence. This characteristic of Islamic laws restricts much the scope of their methodological use in the ordinary sense of the term. It is beyond economists.

***Non-performing loans*:** A loan is nonperforming when payments of interest and principal are past due by 90 days or more, or at least 90 days of interest payments have been capitalized, or refinanced delayed by agreement, or payments are less than 90 days overdue, but there are other good reasons to doubt that payments will be made in full. Non-performing loans normally include

- Real estate owned by foreclosure or a deed in lieu of foreclosure,
- Loans that are of 90 days duration or more or their due date has expired interest on them continues to accrue, and
- Loans which have been placed on nonaccrual (i.e. loans for which interest is no longer accrued and posted to the income statement).

Non-performing loans of financial institutions have generally been on the rise, now more in developing countries, due to factors like moral hazard, managerial corruption, political connivance, and leveraging on equity. Such loans have at times triggered major financial turmoil like the one that started in 2007 with the mortgage debacle in the United States and engulfed the world in no time. Following is an example reflecting the position with regard to NPLs of 16 countries in 2015 based on the World Development Indicators Report 2016. Eight of these countries have the lowest ranks and the other eight have the highest the World average ratio of non-performing loans to total loans estimated at 3.9 for that year

Canada	0.6
Switzerland	0.7
U.K	0.9
US	1.3
Japan	1.4
Malaysia	1.6
China	1.7
Saudi Arab	2.9

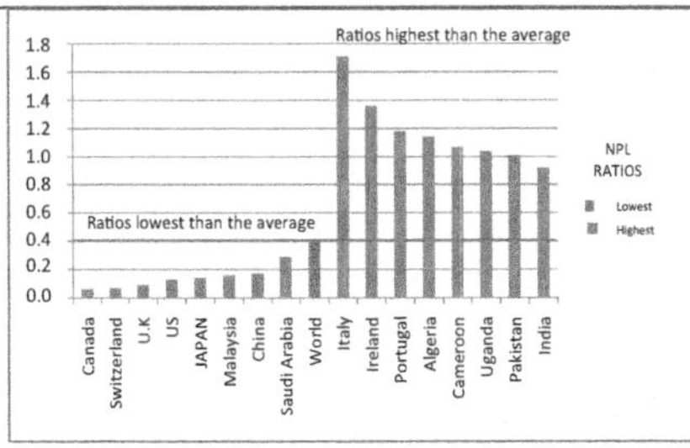

Italy	17.1
Ireland	13.6
Portugal	11.8
Algeria	11.4
Cameroon	10.7
Uganda	10.4
Pakistan	10.1
India	9.2

Ratio of NPLs to total bank loans in 2015 (*Source* Data from World Development Indicator Report 2016)

The point of this state of non-performing loans devastation contextual to the argument of this chapter is that if interest-based finance subsists solely on transferring risk to counterparties, how such massive failures of mainstream institutions could take place?

***Nudge theory*:** Nudge theory presents a concept in behavioural science relating to the social science sphere, especially the formation of political and economic theory. It proposes positive reinforcement of socially beneficial ethical values via indirect suggestions in the decision-making of individuals and groups. The theory attempts to build a bridge between psychology and social sciences to modify rationality results to serve social ends. It underlines in essence the observation Sen makes in his classic essay *Rational Fools*, and it vindicates Islamic economics' emphasis on the pursuit of ethical norms while keeping the independence of choice unimpaired. Nudge theory came into prominence when the 2009 work of Thaler and Sunstein on the subject to won the 2017 Nobel Prize in Economics.

***Profit sharing*:** In the modern era of mass production, profit sharing with labour has emerged as a leading tool for improving industrial peace. This is approved by the Islamic view of distributive justice as well. The justification for sharing is derived from the realization of the indeterminate character of factors' separate contribution to total output. In contrast the notion of combinational or group productivity is sensible. It underlines the justification for sharing business profits with labour.

***Scarcity*:** Scarcity refers to the lack of available resources in relation to their demand over time and space. Thus, relativity is an inherent attribute of scarcity. The concept of absolute scarcity is misleading. Scarcity creates motivation for research, invention, and innovation. Alternative resource uses and multiplicity of wants are in fact sources of human progress and the advancement of civilization. The phenomenon is part of the divine scheme. The scripture is not opposed to this interpretation of the scarcity concept.

***Self-interest*:** The pursuit of self-interest in ingrained in human nature. Its forbidden use caused Adam and Eve's exit from heaven. However, the pursuit of self-interest must not be confused with selfishness. Legal and moral norms accommodate the pursuit of self-interest, but the pursuit of selfishness is or could be exploitative of others, involving efforts to gain at others' cost. The distinction between the two—self-interest and selfishness—is narrow, and at times, barred, but it does separate them. There is no bar on altruism while pursuing self-interest.

***Shari'ah Supervisory Boards*:** Meeting the *Shari'ah* requirements is necessary for each product Islamic banking offers. As such, banks establish *Shari'ah* supervisory boards to advise if a proposed product or service is compliant with the rules. Such a board must have at least three members, non-employees, and specialists in *fiqh muamalat*. Their opinion is binding on the management of the institutions. The appointment of the members is made, and their remuneration set, by a 'general assembly' rather than the institution's board of directors.

***State intervention*:** The days of classical *laissez* faire, as of its modern version, are over. Colossal market failures breeding turmoil has devastated flourishing economies with increasing frequency for too long. Free market economies have learnt that state intervention in modern economies as partners and regulators is unavoidable for peace, stability, and prosperity.

***Sustainability*:** Contextual to material development, sustainability refers to three alternatives: (i) the economy grows at a rate that can be maintained over long periods; (ii) the economy grows at a pace such that the current generation leaves the future generation enough resource availability that allows it to continue to grow at the current rate(in other words, intergeneration equity in development is ensured); and (iii)the pace of growth results in minimal environmental exploitation. Careful analysis of these alternatives shows that they eventually converge to enable the same end—environmental care.

The Islamic Financial Services Board (IFSB): It is an international body that sets standards and offers guidance for Islamic banking and finance and supervisory agencies. It was founded in November 2001 through the cooperation of the governments and central banks of Brunei, Indonesia, and Sudan. But started operations in 2003. Currently, it has 183 members (including full members, associate members, or observer members). It is supported by the Islamic Development Bank (IDB). Interestingly, the IFSB standards are seldom applied by the Islamic financial institutions. It regularly publishes reports containing data and analyses on numerous aspects of Islamic finance. It also organizes workshops, seminars, and conferences on Islamic finance.

UN Developmental Agenda Goals: In September 2015, world leaders at a historic UN Summit adopted a set of 17 Sustainable Development Goals (SDGs) called Agenda 2030, to be pursued over the following 15 years, These new goals universally apply to all countries and are expected to mobilize efforts to end all forms of poverty, fight inequalities, and tackle climate change, while ensuring that no one is left behind—a claim on which there is a big question mark.

Developed countries cannot interfere with small and less developed nations achieving their sustainable development goals by imposing their ambitious plans on them. Meeting the specified goals is not possible without positive cooperation between a country's social, political, and economic systems, geographical conditions, and cultural diversity.

When profit is treated as interest: In income tax laws, interest paid on loans is a deductible expense to assess taxable income profit is not. The provision increases the taxable income reducing profits vis-a-vis a competing conventional bank, other things remaining the same. Some adjustment to remove the handicap is provided in Muslim countries. In the West profit of Islamic banks is treated as interest to a defined extent.

Worldview: The term worldview refers to how a member of a social entity perceives the purpose of life in Allah's creation and his relationship with the Creator. The perception shapes his conduct in various spheres of life. A worldview is architectonic and revolves around a hardcore, which in the Western version is determined by reason while in Islam is faith-driven. A worldview makes value systems, *modus operandi*, property rights, sources of knowledge, and doctrine–reality circuits divergent in the two economic disciplines—the mainstream and Islamic.

Bibliography

AbuSulayman, A. (Ed.). (1995). *Islamization of Knowledge: General Principles and Work Plan*. Washington: International Institute of Islamic Thought (IIIT).

Addas, W. A. J. (2008). Methodology—Secular Versus Islamic. Kuala Lumpur: Research Management Centre, International Islamic University of Malaysia (IIUM).

Agil, S. O. S. (1992). Rationality and Altruism in Islam. In S. L. Tahir (Ed.), *Microeconomics*. Malaysia.

Ahmad, H. (2019, January). Fiscal Policy and Deficit Financing: Islamic Perspectives. *Journal of King Abdulaziz University: Islamic Economics, 32*(1), 79–86.

Ahmad, K. (2007). *Capitalism. Socialism and Welfare State*. IRTI Jeddah Power Point Slides.

Ahmad, M. M., & Pandey, D. (2010). *Are Islamic Banks Better Immunized Than Conventional Banks in the Current Financial Crisis*. 10th Global Conference on Business and Economics, Rome, Italy.

Ahmad, et al. (2014). Empowerment Through Microfinance: The Relation Between Loan Cycle and Level of Empowerment. *World Development, 62*(C), 75–87.

Al 3. (2006). *The Biggest Disruption in History: Massively Accelerated Growth Since the Industrial Revolution*. http://www.nikbergman.com/250/the-biggest-disruption-in-history-masively-ccelerated-growth-since-the-industrial-revolution/.

Z. Hasan, *Leading Issues in Islamic Economics and Finance*,
https://doi.org/10.1007/978-981-15-6515-1

Al-Atas, S. M. N. (1995). *Prolegomena to the Metaphysics of Islam: An Exposition of the Fundamental Elements of Islamic Worldview*. Kuala Lumpur: Malaysian International Institute of Islamic Thought and Civilization.

Al-Suwailem, S. (2014). *Essence of Islamic Finance*. Jeddah: Islamic Development Bank (IDB).

Akhtar, S. (2008, April). *Speech at a Securities Commission Forum on Islamic Finance*. Malaysia.

Antony, B. N. (1970). *Management Accounting, Text and Cases*. Homewood: Richard D. Irwin.

Anwar, Z. (2010). An interview with Anna Maria August/September 2008 downloaded from SC web site. IFSL Research Report on Islamic finance.

Askari, Iqbal, & Mirakhor. (2009). *Globalization and Islamic Finance: Convergence, Prospects, and Challenges*. Singapore: John Wiley & Sons (Asia) Pte Ltd.

Askari, H., Iqbal, Z., Krichene, N., & Mirakhor, A. (2012). *Risk Sharing in Finance: The Islamic Finance Alternative*. Singapore: Wiley.

Askari, H., & Mirakhor, A. (2014). Risk Sharing, Public Policy and the Contribution of Islamic Finance. *PSL Quarterly Review, 67*(271), 345–379.

Aydin, N. (2013, June). Redefining Islamic Economics as a New Economic Paradigm. *Islamic Economic Studies, 21*(1), 1–34.

Bank Negara Malaysia. (2008, October). *Governor's Keynote Address Islamic Finance: A Global Growth Opportunity Amidst a Challenging Environment*. State Street Islamic Finance Congress 2008, Boston.

Baqir al-Sadr. (1984). *Iqtisaduna* [Our Economy, Trans., Vol. 2]. Tehran, Iran: World Organization for Islamic Services (WOIS).

Bernett, C., & Clock, P. (2003). *Governing the Subjects and Spaces of Ethical Consumption*. Internet, Research Projects, Oxford University.

Beverly, S. G. (2002). Consumption and Social Welfare; Living Standards and Their Distribution in the United States (Book Review). *Journal of Sociology and Social Welfare, 29*(4), 172–174.

Bhaswati, Jagdish. (1956). Deficit Financing and Economic Development. *Indian Economic Review, 3*(2), 40–60.

Blaugh, M. (1992). *Methodology of Economics or How Economists Explain* (2nd ed.). Cambridge, UK: Cambridge University Press.

Boulakia, J. D. C. (1971). Ibn Khaldûn: A Fourteenth-Century Economist. *Journal of Political Economy, 79*(5), 1105–1118. https://doi.org/10.1086/259818.

Boulding, K. E. (1963). *Principles of Economic Policy*. London: Staples Press.

Bray, F. S. (1952). *Measurement of Profit*. London, UK: Macmillan.

Break, G. F. (1954). *Capital Maintenance and the Concept of Income*. Berkeley: University of California Press.

Brian, K. (2011). *Introduction to Islamic Banking and Finance*. Hoboken, NJ: Wiley.

Byran, J. B. (2008, May). *Basel I, Basel II and Emerging Markets—A Nontechnical Analysis.* Baltimore, MD: John Hopkins University.

Carroll, J. H. (2014). *Hawser.* Grapnel Books.

Chambers, M. S., Garage, C., & Sehlagehauf, D. (2007). *Mortgage Contracts and Housing Tenure Decisions* (Working Paper). Federal Reserve Bank of St. Louis. Research Division.

Chapra, M. U. (1986). *Towards a Just Monetary System.* Leicester and London, UK: Islamic Foundation.

Chapra, M. U. (1996). *What Is Islamic Economics.* Jeddah: IRTI.

Chapra, M. U. (2000). *The Future of Economics: An Islamic Perspective* (pp. 305–308). UK: The Islamic Foundation.

Chapra, M. U. (2014). *Morality and Justice in Islamic Economics and Finance.* UK: Edward Elgar Publishing.

Choudhory, M. A. (2007). Islamic Economics and Finance: Where Do They Stand. In *Proceedings of 6th International Conference on Islamic Economics and Finance, Advances in Islamic Economics and Finance.* IRTI.

Choudhory, M. A. (2009). Islamic Critique and Alternative to Financial Engineering Issues. *Journal of King Abdulaziz University: Islamic Economics, 22*(2), 205–244.

Cihak, M., & Hesse, H. (2010). Islamic Banks and Financial Stability: An Empirical Analysis. *Journal of Financial Services Research, 38,* 5–113.

Coase, R. W. (1984). Adam Smith's View of Man. In J. C. Wood (Ed.), *Adam Smith: Critical Assessments.* London: Croom Helm.

Cobb, S. (2010). The History and Evolution of Money, UNT Center for Economic Education, Downloaded from (www.wikipedia.org/wiki/History_of_Money), downloaded on January 7, 2011.

Craig, N. (2012). *Islamic Finance: Law and Practice* (D. Eisenberg, Ed.). Oxford: Oxford University Press.

Crowther, G. (1948). *An Outline of Money* (2nd ed., Chapter IX, pp. 277–335). London: Thomas Nelson & Sons.

Crum, W. L. (1932). *Corporate Size and Earning Power.* Harvard University Press.

De Kock, M. H. (1939). *Banks and Banking, Central* (p. 354). London, UK: P. S. King.

Derwish, A. F., & Zain, M. S. (1985). Effect of Zakah on Aggregate Consumption Function in an Islamic Economy. *Journal of Research in Islamic Economics, 2*(2) (Winter, Arabic Section), 121–130.

Di Lorenzo, T. J. (2008, November). *The Corrupt Origin of Central Banking, Mises Daily.* Austria: Ludwig Von Mises Institute.

EckartKoemal, & Malik, M. R. (2012, July 20). Basel III—Is the Islamic Finance Industry Ready? *Islamic Finance News, 8*(29), 1–3.

El-Gamal, M. A. (2009). *Macro vs. Micro- Considerations in Islamic Financial Ijtihad*. Lecture IIFF Istanbul..

El-Gamal, M. A. (2014). *Exploitative Profit Sharing: On the Incoherence of All Contract-Based Approaches to Islamic Finance*.http://www.Elgama.blogspot.com/20l4/01/exploitativeprofit.

El-Hawary, D., Grais, W., & Iqbal, Z. (2007). Diversity in the regulation of Islamic Financial Institutions. *The Quarterly Review of Economics and Finance, 46*(5), 778–800.

Farooq, M. O. (2006). *Islamic L aw and the Use and Misuse of Hathith*. New Horizon.

Faure, A. P. (2015). *Central Banking and Monetary Policy: An Introduction*. bookboon.com.

FDI Stability Report. (2019). *UNCTAD*.

Field, B. C., & Field, M. K. (2002). *Environmental Economics—An Introduction*. Kuala Lumpur: McGraw-Hill.

Finance Congress. (2008). Boston U.S.A.

Fisher, O. (2009). *An Islamic View of the Credit Crisis*, IBF 409 Issue 41.

Friedman, M. (1953). The Methodology of Positive Economics. In *Essays in Positive Economics* (pp. 3–43). Chicago: University of Chicago Press.

Galbraith, J. K. (1969). *The New Industrial State*. USA: Princeton University Press.

Gassan, H. B. (2016). A Consumer and Social Welfare Model Based on the Writings of Shibani (750–805 AD, 131–189 AH). *PSL Quarterly Review, 69*(2), 235–266.

Gide, C., & Rist, C. (1953). *History of Economic Doctrines*. New Delhi: George, Harrap and co.

Goodhart, C. A. E. (2010, November). *The Challenging Role of Central Banks* (BIS Working paper No. 326), Monetary and Economic Department, Bank for International Settlements.

Gorton, G., & Huang, L. (2001). *Banking Panics and the Origin of Central Banking* (Working paper, pp. 1–10), The Wharton School, University of Pennsylvaniaand NBER. gtnews.com (16 December 2008): Commentary – The credit crisis timeline. www.gtnews.com.

Grais, W., & Iqbal, Z. (2007). Diversity in the Regulation of Islamic Financial Institutions. *The Quarterly Review of Economics and Finance, 46*(5), 778–800.

Greenspan. (2010, March 9). Section IV.1. Principles of Reform. In *The Crisis* (pp. 19–37). Second Draft. http://csinvesting.org/wpcontent/uploads/2015/12/BURRY_The_Crisis_By_Alan_Greenspan-3-9-10.pdf.

Guide, C., & Rist, C. (1953). *History of Economic Doctrines*. New Delhi: George Harper.

Gutes, M. C. (1996). The Concept of Weak Sustainability. *Ecological Economics, 17,* 147–156.

Halim, A. (2001). *The Deferred Contracts of Exchange: Al-Qur'an in Contrast with the Islamic Economics Theory on Banking and Finance*. Kuala Lumpur, Malaysia: IKIM.

Halm, G. N.(1965). *Monetary Theory: A Modern Treatment of the Essentials of Money and Banking* (Chapter 12, pp. 171–209). Bombay: Asia publishing House.

Hamoudi, H. A. (2007). Jurisprudential Schizophrenia: On Form and Function in Islamic finance. *Chicago Journal of International Law*.

Hands, D. W. (2012). The Positive and Normative Dichotomy and Economics. *Handbook of Philosophy of Sciences, 3*, 219–239.

Haneef, M. A., & Furqani, M. (2004). Contemporary Islamic Economics and Missing Directions of Genuine Islamization. *Journal of Thoughts on Economics, 19*(4), 28–48.

Haneef, M. A., & Furqani, M. (2011). Methodology of Islamic Economics: Overview of Present State and Future Direction. *International Journal of Economics, Management and Accounting, 19*(1), 1–25.

Haque, M. (1971). Employment and Income Distribution in 1970s—A New Perspective. *Pakistan Economic and Social Review, 9*, 1–9.

Harvard University Forum on Islamic Finance. (2006, April).

Hasan, Z. (1975). *Theory of Profit*. New Delhi: Vikas Publishing House Pvt. Ltd.

Hasan, Z. (1983). Theory of Profit: The Islamic Viewpoint. *Journal of Research in Islamic Economics, 1*(1), 1–17.

Hasan, Z. (1985). Determination of Profit and Loss Sharing Ratios in Interest-Free Business Finance. *Journal of Research in Islamic Economics, 3*(1), 13–27.

Hasan, Z. (1988). Distributional Equity in Islam. In M. Iqbal (Ed.), *Distributive Justice and Need Fulfillment in an Islamic Economy* (Chapter 1, pp. 35–62). Leicester, UK: Islamic Foundation.

Hasan, Z. (1990). Munawar Iqbal; Zakah, Moderation, and Aggregate Consumption in an Islamic Economy-Comments. *KAU Islamic Economics, 2*(2), 91–100.

Hasan, Z. (1992). Profit Maximization: Secular Versus Islamic. In S. Tahir, A. Ghazali, & S. O. S. Agil (Eds.), *Readings in Microeconomics: An Islamic Perspective* (Chapter 20, pp. 239–255). Petaling Jaya, Malaysia: Longman.

Hasan, Z. (1994). Economic Development in Islamic Perspective: Concept, Objectives and Some Issues. *IIUM, Journal of Islamic Economics, 1*(1), 80–111.

Hasan, Z. (1995). Economic Development in Islamic Perspective: Concept, Objectives and Some Issues. *IIUM Journal of Islamic Economics, 1*(1), 80–111.

Hasan, Z. (1996). Book Review of Akram Khan's *An Introduction to Islamic Economics. American Journal of Islamic Social Sciences, 13*(4), 580–585.

Hasan, Z. (1997). Fulfillment of Basic Needs: Concept, Measurement and Muslim Countries' Performance. *IIUM Journal of Economic and Management, 5*(2), 1–38.

Hasan, Z. (1998a). Islamization of Knowledge in Economics: Issues And Agenda. *IIUM Journal of Economics and Management, 6*(2), 1–40.

Hasan, Z. (1998b). Book Review of M. N/ Siddiqi's *Teaching Economics in Islamic Perspective. Islamic Economic Studies, 6*(1), 111–132.

Hasan, Z. (2002a). The 1997–98 Financial Crises in Malaysia: Causes Response, and Results. *Economic Studies, 9*(2), 1–16.

Hasan, Z. (2002b). Maximization Postulates and Their Efficacy for Islamic Economics. *American Journal of Islamic Social Sciences, 19*(1), 95–118.

Hasan, Z. (2002c). Mudarabah as a Mode of Financing in Islamic Banking: Theory, Practice, and Problems. *Middle East Business and Economic Review, 14*(2), 41–53. Sydney, Australia.

Hasan, Z. (2003a). The 1997–98 Financial Crisis in Malaysia: Causes Response and Results:Rejoinder. *Economic Studies, 9*(2), 1–16.

Hasan, Z. (2003b). Globalization, Development, and Muslims, International Journal of Muslim Unity. *IIMU International Islamic University of Malaysia, 1*(1), 41–57.

Hasan, Z. (2004). *The New World Order, Muslim Predicament, and the Way Out* (MPRA Paper 3009). University Library of Munich, Germany.

Hasan, Z. (2005a). Treatment of Consumption in an Islamic Economy—An Appraisal. *Journal of King Abdulaziz University: Islamic Economics, 18*(2), 29–46.

Hasan, Z. (2005b). Islamic Banking at the Cross-Roads: Theory Versus Practice. In R. Wilson & M. Iqbal (Eds.), *Islamic Perspectives on Wealth Creation* (pp. 11–25). Edinburg, UK: Edinburg University Press.

Hasan, Z. (2006). Evaluation of Islamic Banking Performance: On the Current use of Econometric Models in Islamic Economics and Finance. *Islamic Economic Review.*

Hasan, Z. (2007). Evaluation of Islamic Banking Performance: On the Current Use of Econometric Models. In *Proceedings of the 6th International Conference, Advances in Islamic Economics and Finance*, IRTI.

Hasan, Z. (2008). Credit Creation and Control: An Unresolved Issue in Islamic Banking. *International Journal of Islamic and Middle Eastern Finance and Management, 1*(1), 69–81.

Hasan, Z. (2009a). Comments on Masudul Alam Chuodhury: 'Islamic Critique and Alternative to Financial Engineering Issues'. *Journal of King Abdulaziz University: Islamic Economics, 22*(2), 75–81.

Hasan, Z. (2009b). Islamic Banking: Commodity Murabahah Remains in a Lurch – Note. *International Journal of Islamic and Middle-Eastern Finance and Management, 2*(1), 77–79. Emerald.

Hasan, Z. (2010). Profit Sharing Ratios in Mudarabah Contract Revisited. *International Journal of Islamic Banking and Finance, 7*(1), 1–17.

Hasan, Z. (2010). Dubai Turmoil Before and After the Bailout. *International Journal of Islamic Banking & Finance*, Karachi.

Hasan, Z. (2011). Islamic Home Finance in the Social Mirror. *ISRA International Journal of Islamic Finance, 3*(1), 7–24.

Hasan, Z. (2012). Money Creation and Control from Islamic Perspective. *Journal of Islamic Banking & Finance, 29*(1), 70–85.

Hasan, Z. (2013, June). Islamic Norms. The Excel Formula and Home Financing Models. *ISRA International Journal of Islamic Finance, 5*(1), 7–27.

Hasan, Z. (2014a). *Scarcity Self-Interest and Maximization from Islamic Angle.* Jeddah: IDB prize winning lecture.

Hasan, Z. (2014b, June). Basel Accords Financial Turmoil and Islamic Banking. *ISRA International Journal of Islamic Banking and Finance, 6*(1).

Hasan, Z. (2015). *Economics with Islamic Orientation.* Kuala Lumpur, Malaysia: Oxford University Press.

Hasan, Z. (2016a). Risk-Sharing: The Sole Basis of Islamic Finance? Time for a Serious Rethink. *Journal of King Abdulaziz University: Islamic Economics, 29*(2), 23–36.

Hasan, Z. (2016b). PLS Finance and Monetary Policy: A New Measure Mooted. *Journal of Reviews on Global Economics, 5,* 000–000.

Hasan, Z. (2016c). How Islamic Is the Diminishing Musharkah Model Used for Home Financing? *Turkish Economic Review, 3*(3), 443–452.

Hasan, Z. (2016d). *Theory of Profit with Islamic Directions* (pp. 162–178). Paragon, UK: Paragon publishing.

Hasan, Z. (2016e). Risk Sharing: The Sole Basis of Islamic Finance? Time for a Serious Rethink. *KAU Journal: Islamic Economics, 19*(2), 30–31, Section 5.

Hasan, Z. (2017, June). Academic Sociology: The Alarming Rise in Predatory Publishing and Its Consequences for Islamic Economics and Finance. *ISRA Journal of Islamic Finance, 10*(1), (Emerald).

Hasan, Z. (2018a, June). Academic Sociology: The Alarming Rise in Predatory Publishing and Its Consequences for Islamic Economics and Finance. *ISRA International Journal of Islamic Finance, 10*(1), 6–18.

Hasan, Z. (2018b). *Some Higher Education Issues in Muslim Countries with Islamic Economics as an Illustrative Case* (MPRA Paper 90151), University Library of Munich, Germany.

Hasan, Z. (2019). *'Distribution' in Islamic Economics—Applications and Analysis.* Kuala Lumpur: ISRA.

Hasan, Z. (2020). Methodology of Islamic Economics: Is the Subject Worth Discussing? (Chapter 1). In *Methodology of Islamic Economics: Problems and Solutions*. Istanbul, Turkey: IKIM.

Hasan, M., & Dridi, J. (2010). *The Effect of Global Crisis on Islamic and Conventional Banks: A Comparative Study* (IMF Working Paper WP/10/201).

Hassan, A., & Cajee, Z. A. (2002). *Islam, Muslims, and Sustainable Development: The Message from Johannesburg, IMASE*. www.webstar.co.uk/~imase/Old/index.php?fcontent=article9&content=yes.

Hausman Daniel, M. (Ed.). (1984). *The Philosophy of Economics: An Anthology*. Cambridge, UK: Cambridge University Press.

Hausman Daniel, M. (Ed.). (2017). *The Philosophy of Economics; An Anthology*. UK: Cambridge University Press.

Hawley, F. B. (1893). The Risk Theory of Profit. *The Quarterly Journal of Economics, 7*(4), 459–479.

Hicks, J. R. (1946). *Value and Capital*. Oxford: Crandon Press.

Hicks, J. R. (1960). *Social Framework*. Oxford: Crandon Press

Higgs, R. (2012). *Delusions of Power: New Explorations of the State, War, and Economy*. Oakland, California: The Independent Institute.

Honohan, P. (2001, July). *Islamic Financial Intermediation: Economic and Prudential Considerations*. Development Research Group of Financial Sector Strategy and Policy Department, World Bank.

Howladar, K. (2010). *Shariah Risk: Understanding Recent Compliance Issues in Islamic Finance* (Moody's Investor Service Report, p. 1).

Hussein, K. A. (2013). *Islamic Economics: Current State of Knowledge and Development of the Ipline*. The Seventh International Conference on Islamic Economics, Jeddah.

Hutchinson, M. G. (1978). *Economics Thought In Spain, 1177–1740*. London: George Allen & Unwin.

IFSL Research. (2010, January). London.

IMF Conditionality. (2018, March 6). https://www.imf.org/en/About/Factsheets/Sheets/2016/08/02/21/28/IMF-Conditionality.

IMF Survey. (2015). https://www.imf.org/en/News/Articles/2015/09/28/04/53/sores100410a I. On line.

Iqbal, M. (1985). Zakah, Moderation, and Aggregate Consumption in an Islamic Economy. *Journal of Research in Islamic Economics, 3*(1), 45–60.

Iqbal, M. (2008, April 1–3). Contribution of the Last Six Conferences. In *Proceedings 7th International Conference on Islamic Economics*. Jeddah: King Abdulaziz University.

Iqbal, S. A., & Muljawan, D. (Eds.). (2007). *Advances in Islamic Economics and Finance* (Vol. 1). Jeddah: IRTI/IDB.

Islahi, A. A. (2010). Four Generations of Islamic Economists. *Journal of King Abdulaziz University: Islamic Economics, 23*(1), 165–170.

Islamic finance News. (2013, March 26). *Case Study—Abu Dhabi Bank Leads the Way with the World's First Basel III, From Deal of the Year Handbook*, pp. 1–4.

Jose, T. (2016). *What is Deficit Financing? What Are the Different Types of Deficit in the Budget?* https://www.indianeconomy.net/splclassroom/what-is-deficit-financing-what-are-the-different-types-of-deficits-in-the-budget/.

Kahf, M. (1992). The Theory of Consumption. In Tahir et al. (Eds.), *Readings in Microeconomics in Islamic Perspective* (pp. 61–68; 90–105). Petaling Jaya, Malaysia: Longman.

Kamali, M. H. (2002). *Islamic Commercial Law: An Analysis of Futures and Options*. Selangor: Ilmah Publications.

Kazmi, M. Z. (2010, October). *Islamic Dinar Reloaded*. Odalisque: Islamic finance Intelligence (Issue 12–13).

Keynes, J. N. (1890). *Scope and Method of Political Economy*. Kitchener: Batoche Books.

Keynes, J. M. (1930). *A Treatise on Money*. UK: Cambridge.

Keynes, J. M. (1936). *The General Theory of Employment, Interest and Money*. UK: Cambridge University Press.

KFH Research. (2011). *Gold Dinar: Time to return? Monograph* (pp. 1–21) Kuwait Finance House Research Ltd.

Khaldun, I. (1967). *Muqaddimah: An Introduction to History* (F. Rozenthal, Trans., Bollingen Series XLIII, 1980 print, Vol. 2). Princeton University Press.

Khalid, F. M. (2002). *Islam and the Environment, Social and Economic Dimensions of Global Environmental*. Chichester, UK: Wiley.

Khan F. M. (1984). Macro Consumption Function in an Islamic Framework. *Journal of Research in Islamic Economics, 1*(2), 3–25.

Khan, M. A. (1994). *An Introduction to Islamic Economics*. Islamabad, Pakistan: International Institute of Islamic Thought and Institute of Policy Studies.

Khan, M. (1995). *Essays in Islamic Economics*. UK: Islamic Foundation.

Khan, M. A. (2013). *What Is Wrong with Islamic Economics*. Northampton, MA: Edward Elgar.

Khan, M. A. (2018). Methodology of Economics: From Islamic Teachings to Economics. *TUJISE, 5*(1), 35–61.

Khan, M., & Mirakhor, A. (1992). The Financial System and Monetary Policy in an Islamic Economy, 1989. In *Principles of Islamic Financing: A Survey*. Jeddah: IRTI.

Knight, F. H. (1921). *Risk, Uncertainty and Profit*. USA: Mifflin.

Kolata, G. (2017, November). How Faux Journals Are Making Pseudo-Science Legit. *Times of India*.

Kosekla, E., & König, J. (2010). *Can Profit Sharing Lower Flexible Outsourcing?* (HECER Discussion paper No. 310).

Kuran, T. (1989). On the Notion of Economic Justice in Contemporary Islamic Thought. *International Journal of Middle East Studies, 21*(2), 171–191.

Laldin, A., et al. (2013). *Islamic Legal Maxims and Their Application in Islamic Finance*. Kuala Lumpur, Malaysia: ISRA.

Lee, W. S. (2012). What is Inquiry-Guided Learning? https://doi.org/10.1002/tl.20002.

Leibenstein, H. (1978). *General X-Efficiency Theory and Economic Development*. New York: Oxford.

Levy, R. (1957). *The Social Structure of Islam*. London: Cambridge University Press.

Liewellyn, O. A. (1984). Islamic Jurisprudence and Environmental Planning. *Journal of Research in Islamic Economics, 1*(2), 25–49.

Lux, K. (1979). *Adam Smith's Mistake*. US: Shambhala (1990).

Mail Daily. (2010, March 10).

Malik, M. S., Malik, A., & Mustafa, W. (2011). Controversies That Make Islamic Banking Controversial: An Analysis of Issues and Challenges. *American Journal of Social and Management Sciences, 2*(1), 41–46.

Mountz, M. (1951). The Valuation of Business Capital: An Accounting Analysis. *American Economic Review*.

Marshall, A. (1898/1949). *Principles of Economics*. New York: Macmillan.

Marshall, A. (1924). *Principles of Economics*. New York: Macmillan.

Marshall, A. (1946). *Principles of Economics* (18th ed.). UK: Macmillan (print).

McConnell, C., & Brue, S. (1990). *Economics, Principles Problems and Polices* (11th ed.). New York: Mcgrew Hill.

Meera, A. K. (2012). A Critique of Diminishing Balance Method of Islamic Home Financing. *ISRA International Journal of Islamic Finance, 4*(2), 7–23.

Meera, A. K. M., & Razak, D. A. (2009). Home Financing Through the Musharakah Mutanaqisah Contracts: Some Practical Issues. *Journal of King Abdulaziz University: Islamic Economics, 22*(1), 3–25.

Meier, G. M. (Ed.). (1985). *Leading Issues in Economic Development* (4th ed.). Delhi: Oxford University Press.

Melendez, E. D. (2015). *On Governmental Wealth Cost of Crisis Huff Post US*. https://www.huffingtonpost.in/entry/financial-crisis-cost-ao_n_2687553.

Mirakhor, A. (2007). *A Note on Islamic Economics*. Jeddah: IDB, IRTI.

Mirakhor, A. (2014). Foundations of Risk-Sharing Finance: An Islamic View. In K. Lewis, M. Ariff, & S. Mohamad (Eds.), *Risk and Regulation of Islamic Banking*. London: Edward Elgar.

Mirakhor, A. (2015a). *Social Capital and Risk Sharing: An Islamic Finance Paradigm*. New York: Palgrave Macmillan.

Mirakhor, A. (2015b, July 8). *Issues in Islamic Finance: Risk Sharing – An Economic Revolution*. INCEIF: The Global University of Islamic Finance on YouTube. Accessed on 16 October 2015.

Mohammed, N. (2018). *Islamic and Conventional Banking Comparison.* IslamicFinance.com. Accessed 28 March 2018.

Nabil, B. M. A. M. (2013). Conceptual Analysis of Islamic Home Financing Models. *ISRA International Journal of Islamic Finance, 5*(1), 29–88.

Nabil, M. S., & Mirakhor, A. (2015). Risk Sharing and Shared Prosperity in Islamic Finance. *Islamic Economic Studies, 23*(2), 85–115.

Nagar, & Das. (1997). *Basic Statistics.* India: Oxford University Press.

Napier, C. (2009). *Survey Report (2009) on Social Responsibility: Trends in Islamic Financial Institutions.* www.researchgate.net/publication/4737506_Social_reporting_by_Islamic_Bank.

Nasr, S. V. R. (1992). *Islamization of Knowledge: A Critical Overview* (Occasional Paper No. 17). International Institute of Islamic Thought, Islamabad.

Neinhous, V. (2012, November 12–13). Method and Substance of Islamic Economics: Moving Where? In *Workshop on the Future of Islamic Economics* held at Islamic Economics Institute King Abdulaziz University Jeddah, Saudi Arabia.

Nowak, R. A. (2011). *How Effective Is Global Financial Regulation? The Basel Accords' Role in Mitigating Banking Crises.* econ.duke.edu/uploads/assets/NowakRobert.pdf.

NYU.edu. (2014). Chapter 4: How Do we Measure Risk? Retrieved from http://people.stern.nyu.edu/adamodar/pdfiles/valrisk/ch4.pdf.

Osar, J., & Blanchfeild, W. C. (1975). *The Evolution of Economics Thought* (3rd ed.). New York: Haarcourt Brace JovanVish Inc.

Ormerod, P. (2010). Risk, Recessions and the Resilience of the Capitalist Economies. *Risk Management, 12,* 83–99.

Pearce, D., Barbier, E., & Markandya, A. (1990). *Sustainable Development: Economics and Environment in the Third World.* Aldershot: Edward Edgar.

Pearce, D. W., & Turner, R. K. (1990). *Economics of Natural Resources and the Environment.* Singapore: Harvester Wheatsheaf.

Pen, J. (1971). *Income Distribution: Facts, Theories, and Policies.* New York: Praeger.

Pettifor. (2019). *How to Transform an Economic System That Has Driven Us to Disaster* (A Green New Deal Report). https://www.annpettifor.com/2019/09/how-to-transform-an-economic-system-that-has-driven-us-to-disaster/.

Piketty, T. R. (2014). *Capital in the Twenty First Century.* Spiegel.

Planning Commission of India: Indian Economy. https://www.indianeconomy.net/splclassroom/what-isdeficit-financing-what-are-the-different-types-of-deficits-in-the-budgethttpsinancing-what-are-the-different-types-of-deficits-in-the-budget.

Pigou, A. C. (1932). *Economics of Welfare.* UK: Macmillan.

Qutb, S. (1948). *Milestones.* Beirut: The Quran House.

Qutb, S. (1978). *Milestones.* Beirut: The Holy Qur'an Publishing House.

Qutb, S. (n.d.). *Islam, the Misunderstood Religion*. Beirut: Quran House.

Rahman, M. H. (1936). *Islam ka Iqtisadi Nizam ek ajmali khaka (Urdu)—The Economic System of Islam (An outline)*. Dar-ul-Mussan-e-feen, Urdu Bazar, Jama Masjid, Delhi.

Redman, D. A. (1991). *Economics and Philosophy of Science*. Oxford: Oxford University Press.

Repetto, R. (1986). *Skimming the Water: Rent Seeking and the Performance of Public Irrigation Systems*. Washington, DC: World Resources Institute.

Reserve Bank of New Zeeland. (2007). *Capital Adequacy Ratios for Banks-Simplified Explanation and Example of Calculation*. http:/www.rbnz.govt.nzfinstab/banking/regulation/0091769html.

Robbins, L. (1932). *Nature and Significance of Economic Science*. London, UK: Macmillan.

Rodinson, M. (1974). *Islam and Capitalism*. London: Allen Lande.

Roussos, Alex. (2013, January 23). Life Under Basel III: What Will Capital Markets Products Look Like Now? *Islamic Finance News, 10*(3), 1–4.

Rubin, J. (2011). Institutions, the Rise of Commerce and the Persistence of Laws: Interest Restrictions in Islam and Christianity. *Economic Journal, 121*, 1310–1339.

Sadiq, M. (Ed.). (1996). *Economic Development and Islam*. Malaysia: IIUM Press.

Sadr, M. Baqar-as. (1983). *Iqtisaaduna* (Our Economics) (Vol. 2, Part 1). Tehran: WOFIS.

Samuelson, P. A. (1947). *Foundations of Economic Analysis*. Harvard University Press.

Samuelson, P. A., & Nordau, W. D. (2001). *Economics* (17th ed.). New York: McGraw-Hill.

Sen, A. K. (1977). Rational Fools: A Critique of the Behavioral Foundations of Economic Theory. *Philosophy and Public Affairs, 6*(4), 317–344.

Schor, J. (2003). *The New Politics of Consumption: Life Cycle Thinking as a Solution*. Research Projects, Oxford University.

Shari'ati, A. (1982). *Man and Islam*, Lectures (G. M. Fayez, Trans.). Mashhad, Iran: University of Mushhad Press.

Shibani, M. I. A.-H. (1997). *Book of Earning* (1st ed.). Explained by Mohammed Sarkhasi, verified by Abdul Fattah Abu Ghuda. Beirut: Dar Albachaer Alislamia, and Aleppo: Office of the Islamic Publications.

Shinsuke, N. (2012). Critical Overview of the History of Islamic Economics: Formation, Transformation, and New Horizons. *Asian and African Area Studies, 11*(2), 114–136.

Siddiqi, M. N. (1992). Islamic Consumer Behavior. In Tahir, et al. (Eds.), *Readings in Microeconomics in Islamic Perspective* (pp. 49–60). Malaysia: Longman.

Siddiqi, M. N. (1996). *Teaching Economics in Islamic Perspective*. Jeddah: Scientific Publishing Centre, King Abdulaziz University.

Silva, S. S. da, Reis, R. P., & Ferreira, P. A. (2009). Concepts of Nature Value: Are the Particular Characteristics of Nature Goods Being Considered? *VII International PENSA Conference*. Sao Paulo, Brazil.

Slesnick, D. T. (2001). *Consumption and Social Welfare: Living Standards and their Distribution in the United States*. UK: Oxford.

Smith, A. (1776). *An Inquiry Into the Nature and Causes of Wealth of Nations*. University of Glasgow Press.

Stanford Encyclopedia of Philosophy. (2006, June 28). *Substantive Revision Wed February 17, 2016*.

Stieglitz, J. (2009a). *Capitalist Fools*. The Malaysian Reserve, 11 February 2008. https://www.vanityfair.com/news/2009/01/stiglitz200901-2.

Stieglitz, J. (2009b). *Freefall: Markets and the Sinking of the Global Economy*. London: Allen Lane.

Suzanna, E. M., & Ola, A.-S. (2013). Risk Aversion and Islamic Finance: An Experimental Approach. *International Journal of Information Technology and Business Management, 16*(1), 49–77.

Thaler, R. H., & Sunstein, C. R. (2009). *Nudge: Improving Decisions About Health, Wealth and Happiness*. New Haven & London: Yale University Press.

The Seventh Harvard University Forum on Islamic Finance. (2006, April 22–23). *Integrating Islamic Finance in the Mainstream: Regulation, Standardization, and Transparency*. Cambridge, MA: IFP.

Todaro, M. P. (1986). *Economic Development in the Third World*. Longman, UK.

Turner, R. K., Pearce, D., & Bateman, I. (1994). *Environmental Economics—An Introduction*. Singapore: Harvester Wheatsheaf.

UN. (2011). *The Economic and Social Survey of Asia and the Pacific, UN Library*. https://www.un-ilibrary.org/economic-and-social-development/economic-and-social-survey-of-asia-and-the-pacific-2001_1c046692-en.

Ünal, M. (2011, January 19). *The Small World of Islamic Finance: Shariah Scholars and Governance—A Network Analytic Perspective*, v 6.0.

Ursul, A. D. (1983). *Philosophy and The Ecological Problems of Civilization* (2nd ed.). Moscow: Progress.

Usmani, T. (2010). Musharaka and Mudaraba as Modes of Financing. *Journal of Islamic Banking and Finance, 27*(3), 57–76.

Uzair, M. (1982). Central Banking Operations in an Interest-Free Banking System. In M. Ariff (Ed.), xxx.

Waheed, A. (2006, January). *Sustainability and Determinants of Domestic Public Debt of Pakistan, NAGOYA 464-8601* (JAPAN Discussion Paper No. 137).

Weil, L. (2009). *Do Islamic Banks Have Greater Market Power?* (Working paper). http://courmot.ustrasbg.fr/large.

World Inequality Report. (2018). Harvard University Press.

Yosuf, R. M., Wahab, N. A., & Hamza, H. (2017). Does Home Financing Promote Affordability of Home Ownership in Malaysia? An Empirical Analysis Between Islamic and Conventional Banks. *International Journal of Economics, Management and Accounting, 25*(3), 601–627.

Zaidi, N. A. (1987). Profit Rates Policy for PLS Depositors. *Journal of Islamic Banking and Finance, 4*(4), 35–46.

Zaman, A. (2012a). Crisis in Islamic Economics: Diagnosis and Prescriptions. *Journal of King Abdulaziz University: Islamic Economics, 25*(2), 227–250.

Zaman, A. (2012b). Methodological Mistakes and Econometric Consequences. *International Econometric Review (IER) Econometric Research Association, 4*(2), 99–122.

Zein, M. (2010). *Islamic Dinar Revisited*. Opalesque: Islamic Finance Intelligence (Issue 14–15). INCEIF Digital Library.

Zeti, A. A. (2008a). *A Global Growth Opportunity Amidst a Challenging Environment*. Governor's Keynote Address delivered on 8 October at State Street Islamic Finance Congress, Boston, MA.

Zeti, A. A. (2008b). *Keynote Address Delivered on 8 October at State Street Islamic Finance Congress, 2008*. Boston U.S.A.